NFL DRAFT
2017 PREVIEW

By
NOLAN NAWROCKI

ACTA SPORTS

NFL Draft 2017 Preview
by Nolan Nawrocki

Research: Matt Feminis
Research assistant: Eddie Herz
Design and typesetting: Bob Peters

Cover photo credits: Alabama Athletics (left); LSU Communications (center); Texas A&M Media Relations (right); Washington Athletic Communications, Michigan Athletics (spine)

Copyright © 2017 by Nolan Nawrocki

Published by ACTA Sports, a division of ACTA Publications
4848 N. Clark Street, Chicago, IL 60640
(800) 397-2282
www.actasports.com

ISBN: 978-0-87946-585-8

Library of Congress Control number: 2017932657

Printed in the U.S.A. by McNaughton and Gunn

CONTENTS

HAYLEY PENNESI/TENNESSEE ATHLETICS

Derek Barnett

Almost every player in this book was an exceptional college football player or athlete and stands among the best in the country. NFL standards are the most stringent in the world, and it requires immense grit to rigorously compete against the world's most nuanced pros. All players graded were measured against these most demanding measures.

Included with many player profiles is a "Scout's Take," actual feedback reflecting unique and consensus opinions from NFL evaluators, stemming anywhere from veteran area scouts blanketing a region of the country to the savvy GMs going over the top of it when they can fit it into their busy schedules. Much of the information was gathered through the course of the fall, up until the day of publishing this book, and reflects hundreds of conversations aimed at pinpointing the measurables, critical traits, football instincts, work ethic, toughness, competitiveness, leadership, intelligence, temperament, character, scheme fit and league value of the nation's top talent.

Some information and grades might have changed by the time the book is being read, as more workouts, interviews and private workouts take place following the March press date and verified measurements and character research is ascertained.

Much gratitude is owed to everyone who helped contribute to the production of the book in some way, from college coaches and sports information directors to all the NFL executives, scouts and coaches with whom I have had the pleasure to talk football.

A special thank-you belongs to Greg Pierce and the ACTA Sports team for their guidance, Ron Pollack for his draft acumen, Bob Peters for his creativity and Matt Feminis for his diligence and attention to detail. Not to be forgotten is the late Joel Buchsbaum and the PFW family that helped found independent draft analysis. I am so grateful for the patience, toughness and strength of my inspiration, Christie and the A-team.

— *Nolan Nawrocki*

DRAFT OUTLOOK

After a two-year stay in Chicago, the 2017 NFL Draft moves to Philadelphia, returning to its inaugural home in 1936, and for the first time will be held entirely outdoors. Fitting for the NFL city that first welcomed Reggie White, arguably the greatest defensive lineman in NFL history, the ultimate prizes in the 2017 NFL Draft are a pair of defensive linemen, Texas A&M DE **Myles Garrett** and Alabama DT **Jonathan Allen**.

Garrett follows in the path of Texans DL Jadeveon Clowney (2014) and Mario Williams (2006) as a rare athlete with game-changing ability racing the edges. Allen, though he lined up in a 3-4 front at Alabama, profiles as gap-piercing penetrator in the pros more ideally suited for a "40" front. His versatility to play the piano and move anywhere along a line in an even or odd front is unique and sure to command early attention.

Offensively, the most impactful talent in the draft is LSU's **Leonard Fournette**, a generational-type talent in a similar mold as Herschel Walker. Fournette is capable of making the same type of rookie impact as Ezekiel Elliott and Todd Gurley in recent years and brings more fiercely competitive power than Adrian Peterson entering the league. Durability will be his greatest challenge.

Two trades kicked off last year's draft as the Rams and Eagles both vied for their quarterbacks of the future, giving the Titans and Browns additional first-round picks in this year's first round. In 2017, with four early-entry underclassmen heading up the QB class, there's not a passer in the draft who is ready to step into a starting lineup from Day One worth targeting with a trade at the top of the draft. The talent at the position is noticeably down, as many teams have not graded a single quarterback with a true first-round grade.

The most battle-tested passer of the bunch and most definite to fit into the first round following a very strong Combine is Clemson's **Deshaun Watson**, who played his best football on the biggest of stages against Alabama the last two seasons and capped his career with a national championship in which he engineered the game-winning drive with the poise and precision of a savvy veteran. North Carolina's one-year starter **Mitchell Trubisky** has the most upside of the crop; Texas Tech's Air Raid gunslinger **Patrick Mahomes** has the strongest arm; and Notre

Myles Garrett

Dame's **DeShone Kizer** has the best physical tools, though the lowest floor. Though none may warrant true first-round grades, there's a chance all could warrant early-round attention as teams viewing them as eventual franchise quarterbacks could look to move back into the first round coveting the optional fifth year that comes with Round 1 contracts.

Beyond the lack of an elite quarterback, the other greatest void in this year's draft comes on the offensive line. Alabama OLT **Cam Robinson** is the most proven commodity in this year's draft and could be drafted very early because of the scarcity of quality blind-side protectors. Wisconsin's one-year starter **Ryan Ramczyk** and Temple's physical **Dion Dawkins** both could be thrust into starting jobs early and could be forced to adapt on the fly. Utah's **Garett Bolles** has the feet and bend to function at a high level, but his lack of discipline could hinder him from ever reaching his ceiling. On the interior, Ohio State's intelligent **Pat Elflein** and LSU's versatile **Ethan Pocic** both have Day-One starter potential at center, as do guards such as Western Kentucky's efficient **Forrest Lamp**, Indiana's zone-blocking **Dan Feeney**, Pittsburgh's big-bodied **Dorian Johnson** and Western Michigan's massive **Taylor Moton**, who is capable of playing inside or outside.

In stark contrast to the weak tight end crops of recent years, this year's class is the most athletic in NFL history and could feature a pair of impact pass-catchers in the first round for the first time in a decade. Not since 2006 when Vernon Davis and Marcedes Lewis were selected in the first round have a pair been taken in Round 1. Three – Alabama's **O.J. Howard**, Miami (Fla's) **David Njoku** and even Mississippi's **Evan Ingram** – could receive top-round consideration and make an immediate impact in the passing game. Many quality starters could still be found through the fourth round, including South Alabama's athletic **Gerald Everett**, Clemson's soft-handed **Jordan Leggett**, Virginia Tech's explosive **Bucky Hodges** and Michigan's injured **Jake Butt**.

Playmakers will also be in abundance in the backfield beyond Fournette. Stanford's utility weapon **Christian McCaffrey**, Florida State's explosive **Dalvin Cook**, and Ohio State's dynamic multi-purpose threat **Curtis Samuel** all possess immediate impact potential in what is the strongest RB class since 2008, when five backs were selected in the first round and 27 were taken overall, including perennial Pro Bowlers such as Jonathan Stewart, Chris Johnson, Matt Forte, Ray Rice and Jamaal Charles. Oklahoma's **Joe Mixon** also possesses first-round talent if he can overcome his own Ray Rice incident.

A receiving class short on true No. 1 receivers was greatly bolstered by underclassmen, headed by what will become the fastest man in football next season, Washington's electric **John Ross**. Clemson's towering target **Mike Williams**, USC's tough **JuJu Smith-Schuster** and Penn State's physical **Chris Godwin** all could contribute readily. The senior class is loaded with options for the slot, beginning with Western Michigan's competitive **Corey Davis**, East Carolina's savvy **Zay Jones** and Eastern Washington's crafty **Cooper Kupp**.

Headed by Garrett, the DE crop is as good as it has been since 2012, when seven ends were selected in the first round. Stanford's intense **Solomon Thomas**, Missouri's sleek **Charles Harris** and Kansas State's physical **Jordan Willis** all possess double-digit-sack potential. A pair of speed rushers, UCLA's **Takkarist McKinley** and Alabama's **Tim Williams**, and Big Ten stalwarts **T.J. Watt** (Wisconsin) and **Taco Charlton** (Michigan) also have the physical traits to contribute readily.

The interior of the defensive line includes fewer inside terrorizers after Allen, with Michigan's versatile **Chris Wormley**, Florida's disruptive **Caleb Brantley** and Michigan State's enigmatic **Malik McDowell** having physical tools to plug-and-play inside or outside.

Top quality is strong at inside linebacker, beginning with Alabama's impactful, tenacious hitter **Reuben Foster**, who can be equally effective on the outside after cutting weight in 2016. Ohio State thumper **Raekwon McMillan**, LSU's injured **Kendell Beckwith** and Northwestern's **Anthony Walker** all have starter traits on the inside.

Depth is unusually strong at outside linebacker, with Florida's speedy **Jarrad Davis**, Vanderbilt's cerebral **Zach Cunningham** and LSU's ascending **Duke Riley** all possessing starter traits. A pair of college defensive ends, Tennessee's relentless **Derek Barnett** and Temple's **Haason Reddick**, start the conversation among rush linebackers. Alabama's energetic **Ryan Anderson**, Houston's athletic **Tyus Bowser** and Auburn's effortful **Carl Lawson** all have starter potential and will make livings flushing the pocket.

Not since 2010 when the Chiefs selected Eric Berry has a safety heard his name called in the top 5. This year's crop is arguably as strong at the top and deep throughout as any in history, with Day One starters to be found in the middle rounds, and as many as four expected to fit into the first round, beginning with LSU's fierce, tempo-setting **Jamal Adams**, a potential top-5 pick; Ohio State's rangy ballhawk **Malik Hooker**, the most athletic centerfielder since 2004 fifth overall pick Sean Taylor; and Michigan's **Jabrill Peppers**, whose multi-purpose value arising from playing 13 positions in 2016 could also increase demand for his services. Texas A&M's hard-hitting **Justin Evans** could also command Round One interest. Others bolstering the class and having received early-round stamps from evaluators during the fall include Utah's instinctive **Marcus Williams**, North Carolina State's hammer **Josh Jones** and Florida's athletic **Marcus Maye**.

On average, four to five cornerbacks are selected in the first round, and this year fits the norm, with Ohio State's talented **Marshon Lattimore** and long-limbed **Gareon Conley** leading the way. LSU's press corner **Tre'Davrius White** and USC's slot defender **Adoree' Jackson** both could benefit from their return skills, with Jackson's ability to moonlight in offensive packages also increasing his value. The versatility of Colorado's **Chidobe Awuzie** will also pull him into the early-round conversations. It's a good year for finding big cover men, with Alabama's **Marlon Humphrey**, Florida's **Quincy Wilson** and **Teez Tabor**, Clemson's **Cordrea Tankersley**, UCLA's **Fabian Moreau** and Washington's **Kevin King** and **Sidney Jones** fitting among the 21 cornerbacks at the Combine measuring above 6-foot tall. Collectively, it's a deeper cornerback crop than usual, and very noticeably bigger and faster.

The most highly coveted specialist in the draft is Arizona State's accurate **Zane Gonzalez**, the Lou Groza Award winner who finished his career as the FBS leader in field goals made (96) and was nearly 80 percent beyond 50. He's been consistent enough to field interest in the top 100 picks.

QUARTERBACKS

CLEMSON UNIVERSITY

QUARTERBACKS

Nawrocki's TOP 10

◄ 1. DESHAUN WATSON
2. Mitchell Trubisky
3. Patrick Mahomes
4. DeShone Kizer
5. Davis Webb
6. Josh Dobbs
7. Nathan Peterman
8. C.J. Beathard
9. Brad Kaaya
10. Trevor Knight

EDITOR'S NOTE:

e — Measurement is estimated.
#00 — Player's jersey number.
GRADE — Nawrocki's league grade
Draft Projection — Consensus league value where player will likely be drafted.

On all positions, 40-yard-dash times are taken from the Combine when available and are curved to account for conditions (turf, wind, track shoes).

QB C.J. BEATHARD, #16 (Sr-5)

IOWA   ▶ GRADE: 5.29

Ht: 6-2 1/2 | Wt: 219 | 40: 4.90e | Arm: 30 5/8 | Hand: 9 3/8

History: He and his girlfriend, Madelyn, are the parents of daughter, Lyla. Grandson of Bobby Beathard, former Redskins and Chargers GM. Four-year letterman in both football and baseball as a prep in Tennessee, where he was the state's leading passer. Redshirted in 2012. Saw limited action in five games in '13, completing 9-of-27 pass attempts (33.3 percent) for 179 yards with one touchdown and two interceptions. In '14, recorded 52-92-645-5-2 (56.5) in nine games (one start). Outplayed Jake Rudock (Lions) in the Hawkeyes' bowl game against Tennessee to earn the starting job as a junior. Despite playing through a sports hernia injury which required post-season surgery, started all 14 games in '15, and produced 223-362-2,809-17-5 (61.6). Sprained his left knee during '16 fall camp — wore a brace during the season, and totaled 170-301-1,929-17-10 (56.5) in 13 starts. Had 224 career rushes for 429 yards (1.9-yard average) and 10 touchdowns. Had ten fumbles the last three seasons. Went 21-7 as a starter. Two-year team captain and offensive MVP graduated with a leisure studies degree (Recreation and Sport Business). Opted not to run the 40-yard dash at the Combine and did not perform shuttles because of a right hamstring injury.

Strengths: Good short-to-intermediate accuracy and deep-ball touch. Very competitive and physically tough to play through injuries, as he did much of his junior season. Very poised under duress and is not rattled by big stages (see

Michigan). Stands in the pocket and courageously takes some big shots knowing pressure is coming to deliver the ball. Confident with an outstanding football IQ — handles audibles at the line and has an understanding of coverages and situational football. Played in a pro-style offense. Strong on-field leadership qualities. Carries an unselfish, team-first attitude. Has a .750 career winning percentage.

Weaknesses: Has short arms and small hands and grip could be affected in bad weather. Average athlete. Takes too many needless sacks locking in and not feeling oncoming pressure. Struggles to escape the pocket and throw with precision on the move from a variety of arm slots. Loses some velocity on deep outs and does not consistently drive the ball with high RPMs. Not a decisive triggerman comfortable throwing receivers open. Measured 17 percent body-fat percentage, greater than some lean linemen, and could stand to improve conditioning.

Future: A caretaker who excelled more as a junior with a stronger supporting cast. An ideal backup in the mold of a Kyle Orton with enough toughness and intelligence to manage games as an NFL starter if thrust into the role. Will require time to acclimate to the speed of the NFL game.

Draft projection: Fourth-round pick.

Scout's take: "He's limited. He has all the intangibles and none of the talent. He's a backup game manager in the same category with (Eagles' 2013 fourth-round pick) Matt Barkley. He makes more plays with his feet than Barkley. If (Beathard) is your starter, you'll always be left wanting more."

QB JOSH DOBBS, #11 (Sr-4)

TENNESSEE ▶ GRADE: 5.38

Ht: 6-3 3/8 | Wt: 216 | 40: 4.64 | Arm: 32 5/8 | Hand: 9 1/4

History: Also played baseball as a Georgia prep. In 2013, started 4-of-5 games played as a true freshman — completed 72-of-121 pass attempts (59.5 percent) for 695 yards with two touchdowns and six interceptions. Was slated to redshirt as the Vols' third quarterback in '14, but an injury to the starter opened the door for Dobbs to overtake Nathan Peterman by season's end — started five of the final six games, and produced 112-177-1,206-9-6 (63.3). Entrenched as the starter, started all 26 games the next two seasons — posted 205-344-2,291-15-5 (59.6) in '15; and 225-357-2,946-27-12 (63.0) in '16, while earning the TaxSlayer Bowl MVP. Was the most productive rushing quarterback in school history, piling up 438 carries for 2,160 yards (4.9-yard average) and 32 touchdowns. Had 30 career fumbles. Went

23-12 as a starter. One of four quarterbacks in Southeastern Conference history to have 50 career passing touchdowns and 25 career rushing touchdowns (Tim Tebow, Johnny Manziel, Dak Prescott). Team captain is on track to graduate with an Aerospace Engineering degree, for which teammates nicknamed him "Astro."

Strengths: Good release quickness — snaps the ball with fluidity and can manipulate his arm and throwing platform and deliver from a variety of angles. Good balance and body control. Very good athlete. Creates some magic in the pocket eluding the rush — flashes playmaking ability and consistently extends plays with his feet. Recorded the fastest 3-cone-drill time (6.75 seconds) of any quarterback at the Combine, indicative of very good agility and hip flexibility. Extremely intelligent. Outstanding personal and football character. Very humble with an even-keeled demeanor and is not easily rattled. Physically tough and durable. Had a .657 career winning percentage in 35 games.

Weaknesses: Has a thin frame and average hand size. Needs to take better care of the football (30 career fumbles). Operated primarily out of the shotgun and is still adapting to taking drops from underneath center and learning how to diagnose coverages. Developing triggerman — still takes too many chances fitting the ball into tight, man coverage and ball placement could stand to improve. Footwork and mechanics could use more refinement. Almost too intellectual processing what he sees and overanalyzes the game.

Future: A thin-framed, quick-footed, rubber-armed quarterback with natural leadership qualities and a developing calmness in his play. Scouts remained concerned that Dobbs is more smart than instinctive and consequently will require patience to become more of a quick decision-maker than over-thinking processor. Played his best football late in the season and is very driven to succeed. Is still more of a thrower than a passer and has upside if he could be paired with a nurturing coach willing to teach him the nuances. Could bring sustainable value to a stable franchise and emerge in three years as a solid NFL starter.

Draft projection: Third- to fourth-round pick.

Scout's take: "His engineering curriculum was so demanding that it was difficult for him to give football enough attention. Does he love football? If he goes all-in with it for the first time in his life, he will improve. Even though he has a lot of experience, he's never invested fully in the game. You won't find a better person. The way he interacts with his teammates and lifts them up is pretty special. It's going

QUARTERBACKS

to take him a little time, but you get him in the same system for a few years and you could have something."

QB JEROD EVANS, #4 (Jr-4)

VIRGINIA TECH ▶ GRADE: 5.18

Ht: 6-2 3/4 | Wt: 232 | 40: 4.82 | Arm: 33 1/8 | Hand: 9 3/8

History: One of nine children. Prepped in Texas. Signed with Air Force, but did not play in 2013 after tearing his right ACL. Opted out of the military and transferred to Trinity Valley Community College (TX). Backed up Kyle Postma in '14, but saw action in 10 games, and completed 70-of-107 pass attempts (65.4 percent) for 1,001 yards with 14 touchdowns and two interceptions. Took over the starting job in '15, and produced 179-287-3,164-38-3 (62.4) in eight games. Missed the last two weeks of the season because of a fractured left (non-throwing) wrist. Had 132 junior-college carries for 772 yards (5.8-yard average) and nine touchdowns. Became first commit to first-year VT head coach Justin Fuente. Was the Hokies' MVP in '16 after setting school single-season records for passing yards, touchdown passes, and total offense (4,398 yards) — started all 14 games, and produced 268-422-3,552-29-8 (63.5) through the air with 204-846-12 (4.1) on the ground. Sprained his right ankle against Pittsburgh. Had 10 career fumbles. Had a 10-4 starting record at Virginia Tech.

Strengths: Has a strong, athletic build with good size and looks the part. Nifty runner with good vision — see 55-yard TD run vs. East Carolina where avoided seven tacklers. Good run instinct and strength on designed runs and speed options. Has escapability to extend plays when protection breaks down. Adequate arm strength. Good touch in the red area.

Weaknesses: Operated a simplified, spread tempo offense with a lot of quick slants, flares and bubble screens and was not tasked with making pro-style, progression reads. Is quick to pull down the ball and run if a patch of grass opens. Mechanics in the pocket could stand to improve — has a long release and throws a heavy ball. Needs to protect the ball better. Sporadic ball placement and accuracy. Recorded a 26 1/2-inch vertical jump, the lowest of any quarterback at the Combine and indicative of limited explosiveness. Will require time to assimilate a complex playbook.

Future: Athletic, zone-read quarterback ideally suited for a simplified, pocket-moving offense where he could make half-field, high-low reads. Carried a season-high 22 times in the Belk Bowl vs Arkansas and 21 times in each of two biggest matchups against North Carolina

and Clemson, totaling 204 carries in an unsophisticated system that relied on his legs more than his arm. Could warrant some interest as a tight end conversion.

Draft projection: Fifth- to sixth-round pick.

Scout's take: "(Evans) sprays the ball. He is not a go-thru-the-process guy. He has some physical talent but he is not ready. It was a shocker that he (declared) early. He's in the same simple offense as (Broncos QB Paxton Lynch) was at Memphis. There's going to be a big learning curve."

QB BRADY GUSTAFSON, #3 (Sr-5)

MONTANA ▶ GRADE: 4.97

Ht: 6-5 3/8 | Wt: 239 | 40: 5.04 | Arm: 34 | Hand: 9 3/8

History: Montana native also won a state basketball championship in high school. Accepted his only scholarship offer. Redshirted in 2012. Saw very limited action 2013-14 — completed 2-of-6 pass attempts (50.0 percent) for 40 yards with zero touchdowns and zero interceptions in 10 appearances. Head coach Bob Stitt arrived in '15, and Gustafson beat out six other quarterbacks for the No. 1 job — started all seven games he played, managing 167-290-1,984-12-9 (57.6), though he suffered a broken right fibula against Liberty and missed six mid-season contests. In his first career start, beat Carson Wentz's (Eagles) North Dakota State team. In '16, staved off competition from an FBS transfer (Reese Phillips from Kentucky) — was the Grizzlies' team MVP after starting all nine games played, totaling 260-396-2,785-25-8 (65.7). Sat out against Idaho State and Northern Colorado because of a sprained AC joint in his right (throwing) shoulder. Had 11 career fumbles. Went 9-7 as a starter. Team captain. Graduated.

Strengths: Excellent height, size and pocket stature with a sturdy build. Smart, understands passing concepts and can handle audibles at the line. Processes information quickly for limited starting experience. Will deliver the ball in the face of pressure. Unselfish, humble and diligent in his approach.

Weaknesses: Heavy-footed with limited escapability. Tends to throw flat-footed. Has a bit of a push delivery and tends to short-arm the ball from close range. Has an elongated deep-throwing motion and needs to learn to hasten his release. Sporadic ball placement — consistently off the mark and makes his receivers work hard for it. Needs to improve anticipation and deep accuracy and could stand to get stronger in the pocket to withstand the rush. Needs to learn to move safeties with his eyes. Not a confident, vocal triggerman. Often looks to the sideline for checks and pre-determined reads. Ball security has been an issue (11 fumbles in 16 starts). Only a one-and-a-half-year starter.

Future: Big-framed, pocket passer with enough size, toughness and arm talent to warrant developmental consideration. Excelled running a hurry-up offense with a weak supporting cast and has the intelligence and work ethic to attempt molding.

Draft projection: Priority free agent.

QB **BRAD KAAYA**, #15 (Jr-3)

MIAMI (FLA.) ▶ GRADE: 5.27
Ht: 6-3 7/8 | Wt: 214 | 40: 4.90e | Arm: 32 | Hand: 9 3/4

History: Los Angeles native won a state title at Chaminade College Prep. Recruited by then-head coach Al Golden. Made an immediate impact by starting all 13 games in 2014, completing 221-of-378 pass attempts (58.5 percent) for 3,198 yards with 26 touchdowns and 12 interceptions. Started all 12 games played in '15, and passed 238-389-3,238-16-5 (61.2). Did not suit up against Duke (concussion). Playing in Mark Richt's pro-style offense in '16, totaled 261-421-3,532-27-7 (62.0) in 13 starts. Hurt his right (throwing) shoulder against Florida State, and was limited in practice leading up to the North Carolina contest. Had 14 career fumbles. Went 22-16 as a starter. Three-year captain and two-time team MVP is Miami's all-time leading passer (9,968 yards). Opted not to run or jump at the Combine.

Strengths: Experienced, three-year starter. Confident decision-maker. Carries a swagger. Has worked from under center and in the shotgun in multiple offenses, including a pro-style set featuring progression reads and pro-style concepts — and it showed in his footwork at the Combine. Has enough arm strength to make all the throws, with a knack for making back-shoulder throws and delivering the deep fade. Consistently finds open throwing lanes and only had two batted passes in 2016. Delivers the ball under duress with defenders at his feet and side-steps the initial wave of pressure — fine footwork in the pocket. Good football intelligence.

Weaknesses: Has an elongated, slingshot delivery with some upper-body stiffness and tightness in his throwing motion and struggles to hasten his delivery on the move. Barely adequate foot speed to effectively roll out and play with precision outside the pocket or make plays with his feet — gets tracked down. Tends to throw a flat deep ball between the numbers and needs to learn to use more touch on posts, seams and crossing routes. Does not stand tall in the pocket or feel backside pressure well and really labors to escape it. Was

surrounded by a strong supporting cast that produced highly after the catch and made his receivers work too hard for the ball (placement and anticipation). Frequently checks down and does not have an advanced understanding of cycling through progressions.

Future: An efficient pocket passer lacking the arm and escapability desired in a front-line starter, yet possesses ample, pro-style experience, clean footwork and functional decision-making to survive with a talented supporting cast. Has some similarities to Bengals 2014 fifth-round pick (164th) AJ McCarron. Operated multiple offenses in college and could benefit from running the same system for an extended time in the NFL.

Draft projection: Fourth- to fifth-round pick.

Scout's take: "Coaches (at Miami) sell him hard, saying he is raw but talented and could be a first- or second-round pick. He is a bad athlete with a bad body and cannot get himself out of trouble (from the pass rush). I didn't like him nearly as much on film as he was described."

QB **CHAD KELLY**, #11 (Sr-5)

MISSISSIPPI ▶ GRADE: 5.10
Ht: 6-2e | Wt: 220e | 40: 4.85e | Arm: 31 7/8 | Hand: 9 1/4

History: Nephew of Hall of Famer Jim Kelly. Had a checkered prep career in New York, where he also played basketball and lacrosse. Was suspended the final seven games of his high school freshman football season and kicked off the team as a sophomore. Transferred to St. Joseph's and took his team to a pair of state championship games, winning as a junior. Committed to Clemson, and before setting foot on campus aimed a tweet at Tigers backup quarterback Cole Stoudt, saying Stout was "on the bench for a reason!" Redshirted in 2012. Tore his left ACL during '13 spring game, but saw action in five games and completed 10-of-17 pass attempts (58.8 percent) for 58 yards with zero touchdowns and zero interceptions. In April '14, was a passenger in a car that backed into the vehicle of a Clemson football intern. According to the intern, when she mentioned filing a police report, Kelly "got out of the car asking me not to call [police]. He became very agitated and was extremely disrespectful." Soon after, Kelly was benched during the spring game for verbally disrespecting coaches. He was dismissed for conduct detrimental to the team, and landed at East Mississippi Community College. In 12 games that fall, Kelly racked up 303-453-3,906-47-8 (66.9) passing and ran 69 times for 446 yards (6.5-yard average) and four touchdowns for the NJCAA national champs. Less than two weeks after committing to Ole Miss, was arrested in December when he refused to leave a Buffalo bar. According to reports, Kelly fought with bouncers, threatened to "spray this place" with an AK-47, and resisted officers when they tried to arrest him. Kelly was initially arraigned on seven charges, but ultimately pleaded guilty to non-criminal disorderly conduct and received 50 hours community service. Resurfaced with Ole Miss in '15, producing 298-458-4,042-31-13 (65.1) in 13 starts, including an MVP performance in a Sugar Bowl win over Oklahoma State. Became the first Rebels quarterback to defeat Alabama, Auburn, and LSU in the same season (five total victories of top-25 teams) while breaking or tying 14 school single-season records. Missed the final week of '16 spring practice because of sports hernia surgery. In the fall, started the first nine games and managed 205-328-2,758-19-8 (62.5) before suffering a torn right ACL and lateral meniscus — underwent season-ending surgery, and did not participate at Senior Bowl. Totaled 202-963-16 (4.8) as an FBS rusher. Had 18 career fumbles. Made headlines in November when he charged onto the field during his younger brother's high school game, entered a brawl — stemming from a late hit on his brother — and had to be restrained. Also gained notoriety — once in September and again in October — for direct messaging unwanted overtures to an adult film actress' Twitter account. Went 14-8 as a starter. Graduated. Invitation was rescinded from the Combine.

Strengths: Very good arm talent to fire the ball into small windows against tight, man coverage. Ultra-competitive and plays the game with moxie. Good football intelligence. Physically tough. Can withstand big hits and pop back up. Has NFL pedigree. Has a .636 career winning percentage as a starter and shown he can handle pressure rising to the occasion on big stages. Good run strength. Extremely passionate about football and works tirelessly to prepare for the game. Exceptional weight-room worker.

Weaknesses: Unorthodox throwing mechanics, frequently off his back foot with a low release point, leading to 30 batted passes the last two seasons, including a nation-leading 22 in 2015. Plays flat-footed with limited escapability and minimal scrambling talent. Consistently forces the ball into traffic. Excessive emotional outbursts have led to trouble on and off the field and his intense, abrasive personality has been difficult for coaches to manage. Off-field decision-making has brought needless distractions. May not be fully recovered from knee injury for training camp.

Future: Has desirable competitive zeal and intensity and has captained the Rebels to some program-defining victories, yet mechanics and maturity still are in need of much refinement to earn an NFL role and the extra maintenance involved with managing him could be more than many teams are willing to take on. Toughness and competitiveness could carry him to having a solid career if he is able to buy into the team concept. Draft position should provide extreme motivation to disprove critics.

Draft projection: Priority free agent.

Scout's take: "He's a loose cannon coming off an ACL injury and has a lot of (baggage) in his past. He got pulled from the Combine. It feels like Johnny Manziel all over again — too much entitlement and issues stacked on top of issues. For me, he's a free agent for someone else."

QB DeSHONE KIZER, #14 (Soph-3)

NOTRE DAME ▶ GRADE: 5.62

Ht: 6-4 1/4 | Wt: 233 | 40: 4.87 | Arm: 33 1/8 | Hand: 9 7/8

History: Toledo, Ohio, native won a state football championship in addition to playing baseball and basketball. Redshirted in 2014. Played all 13 games in '15, starting the final 11, and completed 211-of-335 pass attempts (63.0 percent) for 2,884 yards with 21 touchdowns and 10 interceptions. Began the '15 season sharing time with Malik Zaire, but took over in Week Three when Zaire was lost to injury. In '16, competed with Zaire for the starting job, and split time despite starting but was handed the reins one week into the season following strong performance vs. Texas in the season opener — passed 212-361-2,925-26-9 (58.7) in 12 starts, earning ND's team MVP award. Was benched midway through third quarter of 17-10 loss to Stanford after throwing interceptions on back-to-back drives, including a pick-six. Had 264 career rushes for 997 yards (3.8-yard average) and 18 touchdowns. Fumbled 10 times in two seasons. Finished 12-11 as a starter. Will be a 21-year-old rookie.

Strengths: Excellent size and fine movement skill for a big man — extends plays with his feet and scans the field well outside the pocket. Can zip the ball into tight spots, make every NFL throw and effortlessly uncork it 70 yards (see Michigan State). Good pocket strength. Can hasten his release and get rid of it quickly when needed. Good run skill on designed QB draws and zone reads. Very articulate during the interview process at the Combine.

Weaknesses: Marginal pocket poise — easily rattled and drops his eyes to the rush when live bullets start flying. Lack of timing and anticipation negates accuracy — is late to release the ball and misses too many wide-open receivers.

Takes needless sacks. Recorded the slowest 10-yards split (1.78 seconds), 20-yard shuttle (4.57) and 3-cone-drill time (7.41) of any QB at the Combine, indicative of limited burst, agility and hip flexibility. Leads receivers into traffic and will force it into double coverage, pressing and trying to do too much. Footwork requires refinement — base tends to widen and diminish ball velocity. Operates heavily out of the gun and will need to acclimate to playing under center. Very young, immature and susceptible to the trappings of the game. Has not demonstrated the competitive will to win or take-charge leadership that great quarterbacks possess. Too often approaches the game as if he has already made it and will need to learn what it means to work like a pro to succeed.

Future: A big pocket passer likely to be overdrafted on upside, Kizer looks every bit the part, with a hose of an arm and all the physical talent needed to thrive, yet he has not shown the accuracy, anticipation, passing instincts or all-in wiring desired in an NFL starter. Could struggle to sustain more than flashes of success until and unless he learns to appreciate the nuances of preparation. Boom-or-bust prospect that could disappoint a team with grand expectations. Played better in 2015 with a stronger supporting cast that featured a top-10 left tackle (Ronnie Stanley) and first-round receiver (Will Fuller) than he did in 2016. Similar talent to 2011 first-round (10th overall) selection Blaine Gabbert, who has had a different head coach, offensive coordinator and QB coach in each of his six seasons in the NFL and struggled to find stability after also entering the NFL as a 21-year-old sophomore.

Draft projection: Top-50 pick.

Scout's take: "You love his size and arm strength when you see him in person. He throws the ball with velocity. He's just not that accurate or consistent. He struggles with anticipation and overall accuracy. He is very streaky. I charted him 0-for-9 on pressure throws (in one game). I see his ceiling as a backup. Someone is going to draft him expecting him to be a lot more than that. Some of our scouts have first-round grades on him. I think they have been paying too much attention to the group-think. One question — when was the last time a quarterback that was benched for underperforming during the year selected in the first round?"

QB TREVOR KNIGHT, #8 (Sr-4)

TEXAS A&M   ▶ GRADE: 5.21

Ht: 6-1 3/8 | Wt: 219 | 40: 4.58 | Arm: 30 5/8 | Hand: 9 7/8

History: Twin brother, Connor, played at Oklahoma. Trevor prepped in Texas, and be-

gan his college career at Oklahoma. Wore jersey No. 9. As a true freshman in 2013, started 5-of-8 games played and completed 79-of-134 pass attempts (59.0 percent) for 819 yards with nine touchdowns and five interceptions, including an MVP performance in the Sugar Bowl against Alabama. Opened the season as the No. 1 for new offensive coordinator Lincoln Riley, but Knight bruised his knee against West Virginia and relinquished the job to Blake Bell. Despite suffering a separated shoulder against Oklahoma State, started the final three games in place of the injured Bell. Started all 10 games played in '14, producing 179-316-2,300-14-12 (56.6). Added a receiving touchdown. Missed the final three regular season contests after suffering a transient quadriplegia injury (cervical spine injury normally caused by hyperextension of the neck). In '15, tossed 22-40-305-2-2 (55.0), as he was overtaken by Baker Mayfield. After earning a finance degree from OU, joined Texas A&M as a graduate transfer for the '16 season — started all 11 games played, and totaled 193-362-2,432-19-7 (53.3) for offensive coordinator Noel Mazzone. Injured his right (throwing) shoulder against Mississippi State, and did not play against Ole Miss and UTSA. Exited the LSU game in the fourth quarter with a left knee injury. Ran 253 times in his career for 1,467 yards (5.8-yard average) and 18 touchdowns. Had 14 career fumbles. Team captain won the Wuerffel Trophy, which honors commitment to community service. Produced an 18-8 career starting record. Was the only quarterback to run the 60-yard shuttle (11.28 seconds) and ran faster than many receivers.

Strengths: Very good athlete, as evidenced by top vertical jump (35 1/2 inches) and broad jump (10'5") of any Combine QB. Has quick feet, as confirmed by 20-yard shuttle time (4.14 seconds) and the scrambling ability to avoid the first wave of pressure and find rushing lanes when the pocket breaks down. Can sling the ball off-balance from various arm angles — excels improvising in the pocket and hastening his release. Has displayed moxie in the clutch, captaining a Sugar Bowl win over Alabama as a true freshman and leading a double-overtime victory against Tennessee in '16. Quick snap delivery. Flashes ability to drop it in a bucket downfield and throw with velocity, tying for the second-highest ball speed (59 m.p.h.) at the Combine. Competitive. Strong personal and football character. Good weight room worker. Mature leader. Takes the game very seriously. Tough and will battle through injuries.

Weaknesses: Below-average size, measur-

QUARTERBACKS

ing the shortest of any passer at the Combine. Risk-taking decision-maker who tends to throw off balance without his feet set and the ball tends to sail and veer off-target as a result, responsible for a dismal 55.5 career completion percentage. Seldom climbs the pocket, tending to flee when it breaks down. Benefited from a big receiving cast that attacks the ball in the air at Texas A&M. Has never made it through a full season healthy given his scrambling style.

Future: An athletic, run-around, sandlot style quarterback lacking ideal size, field vision and accuracy for the NFL game. Best fit could come in a reserve role for an offense featuring a lot of play-action passing and moving pockets such as Seattle, Green Bay or Kansas City.

Draft projection: Priority free agent.

QB MITCH LEIDNER, #7 (Sr-5)

MINNESOTA ▶ GRADE: 5.09
Ht: 6-3 1/2 | Wt: 226 | 40: 4.98 | Arm: 33 3/4 | Hand: 10

History: Younger brother, Matt, is a center for the Gophers. Minnesota native also played basketball in high school. Recruited by then-head coach Jerry Kill. Redshirted in 2012. Made ten appearances in '13, drawing four starts, and completed 43-of-78 pass attempts (55.1 percent) for 619 yards with three touchdowns and one interception. Took ownership of the position in '14 by starting all 12 games played and passing 122-237-1,798-11-8 (51.5). Strained his left MCL against Middle Tennessee State, then was sidelined against San Jose State because of torn ligaments and dislocated toes in his left foot. In '15, re-injured his foot in September versus Kent State, but started all 13 games, and produced 242-407-2,701-14-11 (59.5). Had post-season surgery to repair damaged ligaments. After three years playing for offensive coordinator Matt Limegrover, transitioned to Jay Johnson in '16 when he started all 12 games played, totaling 173-307-2,169-8-12 (56.4). Did not play against Maryland (concussion). Had 446 career rushes for 1,495 yards (3.4-yard average) and 33 touchdowns. Also caught two passes for 25 yards (12.5-yard average). Had 28 career fumbles. Went 25-16 as a starter. Three-time captain garnered team awards for MVP, most courage, and love of the game (twice), as well as unselfishness. Graduated with a kinesiology degree.

Strengths: Excellent size with long arms and a high release point. Experienced, three-year starter. Comfortable working from underneath center. Good pocket strength. Good ball placement and accuracy driving the ball on deep outs — can fit the ball into tight spots. Athletic enough to dart for the sticks and throw with

accuracy on the move. Strong personal character. Competitive goal-line runner (33 career rush TDs).

Weaknesses: Delivery is a bit elongated and has to wind up to uncork it. Average football intelligence. Is not a decisive triggerman — locks onto receivers and forces the ball into coverage too often. Needs to improve his timing and anticipation and learn how to use his eyes to manipulate coverage. Often does not recognize robber coverage and routes are undercut. Presses too much and does not show the moxie, confidence or poise desired at the QB position. Has a 36-32 career TD-INT ratio combined with 28 career fumbles.

Future: A good-sized, strong-armed thrower with the toughness and big-play capability to fit as a backup in a vertical-power offense and produce chunk plays. Will require years holding a clipboard and learning the game before he is ready, though could have a Drew Stanton-like career as a long-term backup. Best fit would be with a big-strike, downfield passing attack such as in Arizona, Tampa Bay or Pittsburgh.

Draft projection: Late draftable pick.

QB SEFO LIUFAU, #13 (Sr-4)

COLORADO ▶ GRADE: 4.94
Ht: 6-3 3/8 | Wt: 232 | 40: 5.11 | Arm: 33 1/2 | Hand: 10 3/4

History: Uncle, Jack Thompson, was drafted third overall in 1979 and had a six-year career as a quarterback with the Bengals and Buccaneers (1979-84). Uncle, Sale Isaia, was an offensive lineman who started 14 games for the Patriots in 2000. As a Washington prep, Liufau also lettered four times in basketball and averaged nearly a double-double his last two seasons. Originally committed to Colorado (his only offer) and then-head coach and current 49ers TE coach Jon Embree, and honored his commitment when Mike MacIntyre arrived. Was slated to redshirt in 2013, but was thrust into action in Week Five — started 7-of-8 games played and completed 149-of-251 pass attempts (59.4 percent) for 1,779 yards with 12 touchdowns and eight interceptions. Started 11-of-12 games in '14 — set 51 school records by passing 325-498-3,200-28-15 (65.3). Sustained a concussion against Arizona, and did not start against Oregon. Added two receptions for 24 yards (12.0-yard average) and one touchdown. In '15, started the first 11 games, managing 214-344-2,418-9-6 (62.2) before suffering a season-ending Lisfranc injury to his left foot (missed '16 spring practice). In the fall, started 10-of-11 games played, and tossed 200-319-2,366-11-6 (62.7). Sprained his right ankle against Michigan — missed the next two games and did not start against USC, then aggravated the injury in the Pac-12 championship against Washington. Recorded 383 career rushes for 931 yards (2.4-yard average) and 13 touchdowns. Had 20 career fumbles. Went 16-24 as a starter. Owns 98 CU records — including total yards (10,509), passing yards (9,568) and quarterback starts (39) — and was the first three-year Buffaloes captain since the 1890s.

Strengths: Experienced, four-year starter. Excellent career production re-writing Colorado's record books. Very tough — consistently hangs onto the ball and delivers in the face of pressure. Good personal and football character. Showed resiliency helping turn around a downtrodden program during four-year stay.

Weaknesses: Marginal foot speed to escape the rush or create with his feet. Limited arm strength. Tends to birddog his primary target. Does not anticipate well and makes too many errantly, mistimed throws behind receivers for a four-year starter. Accuracy is consistently off the mark. Has not been asked to make many full-field, NFL style progression reads and most throws are pre-determined. Could stand to speed up his set-up and delivery. Has been dinged a lot and needs to learn to do a better job protecting his body and sliding.

Future: Very good-sized, streaky, shotgun spread quarterback with intriguing size and toughness. Needs to improve his timing, touch, anticipation and accuracy to earn an NFL role holding a clipboard.

Draft projection: Priority free agent.

Scout's take: "(Liufau) didn't look like he belonged at the Senior Bowl."

QB **WES LUNT**, #12 (Sr-5)

ILLINOIS ▶ GRADE: 5.06
Ht: 6-4 1/4 | Wt: 222 | 40: 4.86 | Arm: 32 | Hand: 9 1/4

History: Illinois native won a pair of state championships in high school (also earned three basketball letters). Broke his right foot while lifting weights the summer prior to his senior season. Began his college career at Oklahoma State, where he started 5-of-6 games played as a true freshman in 2012 — completed 81-of-131 pass attempts (61.8 percent) for 1,108 yards with six touchdowns and seven interceptions. Dislocated his left kneecap against Louisiana-Lafayette, and sustained a concussion against Kansas State. Slid down the depth chart by the end of '13 spring practice, at which time he decided to transfer. Joined U of I that summer, and sat out the season per NCAA transfer rules. In '14, started 7-of-8 games played, and tossed 153-241-1,763-14-3 (63.5). Sprained his

right knee against Texas State, and did not play against Nebraska. Broke his left fibula against Purdue, sidelining him for three weeks. Did not play against Northwestern, and did not start the bowl game against Louisiana Tech (coach's decision). Led the Big Ten in attempts and completions in '15 when he started all 12 games, and produced 270-481-2,761-14-6 (56.1). Started 7-of-8 games played in '16, managing 127-232-1,376-8-3 (54.7). Suffered a back injury against Purdue — missed four games, and did not start against Wisconsin. Had nine career fumbles. Team captain played for three different coaching staffs at Illinois, and had five different quarterback coaches in five years. Graduated with a sports management degree. Produced a 13-18 career starting record.

Strengths: Good size and arm strength. Shows better ball placement and more accuracy than his low completion percentage would indicate given his weak supporting cast and frequent drops (42 by Illini targets in 2015). Throws a fine deep ball and can drop it in a bucket. Very smart with good football IQ. Had a 42-19 career TD-INT ratio with a modest supporting cast. Takes the game seriously.

Weaknesses: Has a linear build susceptible to injury. Lacks leadership qualities and is not a vocal, take-charge field general capable of inspiring confidence in a huddle, carrying an offense or calling out teammates. Is a career 58.2-percent passer and timing needs to improve. Lacks pocket awareness and has very limited mobility, likely to lead to greater injuries. Has been slowed by back injuries, and long-term durability must be evaluated carefully.

Future: A good-sized, strong-armed pocket passer lacking the intangibles and durability to survive in more than a reserve role. Intelligent, introverted potential backup with a chance to stick as a clipboard holder, capable of learning weekly game plans with minimal repetition.

Draft projection: Priority free agent.

Scout's take: "Lunt has some physical talent, but he is not a leader. He is a draftable talent, but he does not have the personality you need to lead at the position. He just doesn't have it in him. He does have enough traits to get you through a game as a backup."

QB **PATRICK MAHOMES**, #5 (Jr-3)

TEXAS TECH ▶ GRADE: 5.98
Ht: 6-2 | Wt: 225 | 40: 4.82 | Arm: 33 1/4 | Hand: 9 1/4

History: Father, Pat, was an 11-year MLB pitcher. Patrick was a three-sport star as a Texas prep. As a senior, amassed 5,567 total yards and 65 touchdowns, averaged 19 points on the hardwood, and was drafted by the Detroit Ti-

QUARTERBACKS

gers. As a true freshman in 2014, started 4-of-7 games played, and completed 105-of-185 pass attempts (56.8 percent) for 1,547 yards with 16 touchdowns and four interceptions, including a Big 12 freshman-record 30-56-598-6-1 (53.6) performance against fifth-ranked Baylor. Sustained a concussion against Texas. In '15, led the country in total offense (393 yards per game) and the conference in passing — piled up 364-573-4,653-36-15 (63.5) in 13 starts, including a historic game against Oklahoma when he set the NCAA single-game total offense record with 819 yards (734 passing, 85 rushing). Is the youngest quarterback in FBS history to record 5,000 yards of total offense in a season. Took home the Sammy Baugh award and paced the country in passing yards, total touchdowns (53), and total yards (5,337) in '16 by racking up 388-591-5,052-41-10 (65.7) in 12 starts. Sprained the AC joint in his right (throwing) shoulder against Kansas. Recorded 308 career rushes for 845 yards (2.7-yard average) and 22 touchdowns. Had 18 career fumbles. Went 13-16 in 29 career starts, totaling 11,252 passing yards, 12,097 total yards, and 115 touchdowns. Team captain.

Strengths: Good size and strength in his body. Outstanding arm talent — can drive the ball with top velocity and high RPM's, evidenced at the Combine where he was the only quarterback to register a ball speed of 60 m.p.h. Throws with fine downfield touch and accuracy from any location. Manipulates his arm and throwing platform with ease and can alter his release point, using an over-the-top, sidearm or a 3/4 delivery from a variety of angles. Makes some rare, John Elway-esque "wow" throws and possesses the best arm rifle of any passer in the draft. Very good awareness and feet to maneuver, spin out of pressure to find open throwing lanes and buy a second chance. Recorded the best 20-yard short shuttle time (4.08 seconds) of any quarterback at the Combine and is effective sidestepping the initial wave and improvising on rollouts and bootlegs, where he has the ability to create magic on the move and convert broken plays into big-chunk gains. Functional run strength on zone-read option runs. Exceptional competitor and overall production.

Weaknesses: Erratic decision-maker with double-digit interception totals the last two seasons. Operates heavily in a simplistic, shotgun, spread offense that calls for one-look reads to many stationary targets. Overly reliant on his extreme arm talent and gets careless with his mechanics and unorthodox delivery, too often throwing off his back foot from odd angles and even attempting left-handed passes on the move (see Oklahoma). Has average agility and scrambling ability — avoids few tacklers in the open field. Will press to make plays and force the ball into tight spaces. Measured 17.6 percent body-fat percentage, greater than some lean linemen, and could stand to improve conditioning. Needs to take better care of the football on the move and cut down on 18 career fumbles. Has a .448 career winning percentage.

Future: Fearless, improvisational, pocket-passing, play-action, Air-Raid gunslinger with a flair for the big play, yet a knack for still making too many boneheaded, high-risk throws. Runs to set up the pass and can invoke fear in defensive coordinators with his flame-throwing arm talent, Houdini magic and pocket-moving passing skill. An unrefined gamer with terrific upside, Mahomes could ideally fit in a downfield passing attack such as Arizona, Buffalo or Pittsburgh. Could ideally use a year as a backup in an NFL offense to acclimate to the sophistication of NFL terminology and become familiar with the complexity of coverages he will see in the pros. Pure physical talent could allow him to have the longest career of any passer in the draft.

Draft projection: Top-40 pick.

Scout's take: "Mahomes is as talented as they come with his arm talent. He is very impressive. He's not a great athlete. You see it with some of the hits he takes that he cannot avoid. He has some stiffness in his body, but boy can he throw it. I'm not a fan of the offense he ran and there are times you ask yourself — 'what was he thinking?' — though he is tough as (iron)."

QB-SS **NICK MULLENS**, #9 (Sr-4)

SOUTHERN MISSISSIPPI　▶ GRADE: 4.92

Ht: 6-0 3/4 | Wt: 207 | 40: 4.70e | Arm: 30 1/4 | Hand: 9 1/4

History: Fiancé, Haleigh, was a Southern Miss cheerleader. Nick also played baseball as a prep in Alabama, where he was honored as the state's Gatorade Football Player of the Year — led Spain Park High to its first regional title in school history. Flipped his commitment from Jacksonville State to UAB before settling on Southern Miss. As a true freshman in 2013 (wore jersey No. 14), completed 136-of-276 pass attempts (49.3 percent) for 1,776 yards with 13 touchdowns and 14 interceptions in nine games (started the final six). Started all 10 games played in '14, totaling 218-365-2,470-12-9 (59.7). Missed two games after suffering a joint capsule injury in his right foot. Was the Conference USA Offensive Player of the Year in '15 — started 14 games, and piled up 331-521-4,476-38-12 (63.5). In '16, transitioned from head coach Todd Monken to Jay Hopson — started all 11 games played, and managed 243-384-3,272-24-11 (63.3). Dislocated the thumb on his right (throwing) hand against UTSA — the bone protruded through his skin, but he returned to the game. Sustained a concussion against Charlotte, and did not play against Old Dominion and North Texas. Became the Golden Eagles' all-time leading passer with 11,994 passing yards and 87 touchdown passes. Had 23 career fumbles. Went 20-21 as a starter. Spent four years under the tutelage of Chip Lindsey — two years in high school and two years at Southern Miss. On pace to graduate with a marketing degree.

Strengths: Three-and-a-half-year starter with outstanding career production, holding nearly every passing record in school history. Physically tough and will battle through injuries — asked to have the bone sticking through his thumb to be pushed in and stitched, only to re-enter the game and throw another TD pass. Good release quickness. Smart and articulate.

Weaknesses: Very marginal size with small hands and a frame not built to withstand heavy contact in the pros. Limited arm talent and escapability, resulting in too many direct hits. Throws the ball to spots and too often up for grabs, with 46 career interceptions. Struggles finding open throwing lanes and had 23 batted passes the last two seasons. Very inconsistent deep accuracy.

Future: Undersized, unassuming passer excelled most as a junior before the departure of Rams sixth-round pick Mike Thomas and Tampa Bay Buccaneers offensive coordinator Todd Monken. A good, tough football player with the toughness and competitiveness to prove more than an arm in a camp. Has some Jeff Garcia qualities to emerge over time if he pursues his passion, though might require a stop in the CFL. Might have a chance as a developmental NFL safety if he runs well enough.

Draft projection: Priority free agent.

Coach's take: "He's a football player. I can't say that any other way. I have told a lot of guys that I have had the opportunity in the past to be around guys like Byron Leftwich and Chad Pennington. Nick Mullens throws the ball as well as any quarterback that I've ever been around. He is a tremendous football player. He is all that he is advertised to be and more."

— *Southern Miss Head Coach Jay Hopson*

QB **NATHAN PETERMAN**, #4 (Sr-5)

PITTSBURGH ▶ GRADE: 5.36

Ht: 6-2 1/2 | Wt: 226 | 40: 4.81 | Arm: 32 | Hand: 9 7/8

History: Dad is a pastor. Married. Prepped in Florida. Committed to Tennessee and then-

head coach Derek Dooley. Began his college career at Tennessee, where he fractured a finger in the spring of 2012 before redshirting. In 13 (wore jersey No. 12), appeared in four games, and completed 10-of-23 pass attempts (43.5 percent) for 45 yards with zero touchdowns and two interceptions before tearing ligaments in his right (throwing) hand against Florida (lone start) and undergoing season-ending surgery. Began '14 as a backup to Justin Worley, and finished the season behind Joshua Dobbs. In seven games (one start), recorded 10-20-49-0-0 (50.0). After graduating with a communications degree in three years, transferred to Pittsburgh to play for offensive coordinator / QB coach Jim Chaney, who helped recruit Peterman to Tennessee. Played all 13 games in '15, starting the final 11 games, and produced 193-314-2,287-20-8 (61.5). Started all 13 games in '16 — under OC Matt Canada — and totaled 185-306-2,855-27-7 (60.5). Sustained a concussion in the Pinstripe Bowl against Northwestern. Recorded 172 career rushes for 525 yards (3.1-yard average) and five touchdowns. Had 16 fumbles. Went 14-10 as Pittsburgh's starter and 0-2 for the Vols. Earned his MBA.

Strengths: Operated a pro-style offense with checks and audibles and appears very comfortable selling play-action fakes and dropping from underneath center. Outstanding passing mechanics — well-coached and in rhythm. Very good football intelligence. Understands route concepts and how to manipulate coverage defenders. Very efficient and was the only quarterback to direct an upset victory over eventual national champion Clemson, proving he can handle the pressure of playing on a big stage. Good short-to-intermediate timing, anticipation and accuracy — hits receivers in stride. Sees the field and distributes the ball with fine touch and anticipation. Adequate athlete able to slide in the pocket, roll out and create some plays with his feet. Registered 7.9 percent body fat at the Combine, the only quarterback to measure in single digits and indicative of a highly-conditioned athlete and diligent weight-room worker. Very professional approach. Intense competitor. Film junkie. Learns quickly. Commands respect in the huddle and is a strong communicator.

Weaknesses: Does not drive the ball downfield and arm talent is just adequate. The deeper he throws, the more sporadic his ball placement. Could stand to improve his pocket presence — takes time to process what he sees at times and can be late to feel pressure. Had a strong supporting cast.

Future: Has the charisma of Tony Romo

and intangibles of Kirk Cousins and comparable arm talent to both. Is not ready to step into prime time and take over as an immediate starter, yet possesses the intelligence and leadership qualities to emerge as an eventual starter in Year Two with continued refinement.

Draft projection: Third- to fourth-round pick.

Scout's take: "Peterman does not belong in the second round, but some scouts have graded him up there. You have to keep in mind what he had around him — a strong running game and one of the best (offensive) lines in the country. He is a smart guy that understands the system they ran. He is just a bit limited with his physical traits."

QB **ANTONIO PIPKIN**, #2 (Sr-4)
TIFFIN (OHIO)　　　　　　　▶ GRADE: 4.96
Ht: 6-0 7/8 | Wt: 225 | 40: 4.66 | Arm: 32 1/4 | Hand: 10

History: Gary, Ind. native also played basketball and baseball in high school. Played all 44 games of his career, starting the final 41. As a true freshman in 2013, completed 254-of-382 pass attempts (66.5 percent) for 2,316 yards with 12 touchdowns and 12 interceptions. In '14, passed 260-409-2,863-19-8 (63.6). Was on the Dragons' basketball team his first two years. Focusing solely on football in '15, produced 250-390-3,227-32-6 (64.1), earning Great Lakes Intercollegiate Athletic Conference Back of the Year. In '16, was a Harlon Hill Trophy finalist (Division II MVP) and the GLIAC Player of the Year — recorded 216-333-2,534-25-6 (64.9). Logged 509 career rushes for 2,207 yards (4.3-yard average) and 25 touchdowns. Had 20 career fumbles. Two-year captain. Rewrote Tiffin's passing records. On track to complete his sports management degree. Was only the third Division II quarterback ever invited to the Senior Bowl. Had a 20-21 career record as a starter.

Strengths: Has a strong, compact frame well built to withstand contact. Outstanding arm strength to drive the ball and uncork it deep. Very good escapability to shake the rush and create with his feet outside the pocket — scorched DII competition with regularity and could move the sticks improvising. Good run strength.

Weaknesses: Footwork needs refinement — does not throw on balance and forces the ball too much. Operated heavily out of the gun and did not cycle through NFL-style progression reads in a simplified offense. Threw a pair of interceptions in the Senior Bowl and did not adapt well to facing better competition. Needs to learn to take better care of the football.

Future: An athletic, quick-footed dual-threat quarterback with the physical talent to develop into a No. 3 with continued refinement. Did not prove he was more than a big fish in a small pond at the Senior Bowl and will require time to be molded.

Draft projection: Priority free agent.

Scout's take: "I thought he struggled more as the Senior Bowl week went on. The stage looked too big and the game looked too fast for him. He has some tools to work with, but he's going to need a lot of time."

QB **COOPER RUSH**, #10 (Sr-5)
CENTRAL MICHIGAN　　　　▶ GRADE: 5.07
Ht: 6-2 5/8 | Wt: 228 | 40: 4.93 | Arm: 32 3/8 | Hand: 9 1/8

History: Michigan native also played basketball as a prep. Was the state's Gatorade Player of the Year as a senior, accounting for 4,760 total yards and 64 touchdowns, including 48 passing (single-season state record). Redshirted in 2012. After the starting quarterback was injured in the '13 season opener, Rush started the final 10 games and completed 177-of-312 pass attempts (56.7 percent) for 2,349 yards with 15 touchdowns and 15 interceptions. Started all 39 games his last three seasons — totaled 243-382-3,157-27-13 (63.6) in '14; 324-489-3,848-25-11 (66.3); and 278-465-3,540-23-16 (59.8) in '16. As a junior, transitioned from head coach Dan Enos to John Bonamego. Had 24 career fumbles. Went 25-24 as a starter. Two-time team captain graduated with an actuarial science degree, and was a Campbell Trophy finalist ("Academic Heisman"). Pulled his hamstring on the second 40 but completed on-the-field workout at the Combine.

Strengths: Experienced, four-year starter in a pro-style offense where he consistently operated from underneath center and out of the shotgun. Tough and very competitive. Good poise — climbs the pocket to buy time and keeps scanning with bodies around him. Fine touch and anticipation. Very intelligent. Makes the line calls and processes coverages quickly. Understands route concepts. Decisive trigger. Good football character — could absorb a playbook quickly. The game is very important to him and he takes it seriously.

Weaknesses: Limited arm strength, weakened by a tendency to throw off his back foot, and confirmed by ball speeds that did not reach 50 mph at the Combine. Struggles fitting the ball into tight windows — hangs the ball and delivers too many floaters that will be preyed upon by NFL defensive backs. Has a low release point and struggles to find open throwing windows, leading to 30 batted passes the last three years. Has very small hands that have contributed to too many fumbles (24) throughout his career and will affect grip in rain and snow. Marginal foot quickness — short-stepper with limited scrambling ability. Quiet-natured for a leadership position.

Future: Productive, mid-major quarterback with physical limitations that will challenge him to acclimate to the speed of the NFL game. Could carve a niche in a dink-and-dunk, rhythm-timing passing game. Shows some similarities to Packers 2016 undrafted free-agent Joe Callahan.

Draft projection: Priority free agent.

Scout's take: "He could compete for a third spot in a camp. Some team might take a flier late (in the draft) on his (experience). He doesn't have a big arm. I didn't give him a draftable grade."

QB SETH RUSSELL, #17 (Sr-5)

BAYLOR ▶ GRADE: 5.04

Ht: 6-2 5/8 | Wt: 213 | 40: 4.75e | Arm: 32 1/4 | Hand: 9 5/8

History: Engaged to be married to former Baylor soccer player Ashleigh James. Texas native also lettered in basketball and track. Junior season was hampered by a broken finger on his right (throwing) hand. Redshirted in 2012. Backed up Bryce Petty the next two years. Appeared in seven games in '13, completing 26-of-43 pass attempts (60.5 percent) for 427 yards with three touchdowns and three interceptions. In '14, tossed 48-85-804-8-1 (56.5) in eight games (one start). Started the first seven games in '15, and produced 119-200-2,104-29-6 (59.5) before suffering a season-ending neck fracture. Broke single-season school record with 10.06 yards per play. Started the first nine games in '16, and totaled 152-278-2,126-20-8 (54.7) before suffering a fractured left ankle and undergoing season-ending surgery (did not participate at Senior Bowl). Was in concussion protocol after the Texas game, but did not miss a start. Recorded 199 career rushes for 1,240 yards (6.2-yard average) and 20 touchdowns. Had 11 career fumbles. Went 14-3 as a starter. Graduated with a communication studies degree.

Strengths: Very good athlete to maneuver around the pocket and sling it. Very quick release. Physically tough to stand tall with the rush closing in and deliver. Will drop his shoulder, barrel through contact and make plays with his feet as a scrambler. Has a good football-playing temperament and is very coachable. Outstanding intangibles — very polite, respectful and respected team leader. Has a .824 career winning percentage as a starter.

Weaknesses: Ran a simplified shotgun spread offense featuring little NFL sophistication and tries fitting the ball into coverage too much. Is not asked to decipher coverage with a lot of one-look, quick-toss concepts. Marginal timing and anticipation. Deep ball tends to sail. Was a 56.9-percent career passer with only 17 career starts. Did not drive the ball with the same torque or velocity as a senior following neck injury in 2015, and injuries have continued to mount and raise concerns about his durability. Measured both the lightest (213 pounds) and highest body-fat percentage (17.7) of any QB at the Combine, greater than some lean linemen, and could stand to improve conditioning.

Future: A good-sized, athletic, system quarterback with enough physical talent, intangibles and upside to warrant developing. Injury history is concerning, and future looked brighter prior to neck injury. Developmental project.

Draft projection: Priority free agent.

QB ALEK TORGENSON, #10 (Sr-4)

PENN ▶ GRADE: 5.19

Ht: 6-1 3/4 | Wt: 215 | 40: 4.91 | Arm: 32 5/8 | Hand: 9 1/4

History: Prepped in California. Played one game (season finale) as a true freshman in 2013, and completed 6-of-10 pass attempts (61.8 percent) for 109 yards with two touchdowns and zero interceptions. Started all 10 games in '14, and recorded 260-421-2,689-14-11 (61.8). Started all nine games played in '15, and totaled 163-236-1,996-19-3 (69.1) in a newly installed up-tempo, spread offense. Sat out against Fordham (concussion). Led the Quakers to their second consecutive share of the Ivy League championship in '16 — started all 10 games, and produced 198-296-2,231-17-4 (66.9). Totaled 319 career rushes for 912 yards (2.9-yard average) and 18 touchdowns. Had 20 career fumbles. Went 16-13 as a starter. Penn's all-time leader in passing touchdowns (52), completion percentage (65.1), and total offense (7,937 yards).

Strengths: Well-built. Sets his feet quickly and makes quick decisions. Good caretaker — takes what the defense gives and does not force it into coverage. Good on-field leadership qualities to direct an offense. Fearless runner when he tucks and runs. Good run strength. Very intelligent. Proved he belonged at the NFLPA all-star game and adapted well to the competition.

Weaknesses: Below-average hand size that weakens grip and has contributed to too many fumbles (20). Has not regularly faced top competition in the Ivy League. Operates exclusively from the shotgun and will need to adjust to taking snaps under center (footwork and

QUARTERBACKS

17

rhythm). Will need to learn how to diagnose coverages and move safeties with his eyes — birddogs too much. Consistently overshoots the deep ball throwing the ball away from coverage and needs to develop more deep touch.

Future: A savvy, dink-and-dunk, rhythm-timing passer who opened some eyes against post-season all-star competition. Has the intelligence and precision to be developed into a potential backup.

Draft projection: Late draftable pick.

Scout's take: "The Penn quarterback is the best of the group (at the NFLPA all-star game). He has the best arm. He can roll out in the pocket. I'm not sure yet if he is a better CFL quarterback or NFL backup, but he has talent you'd like to work with. He's smart and athletic."

QB MITCHELL TRUBISKY, #10 (Jr-4)

NORTH CAROLINA ▶ GRADE: 6.12

Ht: 6-2 1/8 | Wt: 222 | 40: 4.67 | Arm: 32 | Hand: 9 1/2

History: Nickname is Mr. Biscuit. Was Ohio's "Mr. Football." Finished his prep career ranked amongst the top 10 passers in state history — racked up 9,126 passing yards and 92 touchdowns, as well as 1,559 rushing yards and 33 touchdowns. Redshirted in 2013. For two years backed up Marquise Williams, who was undrafted and signed, only to be cut. Made 10 appearances in '14, and completed 42-of-78 pass attempts (53.8 percent) for 459 yards with five touchdowns and four interceptions. Made nine appearances in '15, and tossed 40-47-555-6-0 (85.1). Broke out in '16 when he set UNC single-season records for passing attempts, completions, passing yards, touchdown passes, and total offense (4,056 yards) — started all 13 games, and produced 304-446-3,748-30-6 (68.2). Had 120 career rushes for 439 yards (3.7-yard average) and eight interceptions. Fumbled seven times. Team captain. Finished season 8-5 as a starter.

Strengths: Very good accuracy and can make all the throws and lay in the deep ball very nicely. Good agility to create extra time in the pocket and dash for the sticks — can buy a second chance and keeps his eyes downfield looking to throw. Recorded a 1.56-second 10-yard time, second only to Deshaun Watson at the Combine. Has a rapid release with a smooth, natural delivery and can snap it quickly in the face of pressure. Comfortable in the pocket. Throws a very catchable ball. Good timing and anticipation, especially on intermediate crossers — throws receivers open. Had a 5-1 TD-INT ratio as a junior. Commanded game-winning drives in the final seconds of victories against Pittsburgh and Florida State in back-to-back weeks.

Weaknesses: Below-average size. Operated a spread offense featuring a lot of hitches, screens and confidence-building, lateral tosses — often throws to wide-open receivers. Looked to the sideline for play calls and has very limited experience reading defenses and making progression reads. Rarely played underneath center and footwork will require a lot of refinement. Has difficulty adjusting under duress, and ball loses velocity on the move. Arm strength is not elite and arm tops out at 55 yards (in five games viewed), resulting in underthrows (see Duke, Pittsburgh and Stanford). Only converted 38 percent of third downs (in five games viewed) and does not consistently keep the chains moving. Only a one-year starter. Does not have a strong grasp of diagnosing coverages and will birddog his primary target — eyes are not advanced. Can easily be confused by disguised coverages and nickel robbers (see pick-six vs. Stanford). Needs to gain a better understanding of situational football — took a sack on third-down instead of throwing the ball away and was knocked out of field-goal range in the 25-23 loss to Stanford in the Sun Bowl. Threw game-losing interception in final minutes vs. Duke and could not close out victories on last drive in final two games vs. NC State and Stanford, tailing off at season's end.

Future: A raw, ascending passer whose best football is ahead of him, Trubisky has the accuracy, release quickness and athletic ability to fit in a precision-matchup offense such as the 49ers, Bears or Jets. Does not have a rifle arm and he is going to require a lot of patience adapting to NFL terminology, learning to diagnose coverages and handling complex pressure packages. Though his resume is far from complete, he has eventual starter traits and is likely to be overdrafted on upside to the detriment of his NFL development if it forces him to be thrust into the lineup prematurely.

Draft projection: First-round pick.

Scout's take: "He is by far not a franchise quarterback. He's a system quarterback in a high-percentage offense that throws five screens a game and a lot of flares, hitches, digs and dumpoffs. He doesn't make a lot of downfield NFL throws, and he throws into coverage a lot. He's probably not much different than the quarterbacks drafted in the first round last year from Memphis and Cal who weren't ready by any means to be drafted that early. He's arguably the best (quarterback) of the class, but you're going to make him the first pick in the draft and put a billion-dollar franchise on his back? Ownership better be on board with a long-term plan. He's sitting in the top of the (second round) for me." I'm expecting he'll be one of the first players selected with the way quarterbacks come off."

QB DESHAUN WATSON, #4 (Jr-3)

CLEMSON ▶ GRADE: 6.18

Ht: 6-2 1/2 | Wt: 221 | 40: 4.68 | Arm: 33 | Hand: 9 3/4

History: Watson grew up in Georgia, raised, along with three siblings, by his single mother, Deanne, who received a Habitat for Humanity home presented by Warrick Dunn. Deanne endured tongue cancer during Deshaun's freshman and sophomore high-school years. Watson also played basketball, but quickly emerged as a blue-chip signal caller. A four-year varsity starter, he led his team to its first state championship in over a century, was named Georgia player of the year three times, and won the state's Gatorade Player of the Year award as a senior. He amassed 13,077 passing yards, 155 passing touchdowns, 4,057 rushing yards, and 63 rushing touchdowns, and owns state career records for total offense (17,134 yards) and total touchdowns (218). Watson committed to Clemson during his sophomore year, and honored the commitment despite finishing his high school career as a consensus All-American and consensus No. 1 dual-threat quarterback recruit. As a true freshman in 2014, started 5-of-8 games played, and completed 93-of-137 pass attempts (67.9 percent) for 1,466 yards with 14 touchdowns and two interceptions, including a six-touchdown performance in his first career start against North Carolina. Broke his right (throwing) hand against Louisville, sidelining him for three games. Suffered a sprained MCL and bone bruise in his left knee against Georgia Tech, then tore the ACL in practice the following week — sat out against Georgia State, but played through the injury in a win over South Carolina before undergoing season-ending surgery prior to the Tigers' bowl game versus Oklahoma. Missed '15 spring practice, but returned to start all 15 games in the fall — produced 333-491-4,104-35-13 (67.8) for the national runners-up, becoming the first player in FBS history with at least 4,000 passing yards and 1,000 rushing yards in a season. Was the Atlantic Coast Conference Player of the Year, ACC Championship MVP, Orange Bowl MVP, and a finalist for the Heisman, Maxwell, and Walter Camp Awards. Bulked up 15 pounds entering his junior season. In '16, led the Tigers to a national championship and finished second in the Heisman voting — totaled 388-579-4,593-41-17 (67.0) in 15 starts, setting the ACC single-season touchdown passes record

and breaking his own single-season school record for total offense (5,222 yards). Bruised his right (throwing) shoulder against Syracuse, and sat out the second half for precautionary reasons. Totaled 434 career rushes for 1,929 yards (4.4-yard average) and 26 touchdowns. Had seven career fumbles. In two national championship games against Alabama, passed 66-103-825-7-1 (64.1), including an MVP performance as a junior. Took home the Johnny Unitas, Archie Griffin and Bobby Bowden Awards; won the Davey O'Brien and Manning Awards for the second straight year; and was named to the AFCA Good Works Team. Posted a 32-3 career record. Team captain graduated in three years with a communication studies degree. Medical exclusion from the bench-press test at the Combine because of a right shoulder injury.

Strengths: Has a quick trigger and can hasten his release under duress. Spins a tight spiral and layers the ball at every level with accuracy. Throws on balance and is very effective creating plays when the pocket moves. Very agile with good run instincts to create on designed runs and excel with zone-read concepts, as evidenced with a QB-best 1.52-second 10-yard time at the Combine. Physically tough to withstand contact, spin off the rush and bounce up after absorbing big hits. Played his best on the biggest of stages in the past two National Championship games and against top competition and has proven he could command his team in the clutch (see 4th quarter vs Louisville, Florida State and Alabama). Confident and competitive. Understands coverages. Good decision-maker with a 3:1 career TD-INT ratio. Exceptional career production with a .914 career winning percentage. Suberb intangibles.

Weaknesses: Small-framed, and durability could be tested in the pros the way it was early in his college career if he does not continue to get stronger. Stares down his primary target and will need to learn how to manipulate the eyes of deep safeties to cut down on interceptions and limit the number of batted balls at the line (25 the last two years). Hits a lot of stationary targets on screens and could stand to improve timing and anticipation. Operated with a very strong supporting cast of receivers capable of creating after the catch that padded production. Post-snap decision-making and coverage recognition will need to improve in the pros to cut down on 30 interceptions the last two years. Some of deep outs died in passing drills at the Combine — ball velocity did not break 50 m.ph. and averaged (46.8) the second-lowest of all quarterbacks

QUARTERBACKS

at the Combine.

Future: A very athletic, high-percentage ball distributor with dual-threat capabilities most ideally suited for an offense that features run-pass options. Played in a well-designed, creative offense featuring a lot of talent that accentuates the strengths of athletic passers and minimizes their deficiencies. Shares some similarities to 49ers 2005 first overall pick and Chiefs QB Alex Smith and has the football intelligence, discipline and makeup to become a quality NFL starter.

Draft projection: First-round pick.

Scout's take: "I think (Watson) can be a franchise (quarterback). He is young, smart and humble. He is a gamer. It is important to him. He has all the intangibles. This kid is about football and the team. He is not ready or a finished product by any means. You're going to have to take him higher than you want. Too many teams need a quarterback, and they are not easy to find. A lot of (evaluators) are going to bag on him, but he has shown improvement every year. They asked the kid to do a lot in their offense, and he worked his (butt) off to get where he is."

QB **DAVIS WEBB**, #7 (Sr-4)

CALIFORNIA   ▶ GRADE: 5.42

Ht: 6-4 5/8 | Wt: 229 | 40: 4.83 | Arm: 33 1/8 | Hand: 9 1/4

History: Coach's son. Prepped in Texas. Began his college career at Texas Tech, where a stomach virus caused him to lose 35 pounds his freshman year. Despite enrolling early, Webb split snaps with walk-on Baker Mayfield in 2013, completing 226-of-361 pass attempts (62.6 percent) for 2,718 yards with 20 touchdowns and six interceptions in 10 games (six starts). Mayfield and Michael Brewer transferred after the season, opening the door for Webb to take over in '14 when he started all eight games played, passing 211-345-2,539-24-13 (61.2). Tore the labrum in his left (non-throwing) shoulder against Oklahoma State and in late October suffered a season-ending left ankle injury against TCU. Also had the shoulder surgically repaired. Took a back seat to Patrick Mahomes in '15, producing just 22-41-300-2-0 (53.7) in five games. In '16, joined Sonny Dykes' Cal Bears as a graduate transfer following the hire of new offensive coordinator Jake Spavital, a Kliff Kingsbury protégé — started all 12 games, and produced 382-620-4,295-37-12 (61.6). Added seven punts for a 39.3-yard average with four inside the 20-yard line. Set school single-season records for passing attempts and completions, and tied the mark for touchdowns responsible for (43). Injured his right (throwing) hand on the second possession of the Oregon State contest. Despite negative yardage as a runner, scored nine career touchdowns. Had 14 career fumbles. Team captain and Offensive MVP. Recorded a 11-15 career starting record. Named Senior Bowl MVP after throwing 11-16-165-1-0 (69%).

Strengths: Has a smooth stroke with a clean release and can hum the ball effortlessly. Outstanding arm strength — registered 59 mph ball speeds at the Combine and can zing the ball into tight spots. Is keen to pull safeties with his eyes and understands how to manipulate coverage, as he also showed in the Senior Bowl. Very good field vision. Can drop it in a bucket — delivers a nice deep ball. Film junkie with very good preparation work habits. Effective pooch punter.

Weaknesses: Marginal foot athlete — very deliberate in his set-up and struggles to escape the rush. Streaky passer — needs to be comfortable in the pocket to throw with accuracy. Is too easily flustered under duress, resulting in bad decisions (see pick-6 on screen pass vs. San Diego State) and does not carry a swagger in the clutch (see game-losing interception vs. Aztecs). Not decisive triggering and tends to cruise on auto-pilot in an unsophisticated passing game not requiring many pro-style progression reads, sight adjustments or audibles. Needs to learn how to better gauge his arm strength, especially from short-to-intermediate ranges. Ball placement is too erratic, throwing some dirtballs and wide overshots — inconsistent mechanics.

Future: Similar to Ravens 2007 first-round pick Joe Flacco, Davis is not a naturally confident triggerman who is going to inspire confidence in teammates and needs a clean pocket to operate. Nonetheless, he possesses the size, stature, arm talent and competitiveness to emerge as a functional, winning starter down the road when the game slows down for him and he learns the nuances of an NFL passing game. Will require at least a few years of seasoning before he is ready.

Draft projection: Third- to fourth-round pick.

Scout's take: "I was not a big (Jared) Goff fan. I didn't grade him in the first (round). If you go off where Goff went, Webb might be a first-rounder. He can lay it in the window and sling it and has more upside than Goff did. I think he does. ...I don't think (Davis) belongs in the first (round). He doesn't grade that highly. You can make an argument for it though, and quarterbacks get overdrafted every year with the premium on the position."

RUNNING BACKS

LSU ATHLETICS

Nawrocki's TOP 10

1. **LEONARD FOURNETTE**
2. **Christian McCaffrey**
3. **Dalvin Cook**
4. **Curtis Samuel**
5. **Samaje Perine**
6. **Alvin Kamara**
7. **Joe Mixon**
8. **D'Onte Foreman**
9. **Donnel Pumphrey**
10. **James Conner**

RB CHRIS CARSON, #32 (Sr-4)

OKLAHOMA STATE ▶ GRADE: 5.12

Ht: 5-11 3/4 | Wt: 218 | 40: 4.58 | Arm: 33 1/4 | Hand: 9 5/8

History: Was a non-qualifier coming out of Mississippi. Attended Butler Community College (Kan.) in 2013 — played 11 games, and carried 109 times for 611 yards (5.6-yard average) and eight touchdowns. Played nine games in '14, and toted 139-994-9 (7.2). Originally committed to Georgia, but flipped to OSU because of a much thinner depth chart. With the Cowboys in '15, started 9-of-12 games, and recorded 131-517-4 (3.9) rushing with 17-170-0 (10.0) receiving. Sprained his right ankle against Texas, and sat out against Kansas State. Played nine games in '16, starting the first two, and contributed 82-559-9 (6.8). In Week Two, suffered a broken right thumb against Central Michigan, and missed the next four games. Recorded 49 career receptions for 455 yards (9.3-yard average) and three touchdowns. Also completed 2-of-3 pass attempts (66.7 percent) for 31 yards. Had 11 career fumbles in 491 touches, averaging 5.1 yards per carry the last two years and losing a pair of fumbles (nine came in junior college).

Team captain was voted the Cowboys' Most Outstanding Offensive Player. Pulled a hamstring in skill drills at the Combine and did not perform shuttles.

Strengths: Well-built and looks every bit the part, carrying the lowest body-fat percentage (3.1%) of any player at the Combine. Measured the longest arms and wingspan (79 3/8 inches) of any back at the Combine, increasing his catching radius. Runs hard inside with good body lean on contact and lower-body strength to drive through tacklers. Is a load to bring down and has the power to run over defensive backs (see punishing, multiple-tackle-breaking runs vs. TCU and Texas Tech). Good leg churn through contact and carries defenders on his back for big chunks (see Kansas State). Goal-line hammer. Athletic enough to hurdle tacklers (see Kansas) and flashes a nice spin move. Good blitz recognition in pass pro. Effective chip blocker. Skilled passer. Good weight-room worker.

Weaknesses: A bit high-cut and tight-hipped and rigid as a route runner. Does not easily adjust to the thrown ball. Takes times to get rolling and is too quick to bounce outside. Could

RUNNING BACKS

stand to improve sustaining in pass protection — one-shot blocker. Has missed time to injuries the last two years and never shown he could carry a full workload or make it through a full season healthy. Must learn to do a better job protecting the ball (fumbled every 45 touches).

Future: A big, strong grinder with an all-around skill set to earn a complementary role if he can correct his fumbling flaw. Has a lot of tread left on his tires, though must still prove he is a better football player than body builder.

Draft projection: Late draftable pick.

RB COREY CLEMENT, #6 (Sr-4)

WISCONSIN　　　　　　　　▶ GRADE: 5.32
Ht: 5-10 1/8 | Wt: 220 | 40: 4.71 | Arm: 30 1/2 | Hand: 9 3/4

History: Prepped in New Jersey. Appeared in 12 games as a true freshman in 2013, and carried 67 times for 547 yards (8.2-yard average) and seven touchdowns. Played all 14 games in '14, drawing one start, and recorded 147-949-9 (6.5). Was limited the last four games by a right AC joint sprain. Played four games in '15, drawing one start, and managed 48-221-5 (4.6). Missed eight games because of a sports hernia which required two surgeries. Was suspended for the Minnesota contest after he was cited for two counts of disorderly conduct — found to be the verbal and physical instigator of an altercation with a group of people at his apartment complex. Sprained his left ankle against Northwestern, and tweaked the injury in the bowl game against USC. Missed time early in '16 fall camp (hamstring), but was the Badgers' Offensive Player of the Year after starting all 13 games played and totaling 314-1,375-15 (4.4). Sprained his left ankle against Akron, and did not play against Georgia State. Recorded 29 career receptions for 279 yards (9.6-yard average) and two touchdowns. Had seven career fumbles in 608 touches averaging 5.4 yards per carry. Opted not to perform shuttles at the Combine.

Strengths: Runs hard between the tackles and is aggressive attacking downhill. Very good balance, leg churn and finishing strength to power through contact and fall forward — creases defenses running the same play repeatedly (see LSU). Strong goal-line runner (38 career TDs) — can generate a surge and push the pile. Highly driven and competitive. Creates a lot of yardage after contact. Flashes some jolt in his hands in pass protection and is functional in pass protection. Catches the ball with ease.

Weaknesses: Duck-footed. Overly-muscled and tight. Average creativity and elusiveness

to avoid tacklers. Lacks top-end finishing speed and ran poorly at the Combine. Not an advanced pass protector or nifty route runner. Could stand to do a better job of taking care of the football. Has been slowed by durability issues and missed time each of the last three seasons and likely to struggle staying healthy given how wound tight he is.

Future: A strong, physical, downhill runner capable of contributing readily in the pros. Has the run strength, instincts, competitiveness and power to develop into a steady, workman-like starter. Bid his time behind Melvin Gordon and suffered through some injuries and adversity off the field before emerging as a force as a senior, and must prove he can stay focused and out of trouble in the pros to fulfill his potential.

Draft projection: Fourth- to fifth-round pick.

Scout's take: "He's wound tight. He's doesn't run very well. He's had some issues there. He has some talent. I didn't see a lot to get excited about."

RB-RS TARIK COHEN, #28 (Sr-4)

NORTH CAROLINA A&T STATE　　▶ GRADE: 5.21
Ht: 5-6 1/2 | Wt: 179 | 40: 4.41 | Arm: 29 3/4 | Hand: 10 1/8

History: Nicknamed "the human joystick" for his cutback style. Was part of a North Carolina state champion 4x100 meter relay team in high school. As a true freshman in 2013, started 6-of-11 games and carried 195 times for 1,148 yards (5.9-yard average) and eight touchdowns with 11 receptions for 152 yards (13.8-yard average) and one touchdown. Started all 11 games played in '14, and produced 197-1,340-15 (6.8) rushing and 25-237-1 (9.5) receiving. Did not play against Howard (right knee sprain). Started all 24 games the next two seasons — totaled 264-1,543-15 (5.8) rushing and 25-217-0 (8.7) receiving in '15; and 212-1,588-18 (7.5) rushing and 37-339-1 (9.2) receiving in '16. Has completed 3-of-4 passes in career and returned one punt for 4 yards and a kickoff for 26. Had surgery to repair his left labrum after his junior season. The leading rusher in Mid-Eastern Athletic Conference history (5,619 yards), Cohen was a four-time all-conference honoree, and was the Offensive Player of the Year as a junior. Owns school records for career all-purpose yardage (6,564) and touchdowns responsible for (61). Had eight career fumbles in 993 touches averaging 6.5 yards per carry. Also competed as a sprinter on the track team. Opted not to perform shuttles at the Combine.

Strengths: Compact and very agile. Strong for his size with rapid foot turnover and can

RUNNING BACKS

string some moves together. Has the fastest 10-yard time (1.47 seconds) of any back at the Combine. Extremely competitive — takes a lot of hits, spins off contact and pops right back up off the ground. Good anticipation to see cutback lanes developing, set up his blocks and create in the open field. Has big, soft hands and decisive run-after-the-catch ability.

Weaknesses: Marginal size, measuring the shortest of any player at the Combine. Can get lost in traffic and swallowed up running inside, with limited tackle-breaking strength for the pro game. A bit straight-linish. Did not regularly face top competition. Underpowered blocker who will be mismatched in pass protection.

Future: Diminutive scatback with limited contributions in the return game, yet the skill set to warrant a chance as a returner and situational, third-down back in the pros. Although track speed and rare production could open doors, limitations in pass protection and inexperience in the return game could restrict opportunities.

Draft projection: Late draftable pick.

RB JAMES CONNER, #24 (Jr-4)

PITTSBURGH ▶ GRADE: 5.32

Ht: 6-11/2 | Wt: 233 | 40: 4.64 | Arm: 31 1/4 | Hand: 9 7/8

History: Pennsylvania native earned all-state honors at both running back and defensive end. As a true freshman in 2013 (wore jersey No. 40), dinged his left shoulder during fall camp, but carried 146 times for 799 yards (5.5-yard average) and eight touchdowns in 12 games. Hurt his shoulder against Virginia Tech, and sat out against Old Dominion. Sprained his left knee during '14 spring practice, but started all 13 games in the fall — was the Atlantic Coast Conference Player of the Year after producing 298-1,765-26 (5.9). Set a conference single-season record for touchdowns (26). Sat out the second half against Syracuse (hip pointer). In '15, recorded 8-77-2 (9.6) against Youngstown State, but suffered a season-ending torn right MCL injury. After having surgery, Conner experienced fatigue, insomnia, night sweats and bloating. An X-ray led to a PET scan, and Conner was diagnosed with Hodgkin's lymphoma in late November. Received support and advice from noted athletes and cancer survivors Eric Berry, Merrill Hoge and Mario Lemieux, among others. Participated in winter workouts while undergoing chemotherapy and cancer was in remission by late May '16. In the fall, returned to start all 13 games and post 216-1,092-16 (5.1), breaking ACC records for career rushing touchdowns (52) and total touchdowns (56) in the process. Sustained a concussion in the Pinstripe Bowl against Northwestern. Received the Disney Sports Spirit Award (college football's most inspirational figure) and Brian Piccolo Award (most courageous). Had 30 career receptions for 412 yards (13.7-yard average) and four touchdowns. In 39 career games, amassed 3,733 yards, which ranks second in program history behind Hall of Famer Tony Dorsett. Had six career fumbles in 698 touches averaging 5.6 yards per carry. Two-time team captain. Did not perform shuttles at the Combine because of a left ankle injury.

Strengths: Slams into the line with authority and is a load to tackle, barreling over linebackers and punishing tacklers. Very good lower-body strength, base and balance to absorb contact and continue driving. Has fairly nifty feet for as big as he is and can make subtle cuts to sidestep tacklers. Strong, willing, face-up blocker. Natural hands. Flashes a strong stiff-arm. Determined weight-room worker. Inspirational leader. Respected community worker. Has represented the program with class.

Weaknesses: Tight-hipped and runs a bit upright and segmented. Limited burst and acceleration to make defenders miss. Lacks top-end speed to take the corner or pull away in the open field. Could struggle to create separation in man coverage. Weight climbed past 250 pounds earlier in his career and has fluctuated. Was far more productive in 2014 (1,765 yards) than upon his return from beating cancer in 2016 (1,092 yards) and is still working back to early form.

Future: A powerful, between-the-tackles chunk runner, Conner showed rare mental strength to continue training through winter conditioning while overcoming cancer. Has the bulk strength, balance, patience and sheer power to earn a starter's job for a physical, downhill running game such as the Steelers, Bears or Ravens. Similar to Patriots' 2011 fifth-round pick and OT Marcus Cannon who was found to have cancer prior to the draft at time when some teams had graded him as a first-round talent, the looming risk of cancer returning could push down Conner's draft stock and provide even greater motivation to a very determined runner to return with a vengeance.

Draft projection: Fourth- to fifth-round pick.

Scout's take: "(Conner) was not the same player early in the season that he was late. He improved as the season went along. Not many people could have overcome what he did. He is a warrior. He will be a great representative

RUNNING BACKS

in the community. He was the face of (Pittsburgh's) program."

RB DALVIN COOK, #4 (Jr-3)

FLORIDA STATE ▶ GRADE: 6.06

Ht: 5-10 3/8 | Wt: 210 | 40: 4.49 | Arm: 32 3/8 | Hand: 9 1/4

History: Blue chipper out of Miami Central High, where he won a state championship and garnered USA Today All-American honors. Played through a torn right rotator cuff as a sophomore before having off-season surgery. Received a citation in June 2014 for a BB gun incident that left car windows broken and a pair of citations resulting in a $550 fine the following month from Tallahassee Animal Services after chaining three pit bull puppies together by the neck. Despite not playing the 2014 season opener against Oklahoma State, posted the most productive season by a Seminoles freshman running back — carried 170 times for 1,008 yards (5.9-yard average) and eight touchdowns with 22 receptions for 203 yards (9.2-yard average) and zero touchdowns in 13 games (three starts). Was arrested in July '15 on battery charges after he was accused of hitting a woman at a Tallahassee bar — reportedly attempted to play peacemaker during the escalation of a verbal altercation between the woman and FSU players, but the woman, who was intoxicated, claimed Cook yelled at her and punched her in the mouth. Cook initially lied about his involvement, but he, the other players present, and another witness insisted Cook did not throw a punch. Cook was suspended until the case went to trial in late August. With no video evidence or convincing proof other than testimony from an intoxicated accuser, a jury needed less than a half-hour to find Cook not guilty. He was immediately reinstated to the team. In the fall, won the Jim Brown Award by setting FSU single-season records for rushing yards and all-purpose yards (1,935) — started all 12 games played, and amassed 229-1,691-19 (7.4) on the ground with 24-244-1 (10.2) through the air. Hurt his left hamstring against Wake Forest. Sprained his left ankle against Georgia Tech, and sat out against Syracuse. Was a Doak Walker Award finalist in '16 — started all 13 games, and toted 288-1,765-19 (6.1) with 33-488-1 (14.8) receiving. Had 13 career fumbles in 766 touches averaging 6.5 yards per carry . The Seminoles' all-time leading rusher (4,464 yards) and rushing touchdown scorer (46), Cook is the first back in Atlantic Coast Conference history to gain 4,000 yards in just three seasons. Team captain. Has

undergone two surgeries on his right labrum — once before his freshman season and again before his junior season.

Strengths: Very decisive runner with good wide peripheral vision and can take the corner with ease. Has fine run strength and balance to keep his feet through traffic and handle running inside. Surprisingly good base strength to consistently churn through contact and accelerate out of it, breaking many tackles using a stutter step and short-area burst. Possesses explosive big-play ability and plays faster than his timed speed. Can spin off contact and creates a lot of extra yardage with subtle cutbacks. Sets up blockers well and converts speed to power. Extremely productive against top competition — see Clemson and Florida the last two years. Very quick healer. Is physically tough and will play through injuries.

Weaknesses: Is not built to withstand a heavy workload between the tackles and grind out tough yardage. Dips his head too much inside, negating his vision. Will flag the ball away from his body while making sharp cuts in the open field and needs to do a better job of keeping it high and tight and securing it more soundly — fumbled every 59 touches. Rigid route runner that shows some upper-body stiffness adjusting to the thrown ball, resulting in drops. Tight in the hips and lacks fluidity changing direction, as confirmed by slowest 20-yard shuttle (4.57 seconds) and among the slowest 3-cone drill times (7.29) among backs at the Combine. Recorded a 30 1/2-inch vertical jump, indicating marginal lower-body explosion. Has had multiple shoulder surgeries that invite closer scrutiny. Was not used heavily in pass protection and has not shown the desire to handle blocking. Has run into a string of off-field issues and character must be vetted closely.

Future: Cook does his best work running outside and is most ideally suited for a stretch-zone running game such as the Seahawks, Packers or Redskins. Explosive big-play ability, head-dipping on contact and background / medical history are reminiscent of Titans 2008 first-round pick (24th overall) Chris Johnson, though Cook is stronger, more compact and not as explosive. History of off-field and durability issues could diminish draft value.

Draft projection: First-round pick.

Scout's take: "Some teams don't care about any of the baggage off the field. Al Davis' Raiders were always that way. It's going to take a team like that to roll the dice on (Cook). He's talented, but there's some buyer beware

RUNNING BACKS

with him. You're going to have to manage him."

RB LeSHUN DANIELS, #29 (Sr-4)

IOWA ▶ GRADE: 5.10

Ht: 5-11 1/4 | Wt: 225 | 40: 4.55e | Arm: 30 3/4 | Hand: 9 1/2

History: First name is pronounced "Luh-SEAN." Father, LeShun, had a short stint with the Minnesota Vikings (1997) as an offensive linemen. Brother, James Daniels, was the starting center for the Hawkeyes. LeShun also ran track as an Ohio prep. Played seven games as a true freshman in 2013, carrying 36 times for 142 yards (3.9-yard average) and zero touchdowns. Played five games in '14, running 15-49-1 (3.3). Was a non-factor from September on — seven weeks into the season suffered a stress fracture in his right ankle, which required surgery. Played 12 games in '15, starting five, and totaled 145-646-8 (4.5) while dealing with a nagging injury. Suffered a high ankle sprain Week Two against Iowa State — was limited to 18 carries the next three weeks then sat out two games. Aggravated the injury against Purdue in late November, and was limited to 23 carries the last three contests. In '16, started all 13 games, and produced 213-1,058-10 (5.0). Recorded 10 career catches for 81 yards (8.1-yard average) and zero touchdowns. Had six career fumbles in 419 touches averaging 4.6 yards per carry. Team captain.

Strengths: Outstanding size and weight-room strength — is layered with muscle and tests like a phenom. Presses the line and runs hard downhill. Outstanding lower-body strength to drive thru contact. Good eyes to see the cutback developing and can stick his foot in the ground and go. Functional face-up blocker with a good understanding of pass protection. Extremely intelligent.

Weaknesses: Is tight-hipped with a history of ankle injuries that have nagged him throughout his career. Has never been a full-time starter or proven he could carry a full workload. Much of his production is blocked for him behind a strong offensive line. Could stand to do a better job dropping his pads and uncoiling on contact on inside runs. Is not a smooth route runner and has a limited catching radius — minimal receiving experience. Ball security needs to improve.

Future: Very compact, muscular, well-built runner with the patience, vision and short-area burst to earn a complentary power role if he could find a way to stay healthy in the pros.

Draft projection: Late draftable pick

RB-KR JUSTIN DAVIS, #22 (Sr-4)

USC ▶ GRADE: 5.07

Ht: 6-0 5/8 | Wt: 208 | 40: 4.55e | Arm: 31 | Hand: 9 5/8

History: California native also ran track in high school. As a true freshman in 2013, contributed 53 carries for 361 yards (6.8-yard average) and six touchdowns in seven games before tearing a ligament in his right ankle. Played all 13 games in '14, and carried 129-595-4 (4.6). Started 8-of-13 games in '15, and ran 169-902-7 (5.3), while returning 11 kickoffs for 211 yards (19.2-yard average). Did not play against Arkansas State (ribs). Started 7-of-10 games played in '16, and totaled 110-607-2 (5.5). Missed three midseason games after sustaining a high right ankle sprain against Colorado. Honored with USC's Trojan Commitment Award and Lifter of the Year. Recorded 46 career receptions for 400 yards (8.7-yard average) and two touchdowns. Had nine career fumbles in 518 touches averaging 5.3 yards per carry. Played for four different head coaches. Graduated with an economics degree. Did not participate in the East-West Shrine Game (ankle). Was medically excluded (right ankle) from running or jumping at the Combine.

Strengths: Is quick to the corner. Good short-area burst and acceleration to make hard cuts and hit creases. Sets up his blockers and can run through some arm tackles and shake the initial tackler in the open field. Good athlete. Catches the ball naturally. Has a nose for the end zone.

Weaknesses: Thin lower body with an upright running style. Limited tackle-breaking power to push the pile and churn through congestion and handle inside running. Lacks physicality and gets turned and knocked back too easily. Has blocking limitations and will be overmatched in the pros in pass protection. Needs to protect the ball better. Has never carried a full workload (169 max).

Future: A quick, upright, high-cut, change-of-pace back with kickoff return ability and enough open-field run skill to warrant some interest as a contributor. Will need to make a mark on special teams to stick on a roster.

Draft projection: Priority free agent.

RB MATTHEW DAYES, #21 (Sr-4)

NORTH CAROLINA STATE ▶ GRADE: 5.33

Ht: 5-8 5/8 | Wt: 205 | 40: 4.66 | Arm: 30 | Hand: 10 1/2

History: Prepped in Florida. As a true freshman in 2013, had 63 carries for 252 yards (4.0-yard average) and four touchdowns with 10 receptions for 173 yards (17.3-yard average) and one touchdown. Did not play against Wake

RUNNING BACKS

Forest (ankle). In '14, recorded 104-573-8 (5.5) rushing and 32-321-5 (10.0) receiving in 13 games (three starts). Started the first eight games in '15 — totaled 134-865-12 (6.5) rushing with 24-172-0 (7.2) receiving before turf toe (left foot) cost him the final five games. Returned to start all 13 games in '16, toting 249-1,166-10 (4.7) and catching 32-267-0 (8.3). Recorded 28 career kickoff returns for 509 yards (18.2-yard average). Had six career fumbles in 676 touches averaging 5.2 yards per carry. Team captain and MVP graduated with a sociology degree. Opted not to run the 40-yard dash or shuttles at the Combine.

Strengths: Has huge hands that measured the biggest of any back at the Combine. Runs with urgency — sinks his pads and accelerates to and through the hole. Has nifty feet to sidestep oncoming tacklers and shake tacklers in the open field. Very good eyes and anticipation to see lanes developing at the second level and deftly sets up moves. Outstanding stretch-zone vision to see the cutback. Effective on screens and counters. Functional lower-body strength and balance. Strong personal and football character.

Weaknesses: Short and not naturally big boned. Does not show a top gear to finish. Limited blocking power. Limited run-after-the-catch elusiveness. Has a 28-inch vertical jump, the lowest of any back at the Combine and indicative of limited lower-body explosion. Not a big-play threat in the return game.

Future: A strong, compact, stretch-zone runner with an all-around skill set to develop into a solid complementary back. Has a special-teams makeup.

Draft projection: Fourth- to fifth-round pick.

Scout's take: "(Dayes) is not going to wow you in any area. He's a jack of all trades, master of none. He can do everything well. That plays well in our league. I like his versatility and the way he's wired."

RB D'ONTE FOREMAN, #33 (Jr-3)

TEXAS ▶ GRADE: 5.42

Ht: 6-0 | Wt: 233 | 40: 4.55e | Arm: 31 3/8 | Hand: 10 1/8

History: Twin brother, Armanti, is a receiver for the Longhorns. Running back-defensive end who also returned kicks as a Texas prep. Made seven appearances as a true freshman in 2014, carrying 14 times for 74 yards (5.3-yard average) and zero touchdowns. Broke his hand against Oklahoma State, and missed the last two games of the season. In '15, recorded 94-672-5 (7.1) in 10 games. Missed the last two games after having his right pinky finger

surgically repaired. Broke out in '16 when he won the Doak Walker Award — started 10-of-11 games played, and produced 323-2,028-15 (6.3), including a 51-250-2 effort against Kansas. Sat out against UTEP (hamstring), and strained an abdominal muscle against Oklahoma State — his only game of the season with less than 20 carries. Collected 13 career receptions for 146 yards (11.2-yard average) and zero touchdowns. Had nine career fumbles in 446 career touches averaging 6.4 yards per carry. Will be a 21-year-old rookie. Was medically excluded (left foot) from working out at the Combine.

Strengths: Exceptional size and upper-body power to press off blocks. Is a load to tackle. Fine vision to navigate inside, weave thru traffic and pick and slide. Very good hip strength, core power and movement skill for a big back and consequently has been very effective pushing the pile on the goal line and in short-yardage situations. Seldom knocked backwards. Functional pass protector with the bulk to absorb a charge. Only has taken 431 college carries and has a lot of tread left on his tires.

Weaknesses: Only a one-year starter. Has an upright running style and takes some direct hits that will leave him more vulnerable to injury in the pros. Lacks burst and gear change and is late to reach the perimeter. Could stand to be more aggressive facing up blockers in pass pro. Swings the ball away from his frame, and fumbles have been too frequent (every 50 touches), including two untimely vs. Kansas State. Minimal career receiving production and has limited value as a pass-catcher. Much of his production was blocked for him. Weight has fluctuated throughout his career, as he played between 240-245 pounds, and he registered the highest body-fat percentage (15.1%) of any tailback at the Combine.

Future: A thickly-built, downhill runner most ideally suited for a power-running role in the pros, Foreman is surprisingly light and balanced on his feet and can factor readily on early downs if he learns to correct his fumbling tendency and secures the ball better. Ideally suited for a complementary power role and stands a chance to be overdrafted for a single season of production in which he often had big lanes.

Draft projection: Third- to fourth-round pick.

Scout's take: "Seeing him fumble twice against Kansas State and losing the game at the end is difficult to forget. Foreman looked stiff and overrated to me. I know he put up some big numbers, but I think you could find guys like him easily in the fourth or fifth round."

RB LEONARD FOURNETTE, #7 (Jr-3)

LSU ▶ GRADE: 7.70

Ht: 6-0 1/2 | Wt: 240 | 40: 4.51 | Arm: 31 5/8 | Hand: 9 1/4

History: Has a two-year-old daughter, Lyric. Prepped at New Orleans St. Augustine, where he finished his four-year varsity career with 7,619 yards and 88 rushing touchdowns, garnering USA Today National Offensive Player of the Year. Also was the first player in Louisiana history to win Gatorade Player of the Year twice. As a true freshman in 2014, carried 187 times for 1,034 yards (5.5-yard average) and 10 touchdowns in 13 games (six starts). Added 24 kickoff returns for 625 yards (26.0-yard average), including a 100-yard score against Notre Dame. In '15, paced the nation (168.2 yards per game) and established an LSU single-season rushing record by starting all 12 games played and toting 300-1,953-22 (6.5). Was voted a permanent team captain at the team's post-season banquet. Entered his junior year with two $10 million insurance policies. During '16 fall camp, suffered a left ankle injury (high- and low-ankle sprain) which plagued him throughout the season. Started 6-of-7 games played, and managed 129-843-8 (6.5). Answered the bell against Wisconsin in the season opener, but sat out the following week against Jacksonville State, as well as October contests — separated by an off week — against Missouri and Southern Miss. Returned for four games, but shut it down in late November, opting to sign with Roc Nation agency and focus on getting healthy and prepared for the draft rather than play in the Tigers' final two contests against Texas A&M and Louisville (Citrus Bowl). Posted 41 career receptions for 526 yards (12.8-yard average) and one touchdown. Reportedly was not planning to play against Florida, but asked to suit up following a pre-game skirmish that needed to be broken up by security in which he was involved in a shoving altercation with Florida DB coach Dorian Gray. Had eight career fumbles in 682 touches averaging 6.2 yards per carry. Is signed to an endorsement deal with Under Armour. Opted not to bench, broad jump or perform shuttles at the Combine.

Strengths: Runs angry behind his pads with good forward lean and rarely is knocked backwards. Explosive out of his stance from the first level to the second, as evidenced by his RB-best 20-yard split (2.50 seconds) at the Combine that will help rack up chunk runs. Has the top-end speed to run away from defenders. Powerful tackle-breaker who drops his shoulder and steamrolls tacklers (see Mississippi) and carries defenders on his back.

Good eyes and cutback ability. Can stick his foot in the dirt, make sharp cuts and explode upfield. Nice spin move in the hole and much of his yardage comes after contact. Does not go down easy. Strong stiff-arm. Solid face-up blocker and effective chipping defensive ends. Catches the ball easily outside his frame. Extremely tough, competitive and physical. Has big-play potential as a kick returner and shown he can take it the distance.

Weaknesses: Sheer force and violence with which he runs could invite injuries. Seeks to initiate contact so much he will trip over his own feet. Shut down vs. Alabama the last two years — 19-31-1 in '15 and 17-35-0 in '16 albeit against stacked boxes designed to take him away. Limited pass-protection experience — was not often asked to block and could still improve blocking technique, and do a better job bending his knees. Lacks fluidity as a route runner swiveling for the ball and did not consistently catch the ball cleanly in Combine drills. Has a 28 1/2-inch vertical jump, tied for the second lowest among backs at the Combine. Weight has tended to drift north of 230 pounds and increased weight could affect long-term durability. Registered a 14.4% body-fat percentage at the Combine, among the highest for backs at the Combine. Did not lead the team in rushing (sophomore Derrius Grice) due to missed time and nagging injury.

Future: Tough, decisive, downhill runner with the hip strength, body power and physicality to consistently churn through contact and create chunk yardage, yet also possesses the long speed to create explosive big plays. A complete every down back in a rare category of talent physically gifted enough to have made the jump from high school to the pros had he been allowed, Fournette is a generational talent in the same category as all-time greats such as Bo Jackson, Herschel Walker and Jim Brown exiting college. A bellcow capable of carrying an offense and wearing down defenses. Was at his best when healthy in 2015 and would be most optimal playing in the 220's.

Draft projection: Top-10 cinch.

Scout's take: "It's hard to describe how dominant (Fournette) was at 240 pounds, catching, cutting, running people over. He should be the first pick in the draft. He looks big on tape, but when you stand next to him on the field, you get an even greater appreciation — he's a full-grown man. I think he's better than Ezekiel Elliott. Dudes like this only come around once in 20 years. He was not even fully healthy this year — he's a rare talent."

RUNNING BACKS

RB **WAYNE GALLMAN**, #9 (Jr-4)

CLEMSON ▶ GRADE: 5.28

Ht: 6-0 1/2 | Wt: 215 | 40: 4.62 | Arm: 32 5/8 | Hand: 9 1/8

History: Son of a Marine now coaching high school football. Prepped in Georgia. Redshirted in 2013. Started 9-of-13 games in '14, and carried 161 times for 769 yards (4.8-yard average) and four touchdowns with 24 receptions for 108 yards (4.5-yard average) and one touchdown. In '15, started 13-of-14 games and produced 282-1,514-13 (5.4) rushing and 22-226-1 (10.3) receiving. Sat out against Wake Forest (ankle). Lone non-start was against Notre Dame when the Tigers opened the game with five receivers. Started all 15 games for the national champs in '16, toting 232-1,133-17 (4.9) and catching 20-152-0 (7.6). Sustained a concussion against North Carolina State. Had five career fumbles in 741 touches averaging 5.1 yards per carry. Graduated with a degree in communication studies. Suffered a right hamstring injury during skill drills at the Combine.

Strengths: Very competitive with a well-balanced skill set. Runs hard and with patience and allows blocks to set up. Good vision to see the cutback and find creases. Good lateral agility to make hard cuts and dart upfield. Efficient running style — takes what the defense gives him. Dependable receiver. Disciplined practice player. Good weight-room worker, as evidenced by 21 bench-press reps. Excellent career production.

Weaknesses: Has a narrow frame with small hands. Limited inside-run strength to drive a pile or run through tackles. Lacks explosive short-area burst to elude, as confirmed with 1.65-second 10-yard split, and the top-end speed to pull away from the pack. Recorded a 29 1/2-inch vertical jump, indicative of limited lower-body strength and explosion. Lacks anchor strength in pass pro.

Future: A jack of all trades, master of none, Gallman does not have any elite traits, but is consistent and does a lot of things well. Has the tools to become a reliable backup. Reminiscent of Dolphins 2013 fifth-round pick and Bills RB Mike Gillislee.

Draft projection: Fourth- to fifth-round pick.

Scout's take: "Gallman is a good, pick-and-slide, zone runner. He's put together pretty well. He was 215 pounds in training camp. He will be 220 in the pros. He got hurt early (in the season) and doesn't have a lot of help on the O-Line. He has some power."

RB **De'ANGELO HENDERSON**, #31 (Sr-6)

COASTAL CAROLINA ▶ GRADE: 5.13

Ht: 5-7 1/2 | Wt: 208 | 40: 4.46 | Arm: 29 | Hand: 9 1/2

History: Was the leading rusher in South Carolina his senior season — toted 251 times for 2,345 yards (9.3-yard average) and 27 touchdowns. Greyshirted in 2011. Redshirted in '12. Hit the field in '13 when he carried 82-599-6 (7.3) and caught four balls for 39 yards (9.8-yard average) with zero touchdowns in 15 games (four starts). Was behind Lorenzo Taliaferro (Ravens) on the depth chart. Was the featured back in '14 — started all 14 games, and produced 234-1,534-20 (6.6) on the ground with 33-289-1 (8.8) out of the backfield. In '15, was the Big South Offensive Player of the Year — amassed 222-1,346-16 (6.1) rushing and 40-403-3 (10.1) receiving in 12 starts. Started all nine games played in '16, and totaled 183-1,156-16 (6.3) rushing with 20-190-2 (9.5) receiving. Suffered a shoulder injury against Gardner-Webb, sidelining him for three games. Recorded a touchdown in 35 consecutive games, breaking Danny Woodhead's NCAA record. Owns 10 school records, including rushing attempts (721), rushing yards (4,635), touchdowns (64), and all-purpose yards (5,556). Had 16 career fumbles in 818 touches averaging 6.4 yards per carry. Team captain graduated with a degree in recreation and sport management. Did not perform shuttles at the Combine due to cramps.

Strengths: Has a very low center of gravity and can make sharp cuts moving full speed. Outstanding pound-for-pound strength resulting from committed weight-room work ethic. Good leg drive and initial contact balance. Flashes ability to create some magic with repeated sharp cuts. Outstanding career production. Strong football character — the game is very important to him.

Weaknesses: Very short with small hands that have contributed to 16 career fumbles. Tied for having the shortest arms of any back at the Combine. Limited run strength — too often gets dragged down easily by his jersey. Engulfed inside and tends to bounce outside even when there are creases. Small catching radius and limited adjusting to the ball. Could be a liability in pass protection. Lacks breakaway speed as a returner and has no punt-return experience. Has not regularly faced top competition nor did he stand out in the NFLPA all-star game.

Future: Compact, short-stepping, bowling ball-shaped, perimeter runner with enough strength and balance to fend for a job in a camp. Looks well suited for a role as a pinball punt returner, yet has no experience in this area.

Draft projection: Priority free agent.

RUNNING BACKS

RB BRIAN HILL, #5 (Jr-3)

WYOMING ▶ GRADE: 5.23

Ht: 6-1 | Wt: 219 | 40: 4.56 | Arm: 31 3/8 | Hand: 8 7/8

History: Played running back and safety as a prep in Southern Illinois (near St. Louis). Was recruited to Laramie by head coach Craig Bohl. As a true freshman in 2014, carried 145 times for 796 yards (5.5-yard average) and seven touchdowns in 12 games (four starts). In '15, played all 12 games, starting the final 11, and produced 281-1,631-6 (5.8). Broke his own single-season rushing record in '16 — started 13-of-14 games, and piled up 349-1,860-22 (5.3). Did not start the bowl game against BYU (curfew violation). Snagged 41 career receptions for 403 yards (9.8-yard average) and zero touchdowns. Had five career fumbles in 817 touches averaging 5.5 yards per carry. Needed just three seasons to become the Cowboys' all-time leading rusher (4,287 yards). Team captain.

Strengths: Runs with urgency and determination, dropping his shoulder and barreling through contact. Tough, competitive and physical. Presses the line and revels finishing runs instead of stepping out of bounds. Good leg churn. Follows his blockers and almost always falls forward.

Weaknesses: Tends to run tall. Average long speed. Production is inflated from facing Mountain West competition. Has minimal experience in pass protection and could be overwhelmed by the blitz. Inconsistent catcher — at times fights the ball. Still immature, has some small-school entitlement and demands accountability.

Future: A physical, punishing, inside runner who could contribute readily on early downs, yet lacks the savvy desired in pass protection or consistency catching the ball to be a dependable factor on third down.

Draft projection: Fifth- to sixth-round pick.

Scout's take: "I worry about some of the mental parts of the game — scanning in pass pro and picking up a playbook. He hated school. He has enough talent to play at our level."

RB ELIJAH HOOD, #34 (Jr-3)

NORTH CAROLINA ▶ GRADE: 5.17

Ht: 5-11 3/8 | Wt: 232 | 40: 4.65e | Arm: 30 3/8 | Hand: 9 3/8

History: Was North Carolina's AP Player of the Year as a senior, capping a career in which he amassed 8,981 yards and 147 touchdowns. In the summer of 2013, Hood posted a video of him flushing recruiting letters from Alabama down the toilet. Months later, he de-committed from Notre Dame and chose UNC in order to be closer to home. Considered the crown jewel of the Tar Heels' '14 recruiting class, Hood enrolled early and played nine games (one start) as a true freshman, carrying 67 times for 259 yards (3.9-yard average) and four touchdowns. Was injured against Notre Dame, and missed the next four games (carried just once in the two after that). In '15, started all 14 games, and produced 218-1,463-17 (6.7). Started all 11 games played in '16, and totaled 145-858-8 (5.9). Sustained a concussion against Florida State, and did not play against Virginia Tech. Also sat out the Sun Bowl against Stanford for a violation of team rules. Had 40 career receptions for 211 yards (5.3-yard average) and zero touchdowns, grabbing 25-142-0 as a junior. Recorded 7 fumbles in 470 touches averaging 6.0 yards per carry. Was medically excluded (right hamstring) from working out at the Combine.

Strengths: Has a muscular build and looks the part. Runs hard through contact with a strong surge and usually falls forward. Good base, lower-body strength to run between the tackles and bounce off initial contact. Tough and physical and runs through arm tackles. Fine vision to follow his blocks. Good second-effort, short-yardage and goal-line runner able to maintain balance, spin off tackles and push through a crease (see Virginia). Very football smart and can assimilate a playbook quickly. Assignment sound. Solid hands. Functional blocker.

Weaknesses: Average athlete. Has tight hips, gathers to cut and pitter patters too much behind the line of scrimmage. Limited elusiveness. Creates little yardage after the catch — slow transitioning upfield. Lacks perimeter speed to take the corner. Needs to improve ball security. Split time in the backfield with T.J. Logan and has not shown he can carry a full workload.

Future: A strong, hard-charging, north-south runner ideally suited for a single-back role in a power offense such as the Panthers or Steelers. Could warrant some interest as a do-it-all West Coast offense fullback.

Draft projection: Fifth- to sixth-round pick.

Scout's take: "(Hood) has been hurt all season and he is so tight as it is — I don't know how he stays healthy. I'm surprised he came out early. Sometimes people closest to you can give you bad advice."

RB KAREEM HUNT, #3 (Jr-3)

TOLEDO ▶ GRADE: 5.29

Ht: 5-10 1/2 | Wt: 216 | 40: 4.59 | Arm: 31 3/8 | Hand: 9 5/8

History: Also played basketball and competed in high jump and long jump as a prep in Ohio, where he piled up 5,200 yards and

RUNNING BACKS

83 touchdowns his last two seasons. As a true freshman in 2013, carried 137 times for 866 yards (6.3-yard average) and six touchdowns with 12 receptions for 68 yards (5.7-yard average) and zero touchdowns in 12 games (three starts). Was the Mid-American Conference's leading rusher in '14 — rushed 205-1,631-16 (8.0) and caught 9-39-0 (4.3) in 10 starts. Missed three mid-season games because of a right ankle sprain. Dealt with a Lisfranc injury (right foot) in the spring of '15, then was suspended for the season opener against Arkansas (violation team rules). On the season, started 7-of-9 games played, and totaled 178-973-12 (5.5) on the ground with 11-45-0 (4.1) through the air. Sat out against Arkansas State and Ball State while nursing a left hamstring strain. Led the MAC once again in '16 when he started all 13 games, and produced 262-1,475-10 (5.6) rushing with 41-403-1 (9.8) receiving. Toledo's all-time leading rusher (4,945 yards). Fumbled just once in his career in 855 touches averaging 6.3 yards per carry. Did not perform shuttles at the Combine because of a left hip flexor injury.

Strengths: Has a thick powerful trunk and runs with good leg drive after initial contact. Good eyes to find creases. Hits the hole with urgency and can sort out second-level congestion and shimmy through tight spaces. Recorded a 36 1/2-inch vertical jump at the Combine, indicating good lower-body strength and explosion. Outstanding ball security. Tracks the ball well in the air and catches outside his frame. Solid showing at the Senior Bowl. Has risen to the occasion on big stages, rushing 15-148-3 vs. Missouri in 2014, 32-271-5 in 2014 Bowl vs. Arkansas State and 20-200-1 vs. an undefeated Western Michigan in 2016.

Weaknesses: Does not show elite top-end speed and gets trapped behind the line of scrimmage too often, gathering to cut and overly relying on the jumpcut. Production is inflated from facing Mid-American competition. Could stand to do a better job chip-blocking defensive ends — too passive in pass protection. Weight measured 237 pounds in the spring of 2016, 208 at the Senior Bowl and 216 at the Combine, inviting questions and concerns about why the fluctuations have been so wide-ranging.

Future: A strong, downhill runner who showed up at the Senior Bowl more than 20 pounds lighter than he played during the spring and overhauled his body, appearing a half-step quicker than he did in the fall. Has been a solid, workman-like, productive college back with exceptional ball security and

could fill a serviceable role as a between-the-tackles grinder.

Draft projection: Fourth- to fifth-round pick.

Scout's take: "Hunt can't run. He's productive, but what does he do for you as an NFL back? We have him sitting in the sixth round."

RB AARON JONES, #29 (Jr-4)

UTEP   ▶ GRADE: 5.21

Ht: 5-9 1/2 | Wt: 208 | 40: 4.51 | Arm: 32 1/2 | Hand: 9 1/2

History: Comes from a military family, and his twin brother, Alvin, is a UTEP linebacker. Aaron also played basketball and ran track as a Texas prep. Played nine games as a true freshman in 2013, starting six, and carried 155 times for 811 yards (5.2-yard average) and four touchdowns. Suffered broken ribs against North Texas, and missed the final three games. Started all 12 games played in '14, and produced 242-1,321-11 (5.5). Did not play against Western Kentucky (knee). Was limited to two starts in '15 — managed 32-209-1 (6.5) before undergoing season-ending surgery to repair a torn left ankle ligament. In February '16, was arrested for DWI — entered a pretrial diversion program with conditions that included a probation officer, alcohol and drug tests, and DWI-related classes. In the fall, set the UTEP single-season rushing record with 229-1,773-17 (7.7). Also tossed a 23-yard touchdown pass. Posted four 200-yard games, including 24-301-4 (12.5) in the season finale against North Texas. Suffered a sprained right ankle against Southern Mississippi. Recorded 71 career receptions for 646 yards (9.1-yard average) and seven touchdowns. Had nine career fumbles in 731 touches averaging 6.3 yards per carry. Two-year captain is UTEP's all-time leading rusher (4,114 yards) despite missing 14+ games.

Strengths: Has nimble feet and good hip flexibility to make sharp cuts and suddenly change direction, as evidenced in outstanding 20-yard shuttle (4.20 seconds) and 3-cone drill (6.82) times. Very good long speed and acceleration (1.53-second 10-yard split was among best RBs at the Combine) and can pull away from a pack and create big plays. Natural hands to snag the ball out of the air, as confirmed at the Combine. Good body control to adjust to the low ball and track it deep. Very good career production. Competes on the punt team and has some special-teams experience.

Weaknesses: Has very thin legs that will be more susceptible to injury in the pros. Lacks anchor strength in pass protection. Production inflated vs. lesser competition. Durability has been an issue throughout his career. Not a crafty or refined route runner and not often used in the slot as a receiver.

Future: A quick-footed slasher who flashes some big-play ability, yet lacks the lower-body build, ball security and balanced skill set to be more than a situational, change-of-pace runner in the pros and will have to make a mark on special teams to find a role.

Draft projection: Late draftable pick.

Scout's take: "He's just a guy."

RB-PR ALVIN KAMARA, #6 (Jr-4)

TENNESSEE ▶ GRADE: 5.48

Ht: 5-10 1/4 | Wt: 214 | 40: 4.62 | Arm: 32 3/4 | Hand: 9 1/4

History: Prepped in Georgia, where he was named class 6A player of the year. Began his college career at Alabama — redshirted in 2013 (had his right knee scoped during fall camp). Missed a week of practice in November ("behavioral issues") then was suspended for the Sugar Bowl. Faced an uphill battle to climb a loaded depth chart, and was granted his release to transfer in January '14. In February was caught driving without a license. Played at Hutchinson (Kan.) Community College in the fall, and was the Kansas Junior College Offensive Player of the Year after carrying 172 times for 1,211 yards (7.3-yard average) and 18 touchdowns with 18 receptions for 219 yards (12.4-yard average) and three touchdowns in nine games (wore jersey No. 1). With the Vols in '15, recorded 107-698-7 (6.5) rushing and 34-291-3 (8.6) receiving in 13 games (one start). Started 7-of-11 games played in '16, and totaled 103-596-9 (5.8) on the ground with 40-392-4 (9.8) through the air. Injured his left knee (LCL, meniscus) against Alabama, and did not play against South Carolina or Tennessee Tech. Had 26 career punt returns for 284 yards (10.9-yard average), including one score. Fumbled seven times the last two seasons in 311 touches averaging 6.2 yards per carry. Team captain.

Strengths: Very good size with long arms. Good run skill with stop-and-start acceleration, balance and burst. Unique leaping ability to hurdle tacklers and weave through traffic. Paced all backs at the Combine with a 39 1/2-inch vertical jump and 10'11" broad jump. Very good cutback ability to stick his foot in the ground and go. Runs with good forward lean. Very effective weapon on screens and misdirection and has a knack for making tacklers miss in space. Flexes wide in the slot and can get in and out of breaks quickly. Nifty route runner. Natural hands — catches in stride. Competitive blocker. Has punt return

experience and the feet, body control and traffic burst to be effective in the pros.

Weaknesses: Not an elite burner with the top gear to pull away from the pack — gets tracked down from behind. Average run strength and power to consistently handle the grind between the tackles. Runs too narrow-based, lacks physicality and goes down easy on contact. Misses some open holes and peripheral vision could stand to improve — runs up the backs of blockers and could benefit from more patience. Limited blocking power. Fumbled once every 44 carries — carries the ball too loosely and at times in the wrong arm. Ran out of a spread offense that opened the field and took defenders out of the box. Only a half-year starter and has never proven he could carry a full workload.

Future: Perimeter space runner with the explosive burst and sudden movement skill to contribute as a third-down specialist, slot receiver and punt returner if he learns to correct his fumbling flaw.

Draft projection: Third- to fourth-round pick.

Scout's take: "(Kamara) looked good (at the Combine). He didn't interview very well. He was rough around the edges. He said a disagreement with the position coach was the reason he left Alabama, and it had nothing to do with the stable of running backs they had, even though he had to go the JUCO route and open up recruiting again. It didn't add up and it was clear he was agitated with the questions about it."

RB-KR T.J. LOGAN, #8 (Sr-4)

NORTH CAROLINA ▶ GRADE: 5.25

Ht: 5-9 1/2 | Wt: 196 | 40: 4.37 | Arm: 32 | Hand: 9

History: North Carolina native won a state title, and piled up 5,614 yards and 85 touchdowns his last two high school seasons (despite playing in the fourth quarter of just two games as a senior). Made an immediate contribution as a true freshman in 2013 — carried 93 times for 533 yards (5.7-yard average) and four touchdowns; caught 10 balls for 124 yards (12.4-yard average) and zero touchdowns; and returned 19 kickoffs for 511 yards (26.9-yard average), including two scores, in nine games (four starts). Started 9-of-13 games in '14, and produced 119-582-3 (4.9) rushing, 26-144-0 (5.5) receiving, and 16-405-1 (25.3) on kickoff returns. Ceded carries to Elijah Hood and Marquise Williams in '15 — recorded 66-400-5 (6.1) on the ground, 11-151-1 (13.7) as a receiver, and 21-492-0 (23.4) as a kickoff returner in 14 games (three starts). Played all

13 games in '16, drawing three starts, and totaled 120-650-7 (5.4) rushing, 29-244-3 (8.4) receiving, and 21-690-2 (32.9) returning kickoffs. Had six career fumbles in 556 touches averaging 5.4 yards per carry. Did not perform shuttles at the Combine because of cramps.

Strengths: Good athletic ability, balance and body control. Creative in the open field and understands how to set up blocks and anticipate angles to avoid tacklers. Clocked the fastest 40 time (4.34 seconds) of any running back at the Combine and tied for the fastest 20-yard split (4.50) with Leonard Fournette. Very good second- and third-level vision once he is in the clear. Clean catcher effective on screens. Active and energetic with the ball in his hands. Nifty returner with good anticipation (see Cincinnati and Old Dominion 2015). Unselfish team player. The game is important to him.

Weaknesses: Very lean frame and is not built to withstand a high volume of touches. Marginal run strength. Is not dynamic with the ball in his hands stringing moves together. Has a small catching radius and did not consistently catch the ball cleanly at the Combine. Lacks strength to hold ground in pass protection. Was never a full-time starter, splitting time with Elijah Hood.

Future: A quick-footed, refined rotational runner displaying some big-play ability as a kickoff returner. Most ideally suited for a situational, third-down role. Very workman-like and will carve out a position.

Draft projection: Fourth- to fifth-round pick.

Coach's take: "The guy's always got a smile on his face — he'll do whatever you ask him to do. Whether it's punt return, kickoff return, you put him on the field, whether he's got a block, he's got to do his job — he's going to get his job done. He's a tremendous teammate." —Larry Fedora, UNC Head Coach

RB MARLON MACK, #5 (Jr-3)
SOUTH FLORIDA ▶ GRADE: 5.24
Ht: 5-11 3/8 | Wt: 213 | 40: 4.51 | Arm: 32 | Hand: 9

History: Florida native played running back and linebacker in high school. Made an immediate impact in 2014 — started all 12 games, and carried 202 times for 1,041 yards (5.2-yard average) and nine touchdowns with 21 receptions for 160 yards (7.6-yard average) and zero touchdowns. In '15, was the American Athletic Conference's leading rusher for the second straight year — totaled 210-1,381-8 (6.6) rushing and 16-111-1 (6.9) receiving in 12 starts. Did not play against SMU (hamstring strain). Started all 12 games

played in '16, totaling 174-1,187-15 (6.8) on the ground with 28-227-0 (8.1) through the air. Sustained a concussion against Towson, and did not play against Northern Illinois. Had 12 career fumbles in 651 touches averaging 6.2 yards per carry. USF's all-time leading rusher (3,609 career yards) with 20 100-yard rushing games. Did not perform shuttles because of a left eye injury.

Strengths: Good muscularity. Productive, three-year starter. Runs with good anticipation, sets up blocks in the open field and takes good angles. Nifty feet to sidestep tacklers. Urgent to and through the hole, as confirmed by 1.50-second 10-yard split at the Combine, tied for the fastest among backs. Competes hard. Catches the ball easily and without breaking stride. Adjusts well to the low ball and can snag it outside his frame. Has slot experience. Solid Combine performance.

Weaknesses: High-hipped, a bit leggy and runs upright, negating power and leaving his body open to take direct hits. Could be prone to lower-body injuries. Not a strong tackle-breaker or ideally built to run inside and likes to bounce wide. Average long speed. Much of his production is blocked for him. Fumbled every 54 touches, and could stand to do a better job securing the football. Limited blocking strength — is easily discarded.

Future: A lean, upright glider with a finesse running style most comfortable in space and is ideally suited for a situational, third-down role in the pros. Durability could be tested against better competition.

Draft projection: Fifth- to sixth-round pick.

RB-WR [F]-RS CHRISTIAN McCAFFREY, #5 (Jr-3)
STANFORD ▶ GRADE: 6.33
Ht: 5-11 1/4 | Wt: 202 | 40: 4.48 | Arm: 30 | Hand: 9

History: Comes from an exceptionally athletic family. Father, Ed, was a 13-year NFL receiver (two-time Super Bowl champion), most notably with the Broncos; mother, Lisa, played soccer at Stanford; grandfather, David Sime, was a decorated Olympic sprinter; and several more aunts and uncles played college sports. Older brother, Max, is a second-year receiver for the Green Bay Packers, and younger brother, Dylan, will be a highly touted freshman QB at Michigan. A Colorado native, Christian was the state's top recruit after winning four state titles and a pair of Gatorade Player of the Year awards at Valor Christian. Finished his career with state records for career points (848), touchdowns (141), and all-purpose yards (8,845). Also earned four track letters, and was part of a 4X100 state championship team. As a true freshman in 2014 (wore jersey No. 27), played all 13 games, and carried 42 times for 300 yards (7.1-yard average) and zero touchdowns with 17 receptions for 251 yards (14.8-yard average) and two touchdowns. Posted a historic season in '15 when he broke the NCAA single-season all-purpose yardage record (3,864), set the Cardinal's single-season rushing record, and took home AP Player of the Year and Pac-12 Offensive Player of the Year — racked up 337-2,019-8 (6.0) rushing and 45-645-5 (14.3) receiving in 14 starts. Also tossed a pair of touchdown passes. Was the Pac-12 Championship Game MVP (461 all-purpose yards) and Rose Bowl Offensive Player of the Game (368 all-purpose yards, game record). The only FBS player to lead his team in rushing and receiving, McCaffrey won the Hornung Award (nation's most versatile), and was a finalist for the Heisman, Walter Camp, Maxwell, and Doak Walker. In '16, was the nation's leading all-purpose gainer (211.6 per game) and the Pac-12's leading rusher — started all 11 games played, totaling 253-1,603-13 (6.3) rushing and 38-317-3 (8.3) receiving, including a school-record 31-284-3 against Cal. Suffered a hip injury against Washington State and did not play against Notre Dame. Opted not to play in the bowl game against North Carolina in order to begin draft preparation. Was named CoSIDA Academic All-American of the Year. Had 56 career kickoff returns for 1,479 yards (26.4-yard average), including a 96-yard score against UCLA, and 34 career punt returns for 380 yards (11.2-yard average), including a 63-yard score against Iowa in the Rose Bowl (both touchdowns as a sophomore). Had four career fumbles in 823 touches averaging 6.2 yards per carry. Team captain will be a 21-year-old rookie.

Strengths: Extremely quick and sudden, as confirmed in exceptional agility drill times, the fastest of any back at the Combine. Three-cone drill time (6.57 seconds) and 60-yard shuttle (11.03 seconds) were the second-fastest of all players at the Combine and indicative of exceptional agility, balance, flexibility and endurance. Excellent eyes, anticipation and feel for lanes unfolding in the run game. Very good speed to the perimeter. Makes dynamic speed cuts at top gear and can string moves together in the open field. Exceptional functional, football-playing speed. Precise route runner able to separate with acceleration and savvy. Has naturally soft, sure hands and good concentration. Recorded a 37 1/2-inch vertical jump, indicative of excellent lower-body explosion. Willing, competitive blocker. Extremely competitive and driven. Exceptional personal and football character. Has champion NFL pedigree. Physically tough and will battle through injuries as did much of 2016. Outstanding football character. Protects the ball through traffic and has very good ball security. Lives and breathes the game and has a dedicated, professional approach in every phase — weight room, practice, film study, training table/nutrition, recovery. Versatile and can line up all over the field and run, catch and return.

Weaknesses: Has small hands and short arms. Lacks bulk ideally desired to run inside with modest tackle-breaking strength and power. Bench-pressed 225 pounds only 10 times at the Combine and could stand to improve his upper-body strength to help fight off the jam when split wide and anchor in pass protection.

Future: A utility weapon with excellent eyes and instincts to find creases and create with the ball in his hands, McCaffrey can be a swiss-army knife for a creative offensive coordinator that embraces versatility and has a plan for deploying his many talents. Could fit a Randall Cobb role as a jack of all trades with exceptional quick-cutting ability and could prove to be a more impactful slot receiver and returner than running back in the pros, following in the same path as his father.

Draft projection: First-round pick.

Scout's take: "(McCaffrey) is a first-round cinch to me. You can never draft guys like him highly enough. There's no miss factor. He's very talented. He makes the game looks easy. Everything checks out. He won't allow himself to fail. If we were picking in the top 10, I'd have no qualms taking him there and never look back."

RB ELIJAH McGUIRE, #15 (Sr-4)

LOUISIANA-LAFAYETTE   ▶ GRADE: 5.30

Ht: 5-9 3/4 | Wt: 214 | 40: 4.58 | Arm: 31 | Hand: 9

History: Lost his father when he was 12. Had an injury-riddled junior year — missed part of football season because of a broken foot and damaged thumb ligament, then had his basketball season cut short when he suffered another broken foot bone. Was the state's leading rusher his senior year — carried 223 times for 2,603 yards (11.8-yard average) and 31 touchdowns. Asked how he wound up at Lafayette, McGuire told CBS Sports, "Lafayette was the only school who knew my situa-

RUNNING BACKS

tion. I was a late qualifier and was supposed to graduate in 2014 and UL was the only school who knew that. By the time I graduated, bigger schools didn't realize it and I was already at UL." Made an immediate impact as a true freshman in 2013 (wore jersey No. 22) when he rushed 103-863-8 (8.4) and caught 22-384-3 (17.5) in 13 games (two starts). Was the Sun Belt Conference Player of the Year in '14 — produced 166-1,264-14 (7.6) rushing and 45-468-2 (10.4) receiving in 13 games (five starts). Had off-season surgery to repair a torn left labrum. Started all 25 games the last two seasons — totaled 209-1,047-13 (5.0) rushing and 34-304-3 (8.9) receiving in '15 (12 games); and 232-1,127-7 (4.9) rushing and 29-238-2 (8.2) receiving in '16 (13 games). Sustained a foot injury in Week Four against Tulane, and was hampered most of the season. Had 28 career punt returns for 227 yards (8.1-yard average). Had six career fumbles in 874 touches averaging 6.1 yards per carry. Team captain and Offensive MVP. First in his family to graduate. Was the East-West Shrine Game's Offensive MVP before declining an invitation to the Senior Bowl.

Strengths: Very fluid glider with a good feel for setting up blocks with jab steps and jump cuts — creates a lot of additional yardage slithering thru congestion. Is quick and sudden and accelerates to top speed in steps to take the corner, as confirmed by outstanding 2.56-second 20-yard split indicative of long burst. Rushed 19-129-0 against Georgia and showed he can produce vs. better competition. Protects the ball very well — carries high and tight. Catches the ball very naturally. Competitive blocker who will stick his face in and square up. Tough, durable and will play through injuries as he did much of senior season. Emergency punt returner. Good personal and football character.

Weaknesses: Average size with small hands. Lacks the tackle-breaking strength and physicality to slam inside and looks to bounce outside. Runs too narrow-based and at times looks like he's wearing blinders protecting his body. Ran a 4.57-second 20-yard shuttle at the Combine, tied for the worst among backs, and indicative of limited hip flexibility. Not explosive as a blocker and could do a better sinking his hips in pass protection and scanning to pick up the blitz. Too right-hand dominant carrying the ball and could protect it better in outside hand when running to his left.

Future: Compactly built, shifty, patient ball carrier with a well-balanced skill set to effectively run, block and catch and develop into

a Jerick McKinnon-type, third-down contributor. Hobbled by a foot injury since Week Four in 2016 and did not appear to have the same burst he showed earlier in his career.

Draft projection: Fourth- to fifth-round pick.

RB JEREMY McNICHOLS, #13 (Jr-3)

BOISE STATE   ▶ GRADE: 5.27

Ht: 5-8 5/8 | Wt: 214 | 40: 4.49 | Arm: 31 1/2 | Hand: 10

History: Also ran track as a California prep. Was supposed to redshirt in 2014, but was called upon when Matt Miller was injured — recorded 17 carries for 159 yards (9.4-yard average) and one touchdown with 15 receptions for 155 yards (10.3-yard average) and one touchdown in nine games. Started all 12 games played in '15, and produced 240-1,337-20 (5.6) rushing with 51-460-6 (9.0) receiving. Did not play against Utah State (concussion). In '16, led the Mountain West Conference in touchdowns with 314-1,709-23 (5.4) on the ground and 37-474-4 (12.8) through the air in 13 starts. Returned 34 career kickoffs for 554 yards (12.8-yard average). Had nine career fumbles in 702 touches averaging 5.6 yards per carry. Will be a 21-year-old rookie. Did not bench press because of a medical exclusion (right shoulder) or perform the 60-yard shuttle (tight hamstrings).

Strengths: Runs with urgency and good balance to make sharp cuts at top speed. Usually falls forward. Good feet to navigate through traffic. Gets better with a lather and has shown he could carry a full workload. Aligns wide at times and has dependable hands to catch outside his frame. Excellent career production. Has kickoff return experience. Very good weight-room worker.

Weaknesses: Lacks top-end speed to be a home-run hitter and goes down too easily behind the line of scrimmage. Only shows one gear. Does not have a strong lower body to drive through contact or creativity when trapped — takes some direct hits that will invite injury in the pros. Hit-or-miss blocker. Could stand to improve awareness in pass protection. Shut down (19-46-0) by Baylor in the Cactus Bowl, and production is inflated from facing Mountain West Competition.

Future: More quick than fast, stocky, hard-running, well-rounded back with a chance to compete for a backup role. Must prove he can stay healthy to earn the trust of coaches.

Draft projection: Fourth- to fifth-round pick.

Scout's take: "(McNichols) has good contact balance. He's tough. He runs behind his pads. He can block and catch. He's a solid back."

RUNNING BACKS

RB-KR JOE MIXON, #25 (Soph-3)

OKLAHOMA ▶ GRADE: 5.44

Ht: 6-0 3/4 | Wt: 228 | 40: 4.46 | Arm: 30 1/8 | Hand: 10 1/4

History: Also ran track as a prep in California, where he was one of the most highly recruited running backs in the country. In August 2014, OU suspended Mixon from the team for a year after he was charged with misdemeanor "act resulting in gross injury" stemming from an incident in which he punched a woman at a Norman cafe. Mixon entered an Alford plea, avoiding jail time. Instead, he was given one year probation, paid $1,200 in fines, served 100 hours of community service, and attended cognitive behavior counseling. Despite school officials having access to surveillance video of the incident, per Fox Sports, Mixon was allowed back with the Sooners, as he and Samaje Perine formed one of the most talented duos in college football for the next two seasons. In '15, Mixon carried 113 times for 753 yards (6.7-yard average) and seven touchdowns with 28 receptions for 356 yards (12.7-yard average) and four touchdowns in 13 games (four starts). Sustained a head injury in the Orange Bowl against Clemson. In July '16, two years after the cafe incident, the victim sued Mixon, seeking monetary compensation for negligence, willful and wanton misconduct, and intentional infliction of emotional distress. Two of the three claims were dismissed in November, the same month Mixon issued a written apology. Said Mixon, according to The Oklahoman: "At the end of the night, a group of apparently drunk people started harassing us. Some of my teammates were wise enough to leave. I did not, and I am sorry. The situation got tense. Racial slurs were hurled at me. I should have left, but I did not. A woman shoved me. I was upset and I should have left, but I did not. Then, she slapped me, and I reacted poorly — I struck her. It was a bad reaction, one that does not reflect my character or my values. I am sorry." In December, Mixon's attorney filed an Answer to the Complaint, claiming the victim instigated hostility with Mixon. Days later, the surveillance video, sealed since the criminal portion of the case, was ruled public record. The video shows the victim pushing Mixon in the chest seconds before Mixon punches the woman in the face, causing multiple facial fractures. Played 12 games in '16, making five starts, and totaled 188-1,274-10 (6.8) rushing with 37-538-5 (14.5) receiving. Also tossed a 26-yard TD pass. Was suspended for the Iowa State contest after he ripped up a parking ticket in the presence of a parking attendant. Had 22 career kickoff returns for 504 yards (22.9-yard average), including a 97-yard score against Ohio State as a sophomore, and four career punt returns for 25 yards (6.3-yard average). Had six fumbles the last two seasons in 393 touches averaging 6.8 yards per carry. Mixon was deposed on Jan. 24. A civil lawsuit alleging the incident and its aftermath caused emotional distress has been filed by the woman and is still pending.

Strengths: Has a shredded physique with the size desired in an NFL bellcow. Outstanding athlete with the strength, balance and burst to carry an offense. Fine stretch-zone eyes to find a sliver of daylight and accelerate to and through the hole. Has a knack for setting up blocks and following his blockers. Can pull a rabbit out of his hat and turn a two-yard loss into a big gain (see 68-yard TD run at start of third quarter vs. Texas Tech when he makes seven tacklers miss). Occasionally will brandish a powerful stiff arm. Catches the ball naturally in stride on swing, wheel and seam routes and can snag the one-handed grab. Creates separation as a route runner with quickness and acceleration. Possesses big-play ability.

Weaknesses: Not a strong or polished pass protector. Could do a better job of protecting his feet from shoestring and torpedo tackles and can be tripped up too easily. Pitter patters in the backfield waiting for a hole to uncover and gives up his chest too easily. Runs more gingerly inside than he does on the edges. Was not a full-time starter — split time in the backfield with a talented back, but has yet to show he can handle a full workload or grind down defenses. Must prove he has learned from the past, can mature and prove trustworthy as a citizen in the community.

Future: A big, fast, sure-handed, all-around back whose only football deficiency is in pass protection, Mixon displayed every trait desired in an elite back against Texas Tech and possesses Pro Bowl-caliber physical tools and big-play ability. Possesses first-round talent, yet past transgressions place character grades at the reject level for many teams. From a talent standpoint, could be a Tyreek Hill-esque steal of the draft for a veteran locker room with a nurturing coaching staff and strong support programs that believe in second chances, though could struggle to find more than a few, such as the Bengals, Colts and Chiefs, willing to take the PR hit and continue developing his

RUNNING BACKS

maturity.

Draft projection: Fourth- to fifth-round pick.

Scout's take: "Mixon is really talented. With how hard the league is cracking down on domestic issues though, he could be left undrafted. Today's climate is different since the Ray Rice incident. ...When you talk to (Oklahoma staff), they will tell you Mixon is upbeat, personable and captain material. It's all so positive to a point where they are almost trying to create a better kid than he is to save him. I still can't get past it — who in their right mind punches a woman?"

RB-RS KHALFANI MUHAMMAD, #29 (Sr-4)

CALIFORNIA ▶ GRADE: 5.09

Ht: 5-7 7/8 | Wt: 170 | 40: 4.40e | Arm: 29 | Hand: 9 1/4

History: First name is pronounced "CAL-fawn-ee." Father, Malik, was an Olympic sprinter. Khalfani, a California native, was an outstanding track performer — captured back-to-back state championships in the 100 and 200 meters during his junior and senior years, and was named the state's Track and Field Athlete of the Year as a senior. Played 11 games as a true freshman in 2013, drawing one start, and carried 74 times for 445 yards (6.0-yard average) and four touchdowns. Also returned 46 kickoffs for 1,006 yards (21.9-yard average). Did not play against Washington State (concussion). In '15, rushed 46-215-4 (4.7) and returned kickoffs 14-289 (20.6) in 11 games (one start). Did not play against Washington (broken left thumb). Started 5-of-12 games in '15, running 87-586-1 (6.7) and returning kickoffs 3-52 (17.3). Did not play against Stanford (foot). He sat out spring practice in 2015 to run track and soon fell to fourth on the depth chart. Was voted the Bears' Most Courageous Player in '16 when he started 6-of-11 games played, and had 152-827-2 (5.4) on the ground with 24-584 (24.3) on kickoff returns. Did not play against Utah (quad). Totaled 55 career receptions for 571 yards (10.4-yard average) and three touchdowns. Had nine career fumbles in 501 touches averaging 5.8 yards per carry. Tallied 14 tackles his last two seasons on special teams. Competed for Cal's track and field team for three years, posting a personal-best 10.44 100 meters.

Strengths: Has legitimate track speed and is capable of going the distance when he finds a clear path. Quick to the corner and has outstanding acceleration to pull away. Coachable.

Weaknesses: Very diminutive frame. Goes down easy. More straight-line fast than quick and has just adequate elusiveness to make de-

fenders miss in the open field. Tends to bounce outside. Does not string moves together or show much creativity. Fumbles have been too frequent (every 56 touches), and he needs to secure the ball more tightly. Lacks polish as a route runner. Body-catches too much with a small catching radius and can be fazed by traffic. Has no anchor in pass protection. Never has been a full-time starter.

Future: Emerged as more than a track athlete playing football and could add an explosive threat to a ground game if he learns how to secure the ball more securely.

Draft projection: Priority free agent.

RB DARE OGUNBOWALE, #23 (Sr-5)

WISCONSIN ▶ GRADE: 5.21

Ht: 5-10 3/4 | Wt: 213 | 40: 4.66 | Arm: 31 3/8 | Hand: 9 1/8

History: Pronounced "DAR-ay / oh-goon-bo-WALL-ay." Comes from an athletic family — mother, Yolanda, played softball at De-Paul; Sister, Arike, plays basketball at Notre Dame; and cousin, Diamond Stone, plays for the L.A. Clippers. Oluwadare also competed in basketball and track as a Milwaukee prep. Did not play football until junior season. Red-shirted in 2012. Made eight appearances in '13, recording a pair of special-teams tackles. Converted from cornerback to running back due to team needs in '14 — recorded 34 carries for 193 yards (5.7-yard average) and one touchdown in 14 games. Added 10 tackles. Injuries to Corey Clement opened the door for Ogunbowale to start 10-of-13 games in '15, and he responded with 194-819-7 (4.2) rushing and 36 receptions for 299 yards (8.3-yard average) and one touchdown. Returned to a backup role behind Corey Clement in '16 when he ran 91-506-5 (5.6) and caught 24-208-1 (8.7). Had 11 career kickoff returns for 232 yards (21.1-yard average). Had 0 career fumbles in 390 touches averaging 4.8 yards per carry. Walk-on-turned-captain earned a scholarship as a junior. Graduated with an economics degree.

Strengths: Functional outside stretch-zone runner. Runs hard and battles for extra yardage after the catch. Can sidestep and shake tacklers in the open field. Takes excellent care of the ball — carries high and tight. Effortful blocker showed he could handle pass protection at the Senior Bowl. Extremely intelligent and assignment sound. Excellent weight-room worker. Terrific personal and football character. Represents the program well (volunteer tutor). Very durable and has not missed any time to injury. Quick learner. Has kickoff return experience and initially earned his way on special teams.

Weaknesses: Very lean build with small hands. Below-average foot speed for a third-down back with developing run instincts — stutter-steps too much and does not accelerate to and through the hole. Showed ordinary agility in Combine drills. Marginal tackle-breaking strength to carry a load between the tackles and tends to run a tad upright, leaving his body susceptible to contact. Has some tightness in his body noticeable when adjusting to the thrown ball, resulting in drops. Has a 28 1/2-inch vertical jump, tied for the second lowest among backs at the Combine. Lacks power in pass protection and can be overwhelmed by the blitz.

Future: Classic overachiever with the intelligence, toughness and wiring to contribute readily as a core special teamer and potentially work his way into a rotation on third downs. Lack of foot speed could limit opportunities in the backfield.

Draft projection: Fifth- to sixth-round pick.

Scout's take: "(Ogunbowale) is one of my favorite people in the draft. Both his parents are educators. He's sharp as a whip. He's charismatic. He's a grinder. He's got all the intangibles you want. He's not the most talented player, but he will be difficult to cut once he gets in the building. He'll earn his way on special teams and make a team."

RB SAMAJE PERINE, #32 (Jr-3)

OKLAHOMA ▶ GRADE: 5.64

Ht: 5-10 5/8 | Wt: 233 | 40: 4.59* | Arm: 30 3/8 | Hand: 10

History: (*Improved 40-time at pro day workout after running 4.66 at the Combine with a strained pectoral muscle.) Pronounced "suh-MAH-jay P-rine." Engaged to be married. Texas prep tore his left MCL and LCL at the end of his sophomore season. Chose OU over Alabama. Broke out with a sensational freshman season in 2014 — started 8-of-13 games, and racked up 263 carries for 1,713 yards (6.5-yard average) and 21 touchdowns, including an FBS single-game record 34-427-5 (12.6) against Kansas. Sprained his left ankle against Oklahoma State. Started all 13 games in '15, producing 226-1,349-16 (6.0). Hurt his right hand against Tulsa. Had post-season surgery to repair ligament damage in his left ankle, and sat out '16 spring practice. In the fall, started 9-of-10 games, and totaled 196-1,060-12 (5.4). Was limited to six carries in the season opener versus Houston (left shoulder), then pulled a hamstring against Kansas State, and missed three mid-season contests. Accumulated 40 career receptions for 321 yards (8.0-yard average) and two touchdowns. Had six career fumbles in 725 touches averaging 6.0 yards per carry. Team captain needed just three seasons to break OU's all-time rushing record (4,122 yards).

Strengths: Has a very thick trunk. Exceptional base, lower-body strength and balance to power through contact and barrel over defenders. Keeps his shoulders squared to the line of scrimmage and runs with very good pad level and authority, brushing off defenders with ease. Great eyes and anticipation — patiently follows his blocks. Surprisingly light on his feet and efficient in his movement making subtle cuts. Unleashes a powerful stiffarm. Can create a strong goal-line surge (see Baylor, Texas, Clemson) and be his own blocker. Very tough and physical. Will battle through injuries. Reliable outlet receiver. Very stout in pass pro and scans to pick up the blitz. Weight-room warrior with superhuman strength. Bench-pressed 225 pounds the most times (30) of any back at the Combine and it shows brushing off defenders on contact. Excellent career production. Preserved his body splitting time in a talented backfield with Joe Mixon. Very confident and never sought to transfer or wavered in his commitment with Mixon joining the backfield. Outstanding personal and football character. Smart, articulate and diligent in all facets of the game.

Weaknesses: Lacks top-end speed to regularly take the corner and break away from the pack. Average stop-and-start acceleration and fluidity to create in space. A bit of a short stepper with limited knee drive. Can do a better job avoiding some low-filling tacklers. Is not a fluid route runner ideally suited to flex wide in the slot. Has been dinged the last two years and runs with so much power that durability could become an issue. Limited special teams experience.

Future: A very strong, compactly built, rolling ball of butcher knives able to hammer the ball inside, yet also runs with patience, vision and surprising agility for a man his size. A power back very capable of earning a living between the tackles and factoring every down.

Draft projection: Second- to third-round pick.

Scout's take: "He's a good three-down back who probably lands early in the third (round) in this draft, being as strong a class as it is. He's not as talented as (teammate Joe) Mixon, but he's solid. He was hurt this year too, so durability will play into it. That could knock him down a peg."

RUNNING BACKS

RB DONNEL PUMPHREY, #19 (Sr-4)

SAN DIEGO STATE ▶ GRADE: 5.37

Ht: 5-8 1/4 | Wt: 176 | 40: 4.49 | Arm: 29 | Hand: 8 1/2

History: Has a daughter, Maliya. Las Vegas native was named Nevada's Gatorade Player of the Year after piling up 160 carries for 1,491 yards (9.3-yard average) and 19 touchdowns. Also ran track in high school. As a true freshman in 2013, contributed 125-752-8 (6.0) rushing with 22 receptions for 234 yards (10.6-yard average) and two touchdowns. Added four kickoff returns for 63 yards (15.8-yard average). Started all 41 games the next three seasons — totaled 276-1,876-20 (6.8) rushing and 23-160-0 (7.0) receiving in '14 (13 games); 309-1,653-17 (5.3) rushing and 27-414-3 (15.3) receiving in '15 (14 games); and 349-2,133-17 (6.1) rushing and 27-231-0 (8.6) receiving in '16 (14 games). Doak Walker Award finalist. Leading rusher in FBS history (6,405 yards). First player in history with at least 5,000 rushing yards and 1,000 receiving yards. Two-time Mountain West Offensive Player of the Year and the only three-time team MVP in program history. Had 11 career fumbles in 1,164 touches averaging 6.0 yards per carry. Opted not to run shuttles at the Combine.

Strengths: Extremely competitive, determined and decisive runner. Has a knack for finding small creases and squirting through cracks to find open space. Very good functional play speed to the perimeter and gear change to plant his foot in the dirt and re-direct. Recorded a 1.50-second 10-yard split at the Combine, tied for the fastest among backs and indicative of exceptional short-area burst. Good spin move in the hole. Has a knack for avoiding tacklers with subtle jab steps and short-area burst and consistently produces chunk runs. Surprisingly strong stiffarm for a small back. Aligns in the slot at times and has the quickness to create some separation and get open. Has proven he can handle a heavy workload and has been very durable, playing through hand and ankle injuries in 2015 and never missing any time. Exceptional career production. The game is very important to him.

Weaknesses: Skinny-framed and smallish with short arms, very small hands, both the smallest of any back at the Combine. Lacks run strength and power. Does not have the bulk to withstand the grind of running inside. Only bench-pressed 225 pounds a Combine-low 5 times. Tends to drift in his routes and is not a crafty or refined route runner. Extremely small catching radius, as shown with smallest wingspan (67 3/4 inches) of any skill player at the Combine, even more noticeable by difficulty of quarterbacks connecting in passing drills. Underpowered blocker with no anchor strength. Was not regularly challenged against top competition. Is not a dynamic return man.

Future: On paper, measurables look like a free agent. On the field, had the production of a future all-pro, running with a relentless determination that refused to be denied. More quick than fast, Pumphrey is a very good football player with the wiring and all-around utility to earn a multi-purpose role as a specialty back, slot receiver and punt returner in the pros. Would be most optimized playing for creative offensive minds such as those in New Orleans, Kansas City or Philadelphia.

Draft projection: Fourth- to fifth-round pick.

Scout's take: "He's a special little back. He's just little. He's faster than Darren Sproles and probably quicker. If you were standing next to him, you'd never think he could tear up defenses the way he does."

RB DEVINE REDDING, #34 (Jr-3)

INDIANA ▶ GRADE: 5.06

Ht: 5-8 1/4 | Wt: 205 | 40: 4.76 | Arm: 29 1/4 | Hand: 9 5/8

History: Was sidelined for five games his senior year after transferring to play for Ted Ginn, Sr., at Glenville (OH) High. Saw limited action in 10 games as a true freshman in 2014, carrying 29 times for 118 yards (4.1-yard average) and one touchdown. In '15, was part of one of the best one-two punches in the country — teamed with Jordan Howard (Bears), and produced 226-1,012-9 (4.5) in 13 games (four starts). Was the workhorse in '16 when he toted 253-1,122-7 (4.4). Posted 40 career receptions for 245 yards (6.1-yard average) and two touchdowns. Had five career fumbles in 548 touches averaging 4.4 yards per carry. Will be a 21-year-old rookie.

Strengths: Good feet and anticipation to feel lanes developing. Reads blocks and sifts through traffic. Good forward lean to fall forward. Functional in pass protection to pick up the blitz and get in the way. Reliable hands as an outlet receiver. Very disciplined worker who never missed a day of practice. Unselfish team player.

Weaknesses: Average size and run strength to break tackles. Does not generate power through his lower half or drive piles. Modest athletic ability. Only shows one gear, clocking the slowest 40 time (4.82 seconds) and 60-yard shuttle (12.03) of any running back at the Combine. Lacks finishing speed and gets

RUNNING BACKS

tracked down from behind. Has tightness in his body and does not have the wiggle or acceleration to shake many tacklers in space.

Future: Adequate-sized zone runner takes what the defense gives him and has enough size, toughness and run skill to compete for a job in a camp. Will need to make a mark on special teams to stick on a roster. Has make-it qualities.

Draft projection: Priority free agent.

Scout's take: "He has good vision and instincts and is a solid runner, but he lacks speed. He doesn't upgrade us at all. Someone will draft him late."

FB SAM ROGERS, #45 (Sr-4)

VIRGINIA TECH ▶ GRADE: 5.12
Ht: 5-10 1/4 | Wt: 231 | 40: 4.89 | Arm: 30 1/4 | Hand: 9 3/4

History: Earned letters in football (four), basketball (three), and lacrosse (one) as a prep in Virginia, where he garnered all-state recognition by playing all over the field. Had FCS offers, but opted to join Virginia Tech as a preferred walk-on. Earned the starting job and a scholarship during his true freshman season. Played all 54 games of his career (2013-16), drawing 25 starts — carried 165 times for 692 yards (4.2-yard average) and four touchdowns; caught 72 balls for 802 yards (11.1-yard average) and seven touchdowns; completed 3-of-4 pass attempts (75.0 percent) for 32 yards with one touchdown and zero interceptions; and logged 14 career tackles. Fractured his left elbow in the '14 Military Bowl. Was honored with the No. 25 jersey on Senior Day — a tribute to Frank Beamer typically reserved for the special-teams player of the week — because head coach Justin Fuente said Rogers epitomized what it means to be a Hokie. After beating Maryland that afternoon, Rogers proposed — in the end zone — to his girlfriend Lauren. Had three career fumbles in 240 touches averaging 4.2 yards per carry. Graduated with a degree in human nutrition, foods and exercise.

Strengths: Plays with urgency. Good pound-for-pound strength to run through defensive backs after the catch. Splits wide and takes good angles as a crack-back blocker and gets in the way. Catches the ball very naturally and adjusts easily to it. Specialty passer with an accurate arm. Strong intangibles and natural leadership qualities. Core special teams contributor. Outstanding practice habits and football intelligence — very focused and does a lot of extras. Excellent weight-room worker. Very

durable.

Weaknesses: Small-framed with short arms. Tight-hipped and gathers to cut. Undersized to match up against linebackers. Does not consistently sustain blocks and needs to play with more consistent knee bend.

Future: Very strong, high-effort overachiever with the toughness, competitiveness and football character to become a fixture on special teams and earn a starting job as versatile, receiving fullback.

Draft projection: Sixth- to seventh-round pick.

RB-WR [F]-RS CURTIS SAMUEL, #4 (Jr-3)

OHIO STATE ▶ GRADE: 5.92
Ht: 5-10 5/8 | Wt: 196 | 40: 4.34 | Arm: 31 1/4 | Hand: 9 1/2

History: Averaged 13.7 yards per carry his last two seasons at Brooklyn (N.Y.) Erasmus Hall, where he was the state's Gatorade Player of the Year. Also competed as a sprinter. Backed up Ezekiel Elliott his first year in Columbus. Played all 14 games in '14, drawing one start, and carried 58 times for 383 yards (6.6-yard average) and six touchdowns with 11 receptions for 95 yards (8.6-yard average) and zero touchdowns. In '15, was moved to H-back — hybrid skill position — in order to get him on the field with Elliott. Recorded 22-289-2 (13.1) receiving and 17-132-1 (7.8) rushing. Had post-season foot surgery. Started 12-of-13 games played in '16 — 10 at H-back, two at running back — and totaled 74-865-7 (11.7) receiving and 97-771-8 (7.9) rushing. Added six punt returns for 19 yards (3.2-yard average). Had 21 career kickoff returns for 453 yards (21.6-yard average). Had four career fumbles in 300 touches (107 catches) averaging 7.5 yards per carry. Will be a 21-year-old rookie.

Strengths: Outstanding speed and acceleration to the perimeter to take the corner and run away from defenders (see Penn State). Good eyes and anticipation. Fine cutback ability, on display in multiple runs of game-winning touchdown drive vs. Michigan in which he scored. Runs to the spot and makes some difficult over-the-shoulder grabs (see Rutgers, Nebraska), tracking the ball well downfield. Has the top-end speed to separate vertically vs. man coverage and mismatch safeties. Concentrates in traffic and can make the difficult, contested catch (see Tulsa). Excellent weight-room strength.

Weaknesses: Too straight-linish — will gather to cut and does not elude many tacklers in space, showing some disdain for con-

RUNNING BACKS

tact. Lacks tackle-breaking strength and goes down too easily. Could have difficulty beating physical, press coverage. Tends to cradle-catch even when he goes up for the ball and needs to improve attacking it with his hands and learning how to highpoint. Seldom asked to block. Lacks fearlessness and ideal dynamic lateral agility desired in a returner. Can be a bit careless with the ball and needs to carry it more securely to his frame.

Future: Fast, explosive hybrid back often aligned in the slot with explosive, big-play ability to change games. A poor man's Percy Harvin, Samuel offers unique versatility and potential return skill to contribute readily in the pros.

Draft projection: Top-40 pick.

Scout's take: "Some (scouts) want to grade him as a running back. I think he is on the slight side to do it. He could be a good slot guy — he's twitchy and fast. There is some rawness to him as a receiver, but he is more advanced than (former Buckeye WR) Braxton Miller, who went in the third (round) a year ago. There is a buzz about him sneaking into the late 1st (round) with the way he can run."

RB RUSHEL SHELL, #7 (Sr-5)

WEST VIRGINIA   ▶ GRADE: 4.94
Ht: 5-9 5/8 | Wt: 227 | 40: 4.77 | Arm: 30 | Hand: 9 5/8

History: First name is pronounced "rushell." Has a son, Prince, and twin daughters, Arionna and Amiyah. Had a historic prep career in Pennsylvania — USA Today All-American, AAA Player of the Year, two-time Pittsburgh Post-Gazette Player of the Year, and four-time all-state honoree. Amassed a state-record 9,078 yards and WPIAL-record 110 touchdowns, while setting a national record with 39 straight 100-yard games. Sustained a concussion in October of his senior season. Also played basketball (point guard). With his twins on the way, chose Pittsburgh in order to stay close to home/family. Was suspended for the 2012 season opener against Youngstown State before carrying 141 times for 641 yards (4.5-yard average) and four touchdowns with nine receptions for 103 yards (11.4-yard average) and zero touchdowns in 12 games. Flirted with transferring to UCLA in '13 — ultimately had a change of heart, but was not welcome back at Pittsburgh. Transferred to West Virginia, sitting out the season per NCAA rules. Started 8-of-12 games played in '14, and produced 176-788-7 (4.5) rushing with 21-140-0 (6.7) receiving. Sprained his right ankle against Baylor, and did not play against Oklahoma State. Played all 13 games in '15, drawing three starts, and recorded 161-708-8 (4.4) on the ground and 16-101-0 (6.3) through the air. After backing up Wendell Smallwood (Eagles), was the primary rusher in '16. Despite a concussion during fall camp, ran 113-514-5 (4.5) and caught 12-100-0 (8.3) in 10 games (eight starts). Sprained his ankle against Oklahoma State, and the injury limited him to just 17 carries in the last seven games. Had seven career fumbles in 502 touches averaging 4.5 yards per carry. Completed his sociology and anthropology degree. Suffered a right hamstring injury on his second 40-yard dash attempt and stopped working out after first route drill.

Strengths: Very good bulk. Showed the ability earlier in his career to drop his shoulder, run through multiple tacklers and even hurdle defenders. Good leg churn thru contact. Solid goal-line and short-yardage back — presses the line and has inside-running power. Effective outlet receiver with dependable hands. Willing blocker.

Weaknesses: Tight-hipped and upright runner. Not nifty-footed and lacks finishing speed to pull away or create chunk yards. Plodder who takes time to get rolling and builds to speed, as confirmed with the slowest 10-yard time (1.67 seconds) of any running back at the Combine. Lacks the explosion to reach the corner. Creates no separation as a receiver. Carries the ball loosely and does not change hands to protect it when running to the left. Limited special teams experience.

Future: A plodding, inside runner who peaked in 2014 and would be most optimal playing at a lighter weight than he did as a senior. Lack of speed and special teams experience could restrict his chances.

Draft projection: Free agent.

RB De'VEON SMITH, #4 (Sr-4)

MICHIGAN   ▶ GRADE: 5.24
Ht: 5-10 7/8 | Wt: 223 | 40: 4.65e | Arm: 29 1/2 | Hand: 9

History: Prepped in Ohio. Recruited to Michigan by then-head coach Brady Hoke. As a true freshman in 2013, saw limited action in four games and carried 26 times for 117 yards (4.5-yard average) and zero touchdowns. In '14, recorded 108-519-6 (4.8) with three receptions for 26 yards (8.7-yard average) and zero touchdowns in 12 games (two starts). Started 10-of-13 games in '15, and produced 180-753-6 (4.2) rushing with 19-159-1 (8.4) receiving. Sprained his right ankle against BYU, and did not play against Maryland. Started all 13 games in '16, and totaled 181-846-10 (4.7) on the ground and 16-66-0 (4.1) through the air. Had two career fumbles in 533 touches averaging 4.5 yards per carry. Did not run the 40-yard dash because of a right ankle injury.

Strengths: Outstanding size — has a thick, well-proportioned build with good musculature and a strong trunk. Runs hard downhill with good leg drive, balance and body lean. Strong on contact and does not go down easy — takes a crowd to bring him down. Likes to inflict punishment. Catches the ball with ease. Well-versed in a pro-style offense. Competitive, willing blocker and can hold his ground in pass pro. Effective cut blocker. Showed well in one-on-one blocking drills at the Senior Bowl. Outstanding ball security, fumbling only once every 266 touches and covering the ball with both arms through traffic. Has a passion for the game.

Weaknesses: Has small hands. Limited knee extension and elusiveness in the open field and struggles to get off the track and avoid direct hits, as confirmed by the slowest 20-yard shuttle (4.57 seconds) and 3-cone drill time (7.30 seconds) of any back at the Combine. Presses the line too quickly and runs up the backs of blockers — could stand to improve patience. Is late to reach the perimeter and lacks finishing speed to go the distance. Shows some tightness in his routes. Needs to do a better job scanning to pick up the blitz.

Future: A well-built, hard-charging, power back with the physicality and competitiveness to earn a role grinding between the tackles, yet left too much production on the field failing to see holes developing and instead slamming into piles. A hammer and only a hammer, lacking the creativity to take another tool (vision, cutback ability or elusiveness) out of the toolbox. Has temperament desired to make a living as a core special teams contributor.

Draft projection: Fifth- to sixth-round pick.

Scout's take: "I put (Smith) in the sixth (round). He's a downhill back with some bulk, good pad level and no juice to get outside the tackles."

FB FREDDIE STEVENSON, #23 (Sr-4)
FLORIDA STATE ▶ GRADE: 5.16
Ht: 6-0 1/2 | Wt: 234 | 40: 4.74 | Arm: 32 3/4 | Hand: 9 5/8

History: Florida native. Suffered a broken fibula in November of his junior season. Transitioned from linebacker to fullback upon entering FSU. As a true freshman in 2013 (wore jersey No. 33), appeared in 12 games. Started 7-of-14 games in '14, when he played through a knee injury all season. Injured his right knee during '15 spring practice, requiring surgery.

In the fall, started 10-of-12 games played. Sat out against Chattanooga (concussion). Started 4-of-12 games in '16. Sat out against Charleston Southern (ankle). Had 25 career rushes for 132 yards (5.3-yard average) and five touchdowns; caught 19 passes for 160 yards (8.4-yard average) and two touchdowns; and four kickoff returns for 35 yards (8.8-yard average). Did not have any fumbles in 48 touches. Team captain graduated with a social science degree.

Strengths: Good peripheral blocking vision to find lanes and pave the way as a lead blocker. Understands angles and positioning and is effective sealing linebackers on the second level. Good run strength. Slams the line in short-yardage situations with good forward lean. Tough and will play through injuries. Motivated, mature and responsible.

Weaknesses: Average hip roll and explosion on contact. Not a hammer who is going to drive defenders out of a hole. Limited career production as a runner and receiver. Seldom asked to run routes or carry the ball. Has been dinged a lot with injuries throughout his career.

Future: A tough, blue-collar, converted linebacker ideally suited for a West Coast offense where he could contribute in all phases. Can run, catch and block and immediately earn a role on special teams.

Draft projection: Late draftable pick.

Scout's take: "Stevenson is not going to knock out linebackers or root anyone out of the hole. He's more of a finesse, positional, get-in-the-way type and cuts a lot."

RB-RS JAHAD THOMAS, #5 (Sr-4)
TEMPLE ▶ GRADE: 5.08
Ht: 5-9 3/4 | Wt: 190 | 40: 4.64 | Arm: 30 1/8 | Hand: 9

History: Prepped in New Jersey, where he won a state championship and played on a nationally ranked basketball team. Was a cornerback as a true freshman in 2013 when he appeared in nine games, mostly on special teams. Sat out against Army (knee). In '14, moved to running back — his natural position — and carried 80 times for 384 yards (4.8-yard average) and zero touchdowns with 14 catches for 364 yards (26.0-yard average) and one touchdown in 12 games (four starts). Started 10-of-14 games in '15, producing 276-1,262-17 (4.6) rushing and 22-216-1 (9.8) receiving. Sprained his left MCL in the Owls' bowl game against Toledo. Missed the first two games of the '16 season (dislocated left thumb) before totaling 207-953-13 (4.6) on the ground with 33-418-6 (12.7) through the air. Added eight punt returns for 101 yards (12.6-yard average), as well as 46 career kickoff returns for 1,035 yards (22.5-yard average), including a 100-yard score against Cincinnati as a junior. Had nine career fumbles in 678 touches averaging 4.6 yards per carry. Did not perform shuttles because of a right ankle injury.

Strengths: Natural catcher — extends outside his frame and snags the ball cleanly. Splits wide and shows some savvy to feel coverage and create separation with quickness. Good agility and initial suddenness off spots to shake tacklers in the open field. Displays the vision and burst to be effective in the return game.

Weaknesses: Thin-framed, lacks bulk and runs too tall to handle the grind between the tackles. Marginal power and contact balance — goes down easily with arm tackles and often on first touch. Gets tracked down from behind (see Cincinnati) and lacks finishing speed, as confirmed by slow 40-yard times at the Combine. Not asked to block a lot and does not have the anchor strength to match up.

Future: High-cut, narrow-built space player most valuable as a sure-handed receiving option and returner. Could add a utility weapon to an up-tempo offense, but will need to earn his way in the return game.

Draft projection: Priority free agent.

RB-KR BOOM WILLIAMS, #18 (Jr-3)

KENTUCKY   ▶ GRADE: 5.12

Ht: 5-7 1/2 | Wt: 190 | 40: 4.49 | Arm: 30 | Hand: 8 5/8

History: Also ran track as a Georgia prep (originally verbally committed to University of Georgia). Played 10 games as a true freshman in 2014, carrying 75 times for 488 yards (6.5-yard average) and five touchdowns. Added 19 kickoff returns for 511 yards (26.9-yard average). Was suspended against South Carolina (pellet gun incident), then sustained a concussion against LSU, and did not play against Mississippi State. Dealt with a minor knee sprain during '15 fall camp before starting all 10 games played and totaling 121-855-6 (7.1). Was benched during the Missouri contest then did not play against Eastern Kentucky, as head coach Mark Stoops cited "personal reasons." Did not play against Georgia after dislocating his right elbow against Tennessee (underwent post-season surgery). In '16, started 11-of-13 games and toted 171-1,170-7 (6.8). Recorded 38 career receptions for 292 yards (7.7-yard average) and two touchdowns. Had seven career fumbles in 424 touches and averaged 6.8 yards per carry. Owns school records for career rushing yards (3,609), career all-purpose yards (4,107) and career rushing touchdowns (32).

Strengths: Very quick feet and turnover —

elusive in the open field with explosive big-play ability when he finds a crease. Outstanding athlete. Very light on his feet. Measured the fastest 20-yard shuttle (4.18 seconds) of any back at the Combine, indicative of exceptional change of direction and balance. Effective sifting through traffic on screens. Good short-area burst and acceleration. Adjusts well to the ball. Has kickoff return experience.

Weaknesses: Very small and goes down easy on contact — lacks run strength. Very small catching radius with a 71 1/2-inch wingspan that was among the smallest of backs at the Combine, and provides a very tight window on screen passes. Has some concentration drops. Needs to protect the ball better. Will be a liability in pass protection in the pros. Has been dinged a lot and durability could become a greater issue in the pros.

Future: A track athlete whose best chance of sticking on a roster could come as a return man. Similar to Colts 2013 seventh-round pick and Cardinals RB Kerwynn Williams and could provide roster depth as a change-of-pace back.

Draft projection: Late draftable pick.

Scout's take: "Boom won't run between the tackles or block a lick. He has very average hands, but when he gets to the outside edge, boy, see ya. He came into the room (during the fall) and (scouts) tried to be as direct with him as we could that he won't block and he really didn't care what we were saying to him. He's a little different, but we'll continue doing more work on him."

RB JAMAAL WILLIAMS, #21 (Sr-5)

BYU   ▶ GRADE: 5.22

Ht: 6-0 3/8 | Wt: 212 | 40: 4.59 | Arm: 31 1/4 | Hand: 10

History: Also ran track as a California prep. Was just 17 during his freshman year, but an injury to the starter led to Williams starting 8-of-13 games — carried 166 times for 775 yards (4.7-yard average) and 12 touchdowns with 27 receptions for 315 yards (11.7-yard average) and one touchdown. Was the featured back in '13 when he ran 217-1,233-7 (5.7) and caught 18-125-15 (6.9) in 12 starts. Sustained a concussion and stinger against Utah, and did not play against Middle Tennessee State. Was suspended for the '14 season opener against Connecticut (underage drinking, honor code violation). On the season, started 5-of-7 games played and managed 109-518-4 (4.8) rushing and 8-47-0 (5.9) receiving. Sprained his ankle against Utah State, lasted just one carry against Central Florida, and sat out against Nevada. Suffered a right knee injury against MTSU, and underwent season-ending surgery. Withdrew from school in '15 (personal reasons). In '16, returned to start 9-of-10 games played and total 234-1,375-12 (5.9) rushing and 7-80-0 (11.4) receiving. Bothersome ankle injuries cost him games against Boise State, Southern Utah, and UMASS. Team captain is BYU's all-time leading rusher (3,901 yards). Had five career fumbles in 786 touches averaging 5.4 yards per carry. Opted not to bench press at the Combine.

Strengths: Solid build with well-distributed mass. Runs with intent and slams into contact. Good leg drive. Takes what the defense gives him. Dependable outlet receiver. Carries the ball high and tight, changes hands to protect it when cutting across the field and has good ball security and awareness. Efficient chip blocker. Sees the blitz and is quick to react. Good career production.

Weaknesses: Very tight-hipped with average burst, gear change and long speed, as confirmed by marginal 20-yard shuttle time (4.54 seconds). Runs tall with marginal elusiveness, leading to some direct hits likely to invite injury. Lacks lower-body strength for an inside runner and does not push the pile. Lacks physicality in pass pro. Limited special teams experience. Availability has been an issue every season due to injuries and off-field incidents and trustworthiness is a factor.

Future: Tough, aggressive, hard-charging runner who showed improvement in pass protection as a senior and has the physicality to earn a complementary backup role if he can settle down and mature. Reliability has been an issue throughout his career and could affect his draft standing.

Draft projection: Fifth- to sixth-round pick.

RB JOE WILLIAMS, #28 (Sr-6)

UTAH ▶ GRADE: 5.15

Ht: 5-11 | Wt: 210 | 40: 4.47 | Arm: 30 3/4 | Hand: 9 3/8

History: Engaged (Jasmine). Also ran track as a Pennsylvania prep. Was busted for shoplifting while in high school. Graduated in 2011 before spending the fall semester at Fork Union (Va.) Military Academy. Began his college career at Connecticut, where he saw very limited action in nine games, toting three carries for six yards (2.0-yard average) and zero touchdowns. Was dismissed from the team when someone used a stolen credit card to purchase an expensive, designer backpack for him (reportedly paid $100 cash for a $1,400 item). Got back on the field at Asa College (N.Y.) in '14 (wore jersey No. 2) — played seven games, logging 163-1,093-7 (6.7) rush-

ing and 16-237-3 (14.8) receiving. Added four kickoff returns for 52 yards (13.0-yard average). Was recruited to Utah by recently-retired running backs coach Dennis Erickson. Behind Devontae Booker (Broncos) in '15, Williams contributed 104-477-3 (4.6) rushing and 9-107-0 (11.9) receiving in 10 games (two starts). Stepped into the lead role in '16 when he started all nine games played, and totaled 210-1,407-10 (6.7) on the ground with 9-107-0 (11.9) receiving. Did not play four September/October contests, as he temporarily retired, citing the mental and physical (back, legs, concussions) toll the game had taken on him. Returned to the team with a "My Sister's Keeper" tattoo on his left arm and said it was the nearly-decade-old memory of watching his 7-year-old sister Kylee die of an undiagnosed heart problem that pushed him to retire. Had eight career fumbles in 518 touches and averaged 6.0 yards per carry. Graduated. Will be a 24-year-old rookie.

Strengths: Good eyes to find holes and anticipate running lanes unfolding especially on stretch outside zone runs. Very quick feet and can plant and go and accelerate in a blink when he sees it, as confirmed clocking the second fastest 40 time (as low as 4.41 seconds) of any back at the Combine and the fastest 20-yard shuttle (4.19 seconds). Torched UCLA for 29-332-4 and finished career with renewed vigor following return in mid-October, producing six 100-plus yard games in final seven of career.

Weaknesses: A bit high-cut with a thin lower body and lacks tackle-breaking, run strength. Shies from contact inside and likes to bounce outside. Ran behind a strong, veteran offensive line that created sizable lanes, and much of his production was blocked for him. Very inconsistent hands — double-catches the ball and can be fazed by traffic, as confirmed at the Combine, slowing to catch, letting the ball into his body and cradle-catching. Disinterested blocker. Must do a better job of protecting the football. Questionable personal and football character. Overaged.

Future: A one-cut, zone-running, change-of-pace back who finished his college career with a bang and must prove he can transfer the same energy to the pro level to earn a roster spot. Maturity has been an issue.

Draft projection: Priority free agent.

Scout's take: "(Williams) initially quit because he didn't love football and his body was hurt. He doesn't practice hard. And he doesn't like to get hit. I don't think that is going to play well in our league."

RUNNING BACKS

WIDE RECEIVERS

WASHINGTON COMMUNICATIONS

Nawrocki's TOP 10

◀ 1.	**JOHN ROSS**
2.	**Mike Williams**
3.	**JuJu Smith-Schuster**
4.	**Corey Davis**
5.	**Chris Godwin**
6.	**Zay Jones**
7.	**ArDarius Stewart**
8.	**Cooper Kupp**
9.	**KD Cannon**
10.	**Josh Reynolds**

WIDE RECEIVERS

EDITOR'S NOTE:

Z — Strong, physical flanker
X — Speedy, vertical split end
F — Quick, shifty slot receiver

WR [F] / KR RODNEY ADAMS, #87 (Sr-4)

SOUTH FLORIDA   ▶ GRADE: 5.08

Ht: 6-1 1/4 | Wt: 189 | 40: 4.47 | Arm: 32 | Hand: 9

History: Florida native also played basketball and ran track in high school. Missed time at the beginning of fall camp his senior year because of a misdiagnosed heart condition, according to TampaBay.com. Originally committed to Florida, but changed his mind when receivers coach Aubrey Hill resigned. Adams began his college career at Toledo, where he was recruited by then-head coach Matt Campbell. As a true freshman in 2013, recorded two receptions for 15 yards (7.5-yard average) and zero touchdowns in eight appearances. Dealt with an ankle injury in early October. In November, Adam's mother, Michelle, died in a car accident. He became the legal guardian for his younger brother, and transferred to USF in order to be closer to family (received hardship waiver).

With the Bulls in '14, contributed 23-323-2 (14.0) in 10 games (three starts at "Z"). Sat out a pair of November contests while nursing a left groin strain. Started all 13 games at "Z" in '15, and produced 45-822-9 (18.3). Played through a left knee bruise against UCONN (scored three touchdowns). Moved to the slot in '16, and totaled 67-822-5 (12.3) in 13 starts. Had 40 career rushes for 380 yards (9.5-yard average) and seven touchdowns. Returned 46 career kickoffs for 1,140 yards (24.8-yard average), including a 97-yard score against Navy as a junior. Hurt his ankle in the Birmingham Bowl, and did not participate at the East-West Shrine Game.

Strengths: Good length. Nifty runner with the vision, patience and body control to be effective on jet sweeps, reverses, bubble screens and in the kickoff return game. Sets up blocks and has a knack for slashing through creases. Lulls cover men to sleep with his smooth stride off the line — a glider who flashes the ability to create vertical separation. Competitive with the ball in his hands.

Weaknesses: Has small, inconsistent hands and a very lean frame with a thin lower body that could be more susceptible to injury — has missed time each of the last three years with lower-body injuries. Needs to refine his route-running and learn how to stem and set up defensive backs and more precisely come out of breaks (tends to round). Likes to body catch instead of extending outside his frame. Flags the ball too much in the open field and needs to secure it better. Limited strength as a blocker to get in the way. Tied for fewest bench-press reps (8) among receivers at the Combine.

Future: Very lean, rangy slot receiver with natural run skills and functional kickoff return ability. Could fend for a job as a no. 5 receiver if he is able to earn a role in the return game.

Draft projection: Priority free agent.

WR [X] QUINCY ADEBOYEJO, #8 (Sr-4)

MISSISSIPPI　　　　　　　　► GRADE: 5.25

Ht: 6-2 5/8 | Wt: 197 | 40: 4.39 | Arm: 31 3/4 | Hand: 9 3/8

History: Last name is pronounced "add-ah-BOY-joe." Also ran track as a Texas prep. Played all 13 games as a true freshman in 2013, drawing two starts at split end, and tallied seven catches for 81 yards (11.6-yard average) and one touchdown. Played all 13 games in '14, starting five in the slot, and recorded 26-313-2 (12.0). Started 9-of-13 games in the slot in '15, contributing 38-604-7 (15.9). Gave way to a tight end in non-starts. Moved outside in '16 when he started 11-of-12 games, and totaled 35-456-1 (13.0). Graduated.

Strengths: Very good body length. Has the speed and acceleration to create separation down the field and gain a step on defenders, confirmed by excellent 40-time (as low as 4.34 seconds on one watch) at the Combine. Flashes some run-after-the-catch ability on bubble screens. Showed well at the East-West Shrine game and caught the ball easily.

Weaknesses: Not a polished route runner. Lacks functional strength to beat the jam. Struggles to escape tight man coverage. Not a consistent catcher — double-catches and tends to let the ball into his frame. Can be fazed by traffic. Marginal functional strength — lacks physicality as a blocker. Tied for fewest bench-press reps (8) among receivers at the Combine. Average career production. Limited special teams experience.

Future: Lean, high-cut, leggy vertical threat lacking the special teams experience desired in backup receiver. Long speed could give him a chance to earn a No. 4 or No. 5 role.

Draft projection: Fifth- to sixth-round pick.

WR [F,X] / RS VICTOR BOLDEN, #6 (Sr-4)

OREGON STATE　　　　　　► GRADE: 5.04

Ht: 5-8 3/8 | Wt: 178 | 40: 4.56 | Arm: 31 1/8 | Hand: 9

History: Was also a standout hurdler as a California prep. Played all 13 games during his true-freshman 2013 season, and recorded six receptions for 62 yards (10.3-yard average) and zero touchdowns. However, made his impact on special teams, as he returned 58 kickoffs for 1,198 yards (20.7-yard average), including a 98-yard score against Washington (set Pac-12 single-game records with 12-305). Took over Brandin Cooks' flanker spot in '14 — started all 11 games played, and produced 72-798-2 (11.1). Added four punt returns for 44 yards (11.0-yard average). Sat out against USC after dislocating a finger on his left hand against USC. Started all 12 games in '15, and caught 46-461-3 (10.0) while returning kickoffs 23-580 (25.2), including a 100-yard score against Washington State. Added a 78-yard punt return score against rival Oregon. Was the Beavers' leading receiver for the second straight year in '16 — started all 12 games at the "T" receiver, and totaled 46-542-2 (11.8) while returning kickoffs 27-642 (23.8), including a 99-yard score against Boise State, and returning punts 14-46 (4.6). Was knocked out of the Arizona game thanks to an illegal hit on a punt return. Carried 95 times in his career for 727 yards (7.7-yard average) and three touchdowns. Team captain. Had two head coaches and five offensive coordinators, but was developed for four years by receivers coach Brent Brennan (recently hired as San Jose State's head coach).

Strengths: Quick as a hiccup coming off the line. Good short-area burst and gear change. Outstanding long speed — clocked running 22.5 mph by Catapult GPS. Tracks the ball very well downfield and will lay out and sacrifice his body for the ball. Good sideline awareness — can dot the 'i' and make difficult, acrobatic sideline catches. Good vision and burst in the return game. Tough and competitive and plays with a chip on his shoulder. Works at his craft and described by coaches as the "hardest-working practice player."

Weaknesses: Very wiry frame and lacks strength to fend off the jam and factor as a blocker in the run game. Can be re-routed easily and needs some space to uncover. Drifts too much and does not break off routes sharply. Lacks ideal length to win jumpball situations and could do a better job attacking the ball at times. Limited run strength.

Future: Offering the most immediate value in the return game, Bolden is still unrefined as a slot receiver and might be more impactful playing outside if he can continue improving his hand use and learn to get off the line more cleanly. Strong football character could create path to slot success with a few years of seasoning.

Draft projection: Priority free agent.

WIDE RECEIVERS

WR [Z] KENDRICK BOURNE, #11 (Sr-4)

EASTERN WASHINGTON ▶ GRADE: 5.03

Ht: 6-1 1/8 | Wt: 203 | 40: 4.66 | Arm: 32 1/2 | Hand: 9 1/8

History: Portland, Ore. native whose outlook, behavior, and path changed when he attended a charter school as a senior. Also played basketball and ran track. As a true freshman in 2013, recorded seven catches for 117 yards (16.7-yard average) and one touchdown in 14 appearances. Did not play against North Dakota (right ankle). Teamed with fellow NFL prospect Cooper Kupp to form one of the top receiving duos in the FCS. Was considered the "Z" receiver in the Eagles' prolific spread offense. Started 9-of-14 games in '14, and caught 52-814-10 (15.7). Started 10-of-11 games played in '15, and hauled in 73-998-8 (13.7). Did not start against Sacramento State. Started 13-of-14 games in '16, and totaled 79-1,201-7 (15.2). Did not start against Youngstown State. Had five career rushes for 88 yards (17.6-yard average) and one touchdown.

Strengths: Nice length. Good vision and competitiveness after the catch (see break five tackles vs. after the catch in third quarter vs. Washington State). Adjusts well to the thrown ball and can make difficult, one-handed grabs. Produces in the clutch (see game-tying and game-winning catches against Cal-Poly in 2015).

Weaknesses: Has small hands. Builds to speed and lacks suddenness into his routes and out of his breaks to create separation. Needs to improve his strength to beat the jam and compete for the ball in a crowd. Saw a lot of single coverage matched up away from Cooper Kupp and did not regularly face top competition in the Big Sky Conference. Limited blocking strength. Could require extra time to acclimate to an NFL playbook. Limited special teams experience.

Future: Competitive possession receiver lacking desirable foot speed and football intelligence for the NFL game and will have to learn how to transfer his competitiveness to special teams to stick on a roster.

Draft projection: Priority free agent.

WR [Z] / TE [H] NOAH BROWN, #80 (Soph-3)

OHIO STATE ▶ GRADE: 5.08

Ht: 6-1 3/4 | Wt: 222 | 40: 4.65e | Arm: 31 3/4 | Hand: 9 1/8

History: Played all over the field as a New Jersey prep. In '14, appeared in 13 games as a true freshman (receiver, H-back, special teams), and caught one ball for nine yards (9.0-yard average) and zero touchdowns. Missed the '15 season after breaking his leg (tibia, fibula) during fall camp. Returned to start 12-of-13 games at the "X" in '16, producing 32-402-7

(12.6), including a four-touchdown performance against Oklahoma. Opted not to run the 40-yard dash or jump at the Combine.

Strengths: Outstanding size. Very good strength to power thru press coverage. Bench-pressed 225 pounds 19 times at the Combine, tied for second-best among receivers. Good body strength to shield defenders from the ball and catch in traffic. Strong with the ball in his hand. Capable of making the acrobatic circus catch (see Oklahoma). Solid, competitive blocker — outmuscles defensive backs and consistently sustains.

Weaknesses: Has small hands. Limited playing experience and production. Average foot speed to create separation. Does not play fast. Most of his catches are contested. Unrefined route runner still feeling his way. Has difficulty separating vs. tight coverage. Weight has fluctuated too much in the past and hovered in the 240-245-pound range. Recorded 12.4% body fat at the Combine, abnormally high for a receiver and indicative of a lack of endurance. Does not respond well to hard coaching.

Future: A big-bodied, long-limbed receiver who could warrant interest as an H-back in the pros. Has not compiled a compelling enough playmaking resume or been consistent enough to project as more than a No. 5 or No. 6 receiver.

Draft projection: Late draftable pick.

Scout's take: "Really, take away the Oklahoma game and show me something that he was consistent doing? There are tidbits, but no 'wow' factor. He declared early because he was being pushed aside by underclassmen. He is in the 220-ish range now, but he has been a few meals away from being 250. He could eat his way out of being drafted."

WR [F,X] KD CANNON, #9 (Jr-3)

BAYLOR ▶ GRADE: 5.45

Ht: 5-11 | Wt: 182 | 40: 4.41 | Arm: 30 3/4 | Hand: 8 7/8

History: Has two daughters, Makynlee and Kennedy. Cannon is a native Texan who was a consensus All-American (also ran track). As a true freshman in 2013, started 7-of-13 games at an inside receiver position, and posted 58 receptions for 1,030 yards (17.8-yard average) and eight touchdowns. Started all 13 games at "IR" in '15, catching 50-868-6 (17.4). Added seven kickoff returns for 114 yards (16.3-yard average). In July '16 had his right knee scoped. Played outside in the fall when he started all 12 games played, and racked up 87-1,215-13 (14.0). Did not play against Iowa State (groin). Turns 22 in November. Wore #1 vs. Oklahoma State in honor of injured former teammate Corey Coleman.

WIDE RECEIVERS

Opted not to run shuttles at the Combine.

Strengths: Very good speed and acceleration to take the top off a defense and threaten the field vertically. Explosive release. Easily separates vs man coverage. Tracks the ball well over his shoulder and can make contested catches in a crowd (see Boise State) and sky for the ball. Good leaping ability — has a 37-inch vertical jump. Slippery after the catch on bubble screens and can navigate through traffic.

Weaknesses: Very thinly built with narrow shoulders and marginal strength. Double-catches and uses his body too much. Carries a prima donna attitude and can be demonstrative if the ball is not coming his way. Shows marginal coverage awareness and little awareness for finding soft spots in zones — could stand to do a better job continuing to work to uncover. Ran a limited route tree and will extra require time to assimilate a playbook and adapt to NFL complexities.

Future: A thinly built, fast-flying downfield target most optimally suited to line up in the slot with free releases and win with speed. Could require some time to learn the nuances of route running and adapt to the pro game. Could emerge as a solid No. 3 receiver with continued refinement.

Draft projection: Third- to fourth-round pick.

Scout's take: "I don't think there are any true No. 1 receivers in this draft. There are a glut of guys who are sitting there in the second (round) who could be (No.) 2's. Talent-wise, Cannon is one of them. He can pop the lid off a defense. There are a lot of guys better than him. I could see him pushing down."

WR [F] AUSTIN CARR, #80 (Sr-5)

NORTHWESTERN ▶ GRADE: 5.09

Ht: 6-0 1/8 | Wt: 202 | 40: 4.61 | Arm: 30 5/8 | Hand: 9 1/4

History: Also played basketball as a California prep. Joined NU as a preferred walk-on. Redshirted in 2012 — sliced the tendon to his right pinky finger with a butter knife, and underwent surgery based on "stern recommendation" from his mother, who was concerned about Carr's piano-playing ability. Did not see action in '13. Worked as a slot receiver for the Wildcats. Appeared in 12 games in '14, notching seven grabs for 100 yards (14.3-yard average) and zero touchdowns. Was put on scholarship in '15, and contributed 16-302-2 (18.9) in 12 games (four starts). Went from unknown to a Biletnikoff finalist and the Big Ten Receiver of the Year in '16 by starting 12-of-13 games and racking up 90-1,247-12 (13.9). Non-start was against Michigan State when NU opened with two "superbacks" and an extra offensive lineman. Sustained a concussion against Minne-

sota. Set NU single-season records for receiving yards and touchdown receptions (tie), and was the third player since 1990 to lead the conference in catches, receiving yards, and receiving touchdowns. Team captain and Burlsworth Trophy finalist (most outstanding player who began his career as a walk-on) has a philosophy degree.

Strengths: Adjusts very well to the thrown ball and makes fine in-air adjustments and difficult off-balance, over-the-head snatches. Understands spacing and how to find soft spots in zones to uncover. Catches in stride and hauls in almost every catchable ball thrown his way (95 percent catcher). Very reliable red-zone target. Can take a hit and spin off contact after the catch. Played big vs. best competition — see Wisconsin and Ohio State. Effortful blocker. Very smart.

Weaknesses: Only a one-year starter. Shows some rigidity as a route runner. Lacks top-end speed to separate vertically. Cradle-catches too much. Needs to get stronger. Underdeveloped blocker.

Future: More quick than fast, mechanical, sure-handed slot receiver gained a lot of confidence in his final season. Has the dependability to eventually carve out a role in a lineup piercing underneath zones, though will require a learning curve to adapt to the speed of the NFL game.

Draft projection: Late draftable pick.

Scout's take: "(Carr) is a tough overachiever. He has some size but marginal speed. He's a walk-on from California with a real artsy side. He has some traits to like. I still gave him a free-agent grade."

WR [X] / KR JEHU CHESSON, #86 (Sr-5)

MICHIGAN ▶ GRADE: 5.37

Ht: 6-2 7/8 | Wt: 207 | 40: 4.48 | Arm: 33 3/8 | Hand: 9 1/8

History: Born in Siberia, and grew up in St. Louis. Redshirted in 2012. Learned "X" and "Z" in '13 when he tallied 15 catches for 221 yards (14.7-yard average) and one touchdown in 13 games (two starts). Played 11 games in '14, starting four at "Z," and caught 14-154-0 (11.0). Sprained his right ankle against Rutgers, and sat out against Penn State. In '15, teamed with Amara Darboh as the outside receivers in Jim Harbaugh and Tim Drevno's pro-style offense — started 12-of-13 games at "X", and produced 50-764-9 (15.3). Also returned four kickoffs for 166 yards (41.5-yard average), including a 96-yard score against Northwestern, and blocked a punt vs. Ohio State. Was voted team MVP. Tore his right PCL in the Citrus Bowl against Florida, underwent surgery, and missed '16 spring practice. In the fall, started 7-of-13 games at flanker, and totaled 35-500-

2 (14.3). Had 22 career rushes for 219 yards (10.0-yard average) and three touchdowns. Graduated with a sociology degree.

Strengths: Very good body and arm length to make contested catches. Lays out and sacrifices his body for the ball (see TD catch vs. Rutgers). Competes in a crowd. Understands leverage and positioning and uses his body well to shield defenders. Very scrappy blocker. Quick learner. Has aligned as a gunner on the punt team and has good vision and toughness to carry the ball and function as a kickoff returner.

Weaknesses: Does not play big and appeared to lose speed following offseason knee surgery. Lets the ball into his body and does not consistently extend outside his frame. Leggy, monotone route runner with limited separation ability. Takes long strides and does not explode out of his breaks. Marginal functional strength to beat the jam, as indicated by low 10 bench-press reps at the Combine.

Future: Best season came as a junior when healthy aligned at the "X" position in more of a vertical capacity with better QB play than he had as a senior. Has been trained to play multiple positions in a pro-style offense and has the length and enough speed to develop into a solid No. 3 or No. 4 receiver if he can return to his more dynamic, pre-injury form. Can offer additional value on special teams.

Draft projection: Third- to fourth-round pick.

Scout's take: "(Chesson) is a talented kid. He has pretty good long speed. He's more of a build-up guy than sudden mover. He's an intermediate-level receiver. I think he has some polish and some top-end gear. You can see him separate a little bit. He's more polished than (Carolina Panthers' 2015 second-round pick and former Michigan WR Devin) Funchess was."

WR[F]/RS **STACY COLEY,** #3 (Sr-4)
MIAMI (FLA.) ▶ GRADE: 5.22
Ht: 5-11 7/8 | Wt: 195 | 40: 4.46 | Arm: 32 1/4 | Hand: 9 3/4

History: Florida native. As a true freshman in 2013, played all 13 games — started six in place of the injured Phillip Dorsett (Colts) — and recorded 33 receptions for 591 yards (17.9-yard average) and seven touchdowns. Was the only player in the country to score via rush, reception, kick return, and punt return. Backed up inside and outside in '14 when he started 5-of-12 games, carrying 23-184-0 (8.0). Did not play against Arkansas State (right shoulder bruise). Used primarily in the slot in '15 when he started 8-of-11 games played, and produced 47-689-4 (14.7). Strained his left hamstring in the season opener versus Bethune-Cookman, causing him to miss two of the next three games. Tweaked

his right hamstring during '16 spring practice. Played all 13 games in '16, starting the first nine, and totaled 63-754-9 (12.0). Sprained his left MCL against Florida State. Yielded late-season starts to Malcolm Lewis. Had eight career rushes for 125 yards (15.6-yard average) and one touchdown. Made his mark on special teams, as well — returned 47 career kickoffs for 1,142 yards (24.3-yard average), including one score, and returned 25 career punts for 325 yards (13.0-yard average), including one score. Was flagged 17 times his last two seasons, including eight false start penalties.

Strengths: Has a solid build. Good arm length to pluck the ball outside his frame. Tracks the ball well over his shoulder and flashes the ability to make difficult, acrobatic grabs. Good zone awareness to settle into soft spots. Fine vision, balance and acceleration after the catch. Recorded an explosive 10-yard split (1.52 seconds) and can accelerate to top speed in a blink and has shown big-play return ability.

Weaknesses: Needs to play with more discipline and learn to focus better and cut down on concentration penalties. Undisciplined route runner idles too much and gives up break points. Has some tightness in his stride. Does not consistently attack the ball in the air or win jumpball situations. Average elusiveness and tackle-breaking ability as a returner. Lacks physicality. Soft, overmatched blocker.

Future: A lean, slot receiver with the agility, suddenness and secure hands to earn a slot role if he could learn to continue adopting a more professional approach and play more disciplined. Would highly benefit from a strong veteran mentor and nurturing positional coach to hold him accountable.

Draft projection: Fourth- to fifth-round pick.

WR[Z, F] **AMARA DARBOH,** #82 (Sr-5)
MICHIGAN ▶ GRADE: 5.41
Ht: 6-1 5/8 | Wt: 214 | 40: 4.48 | Arm: 32 5/8 | Hand: 9 7/8

History: Born in Sierra Leone, where his parents were killed during a civil war. After relatives moved them multiple times seeking refuge, they were sponsored by a Christian group, enabling them to start a life in Iowa. At age 17, was legally adopted by the parents of one of his friends. Grew up playing soccer then competed in track and field, basketball and football as a prep. Separated his left shoulder in September of his senior season then had post-season surgery to repair a torn labrum. As a true freshman in 2012, saw limited action in 11 games. Missed the '13 season because of a Lisfranc fracture in his right foot (received medical hardship). In '14, started 8-of-12 games — seven at flanker, one at split

WIDE RECEIVERS

end — and snagged 36-473-2 (13.1). Hurt a finger on his left hand during '15 fall camp. On the season, started 9-of-13 games at "X," and posted 58-727-5 (12.5). Became a U.S. citizen in September. Started 11-of-13 games in '16, and totaled 57-862-7 (15.1). Did not run shuttles at the Combine because of an ankle injury.

Strengths: Well-built with good muscularity, long arms and a strong stride. Tough and physical. Works through press coverage with strength. Plays in a pro-style offense and ran a full route tree. Solid route runner with good balance, tempo and gear change to set up defenders. Runs a variety of patterns. Confident catcher. Makes difficult, contested catches. Good field awareness — navigates zones and finds soft spots. Competitive, willing blocker.

Weaknesses: Drops too many catchable balls, including some key situations. Struggles to separate against press coverage. Lacks suddenness off the line. Did not make an abundance of splash plays. Limited creativity after the catch. Average Senior Bowl week performance.

Future: A good-sized, strong, physical, possession receiver with the toughness to make a living working short-to-intermediate on slants, digs and out routes. Played multiple positions appears most ideally suited to move-the-chains role from the flanker spot or in the slot.

Draft projection: Third- to fourth-round pick.

Scout's take: "(Darboh) is good with shallow routes and moving the chains. I was a little disappointed with what I saw at the Senior Bowl and started to question his speed."

WR [X, F] COREY DAVIS, #84 (Sr-4)
WESTERN MICHIGAN ▶ GRADE: 5.84
Ht: 6-2 3/4 | Wt: 209 | 40: 4.55e | Arm: 33 | Hand: 9 1/8

History: One of seven siblings, Davis grew up with modest means before moving in with his youth football coach's family midway through his time at Illinois' Wheaton-Warrenville South High. Did not have an FBS offer until P.J. Fleck arrived at WMU. Played the "X" receiver for the Broncos. As a true freshman in 2013, caught 67 balls for 941 yards (14.0-yard average) and six touchdowns. Did not play against Kent State (concussion). Started all 12 games played in '14, and produced 78-1,408-15 (18.1). Sat out against Virginia Tech (left hamstring). Started all 13 games in '15, and racked up 89-1,429-12 (16.1). In '16, spearheaded the Broncos' run to the Cotton Bowl — was the Mid-American Conference Offensive MVP, and tied for the national lead in receiving touchdowns with 97-1,500-19 (15.5) in 14 starts. Completed two career passes for 40 yards. Owns the FBS career receiving yards

record (5,278), as well as MAC records for career receptions (332) and touchdowns (52), and is the only player in FBS history with 300 catches, 5,000 yards, and 50 touchdowns. Injured his right ankle in late January and did not participate at the Senior Bowl and was a medical exclusion from workouts at the Combine.

Strengths: Very good body and arm length. Big zone target. Concentrates, tracks and adjusts. Soft hands and strong fingers. Good leaping ability to highpoint and battle for the ball. Opens up his stride in the clear and can create some downfield separation. Intensely competitive and plays very hard. Prepares like a pro and leads with his diligence in all facets of the game, from the weight room to the practice field to the film room — respected team leader. Functional, willing blocker. Experienced, four-year starter with exceptional career production. Racked up 10-154-1 against Michigan State in 2015 and has shown he could match up against better competition.

Weaknesses: Has small hands, made 11 drops as a senior and could be challenged by case of the drops in the pros. At times presses and tries to do too much. Lacks true vertical speed. Has some tightness in his hips and does not transition cleanly out of his breaks. Contained vs. Ohio State (2015) and production is padded from regularly matching up against Mid-American Conference competition that seldom challenged him at the line of scrimmage. Does not consistently sustain as a blocker.

Future: Big-time, mid-major producer with some similarities to No. 2 NFL receivers such as Eagles' 2014 second-round pick (42nd) Jordan Matthews and Cowboys' 2013 third-round pick (74th) Terrance Williams. Has the gritty competitiveness to contribute readily and earn a starting job in the pros, though could struggle to surpass a ceiling of a No. 2 and could require some patience.

Draft projection: Top-50 pick.

Scout's take: "Can (Davis) separate? I didn't think he did very well. I graded him in the third round. I've heard a lot of hype about him. If you are going to draft a receiver in the first round, he better be a No. 1 receiver. I thought Davis was more of a (No.) 2. That's where I think he gets drafted. I was expecting to see more from him. Throw in the injury, competition level, hands and concerns I have about him separating — I'm just not sold. I'd rather buy low."

WR [X] ROBERT DAVIS, #19 (Sr-4)
GEORGIA STATE ▶ GRADE: 5.30
Ht: 6-2 5/8 | Wt: 219 | 40: 4.43 | Arm: 33 | Hand: 9 5/8

History: Warner Robins, Ga. native and son of a sheriff (dad) and deputy warden (mom).

WIDE RECEIVERS

Cousin of Panthers Pro Bowl linebacker Thomas Davis. Robert flew under the recruiting radar — starred on the hardwood, and caught just 11 balls his senior football season. Turned into a diamond in the rough at Georgia State, where he manned the "X" position. As a true freshman in 2013 — the program's first year of FBS membership — recorded 44 receptions for 711 yards (16.2-yard average) and four touchdowns in 12 games (eight starts). Started 11-of-12 games in '14, and caught 50-732-2 (14.6). Did not start season finale against Texas State (Senior Day). Started all 25 games the next two seasons — totaled 61-980-6 (16.1) in '15 (13 games); and 67-968-5 (14.4) in '16 (12 games). Played through a shoulder injury against UT Martin and South Alabama. Finished his career as the program's career leader in receptions (222) and receiving yards (3,391). Is an internship shy of completing his kinesiology degree.

Strengths: Looks the part. Exceptional size and long speed to create separation. Tracks the ball well over his shoulder and consistently catches the ball in stride. Made an inaccurate QB look good. Has explosive leaping ability, as seen hurdling defenders (see Idaho) and evidenced recording a 11'4" broad jump, the highest of any receiver at the Combine. Also recorded a 41-inch vertical jump indicative of rare lower-body explosion. Bench-pressed 225 pounds 19 times at the Combine — and possesses the strength to fend off the jam. Very competitive. Has the size and strength to cover up defensive backs in the run game and is effortful sustaining. Experienced, four-year starter. Has NFL pedigree. Very durable and tough enough to play through injuries.

Weaknesses: Tight in his hips. Raw route runner — not clean at the top of his routes. Not instinctive reading coverages and needs to spend more time learning route concepts not called upon him to do in college and immersing himself in a playbook. Does not use his size or consistently play big and tends to let the ball into his body. Strings few moves together after the catch and is not elusive with the ball in his hands. Not as dominant at the point of attack as a receiver his size could be.

Future: A big, straight-line fast, vertical receiver in a similar mold as Chiefs 2015 third-round pick (76) Chris Conley, Davis possesses a rare size-speed ratio to threaten the field vertically, yet lacks polish and will require some time to refine his craft. Has the physical traits to be molded.

Draft projection: Fourth- to fifth-round pick.

WR [X, F] MALACHI DUPRE, #15 (Jr-3)

LSU ▶ GRADE: 5.42

Ht: 6-2 1/2 | Wt: 196 | 40: 4.54 | Arm: 31 1/2 | Hand: 9

History: Pronounced "mal-uh-kye Doo-pre." New Orleans native was a state-champion in the triple jump, long jump, and high jump, and was a USA Today All-American. As a true freshman in 2014, recorded 14 receptions for 318 yards (22.7-yard average) and five touchdowns in 12 games (two starts at "X"). Sat out the season opener against Wisconsin (ankle), and admitted to not feeling full speed until the latter half of the season. In '15, started 8-of-12 games at "X," and caught 43-698-6 (16.2). Ceded two October starts to Trey Quinn, and gave way to two-tight end personnel in two other contests. Started 9-of-12 games at "X" in '16, and totaled 41-593-3 (14.5) while trying to fend off emerging teammate D.J. Clark. Dupre, who rebounded from five drops in the first two weeks, also spent time in the slot. Will be a 21-year-old rookie.

Strengths: Good length and leaping ability (39 1/2-inch vertical jump) to pluck the ball out of the air. Fluid, limber, flexible athlete with natural bend to adjust to the ball low, high and outside his frame. Good balance and body control to make in-air adjustments. Can make difficult, one-handed snags (see Louisville) and has good sideline awareness in the red zone. Has experience playing in a pro-style offense and produced highly within the scheme.

Weaknesses: Very small hands. Not sudden in his release. Lacks top-end speed to create separation and stretch the field vertically. Not explosive off the line and routes lack polish and suddenness. Limited run-after-the-catch strength and elusiveness to make tacklers miss. Lacks physicality as a blocker.

Future: A rangy, long-limbed, acrobatic receiver who was underutilized in run-first offense featuring an inaccurate quarterback and a cast of talented receivers. Could prove to be a better pro than college player and make a living catching back-shoulder throws and climbing the ladder to secure red-zone fades. Inconsistent QB play and inefficient LSU offense following the September release of Les Miles and offensive coordinator Cam Cameron contributed to declining production, though he still led the team in receiving.

Draft projection: Fourth- to fifth-round pick.

Scout's take: "I graded him in the second (round) early during the fall. The (WR) position is overly saturated with second-round receivers and it's going to push some good players down. He just doesn't get many opportunities in that offense with everything that was going on there."

WR [Z] TRAVIN DURAL, #83 (Sr-5)

LSU ▶ GRADE: 5.21
Ht: 6-0 3/4 | Wt: 202 | 40: 4.56 | Arm: 32 | Hand: 9

History: Louisiana native also starred in football and track (200-meter state champion). Redshirted in 2012 after tearing his left meniscus. Dural was in the shadows of Odell Beckham Jr. (Giants) and Jarvis Landry (Dolphins) in '13 when he caught seven balls for 145 yards (20.7-yard average) and two touchdowns in 12 appearances. Added four punt returns for 12 yards (3.0-yard average). Took ownership of the "Z" position in '14 — started all 13 games, and produced 37-758-7 (20.5). Suffered a head laceration in a September car accident, but did not miss a game. Started 8-of-10 games played in '15, managing 28-533-3 (19.0). Tore his right hamstring against Ole Miss — missed the final two games of the season, had surgery, and endured a long rehab which prevented him from running for nearly six months. In '16, started 9-of-11 games played, and recorded 28-280-1 (10.0). Did not play against Texas A&M (shoulder). Team captain graduated with interdisciplinary studies degree. Was a medical exclusion from the bench press at the Combine because of a left shoulder injury.

Strengths: Good size. Deceptive speed and acceleration at the top of his routes. Can power through arm tackles and sidestep some tacklers. Catches on contact and concentrates in a crowd. Showed the ability to stretch the field and beat man coverage early in his career prior to injury. Functional, willing blocker.

Weaknesses: Has small hands and marginal receiving production. Shows some tightness in his hips and ankles with minimal short-area burst. Had a pedestrian Combine workout, registering a low 30 1/2-inch vertical jump and a slow 20-yard shuttle (4.58 seconds) revealing a lack of agility and explosion. Limited big-play ability. Clocked the slowest 60-yard shuttle (12.28 seconds) of any receiver at the Combine, indicating a lack of flexibility and endurance. Also recorded 14% body fat, abnormally high for a receiver. Marginal blocker.

Future: Flashed most potential early in his career prior to serious hamstring injury that zapped his burst and needs to return to prior form to have a chance of earning a roster spot in the NFL. Production was hindered by offensive struggles that included the September release of Les Miles and offensive coordinator Cam Cameron and inconsistency at the quarterback position.

Draft projection: Fifth- to sixth-round pick.

Scout's take: "(Dural) had his best year in 2014. I thought we would be talking about him as no worse than a (third-rounder). He kind of fell off the cliff this year."

WR [X] AMBA ETTA-TAWO, #7 (Sr-5)

SYRACUSE ▶ GRADE: 5.27
Ht: 6-1 1/4 | Wt: 208 | 40: 4.52 | Arm: 32 | Hand: 9 1/8

History: Name is pronounced "Om-buh Etta-Tah-wo." Born — in the Arabian Peninsula country of Oman — to Nigerian parents, who won a Visa lottery, enabling the family to move to the state of Georgia. Etta-Tawo also ran track in high school. Began his college career at Maryland, where he redshirted in 2012. Played 12 games in '13, starting the final six in place of the injured Stefon Diggs (Vikings), and caught 31 balls for 500 yards (16.1-yard average) and two touchdowns. Played 12 games in '14, starting the final six outside, and chipped in 10-222-1 (22.2). In '15, was passed on the depth chart by freshman D.J. Moore — recorded 20-216-0 (10.8) in 12 games (started first two). Joined Syracuse as a graduate transfer in '16, and broke out in Dino Babers' aggressive, vertical attack. Deployed outside, racked up 94-1,482-14 (15.8) in 12 starts, including a 13-178-5 (13.7) performance at Pittsburgh to cap his college career. Was the Atlantic Coast Conference's leading receiver, and set school single-season records for receptions, receiving yards and receiving yards per game (123.5, second only to Torry Holt in 1998 in the ACC). Team captain. Dislocated a finger during Senior Bowl practice.

Strengths: Good size and arm length. Can create separation vertically and adjusts well to the deep ball. Has some tackle-breaking ability (see Louisville). Good run vision after the catch. Competes for the ball in a crowd (see Florida State) and uses his body to shield defenders.

Weaknesses: Imprecise route runner and needs to have a better plan releasing off the line of scrimmage vs. press coverage. Too stiff and unable to drop his hips and sink into routes. Gathers to cut and opens break points. Does not attack the ball in the air and too often allows it to come into his body. Flags the ball in his hand on bubble screens and needs to secure it better. Limited leaping ability, as confirmed by 31-inch vertical jump. Only a one-year producer. Marginal blocker. Appeared to lack confidence at the Senior Bowl and had a case of the drops before hurting his finger and exiting practice.

Future: An outside-the-numbers, straight-line speed receiver who emerged as a weapon in Dino Babers' aggressive downfield attack, yet lacks the route savvy, hip flexibility, hand confidence and physicality required to make an impact readily in the pros and is suited for a

WIDE RECEIVERS

backup role. Will require a few years to adapt to the complexity of the NFL game and learn to diagnose coverages.

Draft projection: Fourth- to fifth-round pick.

Scout's take: "(Etta-Tawo) is a one-trick pony. He's an 'X' only with marginal hands, and he plays soft. He can't run intermediate routes. Beyond a couple quick hitches or screens, everything has to be outside the numbers because he cannot drop his weight."

WR [F] ISAIAH FORD, #1 (Jr-3)

VIRGINIA TECH ▶ GRADE: 5.31
Ht: 6-1 | Wt: 194 | 40: 4.64 | Arm: 32 5/8 | Hand: 9 1/4

History: Was a two-sport standout as a Florida prep. Originally intended to play football and basketball for Louisville, but changed his mind when then-head coach Charlie Strong went to Texas. Made an immediate impact with the Hokies — started 11-of-13 games at split end in 2014, and produced 56 receptions for 709 yards (12.7-yard average) and six touchdowns. Broke school single-season records for catches and touchdown catches in '15 when he started 12-of-13 games, and piled up 75-1,164-11 (15.5). Set a new catches mark in '16 by hauling in 79-1,094-7 (13.8). Sprained his left ankle against North Carolina. Needed just three seasons to become the Hokies' all-time leading receiver, with 210 receptions, 2,967 receiving yards, and 24 receiving touchdowns. Had 17 career rushes for 84 yards (4.9-yard average) and zero touchdowns. Was not penalized as a junior. Will be a 21-year-old rookie.

Strengths: Good arm and body length. Fine athlete. Has deceptive, competitive speed and a knack for creating some vertical separation. Competes in a crowd and is aggressive going up for the ball. Tracks it very well over his shoulder. Flashes play-making ability. Plays with discipline. Three-year starter with outstanding career production.

Weaknesses: Marginal hand size contributes to a lot downfield cradle-catching and seven drops in 2016. Recorded a 1.69-second 10-yard split, indicative of marginal short-area burst. Struggles beating press coverage. Limited elusiveness after the catch. Cannot take the top off a defense. Finesse, underpowered blocker lacking strength and physicality — whiffs too much and is disinterested mixing it up inside. Has no special teams' experience.

Future: Wiry, athletic, quicker-than-fast, college go-to receiver lacking ideal foot speed to stretch the field and the toughness, physicality and short-area burst desired in the slot. Could challenge for a role as a No. 4 or No. 5 receiver.

Draft projection: Fourth- to fifth-round pick.

Scout's take: "Ford has small hands and a lot of drops, and it shows up on tape consistently. He doesn't run very well. He's a slot receiver — that's all he is."

WR [Z] / KR SHELTON GIBSON, #1 (Jr-4)

WEST VIRGINIA ▶ GRADE: 5.29
Ht: 5-10 3/4 | Wt: 191 | 40: 4.49 | Arm: 32 | Hand: 8 7/8

History: Also ran track as an Ohio prep. Redshirted in 2013. In '14, made four catches for 60 yards (15.0-yard average) and zero touchdowns in 12 appearances. Started all 26 games at wide receiver the next two seasons — totaled 37-887-9 (24.0) in '15 ("Z"); and 43-951-8 (22.1) in '16 ("X"). Also penalized seven times in '16. Had 53 career kickoff returns for 1,244 yards (23.5-yard average), including a 100-yard score against Baylor in '15. Was in on 14 tackles his first two seasons on special teams.

Strengths: Has explosive, big-play ability. Fires off the line into his routes and beats press coverage with quickness and savvy. Very good long speed to gain a step down the field and can beat man coverage, where most of his production is generated. Recorded the fastest 60-yard shuttle (10.71 seconds) of any player at the Combine, indicative of exceptional balance, flexibility and endurance. Tracks the deep ball well and competes for the ball in a crowd. Good body control. Carries a swagger and plays with confidence. Shifty with the ball in his hands and has a knack for cutting back against the grain and finding open space. Very confident and carries a swagger. Good body control and toughness to contribute in special teams' coverage.

Weaknesses: Not a sophisticated or precise route runner and runs a limited tree. Does not have a feel for zones and where to find soft spots in coverage. Tends to cradle catch. Overmatched blocker lacking size and mass. Tied for fewest bench-press reps (8) among receivers at the Combine, indicative of a lack of strength. Has a small catching radius. Average run instincts with the ball in his hand.

Future: An explosive, downfield weapon who plays faster than his timed speed and is capable of making quick speed cuts at top speed to uncover and uncork the lid off defenses. Looks ideally suited for a downfield passing attack such as those deployed in Arizona and Pittsburgh.

Draft projection: Fourth- to fifth-round pick.

WR [Z,X,F] CHRIS GODWIN, #12 (Jr-3)

PENN STATE ▶ GRADE: 5.68
Ht: 6-1 | Wt: 209 | 40: 4.42 | Arm: 31 5/8 | Hand: 9 1/8

History: Prepped in Delaware, where he went to four state championship games (won two), and was the state's Gatorade Player of the Year.

As a true freshman in 2014, recorded 25 receptions for 321 yards (12.8-yard average) and two touchdowns in 13 games (three starts). Started 11-of-13 games at "X" in '15, and produced 69-1,101-5 (16.0). Started all 14 games at "X" in '16, and produced 59-982-11 (16.6). Was very productive in three bowl games, totaling 22-460-3 (20.9). Will be a 21-year-old rookie.

Strengths: Good strength to fend off the jam. Very good in-air body adjustments and catching radius. Works the middle of the field fearlessly. Tracks the deep ball very well and climbs the ladder in a crowd. Clean hands-catcher with outstanding hand-eye coordination. Uses his body well to shield defenders from the ball and make back-shoulder throws. Good leaping ability to secure 50-50 balls. Plays big on the biggest of stages — see three Bowl games, including 9-187-2 final performance vs USC in Rose Bowl. Strong, competitive blocker takes pride in craft. Bench-pressed 225 pounds 19 times at the Combine. Good career production. Good ball skills. Example leader who does a lot of extras and is willing to go the extra mile.

Weaknesses: Shows some tightness in his movement. Still learning how to run routes and set up defenders and has not proven he can consistently beat defenders one-on-one vs. man coverage. Does not create consistent separation and will flag some routes chopping out of his breaks. Likes to cradle-catch with his body. Not a dynamic or elusive runner after the catch.

Future: A well-built, strong, physical receiver who lined up split wide and in the slot and has the versatility to play multiple positions and projects ideally as a "Z" receiver in the pros. Has some similarities to Colts' 2008 sixth-round pick and 49ers WR Pierre Garcon, though Godwin enters the league more proven exiting the Big Ten Conference and is ready to make a more immediate impact.

Draft projection: Second- to third-round pick.

Scout's take: "Godwin is one of the most difficult evaluations in this year's draft. Our grades were all over the place on him, and more of them were low than high. He looks like a quality (No.) 3 (receiver) to me. If you are going to take him in the first two rounds, he has to be a No. 1 or 2, and I just don't see that. I need to do more work on him. I have been wrong before, but that's where I'm at with him."

WR [X] KENNY GOLLADAY, #19 (Sr-5)

NORTHERN ILLINOIS ▶ GRADE: 5.33
Ht: 6-4 | Wt: 218 | 40: 4.52 | Arm: 32 | Hand: 9 3/4

History: Began his college career at FCS North Dakota. As a true freshman in 2012, recorded 30 receptions for 429 yards (14.3-yard average) and one touchdown in 10 games. Started 10-of-11 games at "X" in '13, and caught 69-884-8 (12.8). When the coaching staff was fired after the season, Golladay transferred to NIU, where he sat out the '14 season per NCAA rules. Started all 14 games at wide receiver in '15, and produced 73-1,129-10 (15.5). Started 11-of-12 games in '16, and hauled in 87-1,156-8 (13.3). Non-start was Central Michigan (two tight ends). Had 29 career rushes for 206 yards (7.1-yard average) and three touchdowns. Graduated.

Strengths: Exceptional size. Looks the part with a big frame, good arm length and strong hands to fight off press coverage. Bench-pressed 225 pounds 18 times at the Combine and has good run strength to push through contact. Has a wide catching radius to factor in the red zone, with good in-air body adjustments to make difficult grabs. Tracks the deep ball well. Physical blocker with tenacity to finish and will go hunting linebackers on crackbacks.

Weaknesses: Body stiffness shows in his routes, with tight hips and long legs that create some difficulty bending and breaking off routes cleanly. Does not separate with savvy and needs to learn how to sell his routes better to uncover. Has a tendency to let the ball into his body and basket catch. Does not make many tacklers miss after the catch.

Future: Big, tall, lean, linear athlete with great length and enough foot speed to factor vertically outside the numbers, where he is best. Has a special teams temperament and the physicality to earn more playing time as a receiver for his blocking ability.

Draft projection: Fourth- to fifth-round pick.

WR [Z] CHAD HANSEN, #6 (Jr-4)

CALIFORNIA ▶ GRADE: 5.29
Ht: 6-1 7/8 | Wt: 202 | 40: 4.53 | Arm: 32 1/8 | Hand: 10 1/8

History: Also ran track as a California prep (10.9-second 100 meters). Began his college career at Idaho State, his only scholarship offer. Was listed as a "Z" receiver as a true freshman in 2013 — had 45 receptions for 501 yards (11.1-yard average) and three touchdowns in 11 games (five starts). Did not play against Washington. Transferred to Cal, in part, to be closer to family, particularly an aunt with lung disease. Joined the Golden Bears as a preferred walk-on, and sat out the '14 season per NCAA rules. Played 10 games in '15, and caught 19-249-1 (13.1). Earned a scholarship in '16, and was one of the nation's major breakout players — was the Pac-12's leading receiver with 92-1,249-11 (13.6) in 10 games (nine starts at "Z"). Hurt his left ankle against Oregon State,

WIDE RECEIVERS

and sat out against Oregon and USC.

Strengths: Outstanding hands. Catches the ball cleanly. Physical beating press coverage. Strong runner after the catch and can take slants the distance (see Stanford). Ran a 6.74-second 3-cone drill time, indicating outstanding lateral agility. Keeps working to uncover when the pocket breaks down and is an instinctive, crafty zone-beater. Confident and competitive. Wants the ball in the clutch. Fearless working the middle of the field. Very determined and motivated to succeed with a boulder on his shoulder from being overlooked in the recruiting process.

Weaknesses: Appears stiff releasing off the line. Not explosive at the top of his routes and tends to gather his feet. Lacks explosive top-end speed. Bench-pressed 225 pounds only 11 times and lacks weight-room strength to help ward off physical, press coverage. Not dynamic making tacklers miss in the open field. Could improve physicality as a blocker.

Future: Emerged as Cal's clutch, go-to receiver in first year as a starter and stacked 24-300-2 on San Diego State and Arizona State in September after being told he wasn't good enough to play for either program. Has proven productive at every layer of the field and possesses the hands, toughness and competitive desire to eventually earn a No. 3 role and become a 10-year pro.

Draft projection: Fourth- to fifth-round pick.

WR [Z] KEON HATCHER, #4 (Sr-5)

ARKANSAS ▶ GRADE: 5.07

Ht: 6-1 1/4 | Wt: 212 | 40: 4.69 | Arm: 32 | Hand: 9 1/2

History: Missed games in high school because of a hip pointer. As a true freshman in 2012, had three receptions for 21 yards (7.0-yard average) and one touchdown in 10 appearances. In '13, started 6-of-10 games at the "Z," and caught 27-346-2 (12.8). Missed two September contests while nursing a hamstring injury. Started 12-of-13 games at flanker in '14, and snagged 43-558-6 (13.0). Non-start was versus UAB, as the Razorbacks opened with a fullback. In '15, managed 13-198-2 (15.2) in two starts before suffering a broken left foot (fifth metatarsal) and undergoing season-ending surgery. Was granted a medical redshirt season. Required a second surgery in the spring. Started 8-of-12 at flanker in '16, totaling 44-743-8 (16.9). Sat out against Alcorn State (hamstring). Had 21 career rushes for 259 yards (12.3-yard average) and one touchdown. Also returned 16 career kickoffs for 357 yards (22.3-yard average). Graduated with a sociology degree. Did not perform jumps or shuttles at the Combine because of a right hamstring injury.

Strengths: Outstanding size with a muscular frame. Catches on contact. Is not fazed by traffic. Consistently moves the chains. Good run strength to break arm tackles. Solid career production. Good weight-room worker.

Weaknesses: Marginal lateral agility and long speed. Slow off the line and is moved around the field to allow free releases. Methodical route runner —gathers to cut and is not explosive out of his breaks. Struggles to uncover and separate. Lacks playmaking ability. Makes few tacklers miss. Limited special teams and return experience.

Future: A big-bodied, tight-hipped, possession receiver with a chance to compete for a backup chains-moving, flanker job in a West Coast offense.

Draft projection: Priority free agent.

WR [X] / KR CARLOS HENDERSON, #1 (Jr-4)

LOUISIANA TECH ▶ GRADE: 5.32

Ht: 5-11 | Wt: 199 | 40: 4.51 | Arm: 31 3/8 | Hand: 9 1/8

History: New Orleans native originally committed to Utah, but flipped days before National Signing Day. Redshirted in 2013. Was the Ragin' Cajuns' outside complement to fellow draft prospect Trent Taylor, who worked inside. Henderson was suspended the first two games of the '14 season (violation team rules) before starting 7-of-12 games and catching 29 balls for 569 yards (19.6-yard average) and four touchdowns. Added 25 kickoff returns for 805 yards (32.2-yard average), including two scores. Suffered a finger injury during '15 fall camp, and had surgery which limited him to kick returns only in the season opener against Southern. On the season, started 10-of-11 games played, and snagged 36-774-5 (21.5) with 21-463 (22.0) on kickoff returns. Sat out against Louisiana-Lafayette (hamstring); sustained a concussion against Rice; did not play against Mississippi State (internal injury); and dislocated four toes in the first quarter of the New Orleans Bowl against Arkansas State. Was the Conference USA Offensive and Special Teams Player of the Year in '16 after starting 12-of-13 games and producing 82-1,535-19 (18.7) receiving with 33-826-1 (25.0) on kickoff returns. After sitting out against UTEP (ankle), totaled 20-548-8 (27.4) against Western Kentucky and Massachusetts. Played through a broken hand the final three games. His combined production with Trent Taylor (3,338 yards) is an NCAA single-season record. Had 32 career carries for 267 yards (8.3-yard average) and three touchdowns.

Strengths: Playmaker with the ball in his hands — skilled runner with outstanding vision to make tacklers miss and create in the open field. Good creativity and hand quickness to fend off

WIDE RECEIVERS

the jam and shake free of the press. Catches outside his frame and has natural ball skills to run underneath the ball. Has separation quickness to make plays vertically and accelerates when the ball is in the air. Plays with passion and has very good competitive playing speed, vision and traffic burst as a kickoff returner. Competitive blocker. Is tough and will battle through injury.

Weaknesses: Has some tightness in his hips with a very lean frame that has been vulnerable to injury. Ran a simplified route tree and will require some extra time to acclimate to complex NFL playbooks. Benefitted from playing opposite Trent Taylor and regularly matching up against lesser competition.

Future: A lean, quick-footed, intensively competitive, vertical receiver with the swagger and confidence to eventually earn a role as a No. 3 receiver if he can avoid the high volume of injuries that have been an issue throughout his career. A gamer who will compete readily for a job returning kicks.

Draft projection: Fourth-round pick.

WR [Z] KRISHAWN HOGAN, #80 (Sr-4)
MARIAN (IND.)   ▶ GRADE: 5.18
Ht: 6-3 | Wt: 222 | 40: 4.59 | Arm: 32 1/8 | Hand: 9 7/8

History: Son, KJ, was born two weeks before the Combine. Flew under the radar at Indianapolis Warren Central, where he was on the scout team during his junior season. Began his college career at Walsh University, a below-football-average Division II school in Canton, OH. As a true freshman in 2013 (wore jersey No. 85), had 32 grabs for 393 yards (12.3-yard average) and three touchdowns. Dealt with a right groin strain late in the year. Transferred to Marian University in his hometown of Indianapolis, where he played wide receiver on the most talented team in the NAIA. Was unstoppable from the get-go — started all 14 games in '14, and hauled in 82-1,136-11 (13.9) for the national runners-up. Spearheaded a national championship run in '15 when he racked up 101-1,824-16 (18.1) in 14 starts as an "X" receiver. Led the NAIA in receptions, receiving yards, and receiving yards per game (130.3). Was the Mid-States Football Association Mideast Offensive Player of the Year in '16 after posting 80-1,435-15 (17.9) in 12 starts. Also was used extensively in the 'Wildcat' formation near the goal line his last two seasons, notching 25 touchdowns on 62 carries. Added a two-yard touchdown pass. Oftentimes was not required to play full games, as the Knights won 28 games by three scores or more over three seasons. Scored 402 points in three seasons at Marian, and owns school records for receiving yards (4,395) and touchdowns (42). Team captain.

Strengths: Excellent size with a sturdy build. Caught the ball extremely well at the Combine and at his pro day workout. Extends outside his frame and makes difficult catches in traffic. Very competitive. Extremely motivated. Strong, effortful blocker. Exceptional production.

Weaknesses: Lacks top-end vertical speed to threaten vertically. Tight-hipped and a bit heavy-footed into his routes. Not sudden at the top of his routes. Did not regularly face top competition or distinguish himself at the NFL-PA all-star game.

Future: Dominant small-school receiver who regularly feasted on NAIA competition and has the size, strength and hands to earn a role as a No. 4 receiver in the pros.

Draft projection: Late draftable pick.

Scout's take: "I think he can come to a camp and compete for a fifth (WR) spot. His hands are a little inconsistent. He doesn't have special speed. He is a dominating player at that level and a good athlete, but I don't think he is special and I (viewed) five games last year. I don't think he can beat out our fifth receiver."

WR [X, Z] MACK HOLLINS, #13 (Sr-5)
NORTH CAROLINA   ▶ GRADE: 5.34
Ht: 6-4 | Wt: 221 | 40: 4.51 | Arm: 33 1/4 | Hand: 9 3/4

History: Also played basketball and lacrosse as a Maryland prep. Spent a postgraduate year at Fork Union (Va.) Military Academy. Walked on and redshirted in 2012. Played all 13 games in '13, but did not record receiving stats. Was put on scholarship in '14, played all 13 games, and posted 35 receptions for 613 yards (17.5-yard average) and eight touchdowns. Had the nation's highest yards per catch in '15 — played all 14 games, starting five at flanker, and caught 30-745-8 (24.8). Was ejected in the bowl game against Baylor for a targeting penalty (suspended first half of '16 season opener). In '16, started 4-of-7 games, and managed 16-309-4 (19.3) before suffering a season-ending broken right collarbone injury. Made his mark on special teams — tallied 24 career tackles, and was a four-year special-teams captain. Graduated with a degree in exercise and sports science. Was a medical exclusion from the bench-press test because of a right shoulder injury and did not finish shuttles after being injured running 40-yard dash.

Strengths: Exceptional body and arm length — provides a big, downfield target. Eats up ground with long strides. Deceptive speed to climb the field and create big plays. Very productive, special teams stalwart — all-out, four-phase contributor. Carries a chip on his shoulder and still covers kicks like he's out to earn

WIDE RECEIVERS

a scholarship. Carries a swagger. Vocal leader.

Weaknesses: Leggy long strider struggles making quick cuts. Raw route runner with tightness in his hips. Lacks bulk for as big as he is and goes down easy. Lacks weight-room strength and does not play big. Struggles fending off the jam. Limited blocking strength. Was never a full-time starter. Marginal career production.

Future: Lean, long-limbed vertical receiver with appealing special teams ability to carve a niche as a core contributor readily and eventually work his way into a receiving rotation as a vertical threat.

Draft projection: Fourth- to fifth-round pick.

Scout's take: "Hollins is hurt right now (at the Combine), but he'll get looks in the fourth (round) because of his special teams ability."

WR [Z] BUG HOWARD, #84/13 (Sr-4)

NORTH CAROLINA ▶ GRADE: 5.38

Ht: 6-4 1/8 | Wt: 221 | 40: 4.59 | Arm: 33 1/8 | Hand: 10 3/8

History: Goes by "Bug," the nickname his mother Veronica gave him when he was a toddler. Howard prepped in Georgia, where he racked up 115 receptions for 1,630 yards (14.2-yard average) and 19 touchdowns. Weighed 195 pounds when he arrived in Chapel Hill. Played split end for the Tar Heels. As a true freshman in 2013, had 22 receptions for 278 yards (12.6-yard average) and four touchdowns in 13 appearances. In '14, recorded 42-455-2 (10.8) in 13 games. Saw some reps at tight end during '15 fall camp. On the season, recorded 29-488-4 (16.8) in 14 games (three starts). Started all 13 games in '16, and snagged 53-827-8 (15.6). Took jersey No. 13 in honor of teammate Mack Hollins after Hollins was lost to injury.

Strengths: Exceptional size — offers a huge target and creates mismatches in the red zone with his tremendous body and arm length and leaping ability. Has a 37 1/2-inch vertical jump and skies for the ball. Dangerous fade threat. Catches on contact and hangs onto the ball with very big, secure hands. Uses his body well to shield defenders from the ball and hauls in nearly every ball thrown his way. Good sideline awareness — knows how to use the field. Snagged game-winning catch vs. Pittsburgh and has produced in pressure situations. Can cover up defensive backs in the run game. The game is important to him.

Weaknesses: Comes off the ball too upright and is not quick off the line into his routes. Could be challenged by physical, press coverage. Needs to learn how to stem and set up his routes. Limited initial quickness and separation speed — most of his catches are contested. Struggles to sink his hips, accelerate and create

vertical separation. Not explosive. Lacks elusiveness after the catch. Recorded 14% body fat at the Combine, abnormally high for a receiver and indicative of a lack of endurance. Limited special teams experience.

Future: A big-bodied, long-limbed, strong-handed target with the competitiveness and leaping ability to separate with length, create mismatches in the red zone and produce chunk yardage. Has eventual starter potential as a possession receiver, though Howard received a lot of late-round grades from scouts and draft status might not reflect potential, much like 49ers' 2008 sixth-round pick Josh Morgan and Dolphins' 2012 seventh-round pick and current Titans WR Rishard Matthews.

Draft projection: Fifth- to sixth-round pick.

Scout's take: "(Howard) was a strength of the team. He made a lot of big plays for them."

WR [Z] ZAY JONES, #7 (Sr-4)

EAST CAROLINA ▶ GRADE: 5.63

Ht: 6-2 1/8 | Wt: 201 | 40: 4.48 | Arm: 32 1/2 | Hand: 9

History: Father, Robert, was an ECU All-American and 10-year NFL linebacker (1992-2001) — won three Super Bowls with the Cowboys. Uncle, Jeff Blake, was a 13-year NFL quarterback (made a Pro Bowl with the Bengals). Zay, an Austin, Tex. native, played high school ball for NFL eight-year veteran OT Mike Rosenthal. Also competed in track and field. As a true freshman in 2013, played all 13 games, starting the final eight at "H" (inside receiver) in the Pirates' four-receiver attack — recorded 62 receptions for 604 yards (9.7-yard average) and five touchdowns. Started 9-of-13 games at "H" in '14, producing 81-830-5 (10.2). Played with a torn left labrum in '15 when he started all 12 games at "H," and hauled in 98-1,099-5 (11.2), including a 22-catch performance against South Carolina. After being recruited by and playing for Ruffin McNeil, posted a historic senior season under new coach Scottie Montgomery. Was the nation's leading receiver, and set American Athletic Conference and ECU single-season records for catches and receiving yards — toggled between multiple receiver spots, and amassed 158-1,746-8 (11.1) in 12 starts. Suffered a minor foot bruise against Central Florida. Was a finalist for the Biletnikoff Award and Campbell Trophy ("Academic Heisman"), as well as the Senior CLASS Award. Had 30 career kickoff returns for 598 yards (19.9-yard average). Also completed 3-of-4 pass attempts (75.0 percent) for 36 yards and one touchdown. Team captain walks away as the FBS all-time career receptions leader with 399.

Strengths: Experienced, four-year starter.

Runs precise routes. Instinctive reading coverage and settling into zones. Very good body control to extend outside his frame and make difficult catches. Very natural hands (96-percent catcher). Outstanding concentration tracking the ball over his shoulder (see UCF). Catches in stride. Sells out in a crowd and sacrifices his body. Showed the ability to separate at the Senior Bowl, when he caught a TD and had two others negated. Nifty after the catch. Scrappy blocker. Extremely competitive. Rare college production — NCAA leader. Carries a swagger and has strong on-field leadership qualities and a locker room presence. Very durable and has not missed any time to injury, playing through a shoulder injury most of junior season. Has NFL pedigree and it shows.

Weaknesses: Production was inflated from a lot of lateral tosses in a spread offense. Has some hip tightness and is not a dynamic playmaker after the catch. Was not heavily used downfield as a vertical threat. Could stand to do a better job sustaining blocks.

Future: A tough, competitive, instinctive receiver, Jones made a small mint at the Senior Bowl and continued his ascent at the Combine with a well-rounded showing. A high-impact, low-risk football player. Soaks football knowledge and could contribute readily in the slot in the pros.

Draft projection: Second-round pick.

Scout's take: "One of the questions on (Jones) going into the Senior Bowl was his speed. He was running past guys in the game. He grades out as a third-rounder. I don't think he'll get out of the second after he ran well (at the Combine)."

WR [F,Z] / PR **COOPER KUPP**, #10 (Sr-5)

EASTERN WASHINGTON ▶ GRADE: 5.48
Ht: 6-1 5/8 | Wt: 204 | 40: 4.64 | Arm: 31 1/2 | Hand: 9 1/2

History: Married (Anna). Father, Craig, was a Giants 1990 fifth-round draft pick, and grandfather, Jake, is in the Saints Hall of Fame. Washington native Cooper starred as a receiver-defensive back, and he won a basketball state championship. Redshirted in 2012, and was recognized as the Scout Team Player of the Year. One of the most productive receivers in the history of college football. A four-time consensus All-American for the FCS Eagles, Kupp aligned in multiple spots, but was considered the "X" in the team's spread offense. In '13, won the Jerry Rice Award (top FCS freshman) after setting FCS single-season records for receptions, receiving yards, and touchdowns by a freshman — piled up 93 catches for 1,691 yards (18.2-yard average) and 21 touchdowns (previously held by

Randy Moss) in 15 starts. Started all 13 games in '14, and racked up 104-1,431-16 (13.8). Sat out against Western Montana (right ankle). In '15, won the Walter Payton Award (most outstanding offensive player) and Big Sky Conference Player of the Year — reeled in 114-1,642-19 (14.4) in 11 starts, including an eye-popping 20-275-3 (13.8) against Northern Colorado. Sat out the second half against Northern Iowa (hip pointer). In '16, was second in the Payton voting and shared conference MVP, as he capped his career with 117-1,700-17 (14.5) in 13 starts. Sprained his left AC joint in Week Two against North Dakota State — sat out against Northern Iowa, and re-injured against Portland State and Central Arkansas. Had 17 career rushes for 58 yards (3.4-yard average) and one touchdown; completed 7-of-10 career pass attempts (70.0 percent) for 180 yards and four touchdowns; returned 25 career punts for 426 yards (17.0-yard average, school record), including three scores; and returned five career kickoffs for 90 yards (18.0-yard average). Rewrote the FCS, Big Sky, and EWU record books, notching 52 total records. Most notably, owns the college football record for career receiving yards (6.464); subdivision records for career receptions (428), career touchdown receptions (73), and career receiving yards per game (14.3); conference records for career points (464) and career touchdowns (77); and school all-purpose yardage record (7,038). Two-year captain earned his economics degree with a 3.6 GPA. Invited to the Senior Bowl. Will be a 24-year-old rookie. Opted not to bench press at the Combine and did not finish 60-yard shuttle because of cramping.

Strengths: Experienced, four-year starter with NFL pedigree. Outstanding size. Efficient route runner — makes sharp speed cuts at precise depths and understands how to vary his speed through zones and where to settle. Plays faster than he times and has good functional football-playing speed. Extends outside his frame and makes difficult off-target catches high, low and behind him. Is not fazed by traffic. Helped EWU to 2-2 record vs. Pac-12 competition, piling up 40-716-11 (17.9) against Washington State, Washington, Oregon and Oregon State — rises to the occasion on big stages and proved he could beat better competition. Soft, natural hands (95-percent catcher). Extremely smart and competitive with a high football IQ. Versatile and lines up at every receiver position. Diligently works at his craft and understands football concepts and how an offense is designed — thinks like and aspires to be a coach. Excellent career production. Very durable. Has return experience and serves as

WIDE RECEIVERS

the holder on kicks.

Weaknesses: Could struggle with aggressive press coverage in the pros. Ran a pedestrian 40-time at the Combine. Recorded a 31-inch vertical jump, indicative of a lack of lower-body explosion. Lacks weight-room strength and could stand to improve his physicality as a blocker.

Future: A savvy, smart pro's pro with an advanced understanding of the receiver position, Kupp compensates for a lack of elite physical traits with exceptional toughness, instincts and competitiveness and has the wiring to will his way into a starting role. Physically could be initially challenged by the advanced speed of the NFL game but will overcome it with preparation and has the savvy to acclimate very quickly to a slot role.

Draft projection: Third-round pick.

Scout's take: "(Kupp) is very safe, but he has to be an 'F' (slot receiver) all the way. He is going to get pressed. Against NFL corners, I think he is going to struggle to create separation the way he did in college."

WR [Z] / TE [H] **JEROME LANE**, #7 (Jr-4)
AKRON　　　　　　　▶ GRADE: 4.97
Ht: 6-2 1/2 | Wt: 226 | 40: 4.58 | Arm: 31 1/2 | Hand: 9 3/4

History: Akron native. In high school, played all over the field, as well as competed in basketball, the sport his father, Jerome, played professionally in the NBA and CBA. Jerome Jr. redshirted in 2013. Was used as a linebacker, safety and pass rusher early in his career. In '14, tallied 14 tackles and five sacks in 12 appearances. Converted to receiver in '15 — started 10-of-13 games at the "Z," and produced 39 receptions for 782 yards (20.1-yard average) and eight touchdowns. In '16, played the "X" in the Zips' spread offense, totaling 62-1,018-6 (16.4) in 12 starts.

Strengths: Good size and uses his length to climb defensive backs. Has a 35-inch vertical jump and good leaping ability. Looks the part. Courageous working through the middle. Catches on contact and is not fazed by traffic. Good concentration in a crowd. Tough and physical. Solid inside production. Dependable third-down target. Willing, competitive blocker.

Weaknesses: Rolls off the line with marginal foot speed and only shows one gear. Short-stepper gathers to cut and struggles to drop his hips and transition cleanly out of breaks. Shut down by Pittsburgh in 2015 and held in check by Wisconsin (3-43-0) and Western Michigan (4-42-0) in '16 and piled up stats against mid-major competition. Will struggle to separate with speed vs. NFL defensive backs. Limited elusiveness and burst after the catch.

Future: A bit of a tweener lacking ideal speed

and route savvy for a receiver and the bulk and length desired in an H-back. Has enough athletic ability to continue developing.

Draft projection: Priority free agent.

Scout's take: "(Lane) is good-looking on the hoof — that is it. He's not explosive and doesn't have any other unique traits."

WR [F] **KEEVAN LUCAS**, #2 (Sr-4)
TULSA　　　　　　　▶ GRADE: 5.22
Ht: 5-9 3/8 | Wt: 192 | 40: 4.58 | Arm: 31 7/8 | Hand: 9 7/8

History: Is motivated by the losses of his mother, Kimberly, and grandmother, Bernice, who died three days apart in September 2009. Keevan prepped in Texas (also ran track), but his senior football season was truncated by a torn left lateral meniscus (required surgery). A freshman flanker who enrolled early in January 2013, Lucas recorded 32 receptions for 442 yards (13.8-yard average) and one touchdown in 12 games (five starts). Added five kickoff returns for 102 yards (20.4-yard average). Became one of the nation's most productive slot receivers when he started all 12 games in '14, and produced 101-1,219-11 (12.1). In '15, managed 26-409-5 (15.7) before suffering a season-ending ruptured right patella tendon injury and was granted a medical redshirt season. Returned to start all 13 games in '16, and hauled in 81-1,180-15 (14.6). Had 35 career carries for 238 yards (6.8-yard average) and zero touchdowns. Bypassed his final year of eligibility.

Strengths: Highpoints the ball and plays bigger than his size — attacks the ball in the air and has a surprisingly wide catching radius. Very confident and competitive. Strong on contact and is not fazed by traffic. Sacrifices his body and makes some spectacular, acrobatic grabs (see Cincinnati and Tulane). Plucks the ball easily. Keeps working to uncover on broken plays. Good balance to stay on his feet as a ball-carrier. Diligent weight-room worker. Strong personal and football character.

Weaknesses: Inconsistent hands, including a nation-leading 12 drops in 2016. Has tight hips and limited lateral agility, as confirmed by slow shuttle times, and consequently could have some struggles beating press coverage in the pros. Did not run a diverse route tree and often drifts in his routes. Lacks top-end vertical speed. Is not elusive or dynamic in the open field and does not create a lot of yardage after contact. Was not consistently challenged in the American Athletic Conference.

Future: High-hipped, undersized, competitive slot receiver with the drive and determination to emerge as an effective slot receiver with continued refinement.

Draft projection: Fifth- to sixth-round pick.

WIDE RECEIVERS

WR [X, F] JOSH MALONE, #3 (Jr-3)

TENNESSEE   ▶ GRADE: 5.36

Ht: 6-2 3/4 | Wt: 208 | 40: 4.44 | Arm: 31 3/8 | Hand: 9 5/8

History: Tennessee native was the state's "Mr. Football." Played all 13 games in each of his three seasons in Knoxville. As a true freshman in 2014, recorded 23-231-1 (10.0-yard average) in six starts at the "X." Moved to flanker in '15, catching 31-405-2 (13.1) in 12 starts. After sitting out '16 spring practice (undisclosed surgery), started all 13 games in the fall, and totaled 50-972-11 (19.4, school record). Will be a 21-year-old rookie.

Strengths: Very good size. Dependable catcher, especially tracking and running underneath the deep ball, where he often has to adjust his route and work back to the ball. Exceptional track speed to threaten the field vertically and create explosive big plays. Eats up the cushion of defensive backs with long strides and is effective on intermediate, one-cut routes such as crossers, digs and posts. Functional stalk blocker.

Weaknesses: Struggles to get off press coverage (see Alabama and Georgia). Bench-pressed 225 pounds only 10 times at the Combine and needs to improve his strength to fend off the jam. Not a crisp route runner and does not play to his timed speed. Doesn't attack the ball in the air and consistently lets it come down to him. Mistimes jumps. Measured a 30 1/2-inch vertical jump, among the lowest of receivers at the Combine and indicative of marginal leaping ability. Cradle-catches a lot instead of extending outside his frame and does not trust his hands. Marginal creativity and elusiveness after the catch — little burst or explosion.

Future: A speedy, vertical threat lacking confidence in his hands. Similar to Saints' 2007 first-round pick Robert Meachum, who struggled to ever live up to the expectations of his lofty draft status, Malone is also a deep-ball body-catcher lacking natural receiving skills and instincts. Could be best with free releases and projects as a No. 4 receiver.

Draft projection: Third- to fourth-round pick.

Scout's take: "(Malone) is intriguing because of his vertical speed, but he doesn't excite you on tape. He really doesn't go up and highpoint the ball or pluck it. He's a vertical, build-speed player with adequate hands."

WR [F] GABE MARKS, #9 (Sr-5)

WASHINGTON STATE   ▶ GRADE: 5.01

Ht: 5-11 | Wt: 189 | 40: 4.56 | Arm: 30 3/8 | Hand: 8 3/4

History: Wears jersey No. 9 because that's how old he was when his father was killed in a 2004 drive-by shooting. Marks also ran track as a California prep. Suffered a hip injury during his senior football season. Played the "Z" in Mike Leach's "Air Raid" system. Played all 12 games as a true freshman in '12 (wore jersey No. 84), starting seven, and contributed 49-560-2 (11.4). Played all 13 games in '13, starting the final nine, and posted 74-807-7 (10.9). Was arrested in February '14 — was underage and intoxicated in a bar, and punched an employee, drawing four misdemeanor chargers. Ultimately pleaded guilty to trespassing and frequenting a tavern as a minor, receiving probation and community service. Lost his spot atop the depth chart, and the decision was made to redshirt in '14 (also incurred a staph infection in his pelvis). Returned to start all 13 games in '15, producing 104-1,192-15 (11.5) with 11 punt returns for 106 yards (9.6-yard average). Sprained his right ankle in the regular season finale against Washington. In '16, started all 13 games, and hauled in 89-894-13 (10.0). Owns the Pac-12 career receptions record (316), as well as school marks for receiving yards (3,453) and touchdowns (37). Graduated with sociology degree.

Strengths: Very good ball skills — makes savvy in-air adjustments and tracks the ball very well over his shoulder (see TD grabs vs. Eastern Washington and Arizona). Highly competitive, and it was noticeable at the Combine sacrificing his body to lay out and dive to catch balls. Good effort after the catch.

Weaknesses: Undersized with a thin frame, very small hands, short arms and average football-playing strength. Marginal short-area burst and long speed to create any separation — most of his catches are contested. Recorded a 29 1/2-inch vertical jump indicative of marginal leaping ability. Operated out of a pass-happy, spread offense and did not run a full route tree. Character and durability require careful scrutiny.

Future: A very productive, unrefined, possession receiver that projects to the slot in the pros, where he stands a better chance to release cleanly. Has overcome a lot of adversity to accomplish what he has in his career and been slowed by an assortment of injuries and off-field incidents that could force him to prove his capability in the slot from an undrafted position.

Draft projection: Priority free agent.

WR [F] / RS ISAIAH McKENZIE, #16 (Jr-3)

GEORGIA   ▶ GRADE: 5.31

Ht: 5-7 1/2 | Wt: 173 | 40: 4.41 | Arm: 28 7/8 | Hand: 8 7/8

History: Miami native and American Heritage High product — played on a star-studded team which included UGA teammate Sony Michel and Florida State cornerback Tavarus McFadden, amongst others. Raised by his grand-

WIDE RECEIVERS

mother, McKenzie survived a dangerous part of Miami. He shared details of his upbringing with the Miami Herald, saying he never met his father, saw his drug-addicted mother physically abused, and witnessed three people shot and killed. Worked as a slot/return specialist for the Bulldogs. As a true freshman in 2014, played 12 games (three starts) — caught six balls for 67 yards (11.2-yard average) and zero touchdowns, while returning 19 punts for 230 yards, including two scores. Was suspended for the bowl game against Louisville for what then-head coach Mark Richt said was "an in-house, taking-care-of-business issue." Pulled his right hamstring in the '15 spring game then missed time during fall camp because of a left hamstring injury. On the season, played 10 games (four starts), and recorded 10-123-0 (12.3) receiving with 17-217-2 (12.8) on punt returns. Re-injured his left hamstring against Alabama, sidelining him against Tennessee and Missouri. Also missed the Georgia Tech contest because of a foot injury. Played all 13 games in '16, starting four, and totaled 44-633-7 (14.4) with 23-245-1 (10.7) on punt returns. Dealt with a minor left arm injury against Vanderbilt. Had 37 career rushes for 329 yards (8.9-yard average) and four touchdowns, as well as 17 career kickoff returns for 375 yards (22.1-yard average), including one score. Holds UGA records for punt return scores (five) and total return scores (six).

Strengths: Exceptional long speed that consistently shows up in the return game. Ran a 6.64-second 3-cone drill time, among the fastest at the Combine and indicative of outstanding agility. Caught the ball well outside his frame and tracked it easily over his shoulder at the Combine. Very strong for his size.

Weaknesses: Very small with tight hips more evident weaving during the gauntlet drill at the Combine. Has a tiny 68 1/4-inch wingspan and small catching radius. Minimal career receiving production and experience, with raw route-running skill. Has been dinged a lot throughout his career and durability is an issue.

Future: Diminutive, dynamite returner with explosive big-play ability to factor readily in the return game and contribute in creatively designed packages that put the ball in his hands in space and allow him to turn on the jets.

Draft projection: Fourth- to fifth-round pick.

WR [F] DREW MORGAN, #80 (Sr-4)

ARKANSAS ▶ GRADE: 4.99
Ht: 5-11 7/8 | Wt: 190 | 40: 4.72 | Arm: 30 3/8 | Hand: 9 1/2

History: Arkansas native starred — on both sides of the ball — on two undefeated state championship teams, and was named MVP of both title games. Made ten appearances as a true freshman in 2013, and did not record any stats. A reserve in '14, recorded 10 grabs for 181 yards (18.1-yard average) and one touchdown in 13 games. In '15, stepped in for the injured Keon Hatcher to start 10-of-13 games at the "X," producing 63-843-10 (13.4). Hurt his right shoulder in Week Eight against Tennessee-Martin, and had off-season surgery. Started 9-of-13 games at wide receiver in '16, and caught 65-739-3 (11.4). Added three kickoff returns for 58 yards (19.3-yard average) and four punt returns for 37 yards (9.3-yard average). Tweaked his back against Alabama. Was ejected from bowl game against Virginia Tech for spitting in an opponent's face. Led the Razorbacks with 41 "money" catches (first down and/or touchdown). Graduated with a management degree.

Strengths: Very scrappy competitor. Crafty running routes and sifting through zones to uncover. Physically tough to withstand contact across the middle and catch in congestion. Urgent running upfield on screens and quick-hitting routes. Extremely smart with outstanding football IQ. The game is very important to him, and he works diligently at his craft.

Weaknesses: Undersized and lacks strength and is moved around the field to create free releases. Average athlete with pedestrian speed by NFL receiving standards. Will struggle with press coverage — gets knocked off course. Recorded a 9'0" broad jump, the shortest of any receiver at the Combine and indicative or marginal leaping ability and explosion. Also measured the slowest 40-yard dash (4.79) of any receiver at the event. Underpowered blocker. Minimal return experience.

Future: A determined, quicker-than-fast, slot receiver who compensates for his lack of size, strength and speed with grit, toughness and determination. Marginal showing at the Combine will likely leave undrafted, and fierce competitiveness is likely to allow him to earn a roster spot and evolve into a competitive pro with a few years in an NFL strength program.

Draft projection: Priority free agent.

Scout's take: "(Morgan) is a camp body, that's all. He doesn't have the traits to be drafted. I will say he is one of the toughest kids I (scouted) this year. I won't be surprised if he finds a way to make it."

WR [F] / RS SPEEDY NOIL, #2 (Jr-3)

TEXAS A&M ▶ GRADE: 5.05
Ht: 5-10 5/8 | Wt: 199 | 40: 4.65e | Arm: 30 | Hand: 9 1/4

History: New Orleans native was a consensus five-star recruit as a receiver/athlete. As a true freshman in 2014, started 5-of-12 games at wide receiver, and posted 46 receptions for

583 yards (12.7-yard average) and five touchdowns. Injured his left MCL against Rice, but missed just one game after arthroscopic surgery. Was suspended for portion of '16 spring practice. Explained head coach Kevin Sumlin: "Speedy has some things he's got to complete. . .We asked him to do some things, and while he's doing that he's been away from the program. ...There are guys who mature at different times, and sometimes you have to put some things in place to make sure guys really understand what's expected of them." Played nine games in '15, starting three outside, and tallied 21-226-2 (10.8). Did not play against Arkansas or Mississippi State while nursing a soft tissue injury. Was suspended against Western Carolina in November and for the bowl game against Louisville. Was arrested in April '16 for driving without a license. Did not play the season opener versus UCLA (suspension), but started 8-of-10 games played, catching 21-325-2 (15.5). Sat out against South Carolina (injury). Was suspended for the bowl game against Kansas State after his arrest for marijuana possession. Had 43 career kickoffs for 990 yards (23.0-yard average) and 17 career punt returns for 197 yards (11.6-yard average). Opted not to run the 40 or shuttles and injured his right hip during jumps.

Strengths: Good movement skill. Flashes big-play ability. Recorded the best vertical jump (43 1/2 inches) of any receiver at the Combine along with an 11'1" broad jump, indicating explosive leaping ability. Has the agility and short-area burst to be effective in the return game.

Weaknesses: Modest size. Does not play big or fast nor attack the ball in the air the way an explosive leaper is capable, often allowing the ball to come to him. Cowers working inside and cannot be trusted in critical situations. Marginal football playing instincts. Routes lack precision and polish, and he often turns back to the ball too early and allows break points. Disinterested blocker. Has yet to adopt a professional approach to the game and been suspended four times in three years and not yet learned from his mistakes. Has been nagged by injuries.

Future: An explosive athlete and highly-regarded recruit who has never lived up to his press clippings and seen his development hampered by a consistent lack of maturity. Must prove he loves football and commit to the game to have a chance of earning a roster spot.

Draft projection: Priority free agent.

WR [Z] / KR ZACH PASCAL, #6 (Sr-5)
OLD DOMINION (VA.) ▶ GRADE: 5.26
Ht: 6-1 5/8 | Wt: 219 | 40: 4.64 | Arm: 32 | Hand: 10

History: Played running back, receiver, and cornerback as a Maryland prep. Redshirted in 2012. Primarily an inside receiver his first two seasons then was used all over the field as an upperclassman. Played all 12 games in '13, starting five, and recorded 41 catches for 534 yards (13.0-yard average) and six touchdowns. Started all 12 games at wide receiver in '14, and produced 59-734-7 (12.6). Started 11-of-12 games in '15, and caught 68-970-8 (14.3), while gaining a school-record 1,549 all-purpose yards. Started all 13 games in '16, and hauled in 65-946-9 (14.6). Had 38 career rushes for 310 yards (8.2-yard average) and one touchdown. Returned 32 career kickoffs for 729 yards (22.8-yard average). Team captain is ODU's all-time receptions leader (233). Graduated.

Strengths: Very good size and looks the part. Powers off the line and brushes off press coverage. Solid run strength. Makes some difficult catches look routine with superb concentration. Very competitive working inside and keeps churning his legs after contact. Tracks the ball easily down field, and confirmed ability to adjust well and catch it over his opposite shoulder during Combine drills. Caught 8-104-2 vs. North Carolina State in 2016 and responded to the challenge of facing better competition. Has core special teams experience and contributed in every phase throughout his career.

Weaknesses: Did not run a full route tree — only shows one gear and does not sink his hips and accelerate out of breaks. Could stand to sharpen his patterns. Lacks the top-end speed to separate vertically. Piled up production against modest competition.

Future: A big, strong, physical, competitive, small-school go-to receiver with enough strength and toughness to translate his game to the slot in the pros and fend for a No. 5 receiving job. Has a special teams' temperament to earn a roster spot.

Draft projection: Fifth- to sixth-round pick.

WR [F] / RS JAMES QUICK, #17 (Sr-4)
LOUISVILLE ▶ GRADE: 5.03
Ht: 5-11 7/8 | Wt: 186 | 40: 4.61 | Arm: 30 3/4 | Hand: 9

History: Has a one-year-old son named Jadyn. Prepped at Louisville (Ky.) Trinity High, where he won three state football championships and another in basketball. Holds the state record with 280 career receptions. Was considered the best player in Kentucky, as well as the highest rated recruit ever to sign with UL (had offers from Alabama, Ohio State, and Oregon, amongst others). Also ran track, posting a 20.94-second 200 meters, a state record. As a true freshman in 2013, had six catches for 73 yards (12.2-yard average) and zero touchdowns in nine appearances. Had a 30-yard fumble recovery score on special teams. Was cited in May '14 for marijua-

WIDE RECEIVERS

na possession and drug paraphernalia — caught with 39.5 grams of marijuana, a digital scale, and an herb grinder in his apartment. Charges were dropped during fall camp. On the season, played the "Z" in Bobby Petrino's spread system — started all 12 games played, and caught 36-566-3 (15.7), while returning 20 punts for 148 yards (7.4-yard average) and eight kickoffs for 156 yards (19.5-yard average). Was suspended against Boston College (violation team rules). Moved inside in '15, and responded with 39-624-5 (16.0) in 11 games (eight starts). Sprained his right ankle in the season opener against Auburn, and did not play against Houston or Clemson. Started 10-of-13 games in '16, and snagged 45-769-6 (17.1). Had three position coaches in four years. Graduated.

Strengths: Keeps working to uncover when the pocket breaks and is effective improvising on option routes and finding open pockets in coverage. Uses nods and head fakes to sell his routes. Flashes big-play ability.

Weaknesses: Thinly built with short arms and small hands. Lacks long speed. Makes too many concentration drops (see three dropped TDs vs. Virginia). Posted an ordinary 31-inch vertical jump, indicative of average lower-body explosion and athletic ability. Questionable football instincts and awareness — ran out of bounds short of a first down in a 4th-and-12 situation with 40 seconds remaining against Clemson. Executives remain concerned about off-the-field issues and inconsistent production. Recorded a 4.40-second 20-yard shuttle, revealing a lack of hip flexibility that also showed up weaving in the gauntlet drill at the Combine and at times he stumbles re-directing after the catch. Overwhelmed blocker. Limited return skill.

Future: Very thin, underachieving, short-to-intermediate slot receiver with enough route savvy to compete for a role, though case of concentration drops, limited special-value value and off-field transgressions could limit opportunities. Has some legit skill to surprise if the light ever comes on.

Draft projection: Priority free agent.

Scout's take: "(Quick) has ability if you watch him closely at practice. He just doesn't work at it and does not have much production. He is an enigma. There are times he has really good games, and others where he really struggles catching the ball. ... With the drug issues in his background, I don't think we'd consider him."

WR [F] MICHAEL RECTOR, #3 (Sr-5)
STANFORD　　　　　▶ GRADE: 4.90
Ht: 6-0 1/2 | Wt: 193 | 40: 4.44 | Arm: 32 1/2 | Hand: 9 1/4

History: Receiver-cornerback also punted and returned punts as a Washington prep, as well as competed in soccer and track. Redshirted in 2012. Played all 14 games in '13, starting three, and caught 14 balls for 431 yards (30.8-yard average) and three touchdowns. Played all 13 games in '14, starting two, and caught 24-324-2 (13.5). Stepped into the lineup in '15 when he produced 34-559-7 (16.4) in 14 games (13 starts). Was benched for the first half of the season opener against Northwestern (violation team rules). Started all 13 games in '16, and grabbed 32-367-3 (11.5). Added six kickoff returns for 58 yards (9.7-yard average). Had nine career carries for 110 yards (12.2-yard average) and one touchdown. Graduated with a degree in human biology. Opted not to bench press at the Combine.

Strengths: Good straight-line speed. Will compete for the ball in a crowd. Can create some separation on one-cut, intermediate patterns. Willing blocker.

Weaknesses: Has small hands and a small catching radius. Does not easily adjust to the low ball and likes to secure the ball with his body. Unrefined route runner — builds to speed and gathers to cut. Can be fazed by traffic on shallow crossers. Limited creativity and production with the ball in his hands. Scouts have questioned how much he loves football. Lacks special teams' experience.

Future: An intermediate, possession receiver whose redeeming quality is his speed, though it does not consistently reveal itself on tape. Could provide depth in a camp.

Draft projection: Priority free agent.

WR [X] JOSH REYNOLDS, #11 (Sr-4)
TEXAS A&M　　　　　▶ GRADE: 5.44
Ht: 6-2 7/8 | Wt: 194 | 40: 4.54 | Arm: 31 1/2 | Hand: 9 3/8

History: San Antonio, Tex. native. Played receiver, safety, and kicker/punter, as well as competed in basketball and track. Was a qualifier coming out high school, but did not have FBS scholarship options. At Tyler (Tex.) Junior College in 2013, posted 44 receptions for 782 yards (17.8-yard average) and 12 touchdowns. Was aligned wide to the right for the Aggies. Made an immediate impact in '14 — started 11-of-13 games, and caught 52-842-13 (16.2). Gave way to extra tight end in non-starts. Started all 12 games played in '15, and hauled in 51-907-5 (17.8). Was suspended against Western Carolina (violation team rules). Started all 13 games in '16, and totaled 61-1,039-12 (17.0). Did not bench press at the Combine because of a right shoulder injury.

Strengths: Outstanding length. Has a 37-inch vertical jump and uses it to sky for the ball and win 50-50 balls. Competes and concentrates in a crowd. Eats up defenders' cushion with long strides. Extends outside his frame and can make difficult circus catches. Surprisingly loose-hipped for a big receiver and can sink his hips and pop out of his breaks. Has a feel for zone coverage. Outstanding ball skills and wide catching radius were on display at the Senior Bowl, where he showed the ability to separate in one-on-one drills vs. Tre'Davious White. Has been very durable and not missed any time due to injury.

Weaknesses: Relatively small arms for his height. Lacks suddenness off the line and takes time to build speed. Has a lanky build and is too easily knocked off routes. Could benefit from more time in the weight room and needs to improve functional playing strength. Has room to improve as a blocker.

Future: A lanky, athletic, downfield, jump-ball catcher who consistently produced in the clutch and elevated his draft value with a solid Senior Bowl showing. Has the tools to threaten the field vertically and create matchup issues with his length. Could emerge as an eventual starter within a year with continued strength development.

Draft projection: Third- to fourth-round pick.

Scout's take: "(Reynolds) can get bigger and stronger. I was not a big fan of him when I went through the school. I left him in the third (round) for his size and ball skills."

WR [Z] JALEN ROBINETTE, #9 (Sr-4)
AIR FORCE ▶ GRADE: 5.13
Ht: 6-2 7/8 | Wt: 220 | 40: 4.64 | Arm: 32 3/8 | Hand: 10 7/8

History: Prepped in Ohio, where he played football (running quarterback) and basketball and ran track. As a true freshman in 2013, had 16 receptions for 291 yards (18.2-yard average) and three touchdowns in 12 appearances. Became the go-to receiver in Troy Calhoun's multiple attack. Started 11-of-13 games in '14, and caught 43-806-4 (18.7). Started 13-of-14 games in '15, and grabbed 26-641-5 (24.7). Started all 13 games in '16, and hauled in 35-959-6 (27.4). Led the country in yards per catch. On Senior Day, wore "Rowell" on the back of his jersey to honor his mother, Trine Rowell, who had Jalen when she was just a teenager. Completed 3-of-6 career pass attempts (50.0 percent) for 130 yards (21.7-yard average) and three touchdowns.

Strengths: Looks the part with exceptional size and uses it well to shield defenders from the ball. Competes hard for 50-50 balls and catches with defenders draped on his back. Can maintain balance through the process of the catch and is strong with the ball in his hands. Very good sideline awareness. Towering red zone

target. Shows the ability to separate with length at the last moment. Has good passing skill for specialized toss and double passes. Flashes aggression in the run game with the leg drive and finishing strength to bury defensive backs.

Weaknesses: Comes off the ball too upright and takes time to build to speed. Could struggle beating press coverage. Did not run a full route tree in an option offense. Lacks long speed and many of his catches are contested. Recorded a 31 1/2-inch vertical jump, indicative of marginal leaping ability. Bench-pressed 225 pounds only 13 times and needs to improve his strength to beat the jam.

Future: An excellent-sized, college vertical threat lacking ideal speed to separate downfield in the pros. Operated out of a run-first offense that emphasized blocking on the perimeter and can add an element of physicality to the edges. Most ideally suited for a West Coast offense and has a chance to battle for a job as a No. 5 or 6 receiver. Size and blocking ability are best qualities.

Draft projection: Late draftable pick.

WR [Z] DARREUS ROGERS, #1 (Sr-5)
USC ▶ GRADE: 5.05
Ht: 6-1 1/8 | Wt: 216 | 40: 4.89 | Arm: 32 | Hand: 10 1/8

History: His son, Carter, was born in January. Darreus is a Compton, Calif. native. Greyshirted in 2012. As a true freshman in '13, started 4-of-11 games played (two as a third receiver, two in place of the injured Marquise Lee), and recorded 22 catches for 257 yards (11.7-yard average) and zero touchdowns. Sprained his right ankle against Boston College, and sat out three games. In '14, tallied 21-245-4 (11.7) in 13 games (three starts as a third receiver). Started 11-of-12 games at split end in '15, and grabbed 28-289-3 (10.3). Strained his left hamstring against Arizona State — sat out against Washington State then re-injured the hamstring against Notre Dame, and sat out against Utah. Started all 13 games at split end in '16, and produced 56-696-4 (12.4). Opted not to run the 40-yard dash at the Combine.

Strengths: Well-built. Aggressive release with enough strength to fend off the jam. Has natural receiving skills, displaying deft body control and clean hand placement to make acrobatic grabs outside his frame. Good concentration in a crowd. Very reliable, strong hands. Has a knack for making back-shoulder catches. Willing blocker flashes physicality.

Weaknesses: Marginal foot speed and has some heaviness in his movement. Struggles to create separation with quickness or route savvy. Recorded a 26 1/2-inch vertical jump,

WIDE RECEIVERS

the lowest of any receiver at the Combine and revealing very little leaping ability. Also tied for fewest bench-press reps (8) among receivers at the Combine and could stand to improve strength. Limited career production. Inconsistent effort as a blocker.

Future: A much better football player than athletic tester, Rogers will be challenged by the speed of the NFL game, yet could find a place in the league as a physical, sure-handed, slot receiver capable of getting positioning. Has make-it qualities.

Draft projection: Priority free agent.

WR [F,X] / PR FRED ROSS, #8 (Sr-4)

MISSISSIPPI STATE   ▶ GRADE: 5.23
Ht: 6-0 3/4 | Wt: 213 | 40: 4.53 | Arm: 31 1/4 | Hand: 9 1/4

History: Parade All-American from Texas, where he totaled 185 receptions for 2,929 yards (15.8-yard average) and 36 touchdowns his last two high school seasons. As a true freshman in 2013, caught nine receptions for 115 yards (12.8-yard average) and zero touchdowns in 11 appearances. Sat out the last two games because of a broken collarbone. Played all 13 games in '14, starting one, and tallied 30-489-5 (16.3). In '15, set the MSU single-season catches record — started all 13 games at the "H" (slot) position, and produced 88-1,007-5 (11.4). Sat out '16 spring practice (groin surgery). In the fall, garnered first-team All-Southeastern Conference recognition (Coaches) for the second straight year after catching 72-917-12 (12.7) in 13 starts (worked inside and outside). Returned 38 career punts for 315 yards (8.3-yard average), including one touchdown. His 199 career receptions and 2,528 career receiving yards are school records. Had six career rushes for 87 yards (14.5-yard average) and one touchdown. Also completed three passes for 60 yards and a score. Earned his human sciences degree. Calf tightened after first 40-yard dash at the Combine.

Strengths: Good balance and body control. Crafty route runner capable of sinking his hips and popping out of breaks with little wasted motion. Uses stems and nods to uncover and works back to throws. Makes some spectacular, one-handed snags to off-target throws (see Arkansas). Good vision in the open field and is deceptively nifty with the ball in his hands. Effective punt returner. Lined up inside and outside and can play multiple spots. Solid career production in the Southeastern Conference.

Weaknesses: Has small, inconsistent hands. Struggles escaping press coverage (see Alabama) and could improve upper-body strength. Bench-pressed 225 pounds only 10 times at the Combine and needs to get stronger. Lacks elite

burst and top-end speed and takes time to build speed. Lacks a top gear to take the top off the defense. A fair number of catches are contested.

Future: A refined, possession target capable of becoming an effective No. 4 option, lining up as a slot or flanker and making a living in the short-to-intermediate passing game piercing zones. Punt return skills add to his value.

Draft projection: Fourth- to fifth-round pick.

WR [X,F] / RS JOHN ROSS, #1 (Jr-4)

WASHINGTON   ▶ GRADE: 6.34
Ht: 5-10 3/4 | Wt: 188 | 40: 4.22 | Arm: 31 1/2 | Hand: 8 3/4

History: Long Beach, Calif. native starred as a receiver, cornerback, and kick returner in high school. Also ran track, posting a 10.66-second 100 meters. Recruited to Washington by then-head coach Steve Sarkisian, Ross played the slot as a true freshman in 2013 — caught 16 balls for 208 yards (13.0-yard average) and one touchdown, while returning 31 kickoffs for 720 yards (23.2-yard average), including one score. Added four punt returns for 21 yards (5.3-yard average). Played hurt as a sophomore. Started 7-of-13 games played in '14 — three at receiver, final four at cornerback out of necessity — and recorded 17-371-4 (21.8) receiving; 16 tackles, one pass breakup, and one interception; and 38-938-2 (24.7) on kickoff returns. Tore his right meniscus against Illinois, and did not play against Georgia State, then had postseason microfracture surgery. Tore his left ACL and meniscus the following spring, sidelining him in '15. Broke out in '16 — lined up outside and inside, and posted 81-1,150-17 (14.2) receiving with 17-411-1 on kickoff returns in 14 games (12 starts). Was the Huskies' offensive MVP. Had 20 career rushes for 195 yards (9.8-yard average) and two touchdowns. Ross' four kickoff return touchdowns are a school record. Scheduled for labrum surgery on his right shoulder on March 14th and was a medical exclusion from the bench-press test. Did not run shuttles after calf tightened.

Strengths: Rare explosiveness and top-end speed to close cushion and gain steps of separation vertically, as evidenced in a Combine-best 4.22-second 40-yard dash time that stands as the best ever recorded. Accelerates to top-end speed instantly and knows how to set up routes with stems and stutter steps to open the hips of defenders. Understands zone coverage and where to settle in soft spots. Can convert short catches into explosive big plays. Fearless working across the middle. Outstanding body control and in-air adjustments. Tracks the deep ball very easily. Dynamic with the ball in his hands with excellent vision and has eight career

WIDE RECEIVERS

return TDs. Weapon on reverses, jet sweeps and screens. Extremely determined and focused. Unselfish team player with great humility.

Weaknesses: Lacks ideal length with a thin frame that has been prone to injury, and long-term durability should be a consideration. Has a small catching radius and does not consistently highpoint the ball or attack it in the air. Could stand to refine the depths of his routes and become a more precise route runner. Underpowered blocker lacking the stature to sustain blocks.

Future: A dynamic playmaker in multiple phases of the game, Ross is a threat to score every time he touches the ball and will bring a game-changing presence to an offense and return game. Injury history is concerning given the rare speeds he travels with such a narrow frame, though Ross is extremely tough and shown he will battle through injuries. An instant-impact, big-play weapon.

Draft projection: Top-15 pick.

Scout's take: "Ross is a better athlete with more explosion and twitch than (Browns 2016 1st round pick [15]) Corey Coleman."

WR [F] TRAVIS RUDOLPH, #15 (Jr-3)
FLORIDA STATE ▶ GRADE: 5.13
Ht: 5-11 3/4 | Wt: 189 | 40: 4.63 | Arm: 31 7/8 | Hand: 9 1/4

History: Multiple recruiting services rated him the No. 1 receiver recruit in the country coming out of Florida, where he was coached by former NFL quarterback Steve Walsh. Also ran track. Had his left foot surgically repaired before joining the Seminoles. Was the team's No. 2 receiver by the end of his true-freshman season in 2014 — started 6-of-13 games at the "Z," and recorded 38 catches for 555 yards (14.6-yard average) and four touchdowns. Moved to the "X" in '15 when he started 11-of-13 games, and caught 59-916-7 (15.5). Non-starts went to Kermit Whitfield. In late August '16, generated one of the best 'feel-good' stories of the sports year. While visiting a local school, Rudolph sat down to eat lunch with an autistic boy who was alone in the cafeteria. A picture capturing the moment brought the boy's mother to tears, as she called Rudolph a 'hero' in an accompanying Facebook post which went viral. Missed time during fall camp (hamstring), but was FSU's leading receiver for the second straight season — played outside and inside, and posted 56-840-7 (15.0) (including 13 grabs for 238 yards against Wake Forest) in 13 starts.

Strengths: Enters the middle of the field with confidence, catches on contact and runs through some arm tackles. Surprisingly strong for his size with good balance. Flashes a strong

stiff arm. Urgent with the ball in his hands. Excellent adjusting over his shoulder and can make difficult grabs with strong and dependable hands. Solid production. Competitive, aggressive blocker.

Weaknesses: Very stiff stride with tight hips very noticeable weaving in the gauntlet drill. Recorded the slowest 10-yard split (1.72 seconds) and 20-yard split (2.78) of any receiver at the Combine, indicative of very marginal burst and acceleration. Ordinary leaping ability, confirmed by 31 1/2-inch vertical jump, and often lets the ball come to him instead of attacking it in the air. Recorded a 4.46-second 20-yard shuttle, revealing limited hip flexibility and natural bend.

Future: A better football player than tester, Rudolph lacks ideal physical traits for the pro game and projects to the slot. A competitive gamer who will endear himself to coaches and be difficult to cut. Ability to factor on special teams could determine his roster fate.

Draft projection: Late draftable pick.

WR [Z, F] / KR ARTAVIS "TAY" SCOTT, #3 (Jr-3)
CLEMSON ▶ GRADE: 5.13
Ht: 5-10 1/8 | Wt: 193 | 40: 4.63 | Arm: 31 | Hand: 9 3/8

History: Also competed in track and field as a Florida prep. Had behavior/temper-related issues during his youth — Artavis' mother 'suspended' him for an entire grade-school season, and he also 'earned' benchings as a high-school underclassman. Explained his coach Bob Hudson in the Tampa Bay Times: "We had to wrestle with it. ... It wasn't, like, uncontrollable. ... Tay is one of the most competitive people I've ever been around, and that competitive spirit would just come out in different ways." Worked inside and outside for the Tigers. Led the team in catches as a true freshman in 2014 — played all 13 games, starting six, and produced 76 receptions for 965 yards (12.7-yard average) and eight touchdowns. Started all 15 games in '15, and racked up 93-901-6 (9.7) despite tearing his right meniscus midway through the season against Miami (put off surgery until December). Started all 15 games for the '16 national champs, and contributed 76-614-5 (8.1), in the process breaking Sammy Watkins' career receptions record (245). Returned 39 career kickoffs for 925 yards (23.7-yard average) and 22 career punts for 114 yards (5.2-yard average). Had 18 career carries for 49 yards (2.7-yard average) and one score. Earned his communication studies degree in three years, and was the first third-year junior to participate in the Senior Bowl.

Strengths: Strong-handed to fight off press coverage. Very tough competitor willing to work through the middle of the field. Battles for the ball in traffic. Runs hard upfield after the catch and plays with urgency. Good run strength after the catch, with an outstanding second-effort surge. Plays faster than his timed speed with the ball in his hands — good competitive playing speed. Uses his body well to shield defenders from the ball. Tenacious blocker. Has return experience.

Weaknesses: Marginal size. Slow rolling off the line. Very tight hips, as confirmed by 4.50-second 20-yard shuttle time at the Combine. Consistent body-catcher. Recorded a 31-inch vertical jump, revealing modest lower-body explosion and athletic ability. Limited run-after-the-catch creativity and burst. Benefitted from a very strong supporting cast.

Future: Tight-hipped, tough, highly competitive body-catcher with the strength and determination to work underneath routes out of the slot where he will be able to release more cleanly. Has a special team's mentality, and his best chance to carve a niche could be as a core contributor.

Draft projection: Late draftable pick.

WR [Z] JUJU SMITH-SCHUSTER, #9 (Jr-3)
USC ▶ GRADE: 5.97
Ht: 6-1 3/8 | Wt: 215 | 40: 4.56 | Arm: 32 7/8 | Hand: 10 1/2

History: Added Schuster to his last name when he turned 18 to honor his stepfather. Highly recruited out of Long Beach (Calif.) Poly. Chose USC in order to remain close to home and his local church. Played opposite Nelson Agholor (Eagles) as a true freshman in 2014, producing 54 receptions for 724 yards (13.4-yard average) and five touchdowns in 13 games (12 starts). Started all 14 games at flanker in '15, and racked up 89-1,454-10 (16.3). Broke the fourth metacarpal bone in his right hand against Cal, requiring surgery, but did not miss a game. Sprained his left ankle three weeks later against Oregon. Sprained a toe on his right foot early in '16 fall camp then dealt with back pain during the season, but started all 13 games at flanker, hauling in 70-914-10 (13.1). Fought a cold leading up to the Rose Bowl against Penn State. Had eight career carries for 34 yards (4.3-yard average) and zero touchdowns, and returned 16 career kickoffs for 185 yards (11.6-yard average). Does not turn 21 until November. Opted not to run shuttles at the Combine.

Strengths: Thickly built and muscular. Powers off the line and outmuscles defensive backs. Continues working to uncover on broken plays and presents a huge target. Exceptional catching radius with very good body control and ball skills to attack it in the air. Extremely competitive, plays with confidence and carries a swagger. Plays bigger than his size and consistently wins 50/50 balls. Catches on contact. Strong and physical after the catch and powers through arm tackles. Fearless working across the middle. Consistently works back to the ball and uses leverage and positioning to shield defenders. Passionate about the game.

Weaknesses: Lacks explosive, top-end speed and is not a blazer. Recorded a 32 1/2-inch vertical jump indicative of average leaping ability. Has a tendency to drift in his routes and round off breaks. Is not a precise route runner and could stand to do a better job of selling his routes and avoid freelancing. Inconsistent effort as a blocker — throttles down on the backside and needs to become more consistent. Overly emotional and can be demonstrative when the ball is not consistently being delivered his way. Reportedly involved in fights at practice following opening loss to Alabama and emotions often get the best of him.

Future: Big, strong, physical power receiver with the toughness, competitiveness and run-after-the-catch ability to contribute immediately and emerge as an impact flanker in a West Coast offense. Will readily compete for a No. 2 possession role, with the fire in his belly to emerge as a No. 1.

Draft projection: Top-40 pick.

Scout's take: "(Smith-Schuster) is a (second-rounder). He doesn't run that well. … He wears his emotions on his sleeves. He has some diva in him, but it usually comes across constructively. He's extremely competitive and hates to lose, and it gets him in trouble sometimes."

WR [X] JAMARI STAPLES, #2 (Sr-4)
LOUISVILLE ▶ GRADE: 5.24
Ht: 6-2 7/8 | Wt: 195 | 40: 4.51 | Arm: 33 1/2 | Hand: 9 1/2

History: Jamari's mother, Ametrice, died in a car accident when he was seven. Prepped in Alabama. Began his college career at Alabama-Birmingham, where he played "X" and "Z." Started 8-of-10 games played in '13, and recorded 31 catches for 458 yards (14.8-yard average) and four touchdowns. Sat out two November contests while nursing a high right ankle sprain. Played nine games in '14, starting four, and grabbed 9-190-1 (21.1). Sat out against Alabama A&M (high left ankle sprain) then missed two November contests while recovering from a concussion. Transferred to UL when the UAB program was shut down. Lost his best friend in a car accident in June '15. Primarily an outside receiver for the Cardinals. Missed the first month of the season (torn right MCL), but started 7-of-9 games played, and contributed 37-638-3 (17.2). Hurt his shoulder against Pittsburgh, and managed just two catches the last two games of the year. Started 11-of-12 games played in '16, and caught 36-615-2 (17.1). Missed the Kentucky contest because of a concussion then sustained another concussion at the Senior Bowl. Opted not to bench or run shuttles at the Combine.

Strengths: Very good height and arm length with a giant 78 7/8-inch wingspan. Continues working to uncover when the pocket breaks down and finds open throwing lanes. Recorded a 10'8" broad jump and 36-inch vertical jump, and explosive leaping ability translates to the field. Highpoints the ball and flashes playmaking ability. Good body control to contort his body in the air and pluck the ball out of the sky. Good practice habits and is coachable. Example leader.

Weaknesses: Has a narrow frame that looks nearly maxed out. Below-average initial get-off speed, as confirmed by 1.62-second 10-yard split time. Choppy route runner. Did not catch the ball naturally at the Combine. Takes some awkward hits given his length and leaping ability and needs to become a stronger traffic player to consistently secure contested grabs. Average career production. Lacks physicality as a blocker. Has had a history of injuries and concussion history warrants closer attention.

Future: High-hipped, lean, leggy, long-levered glider with build-up speed to stretch the field and the length and ball skills to mismatch NFL defensive backs. Will need to continue refining his routes and learning how to diagnose coverage to earn more than a no. 4 role in the pros.

Draft projection: Fourth- to fifth-round pick.

Scout's take: "Staples did not come into the year as publicized as the other receiver (James Quick). (Staples) is the one who makes a lot of their big plays."

WR [Z, F] ArDARIUS STEWART, #13 (Jr-4)

ALABAMA ▶ GRADE: 5.59

Ht: 5-11 1/8 | Wt: 204 | 40: 4.49 | Arm: 32 1/2 | Hand: 9 3/8

History: Has a son. Alabama native played quarterback, receiver, running back, and safety in high school. Scored 52 touchdowns his senior season. Redshirted in 2013. Played 13 games in '14, drawing two starts, and grabbed 12 receptions for 149 yards (12.4-yard average) and zero touchdowns. Did not play against Auburn ("stretched knee ligaments"). In '15, started all 15 games at flanker, and produced 63-700-4 (11.1) for the national champs. Played "X" and slot in '16 when he totaled 54-864-8 (16.0) in 12 starts. Combined for 18-283-4 in November contests against Mississippi State and Auburn. Also completed two passes for 36 yards.

Sprained his left knee against Ole Miss, and did not play against Kent State or Kentucky; was suspended against Chattanooga (violation team rules); and was a non-factor in the playoff game against Washington (pulled muscle). Had 13 career carries for 82 yards (6.3-yard average) and zero touchdowns, and returned 10 career kickoffs for 191 yards (19.1-yard average). Opted not to bench and did not run shuttles at the Combine because of a groin injury.

Strengths: Physical fending off the jam. Fights for the ball in traffic and is strong at the catch point. Very good field awareness — understands situational football. Ran a full route tree. Good run strength after the catch. Aggressive clearing out defensive backs when the ball is being run his way and keeps working downfield as a blocker on broken plays. Latches on and finishes blocks. Good football intelligence. Has return skill, passing talent and wildcat experience, and versatility is a plus.

Weaknesses: Lacks elite speed to threaten the field vertically and pull away from defenders and does not consistently separate down the field. Average elusiveness after the catch. Recorded a 1.64-second 10-yard split at the Combine, indicative of marginal initial quickness and short-area burst. Can be slow getting off spots and a lot of catches are contested. Takes some plays off as a backside blocker.

Future: Converted prep wildcat quarterback with the toughness, physicality, football smarts and versatility to contribute readily in the pros. Could emerge as a solid No. 2 receiver and skill set is most optimally suited for a flanker role in a West Coast offense.

Draft projection: Second-round pick.

Scout's take: "(Stewart) received a second-round grade from (the underclassmen advisory panel). He could still land there. I won't be surprised if he slides a round. He's still rough around the edges."

WR [F] / PR RYAN SWITZER, #3 (Sr-4)

NORTH CAROLINA ▶ GRADE: 5.28

Ht: 5-8 1/2 | Wt: 181 | 40: 4.49 | Arm: 28 | Hand: 9 1/4

History: Engaged to Gabie, who was a Tar Heels cheerleader. Decorated high school running back from West Virginia, where he piled up 8,100 all-purpose yards and 103 career touchdowns. Sustained a concussion in the season opener of his senior season. A Parade All-American and two-time state player of the year, Switzer also won a basketball state title, and was part of state championship 4x100 and 4x200 relay teams. Best 100 meters was 11.17 seconds. As a true freshman in 2013, caught 32 balls for 341 yards (10.7-yard average) and three touchdowns in 13 games. However, put himself on the national radar as a punt returner: returned 24 punts for 502 yards (20.9-yard average), including five touchdowns (all in the final five games), which tied an NCAA record. Started 9-of-13 games in '14, and posted 61-757-4 (12.4) with 37-172-0 (4.6) returning punts. Was knocked out of the regular season finale versus NC State with a torso/abdominal injury resulting from an illegal hit. Switzer, who called the play a "cheap shot," was taken to the hospital for precautionary reasons, and was not back to full speed for two weeks. Started 9-of-14 games in '15, and totaled 55-697-6 (12.7) receiving with 22-302-2 (13.7) returning punts. In '16, set a UNC single-season receptions record, and was the Tar Heels leading receiver for the third straight season — started 12-of-13 games (gave way to "22" personnel against Virginia), and punctuated his career with 96-1,112-6 (11.6) receiving and 16-106-0 (6.6) returning punts. In back-to-back wins over Pittsburgh and Florida State, totaled 30 grabs for 366 yards. Recorded 25 career carries for 82 yards (3.3-yard average) and zero touchdowns, and completed 3-of-5 pass attempts for 105 yards (21.0-yard average) and two scores. Had 12 career fumbles. His 244 career receptions and 2,907 receiving yards are school records. Graduated with a degree in exercise and sport science.

Strengths: Excellent agility to win at the line of scrimmage, as confirmed by tying with the fastest 20-yard shuttle (4.00 seconds) of any receiver at the Combine. Instinctive finding soft holes in zones and snapping out of his breaks to uncover. Runs crisp routes at precise depths and can be trusted in critical situations. Sacrifices his body in traffic and shows a healthy disregard for his body with the ball in his hands, especially as a returner early in his career. Extremely confident.

Weaknesses: Poor size. Has small hands and needs to do a better job of securing the ball (12 fumbles). Measured the shortest arms of any player at the Combine and also had the shortest wingspan (68 inches) of any receiver at the event, creating a small catching radius. Has a 32-inch vertical jump, revealing marginal leaping ability. Came across as arrogant in team interviews and scouts have questioned whether he is a team player. Gets discarded easily as a blocker.

Future: A quicker-than-fast, dynamic slot receiver who showed special skills as a punt returner early in his career, Switzer has shown improvement every year of his career and will continue grinding away until he earns a starting job in the slot in the pros. Offers the most immediate value as a punt returner, though must prove he can stay healthy. Lack of size could

challenge an inaccurate quarterback.

Draft projection: Fifth- to sixth-round pick.

WR [F] TAYWAN TAYLOR, #2 (Sr-4)
WESTERN KENTUCKY ▶ GRADE: 5.39
Ht: 5-11 | Wt: 203 | 40: 4.52 | Arm: 32 5/8 | Hand: 9 ¼

History: Kentucky native. As a true freshman in 2013, recorded 24 receptions for 270 yards (11.3-yard average) and zero touchdowns in 11 games (seven starts). Did not play against Army (left wrist). Started 7-of-13 games in '14, and caught 45-767-7 (17.0). As an upperclassman, stacked the two most prolific receiving seasons in school history. Played all 14 games in '15, starting five, and produced 86-1,467-17 (17.1). Broke his own single-season marks in '16 by amassing 98-1,730-17 (17.7) in 14 starts. In the last two seasons, racked up NCAA-best 46 plays of 25-plus yards, including 15 that went for at least 50 yards. Owns school records for receptions (253), receiving yards (4,234) and touchdowns (41). Team captain.

Strengths: Exceptional quickness, registering a 4.01-second 20-yard shuttle time and 6.57-second 3-cone drill time indicative of exceptional hip flexibility, balance and burst. Makes speed cuts at top gear and can create separation with quickness. Catches the ball cleanly outside his frame. Explosive big-play weapon. Outstanding career production. Has return experience.

Weaknesses: Has small inconsistent hands and had 8 drops in 2016. Lacks strength and physicality and can be knocked off routes and pushed around as a blocker. Is still learning how to sharpen his routes. Lacks top-end speed and can be tracked down from behind (see Alabama). Needs to learn to secure the ball better in the open field. Was immature early and relied too much on his natural talents.

Future: A very agile, dynamic football player with the receiving skills, hand quickness and competitiveness to compete for a No. 3 job in the slot readily.

Draft projection: Third- to fourth-round pick.

Scout's take: "(Taylor) is sudden, quick and has good hands. He ran better than I was expecting at the Combine. I can see him possibly sneaking into the third round."

WR [F]/PR TRENT TAYLOR, #5 (Sr-4)
LOUISIANA TECH ▶ GRADE: 5.19
Ht: 5-8 | Wt: 181 | 40: 4.63 | Arm: 28 3/4 | Hand: 8 1/4

History: Louisiana native won a pair of state championships at Evangel Christian Academy. Also competed in basketball, tennis, and track. Louisiana Tech was his only offer, as his high school coach convinced then-head coach Sonny Dykes that Taylor was similar to Wes Welker,

WIDE RECEIVERS

who Dykes coached at Texas Tech. Excelled as a slot receiver for the Ragin' Cajuns. As a true freshman in 2013, had 28 catches for 260 yards (9.3-yard average) and two touchdowns. Started 9-of-14 games in '14, and produced 64-834-9 (13.0). Started 12-of-13 games in '15 (gave way to fullback and tight end against North Texas), and racked up 99-1,282-9 (12.9). Led the country in receiving yards in '16 when he exploded for 136-1,803-12 (13.3) in 14 starts. Kicked an extra point on Senior Day. His combined production with Carlos Henderson (3,338 yards) is an NCAA single-season record. Taylor's 327 receptions are most in school history. Had 58 career punt returns for 482 yards (8.3-yard average). Has seven career fumbles. Team captain.

Strengths: Good football instincts and awareness. Extremely effortful and sells out to make plays. Terrific competitor and runs hard with the ball in his hands and can string a few moves together and make tacklers miss. Very good separation quickness, as confirmed producing the second-fastest 20-yard short shuttle (4.01 seconds) of any player at the Combine. Also paced all receivers with the fastest 3-cone drill time (6.57), revealing superb short-area burst and balance. Very good weight-room worker who can squat nearly three times his weight. Exceptional college production. Has punt-return experience.

Weaknesses: Very small-framed with extremely short arms and is tied for having the smallest hands of any player at the Combine. Marginal timed speed. Small downfield target. Must improve ball security. Lacks ideal strength to be match up with many defensive backs.

Future: A very tiny slot receiver with the quickness, agility and competitive fire to push for a backup slot job in the pros. Best chance to earn a roster spot will likely come as a punt returner. Could emerge as a functional contributor with a few years of seasoning.

Draft projection: Seventh-round pick.

WR [F] NOEL THOMAS, #5 (Sr-4)
CONNECTICUT ▶ GRADE: 5.07
Ht: 6-0 1/2 | Wt: 205 | 40: 4.58 | Arm: 30 | Hand: 8 3/4

History: Coach's son. Connecticut native. As a true freshman in 2013, had three catches for 32 yards (10.7-yard average) and zero touchdowns in five late-season appearances. In '14, recorded 26-305-4 (11.7) in 12 games (five starts at wide receiver). Started 12-of-13 games in '15, and caught 54-719-3 (13.3). Set a school single-season receptions record in '16 by piling up 100-1,179-3 (11.8) in 12 starts. Had 18 career rushes for 82 yards (4.6-yard average) and zero touchdowns. Opted not to run shuttles at the Combine.

Strengths: Competes for the ball in a crowd

and makes acrobatic, in-air adjustments to off-target throws. Versatile and has lined up inside and outside. Good football IQ. Solid improving production. Has been a 4-phase, core special teams' contributor.

Weaknesses: Very small hands and short arms. Unpolished route runner — releases upright and rounds off his breaks with extra steps, flashing indicators to defensive backs. Does not play fast. Lacks creativity to make defenders miss after the catch. Allows the ball into his body too much. Bench-pressed 225 pounds only nine times at the Combine and needs to get stronger to help ward off press coverage. Recorded 16.5% body fat at the Combine, indicative of a lack of endurance. Underpowered blocker. Has produced only 10 career TDs.

Future: Good-sized, slot receiver lacking the release strength, route savvy, competitive speed and conditioning needed to make a living manning the slot. Practice squad candidate.

Draft projection: Priority free agent.

WR [F] / QB GREG WARD, #1 (Sr-4)
HOUSTON ▶ GRADE: 5.01
Ht: 5-10 3/4 | Wt: 186 | 40: 4.60e | Arm: 31 1/8 | Hand: 9 7/8

History: Preacher's son. Texas native was one of the state's most productive prep players. Played receiver as a sophomore before starring as a quarterback — threw for 7,800 yards and 71 touchdowns, and ran for 2,075 yards and 31 touchdowns as an upperclassman. Was a utility man during his 2013 true-freshman season, as he worked as a backup quarterback, receiver, and punt returner — completed 19-of-29 pass attempts (65.5 percent) for 310 yards with one touchdown and zero interceptions in 10 appearances. Also had 10 receptions for 95 yards (9.5-yard average) and one touchdown. In '14, started 12-of-13 games — first four at "Z' receiver, final nine at quarterback — and recorded 15-139-1 (9.3) receiving and 177-263-2,010-12-7 (67.3) passing. Was the full-time quarterback his last two years. Started 13-of-14 games in '15, and produced 232-345-2,828-17-6 (67.2), including an MVP performance against Florida State in the Peach Bowl. Sprained his left ankle against Memphis, and did not start against UCONN (forced into the game on the last drive of 20-17 loss). Broke or tied 17 records. Set UH single-season rushing touchdowns record (21), and joined Deshaun Watson as the only quarterbacks to pass for 2,000 yards and run for 1,000. Despite hurting his right (throwing) shoulder in the '16 season opener against Oklahoma — played hurt the rest of the season — led the American Conference in passing (296.4 yards per game) and total offense (339.6 yards

69

per game). Passed 319-469-3,557-22-13 (68.0) in 12 starts. Received "constant maintenance treatment," according to head coach Tom Herman; sat out against Lamar (MRI revealed no structural damage); and aggravated the injury against Tulane in November. In his career, ran the ball 558 times for 2,375 yards (4.3-yard average) and 39 scores (school record), including 16 games with at least 80 yards on the ground. Had 11 career punt returns for 69 yards (6.3-yard average). Had 22 career fumbles. Finished third in school history behind Case Keenum (Rams) and Kevin Kolb (Eagles '07 second-rounder) with 11,080 yards of total offense. Team captain went 27-5 as a starting quarterback. Opted not to work out at the Combine.

Strengths: Good athlete. Very competitive. Operated behind a mediocre offensive line all season and was forced to improvise and create plays with his feet — flashed playmaking ability. Flashed potential running routes at the NFLPA all-star game. Is physically tough and battled through injury all season. Made a one-handed snag while on the sideline at the NFLPA all-star game and has shown upside as a pass catcher.

Weaknesses: Played quarterback weighing in the 170's with a frame that is susceptible to injury. Poor height for the QB position and will struggle to find open throwing windows. Very limited route-running experience. Not a vocal leader. Very unproven as a receiver.

Future: A quick-footed athlete who showed upside as a slot receiver in limited exposure at the NFLPA game and has a chance to fight for a roster spot and become a functional receiver if he is willing to commit to learning a new position. Developmental project.

Draft projection: Priority free agent.

Scout's take: "I don't know what to do with him. I've seen him light it up (at quarterback), but he's a little guy with a bad throwing motion. He's quick and fast. He's probably a little bit better of a passer than (2016 Seahawks undrafted free agent Trevone) Boykin last year out of TCU."

WR[X]/RS DEDE WESTBROOK, #11 (Sr-5)

OKLAHOMA ▶ GRADE: 5.40

Ht: 5-11 7/8 | Wt: 178 | 40: 4.34 | Arm: 30 5/8 | Hand: 9

History: First name is pronounced "DEE-dee." Has three children: Vincent, Destiny, and Rayleigh. Prepped in Texas, but missed a chunk of his senior season after rupturing his small intestine (was told not to play football again). Did not qualify academically, and did not get back on the field until 2014 at Blinn College (TX), where he primarily played in the slot — reeled in 76 catches for 1,487 yards (19.6-yard aver-

age) and 13 touchdowns in eight games. A split end with the Sooners, Westbrook started all 13 games in '15, catching 46-743-4 (16.2). In '16, was the Biletnikoff winner and Big 12 Offensive Player of the Year, as well as a Heisman and Hornung finalist — totaled 80-1,524-17 (19.1) with nine kickoff returns for 244 yards (27.1-yard average) and five punt returns for 81 yards (16.2-yard average), including a 71-yard score against Kansas. Set an OU single-season record for receiving touchdowns despite not scoring any the first three weeks of the season when he was slowed by a hamstring injury. Did not start against Kansas State — "It was just a team-policy deal," explained head coach Bob Stoops. Sustained a concussion against Oklahoma State. Had 15 career rushes for 118 yards (7.9-yard average) and zero touchdowns. Has a history of alleged domestic incidents. In August '12, was arrested on a family violence charge, but charges were later rejected. In April '13, was arrested for family violence, but the case was dismissed for "inability to locate state's witness"; and in May '16, was arrested for trespassing because of another incident with the same woman. According to the Tulsa World, "The [police] report details a Cameron resident calling police on Westbrook for being on her property. The report says Westbrook was visiting the resident's daughter, but both parties knew Westbrook was not allowed on the property because of a past altercation." Opted not to perform bench-press test at the Combine.

Strengths: Exceptional hands (95-percent catcher) — excellent tracking the deep ball. Great body control and playing speed. Can separate vertically and works back to the ball very well, offering up an easy target for his quarterback. Has a knack for continuing to work free on broken plays and uncovering. Sets up defensive backs with stems, nods and double moves — knows how to open a defender's hips and create separation. Torched Texas (10-232-3) and Texas Tech (9-202-2). Feasted on the play-action passing game and blew the top off defenses. Has vision and competitiveness to produce with the ball in his hands (see bubble screen against West Virginia) and the urgency and balance to run thru weak arm tackles. Willing stalk blocker. Efficient returner.

Weaknesses: Very marginal size with small hands. Rail thin and lacks functional strength to beat press coverage (see Ohio State). Is easily altered at the line of scrimmage and can be fazed by traffic in the middle of the field. Lacks run strength after the catch. Not a precise route runner. Marginal strength as a blocker and is easily discarded. Benefitted from one of the nation's best backfields that frequently drew extra defenders into the box. Is stiff-legged and requires extra stretching at practice. Character and maturity invite closer scrutiny and could require extra maintenance.

Future: Explosive, big-play receiver who put himself on the map with one of the most impactful months of October (40-881-11) in college football history. A natural-handed, silky smooth-striding receiver who must prove he can overcome his size and strength limitations vs. NFL defensive backs and continue maturing to reach his potential.

Draft projection: Third- to fourth-round pick.

Scout's take: "He is probably going to be a little bit underdrafted for the ability that he has. He came into the program at 162 and was 171 (in the fall when I passed through). He has the skinniest legs I have ever seen on a receiver, skinnier than (former Eagles WR) Todd Pinkston. ... He could be a 5th or 6th receiver for us if he has any special teams' ability."

WR [F]/KR **KERMIT WHITFIELD**, #8 (Sr-4)
FLORIDA STATE ▶ GRADE: 5.02
Ht: 5-7 3/4 | Wt: 185 | 40: 4.49 | Arm: 30 | Hand: 8 1/2

History: Nickname "Kermit" comes from his childhood enjoyment of the Muppets. Consensus four-star recruit out of Orlando's Parramore neighborhood. His father, Levonte Sr., was shot and killed in 2006. Levonte Jr. doubled as a track star — captured the state's 3A state championship in the 100 and 200 meters, posting a person-best 10.21 100. Played 12 games as a true freshman in 2013, and had five catches for 89 yards (17.8-yard average) and zero touchdowns. Made his biggest impact on special teams, returning 15 kickoffs for 559 yards (37.3-yard average) and two scores, including a 100-yarder in the BCS National Championship Game against Auburn. Led the nation in kickoff return average, breaking a 59-year-old Atlantic Coast Conference record. In '14, tallied 11-145-0 (13.2) receiving with 32-665 (20.8) on kickoff returns in 14 appearances. Missed time during '15 spring practice with a right hamstring strain. In the fall, produced 57-798-6 (14.0) receiving and 19-507 (26.7) returning kickoffs in 13 games (five starts — three at "Y," two at "X"). Played inside and outside again in '16 — started 7-of-13 games, and totaled 34-395-1 (11.6) receiving and 26-595 (22.9) returning kickoffs. Had 16 career rushes for 148 yards (9.3-yard average) and one touchdown.

Strengths: Very quick off the line and can separate with quickness. Competitive with the ball in his hands and has natural run instincts and top-end speed to be effective on reverses

and open-field runs. Has been very durable despite lack of size. Good eyes, run patience, balance and burst as a kickoff returner and has the long speed to go the distance. Solid showing at the East-West Shrine game.

Weaknesses: Very diminutive stature with small hands and often lets the ball into his body. Lacks savvy as a route runner. Has never been a full-time starter. Modest career receiving production. Breaks few tackles and lacks run strength, as evidenced tying for the fewest bench-press reps (8) of any receiver at the Combine. Undersized, overwhelmed cut blocker. Limited punt return experience.

Future: Small, shifty, short-to-intermediate slot receiver who offers the most immediate value as a kickoff returner. Could warrant late draft consideration as a specialty utility weapon. Most impactful season came in 2015.

Draft projection: Priority free agent.

WR [Z] **MIKE WILLIAMS**, #7 (Jr-4)
CLEMSON ▶ GRADE: 6.11
Ht: 6-3 5/8 | Wt: 218 | 40: 4.57 | Arm: 33 3/8 | Hand: 9 3/8

History: South Carolina native — from a town of less than 200 people. Also played basketball in high school. Played all 13 games as a true freshman in 2013, starting three, and recorded 20 receptions for 316 yards (15.8-yard average) and three touchdowns. Missed four games because of torn ankle ligaments. Started 11-of-13 games in '14, and caught 57-1,030-6 (18.1). Non-starts were games in which the Tigers opened with an extra tight end. In '15, Williams' season ended after 2-20-1 (10.0) in Week One when he suffered a neck fracture. Returned to start all 15 games for the '16 national champs, racking up 98-1,361-11 (13.9). Tweaked his hamstring against Boston College. Sustained a helmet-to-helmet hit in the national championship game against Alabama, but returned to the game. Graduated with a sociology degree. Opted not to run or perform shuttles at the Combine.

Strengths: Rare size, body control and catching radius to extend outside his frame and pluck the ball out of the air. Excellent arm and body length. Very good athlete with the strength to fend off the jam. Has strong hands and the physicality to post up defensive backs, win jumpball situations and create mismatches in the red zone. Feasts on back-shoulder throws. Climbs the ladder and plucks the ball out of the air. Superb tracking and adjusting to the ball in the air. Very good concentration. Functional run strength after the catch. Competitive blocker with the size to cover up defensive backs in the run game.

Weaknesses: Lacks top-end speed to cre-

WIDE RECEIVERS

ate consistent vertical separation and outrun cornerbacks — many of his catches are contested. Mistimes jumps and often catches the ball while descending. Needs to learn how to diagnose coverages. Could stand to improve his route precision and understanding of where the sticks are. Blocking effort could stand to improve — does not dominate in the run game the way he is capable. Injury history must be evaluated carefully.

Future: A big, strong, athletic target with the hand strength, body control and catching radius to contribute readily in the pros and make an inaccurate quarterback look good. Durability has been an issue throughout college and could linger into the pros. Has the length, body control and catching radius to readily emerge as a No. 2 receiver, though lacks the downfield speed and playmaking ability after the catch expected of a true No. 1.

Draft projection: First-round pick.

Scout's take: "(Williams) is a power receiver. He is not a speed guy. He is very productive with great body control and big ol' mitts. He's an ex-basketball guy. He broke his neck (in 2015). That still is a concern."

WR [F] / RS **DONTRE WILSON**, #2 (Sr-4)

OHIO STATE ▶ GRADE: 4.99

Ht: 5-10 1/8 | Wt: 183 | 40: 4.57 | Arm: 30 1/2 | Hand: 9 1/4

History: Was one of the top running backs in Texas, where he also ran track. Played H-back for the Buckeyes. As a true freshman in 2013 (wore jersey No. 2), had 22 receptions for 210 yards (9.5-yard average) and two touchdowns in 14 games (two starts). Ejected from the Michigan game for fighting. In '14, managed 21-300-3 (14.3) in 10 games (three starts). Broke his right foot against Michigan State, and required two surgeries to heal properly. Was suspended for the '15 season opener against Virginia Tech (violation of team rules), and tallied 7-63-0 in nine games (one start). Was a non-factor the second half of the season, in part because he was still bothered by the foot injury (sidelined three games). Played 12 games in '16, drawing two starts, and snagged 27-352-5 (13.0). Did not play in the playoff game against Clemson. Had 65 career rushes for 428 yards (6.6-yard average) and two touchdowns. Returned 53 career kickoffs for 1,280 yards (24.2-yard average) and returned 31 career punts for 243 yards (7.8-yard average).

Strengths: Good athletic ability and body control. Very competitive and has a chip on his shoulder. Functional perimeter runner effective running jet sweeps — shows some creativity in the open field spinning off tacklers and displaying fine run-after-the-catch ability.

Weaknesses: Undersized with small, inconsistent hands. Has never been a full-time starter. Lacks run strength and breaks few tackles. Drifts in his routes and lacks polish. Lacks finishing speed in the return game.

Future: A competitive slot receiver and multi-purpose back slowed by lingering foot injuries early in his career, Wilson saw a reduced role due to the emergence of Jalin Marshall and Curtis Samuel. Could fend for a job as a returner in a camp if he clears medically.

Draft projection: Priority free agent.

Scout's take: "(The coaches) removed him from being the starting punt returner because of fumbles and drops. I don't see him getting drafted."

WR [F] / PR **BOBO WILSON**, #3 (Sr-4)

FLORIDA STATE ▶ GRADE: 5.12

Ht: 5-9 1/4 | Wt: 189 | 40: 4.62 | Arm: 31 3/8 | Hand: 9 3/8

History: Florida native also ran track in high school. As a true freshman in 2013, made three catches for 23 yards (7.7-yard average) and zero touchdowns in 13 appearances. In the summer of '14, was charged with a felony after stealing a scooter. Wound up pleading no contest to misdemeanor petty theft and misdemeanor criminal mischief. Paid restitution, and was sentenced to 30 days jail work camp and one year probation. Served a one-game suspension before starting 7-of-13 games played at the "Y" (slot) spot, catching 42-527-4 (12.5). In '15, was the Seminoles' "Z" receiver — started all 13 games, and caught 58-622-3 (10.7). Had post-season surgery to repair a Jones fracture in his right foot. In '16, started 5-of-8 games played at wide receiver, and recorded 30-390-1 (13.0) before suffering a right foot injury and undergoing season-ending surgery. Returned 44 career punts for 383 yards (8.7), including one untouched, 89-yard score vs. Charleston Southern.

Strengths: Competitive working inside and will catch on contact. Good short-area quickness and burst. Finds open throwing windows and works to uncover. Willing blocker. Good vision setting up blocks in the return game. Physically tough and will play through pain.

Weaknesses: Has some tightness in his hips, as evidenced in slowest 20-yard shuttle (4.58 seconds) of any receiver at the Combine. Tends to catch with his body and cradle-catches too much. Lacks top-end speed to create separation down the field. Marginal durability.

Future: Thinly built, quicker-than-fast slot receiver with the toughness to handle the dirty work inside and compete for a backup job and punt return role.

Draft projection: Priority free agent.

WIDE RECEIVERS

TIGHT ENDS

UNIVERSITY OF ALABAMA

Nawrocki's TOP 10

1. **O.J. HOWARD**
2. **David Njoku**
3. **Evan Engram**
4. **Gerald Everett**
5. **Jordan Leggett**
6. **Bucky Hodges**
7. **Jake Butt**
8. **Jeremy Sprinkle**
9. **Adam Shaheen**
10. **Jonnu Smith**

EDITOR'S NOTE:

Y — Complete, in-line blocker
H — Movement role
F — Slot, receiving role

TE [F] / WR **BILLY BROWN**, #81 (Sr-5)

SHEPHERD (W.V.) ▶ GRADE: 5.16
Ht: 6-3 3/4 | Wt: 255 | 40: 4.71 | Arm: 33 | Hand: 10 3/8

History: Prepped in Maryland. Was recruited by major FBS programs, but didn't qualify academically. Chose Shepherd over junior college, and played "X" receiver for the Division II Rams. As a true freshman in 2012, had 25 receptions for 323 yards (12.9-yard average) and five touchdowns in 11 games (three starts). Tore his left ACL at the end of the season, and was sidelined in '13. Returned to start 9-of-10 games in '14, catching 36-676-6 (18.8). Played part of the season with a cast protecting a torn right thumb ligament. Started all 28 games the next two seasons — totaled 89-1,492-10 (16.8) in '15 for the national runners-up; and 99-1,580-22 (16.0) in '16. Participated in East-West Shrine Game. Will be a 24-year-old rookie.

Strengths: Very good size with long arms and big hands. Presents a big target and competes for the ball in a crowd. Exceptional production. Will battle through injuries.

Weaknesses: Comes off the ball too upright and does not sink his hips and accelerate into his routes. Needs to learn how to use his hands better to avoid the jam. Only shows one gear. Lacks elusiveness to avoid tacklers after the catch. Inconsistent blocking effort — at times looks disinterested. Has not blocked in-line. Regularly matched up against inferior competition and did not stand out at the East-West Shrine game. Has very limited special teams experience. Overaged.

Future: Big-bodied, broad-shouldered, long-limbed college receiver regularly outsized small-school defensive backs and racked up huge production. Must prove he is more than a big fish in a small pond, can adapt to moving from receiver to a detached tight end role and

TIGHT ENDS

learn to become more crafty as a route runner to survive against NFL cover men.

Draft projection: Late draftable pick.

TE [F] **PHARAOH BROWN**, #85 (Sr-5)

OREGON   ▶ GRADE: 5.02

Ht: 6-5 5/8 | Wt: 255 | 40: 4.83 | Arm: 35 5/8 | Hand: 10 3/8

History: Receiver-defensive end also played basketball as an Ohio prep. Recruited to Oregon by then-head coach Chip Kelly. As a true freshman in 2012, had two grabs for 42 yards (21.5-yard average) and zero touchdowns. Suffered a left lower leg injury during '13 fall camp, sidelining him for the first three weeks. On the season, started 5-of-9 games played, and caught 10-123-2 (12.3). Was suspended for the Bowl game against Texas for his role in a snowball fight that got out of hand (pelted uninvolved nearby drivers). In '14, tallied 25-420-6 (16.8) in 10 appearances before suffering a severe, season-ending right knee injury — tore two ligaments and stretched an artery, causing internal bleeding. Redshirted in '15. Returned to start 8-of-9 games played in '16, totaling 33-426-5 (12.9), including 7-129-2 against Arizona State. Did not play against Colorado (ankle) then suffered a hamstring injury against Stanford, and did not play the final two games of the season. In November, The Emerald, a University of Oregon student news source, reported Brown was accused of three acts of violence: "Brown allegedly punched teammate Matt Wogan in the Ducks' locker room in October 2014, rendering Wogan concussed. Eugene Police Department investigated Brown for strangulation in October 2015 following a physical fight with his girlfriend at his apartment. Most recently, Brown allegedly fought former teammate Paris Bostick in the locker room after a verbal dispute during a conditioning session in summer 2016." No charges were filed after the altercation with his girlfriend, who told the Emerald, "I definitely felt like I was an equal part in what happened and maybe even more the reason why it escalated to that point. People are always quick to blame the guy, but sometimes the girl is out of line, too." Opted not to run or jump at the Combine.

Strengths: Very good size with rare arm length and big hands to pluck the ball outside his frame. Limber athlete. Flashes some aggression blocking on the second level and will peel back and pick off defensive backs (see Washington State). Scrappy competitor. Tied for the most bench-press reps (24) among tight ends at the Combine. Can create mismatches in the red zone with his unique length. Measured

an 84 1/2-inch wingspan, the longest of any pass catcher at the Combine.

Weaknesses: Lacks the girth, bulk and functional strength desired as an in-line blocker and weight-room strength does not translate to the field. Too easily knocked off routes and lacks run strength after the catch. Goes down easily. Unpolished route runner lacking precision — tends to drift and gathers to cut. Creates little separation. Not a natural-handed catcher and drops are persistent — hears footsteps and loses concentration. Durability has been an issue — agility was negated following very grossly hyperextended knee injury in 2014. Off-field incidents have been too recurrent and invite questions about ability to fit into a locker room.

Future: A rangy, long-limbed pass catcher showed a promising start at Oregon before injuries and off-field incidents derailed his career. Rebounded as a senior and still possesses enough athletic talent to find a role, though likely will be forced to prove himself as an undrafted free agent.

Draft projection: Late draftable pick.

TE [Y] **JAKE BUTT**, #88 (Sr-4)

MICHIGAN   ▶ GRADE: 5.40

Ht: 6-5 1/2 | Wt: 246 | 40: 4.85e | Arm: 32 | Hand: 10

History: Also played basketball as an Ohio prep. High school teammate of Ohio State offensive lineman Pat Elflein. Recruited to Ann Arbor by then-head coach Brady Hoke. Started 8-of-13 games as a true freshman in 2013, and caught 20 balls for 235 yards (11.8-yard average) and two touchdowns. Tore his right ACL and meniscus during ensuring winter conditioning. In April '14, was cited for public urination — initially denied it, but admitted responsibility and paid a $150 fine. Sat out the '14 season opener and playing just a few snaps in Week Two, but played 10 games, starting five, and recorded 21-211-2 (10.0). Was suspended against Indiana (undisclosed violation team rules). Was the Big Ten Tight End of the Year in '15 — started 11-of-13 games, and produced 51-654-3 (12.8). Won the Mackey Award in '16 after starting all 13 games and hauling in 46-546-4 (11.9), though he tore his right ACL, against Florida State in the Sugar Bowl. Team captain and Senior CLASS Award recipient, graduated with sociology degree. Michigan's all-time leader in receptions (138) and receiving yards (1,646) by a tight end. Was a medical exclusion from the Combine because of right knee injury.

Strengths: Crisp route runner — uses head fakes, jabs and gear change to set up defenders.

TIGHT ENDS

Good body length and body control. Adjusts well to the ball in the air and makes some difficult contested grabs in the red zone. Effective settling into zones on option routes and creating some separation from linebackers. Willing to work across the middle and catch on contact. Urgent turning upfield after the catch and has good run vision to weave through traffic. Willing, get-in-the-way blocker capable of walling off "Sam" linebackers and sealing second-level defenders. Solid football character — humble, unselfish, team player.

Weaknesses: Arms (32 inches) measured the shortest of any tight end at the Combine, with a short 77-inch wingspan. Could stand to add some bulk and improve his core functional football-playing strength to match up against physical, base ends. Not a consistent finisher — allows linebackers to slip off too frequently. Limited body power to barrel through contact and break tackles. Lacks top-end speed and could struggle separating from tight man coverage in the pros. Not a true seam-stretcher. Durability must be evaluated carefully following multiple knee surgeries.

Future: A good-sized, underneath target utilized most effectively on short crossers and drags and capable of contributing in-line or flexed wide. Has potential to emerge as a solid, all-around tight end if he commits to getting stronger and learns to finish in the run game and more aggressively attack the ball in the air. Best traits are his hands, route savvy and short-area receiving skills. Received some second-round grades from scouts during the fall, though uncertainty surrounding knee injury could knock draft value down a round or two and leave him on the PUP list initially as a rookie. Likely will not be back to full health until 2018 and could wind up essentially redshirting as a rookie.

Draft projection: Third- to fourth-round pick.

Scout's take: "I thought he was more of a receiver than a blocker. I put him in the same category with (Denver 2015 third-round pick [92]) Jeff Heuerman."

TE [H] CETHAN CARTER, #11 (Sr-4)

NEBRASKA ▶ GRADE: 5.21

Ht: 6-3 1/4 | Wt: 241 | 40: 4.71 | Arm: 32 3/8 | Hand: 9

History: First name is pronounced "SEETH-un." Played tight end/fullback at Louisiana's Archbishop Rummel, where he won a state championship. Also played basketball. Recruited to Nebraska by then-head coach Bo Pelini. As a true freshman in 2013, started 6-of-13 games, and recorded 10 receptions for

127 yards (12.7-yard average) and zero touchdowns. In '14, started 8-of-9 games played, and grabbed 6-98-1 (16.3). Missed four mid-season contests because of a broken right foot. Missed part of '15 spring practice after having surgery to repair a broken left foot. Was suspended the first two games of the season (undisclosed violation team rules) before starting all 11 games played and catching 24-329-2 (13.7). Started all 10 games played in '16, and posted 19-190-1 (10.0). Sat out three October contests because of a left elbow injury. Will be a 24-year-old rookie. Opted not to perform shuttles at the Combine and his back tightened following the gauntlet drill.

Strengths: Effective on screens and occasional counters, with the lower-body strength and balance to churn through contact. Strong hips to drop his shoulder and run over defenders (see Northwestern and UCLA in 2015). Catches on contact and adjusts in the air to the ball. Plays bigger than his size, runs his legs on contact and flashes ability to generate some push as a move blocker with an angle. Competitive second-level, stalk blocker. Confident and carries a swagger.

Weaknesses: Small-handed and short-armed and lacks ideal bulk to factor in-line in the pros. Shows some hip tightness and overall stiffness in his body as a route runner — does not make sharp cuts or set up defenders in coverage or elude tacklers in the open field. Ran a limited route tree and lacks route savvy. Measured the shortest wingspan (76 1/2 inches) of any tight end at the Combine. Many of his catches are contested and the ball gets on top of him quickly, leading to eight drops in 2016. Could require extra time initially to assimilate a complex playbook. Limited special teams experience.

Future: Aggressive, undersized H-back with the competitiveness and edge desired on special teams, though he has little experience in that phase. Tough football temperament could allow him to earn a roster spot.

Draft projection: Fifth- to sixth-round pick.

Scout's take: "When he was suspended (in 2015), he didn't shut it down. He dominated on the scout team. He's a little rough around the edges in a good way. He's feisty and doesn't back down from a challenge."

TE [F] / WR [Z] DARRELL DANIELS, #15 (Sr-4)

WASHINGTON ▶ GRADE: 5.17

Ht: 6-3 1/4 | Wt: 247 | 40: 4.54 | Arm: 34 1/2 | Hand: 10 1/4

History: First name is pronounced "duh-RELL." Played receiver, safety, and linebacker as a California prep. Recruited by then-head coach Steve Sarkisian, who converted Daniels from receiver to tight end, citing Daniels' similarities to Fred Davis, a former NFL tight end who made the receiver-to-tight end conversion under Sarkisian at USC. Saw special-teams action as a true freshman in 2013, made three tackles in 11 appearances. Transitioned to tight end and played 11 games in '14, drawing four starts, and recording 11 catches for 171 yards (15.5-yard average) and one touchdown. Started 8-of-13 games in '15, and grabbed 19-250-1 (13.2). Played all 14 games in '16, starting six, and caught 17-307-3 (18.1).

Strengths: Has a big frame with outstanding arm length and big hands. Outstanding straight-line speed to create separation in the seam and threaten the field vertically. Catches the ball cleanly and without breaking stride. Competitive stalk blocker —will sacrifice his body. Vocal team leader. Quality special teams contributor as a cover man and gunner on the punt team. Solid NFLPA all-star game showing.

Weaknesses: Just adequate body mass for the TE position and could stand to do a better job of using his body to shield and box out defenders. Tied for the fewest bench-press reps (17) of any tight end at the Combine and has room to get stronger. Has some tightness in his hips and is a bit straight-linish, gathering to cut and bowing when changing direction (extra steps). Could stand to do a better job selling routes and did not run a varied route tree. Was never a full-time starter. Modest career production.

Future: A smooth-striding, straight-line, fast glider with the length, speed and hands to intrigue as a developmental prospect. Must improve his route savvy, blocking technique and football awareness to carve out more than a rotational role in the pros. Special teams could be his ticket.

Draft projection: Fifth- to sixth-round pick.

Scout's take: "I know he has run in the 4.4's (in the past), but he has tight hips, can't drop his weight and has marginal body control. He doesn't help us."

TE [F] / WR [Z] **EVAN ENGRAM**, #17 (Sr-4)

MISSISSIPPI   ▶ GRADE: 6.04

Ht: 6-3 3/8 | Wt: 234 | 40: 4.37 | Arm: 33 1/2 | Hand: 10

History: Prepped in Georgia. Arrived in Oxford weighing 210 pounds, and was used as a flex tight end in Hugh Freeze's system. As a true freshman in 2013, started 6-of-8 games played, and chipped in 21 receptions for 268 yards (12.8-yard average) and three touchdowns. Sustained a high left ankle sprain

against LSU, required surgery, and missed the last five regular-season games. Started all 13 games in '14, catching 38-662-2 (17.4). Started 12-of-13 games in '15, and reeled in 38-464-2 (12.2). Non-start was against Mississippi State (gave way to extra running back). Paced the nation's tight ends in '16 — totaled 65-926-8 (14.2) in 11 starts. Sat out the Egg Bowl against Mississippi State (hamstring). Two-time captain owns Ole Miss tight end records for most catches (162), receiving yards (2,320) and touchdowns (15).

Strengths: Good release quickness off the line. Sinks his hips and accelerates at the top of his routes to create separation. Has a feel for coverage and finding soft spots in zones. Creates mismatches in the slot with his length and has the speed to mismatch linebackers in man coverage. Blazed the fastest 40-yard dash time (4.37 seconds) of any tight end at the Combine, faster than all but three wide receivers, none of whom weighed more than 200 pounds. Tracks the ball well over his shoulder and catches in stride. Can climb the ladder in the red zone and pluck the ball out of the air (see Georgia). Has a 36-inch vertical jump and good leaping ability. Competitive runner after the catch and will run through some defensive backs. Willing, try-hard blocker. Good football intelligence. Respected team leader. Loves football and works at his craft to improve. Registered low 7.1% body fat percentage at the Combine, indicative of exceptional endurance.

Weaknesses: Has a narrow frame that will max out around 240 pounds and lacks the build to be effective blocking in-line. Just adequate playing strength — does not attack the ball in crowds or compete easily for 50-50 balls. Makes some concentration drops in traffic and gets distracted by bodies. Lacks the sand in his pants to anchor or stop a charge.

Future: A quick, athletic receiving tight end who emerged as the team's leading pass catcher as a senior. Similar to Jets' 2008 first-round pick (30th) Dustin Keller, Engram's strong Combine showing enhanced his draft standing and could push him into the first round. Has a rare size-speed ratio and could be a mismatch slot weapon.

Draft projection: Top-40 pick.

Scout's take: "Engram looks like a big receiver. He was 228 when I passed through. Demaryius Thomas and Brandon Marshall look bigger than him. A lot of scouts probably write (Evans) as an 'F' tight end like Jordan Reed. I don't see him that way at all. I think he's really a cross between an X and Z receiver. He's not a true vertical X and he's bigger than your typical Z and can create mismatches. That's where he might wind up."

TE [H, F] **GERALD EVERETT**, #12 (Sr-5)

SOUTH ALABAMA ▶ GRADE: 5.58
Ht: 6-3 | Wt: 239 | 40: 4.61 | Arm: 33 | Hand: 8 1/2

History: Prepped in Georgia, where he was primarily a basketball player while also competing in track (didn't play football until senior year). As a 180-pound receiver, pledged to Bethune-Cookman in 2012. However, he decided he wanted to go to a bigger school. Spent two years at Hutchinson (Kan.) Community College. Returned to the field in '14 for Alabama-Birmingham — caught 17 balls for 292 yards (17.2-yard average) and one touchdown in 12 games (one start). After the program was shut down, transferred to South Alabama, where he started 11-of-12 games in '15, and hauled in 41-575-8 (14.0). Also had four "Wildcat" rushing scores and a seven-yard passing touchdown. Started 11-of-13 games in '16, and totaled a team-leading 49-717-4 (14.6) despite breaking his right pinky finger against Presbyterian (required surgery) in November and played thru the injury the final two games. Suffered a hip injury during Senior Bowl practice. Graduated with a degree in interdisciplinary studies. Aiming to be the first South Alabama player drafted since the program's inception in 2009.

Strengths: Good muscularity and looks the part. Outstanding athlete — fluid strider with graceful movement skill. Very good ball skills and body control to track and adjust to off-target and underthrown balls. Extends outside his frame and can snag the ball out of the air. Has a 37 1/2-inch vertical jump and very good leaping ability. Quick turning upfield and creating after the catch and shows elusiveness making defenders miss in the open field. Capable of stretching the field. Tough competitor who has shown a willingness to play through injury.

Weaknesses: Has extremely small hands, the smallest of any tight end at the Combine. Lacks bulk — is slender and too easily knocked off course. Not a crisp route runner and gives up break points slowing to catch and chopping his steps. Underpowered blocker (needs an angle). Production is padded from regularly facing lesser competition. Was held off the stat sheet in the bowl game against Air Force (though playing through finger injury).

Future: A lean, finesse, flex pass catcher with the athletic ability, ball skills and run creativity to factor readily in the receiving game. Has a lot of upside, though must sharpen his routes and learn to become more competitive as a blocker.

Draft projection: Second- to third-round pick.

Scout's take: "Everett is going to be an H-move guy. He has to be flexed out. He is legit. He is one of the fastest and most athletic, with the best ball skills of the group. He's a lot like (Rams' 1996 second-round pick) Ernie Conwell."

TE [H] **COLE HIKUTINI**, #18 (Sr-5)

LOUISVILLE ▶ GRADE: 5.23
Ht: 6-4 3/8 | Wt: 247 | 40: 4.75e | Arm: 32 3/4 | Hand: 10

History: Last name is pronounced "HICK-a-teen-ie." High school receiver out of California. Began his college career at Sacramento State, where he redshirted in 2012. Played nine games in '13, starting the final four, and posted 21 catches for 204 yards (9.7-yard average) and five touchdowns. With the desire to play at the FBS level, transferred to City College of San Francisco (Calif.), where he recorded 40-658-4 (16.5) in 13 games. Transferred to UL in '15, and snagged 19-348-3 (18.3) in 11 games (three starts). Missed time during '16 spring practice (PCL surgery) then hurt his shoulder in the season opener against Auburn, costing him two-plus games. Rebounded to post very productive senior season from his H-back position, hauling in 50-668-8 (13.4). Was a medical exclusion from the Combine because of right knee injury.

Strengths: Tracks the ball well over his shoulder and climbs the ladder to get it. Catches effortlessly. Effectively works the middle of the field and catches in stride. Understands how to navigate through zones and shield defenders from the ball. Made some strides as a blocker.

Weaknesses: Upright runner after the catch with limited creativity and short-area burst to make defenders miss. Too easily re-routed. Lacks run strength to power through tackles. Marginal blocker with minimal body power. Lacks physicality to play in-line. Only a one-year starter. Durability has been restricting.

Future: Tall, skinny, athletic H-back emerged as a senior and showed fine movement skill, a wide catching radius and enough playmaking ability to contribute in an NFL passing game. Offers little in the way of a blocker and does not have a desirable temperament for special teams, which could limit his chances to earn a roster spot.

Draft projection: Fifth- to sixth-round pick.

Scout's take: "(Hikutini) came out of nowhere this year and caught a (boatload) of balls. Someone will like him as an offset movement guy. I don't think he runs well. He can catch, but he is (very soft) as a blocker."

TIGHT ENDS

TE [F] **BUCKY HODGES**, #7 (Jr-4)

VIRGINIA TECH ▶ GRADE: 5.47

Ht: 6-6 | Wt: 257 | 40: 4.56 | Arm: 32 1/2 | Hand: 10 1/8

History: High school quarterback out of Virginia. Redshirted in 2013. Played all 40 games of his career. Started 10-of-13 games in '14, and recorded 45 catches for 526 yards (11.7-yard average) and seven touchdowns. Was arrested in February '15 for public intoxication. In the fall, caught 40-530-6 (13.3) in 13 starts. Produced 48-691-7 (14.4) in '16 (14 starts). Hodges' 20 career touchdowns tied Heath Miller's Atlantic Coast Conference record for tight ends, and he is the Hokies' all-time leading tight end with a 133-1,747-20 (13.1) career line. Opted not to perform the 3-cone drill.

Strengths: Extremely athletic with a huge frame and giant catching radius. Very good career production. Has big-play speed to threaten the seam and stretch the field vertically. Very good ball skills to locate and snag the deep ball. Recorded a 11'2" broad jump, setting a new Combine record for tight ends and indicating rare lower-body explosion.

Weaknesses: The game does not yet come natural to him — gears down out of his breaks, slows to catch and does not consistently track the deep ball, all confirmed in receiving drills at the Combine. Not creative after the catch. Hand placement can be awkward catching the ball (skillet hands), leading to drops. Looked like a fish out of water in a three-point stance in blocking drills at the Combine, false-stepping with no base — technique will require a lot of refinement.

Future: A converted quarterback still learning the finer points of the game, Hodges has the size and athletic traits to become a mismatch piece in the receiving game. Has a rare size-speed combination and leaping ability to develop into a solid NFL starter with continued refinement, though will require a year of seasoning to emerge.

Draft projection: Second- to third-round pick.

Scout's take: "Hodges has played and been productive since his freshman year. He's 6-6, 255 and can run in the 4.5's. Watch him make plays. They flex him out a lot. How many TE coaches that need a receiving tight end will want a guy (with measurables like his)? He's a lot like Jimmy Graham was coming out."

TE [Y,F] **O.J. HOWARD**, #88 (Sr-4)

ALABAMA ▶ GRADE: 6.21

Ht: 6-5 3/4 | Wt: 251 | 40: 4.56 | Arm: 33 3/4 | Hand: 10

History: Full name is O'Terrius Jabari Howard. Grew up in unincorporated Autauga County, Ala. Two days before he was to begin at football powerhouse Prattville High, state zoning changes forced Howard to attend Autauga Academy, a high school founded in 1969 with the aim of maintaining segregated education. As a junior, was at the heart of a remarkable story when members of the school board discriminated against Howard, directing the headmaster to prevent Howard from bringing his white girlfriend to the prom (ultimately attended with his girlfriend after a community firestorm of outrage and support). Howard was the consensus top-rated tight end recruit in the country. Missed a month of his senior season after suffering a minor left MCL injury in September 2012. Gifted athlete who also starred in basketball and baseball (was considered a Division I-caliber recruit/Major League Baseball prospect). As a true freshman in 2013, had 14 catches for 269 yards (19.2-yard average) and two touchdowns in 13 games (five starts). In '14, caught 17-260-0 (15.3) in 14 games (three starts). In '15, produced 38-602-2 (15.8) in 15 starts, including an MVP performance in the national championship game against Clemson in which he exploded for 5-208-2 (41.6). Was a finalist for the Mackey and senior CLASS awards in '16 when he posted 45-595-3 (13.2) in 15 games (13 starts). Howard did not miss a game during his 57-game career, and was the most productive tight end Nick Saban has coached at Alabama. Graduated with a telecommunications degree.

Strengths: Good body length and catching radius and adjusts easily to the ball. Solid blocking technician in-line and at the second level — understands angles and fits in the run game. Looked like a seasoned veteran in blocking drills at the Combine. Recorded the fastest 10-yard split (1.52 seconds) of any tight end and dominated the shuttles in the TE group, registering the best 20-yard shuttle (4.16 seconds), 60-yard shuttle (11.46) and 3-cone drill (6.85 seconds), demonstrating exceptional balance, burst, flexibility, agility and endurance. Can be dynamic and explosive with the ball in his hands and turn short gains into big plays. Registered 7.7% body fat percentage at the Combine, indicative of exceptional endurance. Stood out at the Senior Bowl. Has a professional approach to the game. Regularly matched up against tough competition in the Southeastern Conference and excelled in all phases. Smart, articulate, humble, team player.

Weaknesses: Lacks bulk and could stand to add some mass to match up better with defensive ends in pass protection and in the run game. Recorded a 30-inch vertical jump at the Combine, among the lowest tight ends at the Combine and indicative of a lack of lower-body strength and explosion. Scouts have raised questions about whether there is enough glass in his diet to avoid coasting.

Future: An athletic, stretch-the-field, playmaking weapon who was underutilized in the passing game as a senior, yet possesses the length, speed, body control and burst to mismatch linebackers and safeties and compete at the point of attack. A safe selection with upside, will only continue to ascend. Profiles as a Day One starter with Pro Bowl potential and could become a better pro than he was a college player in an offense better designed to maximize his seam-stretching, big-play capability.

Draft projection: First-round pick.

Scout's take: "Alabama didn't use him enough, and they know it. It's been a bit of a sore subject there. Lane Kiffin's offense didn't accommodate all of their talent. (Howard) was capable of blowing the roof off defenses and all he ran were a bunch of slants, choice routes, pivots and TE delays — a lot of shallow crossing routes. He is big man who can fly. He can block and he is only going to get stronger — he can be a complete tight end. They just didn't feature him that much."

TE [H] GEORGE KITTLE, #46 (Sr-5)

IOWA ▶ GRADE: 5.28

Ht: 6-3 3/4 | Wt: 247 | 40: 4.54 | Arm: 33 1/8 | Hand: 9 1/4

History: Father, Bruce, was a captain on Iowa's 1982 Rose Bowl team, as well as a coach under Bob Stoops at Oklahoma. Cousin, Henry Krieger-Coble, played for the Hawkeyes before joining the Denver Broncos in 2016. George, who attended three high schools in two states (Iowa, Oklahoma) as a sophomore, was a 200-pound receiver, tight end, safety, and linebacker. Also played basketball as a prep. Jumped at Iowa's last available scholarship. Redshirted in 2012. Played 12 games in '13, starting one, and caught five balls for 108 yards (21.6-yard average) and zero touchdowns. Sat out against Michigan (back spasms). Was fourth on the depth chart in '14, and caught just 1-25-0 (25.0) in 12 appearances. Sat out against Northwestern (ankle). Had his left ankle scoped after the season. Sprained his right MCL in the '15 season opener against Illinois State, and was a non-factor in Week Two against Iowa State. On the season started 6-of-13 games played, catching 20-290-6 (14.5). In '16, recorded 22-314-4 (14.3) in 11 starts. Left the Minnesota contest with an AC joint sprain. Suffered a severe lower right ankle sprain against Purdue — affected him the second half of the season, and sidelined him against Michigan and Illinois. Has his communications degree. Opted not to perform shuttles at the Combine.

Strengths: Aggressive blocker with a physical football-playing temperament. Runs his feet on contact and seeks to bury defenders. Sound technician (leverage, knee bend, balance and hand use) with good finishing strength — plays bigger than his size. Can reach and seal defensive ends on stretch outside zone runs. Recorded a 35-inch vertical jump and 11-foot broad jump, indicative of outstanding lower-body explosion and strength that shows up in the run game. Played in a pro-style offense. Good sideline awareness. Dependable hands. Adjusts well to the ball and catches outside his frame. Clocked as low as a 4.51-second 40-yard dash time and has the speed to stretch the field. Gets upfield fast after the catch. Outstanding weight-room worker — packed on nearly 40 pounds since his arrival. Competitive special-teams performer.

Weaknesses: Has a narrow frame with a linear lower-body build that has been prone to injury throughout his career, and long-term durability needs to be a consideration. Straight-linish with some tightness in his hips (evidenced by weaving in the gauntlet drill at the Combine). Rough route runner — foot pounder with heavy, loud, choppy steps in transition out of his breaks and slows to catch, giving up break points to defenders. Limited career receiving production.

Future: A tenacious blocker with speed to threaten the seam and the competitiveness to seal off defenders in the run game. Could become a solid No. 2 tight end / H-back and would be most ideally suited for an outside stretch-zone running game such as the one used by the Falcons, Seahawks and 49ers. Compares to Seahawks 2013 fifth-round pick Luke Wilson.

Draft projection: Fourth- to fifth-round pick.

Scout's take: "(Kittle) is a high-energy (player). He's self-made, and his body still looks like a receiver. He plays a little bit out of control. I like the way he competes."

TE [F,Y] JORDAN LEGGETT, #16 (Sr-4)

CLEMSON ▶ GRADE: 5.56

Ht: 6-5 1/2 | Wt: 258 | 40: 4.75e | Arm: 33 1/2 | Hand: 10 3/8

History: Prepped in Florida. As a true freshman in 2013, sprained his right MCL during fall camp — sat out two September contests, and wore a brace upon returning. Recorded

TIGHT ENDS

12 catches for 176 yards (14.7-yard average) and two touchdowns in 10 games (one start). Was suspended against Georgia Tech (violation team rules). Started 7-of-11 games played in '14, and managed 14-161-1 (11.5). Tore the meniscus and sprained the MCL in his right knee against Boston College, and did not play against Syracuse. Also sat out the bowl game against Oklahoma after hurting his right knee in practice. Started all 15 games each of the next two years — totaled 40-525-8 (13.1) in '15; and 46-736-7 (16.0) in '16 for the national champs. Two-time Mackey Award finalist. Clemson's all-time leader in receptions (112), receiving yards (1,598), and touchdowns (18) by a tight end. Team captain graduated with Parks, Recreation, Tourism degree. Opted not to run the 40-yard dash at the Combine.

Strengths: Very good size with an athletic frame. Plucks the ball out of the air and can make some very difficult snags outside his frame look easy. Very good body control and ball skills. Efficient route runner. Plays fast with the ball in his hands. Has produced under pressure — caught the game-winning TDs in the 4th quarter vs Florida State and Louisville and has shown he can deliver in the clutch.

Weaknesses: Makes some concentration drops. Not dynamic with the ball in his hands. Stopped running his route on a critical third down midway through the 4th quarter of the national championship against Alabama and competitive fire does not always burn. Coasts too much and effort is hot and cold. Could stand to improve finishing strength and desire as an in-line blocker. Too narrow-based and underdeveloped as a blocker.

Future: Well-built, athletic pass-catcher who showed improvement down the stretch and has the dependable hands, body control, balance and ball skills to make an impact in the receiving game flexed wide, in-line or on the move. Has considerable room for improvement as a blocker and needs to learn how to finish.

Draft projection: Second- to third-round pick.

Scout's take: "(Leggett) is big, fast, athletic and can catch. He is a bigger version of (Redskins TE) Jordan Reed. He is that type of receiver."

TE [Y] DAVID NJOKU, #86 (Soph-3)

MIAMI (FLA.)   ▶ GRADE: 6.16

Ht: 6-4 | Wt: 246 | 40: 4.64 | Arm: 35 1/4 | Hand: 10

History: Last name is pronounced "JOE-koo." One of nine children born to Nigerian parents. Prepped in New Jersey, and was a national champion high-jumper (6 feet, 11 inch-

es). Also competed as a high-jumper for the Hurricanes track and field team. Redshirted in 2014. Played all 13 games in '15, starting four, and caught 21 balls for 362 yards (17.2-yard average) and one touchdown. In Mark Richt's pro-style offense in '16, responded with 43-698-8 (16.2) in 13 games (five starts). Declared for the draft with two years of eligibility remaining and will be a 20-year old-rookie.

Strengths: Solid musculature with extremely long arms. Experienced playing in a pro-style offense. Has a 37 1/2-inch vertical jump and 11'1" broad jump, indicative of rare leaping ability and lower-body explosion that translates to hurdling defenders (see Georgia Tech). Consistently rips through arm tackles and has good run strength. Has explosive big-play ability and can turn short catches into long gains (see Duke, West Virginia). Good speed to separate vertically. Tracks the ball very well downfield and catches with ease over his shoulder and outside his frame. Competitive runner after the catch. Flashes a mean streak. Functional in-line blocker with enough strength to steer and control defensive ends. Very football smart. Registered 6.4% body fat percentage at the Combine, the lowest of any tight end at the Combine, and indicative of a highly conditioned athlete.

Weaknesses: Is not yet a polished route runner and signals break points by leaning and chopping out of his transition. Hip tightness was very noticeable weaving off the line during the Combine gauntlet drills. Lacks bulk needed to survive as an in-line blocker against NFL defensive ends and has much room to improve lower-body strength and leg drive. Has never been a full-time starter and produced modest career receiving production (66-1,060-9). Could not unseat Chris Herndon for a starting role (despite doubling his production in 2016).

Future: Very lean, high-hipped, long, explosive pass catcher who will require a lot of seasoning before he is ready, yet possesses undeniable athletic traits that will pique the interest of NFL teams and could allow him to blossom into a dangerous receiving threat.

Draft projection: First-round pick.

Scout's take: "Njoku is a freak athlete. He's built like Jevon Kearse. He can do it all. He might have the potential to be the most complete tight end to exit in a while. Producing 600+ yards for a tight end is outstanding. I know he's getting beat up for his lack of production in our building, but it's all ahead of him. For a sophomore, he was tearing it up."

TE [Y] **SCOTT ORNDOFF**, #83 (Sr-4)

PITTSBURGH   ▶ GRADE: 5.12

Ht: 6-4 7/8 | Wt: 253 | 40: 4.82 | Arm: 33 1/2 | Hand: 9 5/8

History: Father, Scott, played in the USFL. Pennsylvania native was then-head coach Paul Chryst's first commitment in the class of 2013. As a true freshman, Orndoff recorded six receptions in 50 yards (8.3-yard average) and two touchdowns in nine games (five starts) before suffering a season-ending right knee injury (multiple ligaments). Saw limited action in 10 games in '14, grabbing 4-24-1 (6.0), missing three with a high left ankle sprain. Started 7-of-13 games in '15, and caught 13-244-5 (18.8). Started 11-of-13 games in '16, and produced 35-579-5 (16.5). Gave way to extra receivers in non-starts. Earned his degree in administration of justice.

Strengths: Works across the middle without fear. Good sideline awareness. Quick upfield after the catch and pushes the ball north and south. Solid production in a pro-style offense. Best production came against top opponent in upset victory over national champion Clemson when he caught 9-128-2. Functional, competitive in-line blocker. Plays on his feet with good balance.

Weaknesses: Ordinary short-area burst and acceleration into his routes and out of his breaks, as confirmed by pedestrian 7.43-second 3-cone drill time. Will struggle to separate against man coverage in the pros. Has some tightness in his hips. Hand reactions can be late and the ball gets on top of him quickly, leading to five drops in 2016. Likes to catch with his body. Tied for the fewest bench-press reps (17) and lowest vertical jump (27 inches) of any tight end at the Combine and has room to get stronger. Limited anchor strength.

Future: Lacks ideal physical traits to match up with NFL defensive ends as a blocker, but could fight for a job as a dependable, move-the-chains target, and stick as a No. 3 tight end.

Draft projection: Late draftable pick.

TE [Y] **HAYDEN PLINKE**, #85 (Sr-6)

UTEP   ▶ GRADE: 5.04

Ht: 6-4 1/4 | Wt: 264 | 40: 4.98 | Arm: 32 1/2 | Hand: 10

History: Pronounced "PLINK-ee." Competed in football, basketball, and track (state champion javelin thrower) as an Oregon prep. Greyshirted at Boise State in 2011. Saw limited action in six games in '12, catching 2-20-0 (10.0) while battling through shoulder and knee injuries. Was suspended indefinitely and expelled for undisclosed reasons. Transferred to FCS Portland State for the '13 season — grabbed 3-65-0 (21.7) with 27 carries for 191 yards (7.1-yard average) and one touchdown operating as a wildcat quarterback. Did not play in the season finale (concussion) against Eastern Washington. Transferred to UTEP, and sat out '14 per NCAA transfer rules. Had surgery to repair a hernia before suiting up for the Miners. In '15, started 10-of-11 games played, producing 37-410-0 (11.1). Sprained his right MCL against Rice then broke his left foot against Louisiana Tech, knocking him out of the season finale against North Texas. Started all 12 games in '16, and produced 38-456-8 (12.0). Graduated with a degree in multidisciplinary studies. Turns 25 in December.

Strengths: Has a solid build with a good frame. Very competitive gamer with a competitive football temperament and urgency with the ball in his hands. Plays faster than his timed speed and has adequate competitive speed. Catches the ball naturally and runs hard after the catch. Effortful blocker. Energetic field presence. Has experience in a pro-style offense. Has a love for the game.

Weaknesses: Tight-hipped and gathers to cut. Plodding route runner with no burst or acceleration out of his breaks. Recorded the slowest 10-yard split (1.80 seconds) and second-lowest vertical jump (28 inches) of any tight end at the Combine, indicative of marginal initial quickness and explosion. Lacks seam-stretching speed. Blocks with a narrow base and could stand to do a better job of locking out. Has spent time at three schools in six years, with a history of off-field issues, and requires discipline, structure ànd extra maintenance. Overaged. Durability has been an issue.

Future: A better football player than athletic tester, Plinke must learn what it means to be a pro and how to focus if he is going to have a chance to contribute in the pros. Could develop as a short-to-intermediate pass catcher with a strong support structure. Injury history, off-field issues and lack of foot speed likely will force him to make a team as an undrafted free agent.

Draft projection: Priority free agent.

TE [Y] **MICHAEL ROBERTS**, #80 (Sr-4)

TOLEDO   ▶ GRADE: 5.22

Ht: 6-4 3/8 | Wt: 270 | 40: 4.86 | Arm: 33 | Hand: 11 1/2

History: Grew up in Cleveland. Father was imprisoned when Michael was 12 (released in 2014). Michael starred on the field and hard-

TIGHT ENDS

wood in high school. During his senior year, coped with the deaths of his grandmother and younger brother. Originally committed to Ohio University, but failed to qualify academically and opted to attend Toledo, where he worked multiple jobs to pay for his first year (greyshirted in '12). Saw very limited action in five games in '13. Missed the first four games of '14 after spraining both ankles. On the season, appeared in nine games and caught four balls for 65 yards (16.3-yard average) and two touchdowns. Played all 12 games in '15, starting one, and collected 21-234-4 (11.1). Broke out in '16 when he scored eight more touchdowns than any other tight end in the country — produced 45-533-16 (11.8) in 13 starts. Broke Lance Moore's school single-season touchdowns record. Earned his criminal justice degree. Did not bench press at the Combine because of a muscle strain.

Strengths: Excellent body mass with huge hands, the largest of any player at the Combine. Light on his feet for as big as he is and consistently moved the chains and created mismatches in the red zone with exceptional production (16 TDs). Good body control. Can cover up defenders in the run game with his sheer size, plays with a wide base and walls off defenders.

Weaknesses: Stumbled through a number of routes in receiving drills at the Combine and has a lot of room to improve his precision as a route runner. Lets the ball into his body and double-catches. Recorded a poor 4.52-second 20-yard shuttle time at the Combine, indicative of limited hip flexibility, balance and burst. Dull route runner. Recorded a low 30-inch vertical jump and has below-average leaping ability. Only a one-year starter. Lacks competitive fire. Limited run-after-the-catch creativity and elusiveness. Much of his production came unencumbered against lesser competition, and he produced only one game with more than 61 receiving yards.

Future: Excellent-sized, big-bodied target emerged as a strong red-zone weapon as a senior and possesses the rare size to factor as a blocker and become a strong contributor — if he ever commits fully to the game and learns to compete hard all the time, a big "if". Will require several years to assimilate to an NFL program.

Draft projection: Fourth- to fifth-round pick.

Scout's take: "(Roberts) looks like he is lumbering when he runs. My problem with him is that he is a one-year starter that only won a role because there was no one else to beat out. He has great production, but a lot of his touchdowns were uncovered. Sometimes he looks like a second-rounder and a lot of times he looks like a free agent. For as big as he is, he doesn't block at all. I was hoping to see much better."

TE [F] ERIC SAUBERT, #85 (Sr-5)

DRAKE ▶ GRADE: 5.19

Ht: 6-4 3/4 | Wt: 253 | 40: 4.69 | Arm: 33 1/2 | Hand: 10 3/8

History: Tight end-defensive end also played basketball as an Illinois prep. Had his right labrum surgically repaired after his senior season. Redshirted at Drake in 2012. Started 9-of-11 games in '13, and had 47 receptions for 549 yards (11.7-yard average) and two touchdowns. Started 7-of-8 games played in '14, and caught 32-348-2 (10.9). Missed three October contests because of a right PCL sprain. Started all 11 games in '15, and totaled 55-580-7 (10.6). Was the team's leading receiver for the second straight season in '16 when he hauled in 56-776-10 (13.9). Football Championship Subdivision non-scholarship product earned invitations to the East-West Shrine Game, Senior Bowl, and Combine. Team captain graduated with a degree in actuarial science. Opted not to run the 40-yard dash or shuttles at the Combine.

Strengths: Experienced, four-year starter. Extends outside his frame and can make difficult grabs. Climbs the ladder to take the ball out of the air. Lines up all over the field and has good football smarts. Very intelligent and has a high capacity for learning a complex playbook. Solid showing at the East-West Shrine game. Played on the punt block and kickoff return teams and has special teams experience.

Weaknesses: Thin-waisted with a linear, narrow frame that is not built to support mass and already looks maxed out. Limited power and base as an in-line blocker and lacks functional football-playing strength. Falls off blocks and struggles to sustain. Drifts in his routes, labors to create vertical separation and does not play with precision. Needs to become a more consistent catcher and cut down on concentration drops. Did not regularly match up against top competition and was not often challenged releasing off the line.

Future: Oversized receiver lacking the girth, functional football playing strength and consistent effort to match up with NFL defensive linemen as an in-line blocker. Possesses enough size and receiving skill to warrant a look in an NFL camp as a detached receiver.

TIGHT ENDS

Must prove he has the temperament to contribute on special teams.

Draft projection: Late draftable prospect.

TE [H,F] / WR [Z] RICKY SEALS-JONES, #9 (Jr-4)

TEXAS A&M ▶ GRADE: 5.09

Ht: 6-4 5/8 | Wt: 243 | 40: 4.74 | Arm: 33 1/8 | Hand: 9 5/8

History: Cousin of Hall of Famer Eric Dickerson. Texas native played quarterback and safety in high school and was regarded as one of the top recruits in the country. Reportedly dislocated his left knee cap in September of his senior season (also sprained an ankle upon returning in October). As a true freshman in 2013, had three catches for 84 yards (28.0-yard average) and one touchdown before undergoing season-ending knee surgery (granted medical hardship). Was deployed as a mismatch piece by the Aggies, oftentimes as an inside receiver/H-back. Started 10-of-13 games in '14, and caught 49-465-4 (9.5). Started 11-of-13 games in '15, and snagged 45-560-4 (12.4). Was ejected for targeting against Mississippi State. Started 9-of-11 games in '16, and grabbed 26-333-1 (12.8). Hurt his left ankle against Arkansas, and did not play against South Carolina or Tennessee. Team captain.

Strengths: Experienced three-year starter in the Southeastern Conference. Offers a huge target in the slot with long arms to extend outside his frame and secure the ball. Good grip strength to catch on contact and compete for the ball in a crowd. Fights for the ball at the top of his routes and understands how to use his body and length to fend for positioning and shield defenders. Has enough speed to threaten the seam. Willing blocker with a frame to add upper-body strength and cover up linebackers.

Weaknesses: Lacks the foot speed to split wide and separate as a receiver in the pros. Marginal initial quickness off the ball, takes long strides and struggles to shake tight coverage. Only shows one gear. Most of his catches are contested. Limited run-after-the-catch strength and production. Has a 28-inch vertical jump, indicative of ordinary leaping ability and lower-body explosion. Bench-pressed 225 pounds 17 times, tied for the lowest among tight ends at the Combine. Has no in-line blocking experience and worked primarily out of the slot. Has no special teams experience. Marginal redzone production (10 career TDs).

Future: Excellent-sized, leggy, possession receiver with enough size and foot speed to compete for a detached job as an H-back. Has a

chance to earn a role as a No. 3 tight end.

Draft projection: Priority free agent.

TE [Y] ADAM SHAHEEN, #44 (Jr-4)

ASHLAND ▶ GRADE: 5.36

Ht: 6-6 1/2 | Wt: 278 | 40: 4.81 | Arm: 33 1/2 | Hand: 9 5/8

History: Receiver-safety whose main sport was basketball as a 195-pound Ohio prep. Began his college career on the hardwood at Pittsburgh-Johnstown in 2013-14 (was listed at 215 pounds). Missing football, Shaheen transferred to Division II Ashland, where he was used in-line and detached in the Eagles' pro-style offense. Did not flash until the end of the '14 season, grabbing 2-85-0 (42.5) in nine appearances. Started 8-of-11 games in '15, and produced 70-803-10 (11.5). In '16, set the D2 single-season record for touchdowns by a tight end with 57-867-16 (15.2) in 11 starts. Four years removed from high school, opted to forgo his final year of eligibility.

Strengths: Outstanding size — looks the part, measuring the tallest and heaviest of any tight end at the Combine. Also tied for the most bench-press reps (24) among tight ends at the event. Carries his weight well. Solid hands and hand-eye coordination. Smart and instinctive. Has functional run-after-the-catch ability. Outstanding production. Aligned inside and outside roughly an equal amount of time and has versatility to create mismatches with his length from the slot.

Weaknesses: Allows the ball into his body too much and likes to body-catch. Limited hip flexibility and knee extension to open up his stride. Clocked a 1.71-second 10-yard split, indicative of very ordinary initial burst. Not the dominant blocker expected for his size / competition level and could stand to improve his balance and core, functional football-playing strength. Lunges and overextends too much. Registered 20.3% body-fat composition at the Combine, the highest of any tight end, and ran one of the slowest 60-yard shuttles (12.40 seconds) — could stand to improve conditioning and endurance. Did not regularly face top competition and looked like a man among boys against lesser competition.

Future: Late bloomer with a very intriguing size-speed ratio and sensational Division II production that projects well to the NFL game. Will require a year to adapt to the speed and physicality of the pros, though has upside potential to emerge as an eventual starter.

Draft projection: Third- to fourth-round pick.

Scout's take: "Some people look down on

TIGHT ENDS

the level of competition, but those (DII) schools do produce some players. (Shaheen) might go in the fourth (round). He's a good athlete. He's a willing enough blocker. He will be a 10-year player — I just don't know how much of a 'wow' factor there will be."

TE [F, H] JONNU SMITH, #87 (Sr-4)

FLORIDA INTERNATIONAL ▶ GRADE: 5.33

Ht: 6-2 5/8 | Wt: 248 | 40: 4.63 | Arm: 32 7/8 | Hand: 9 1/4

History: Father, Wayne, died when Jonnu was four. Philadelphia native who came to FIU by way of Ocala, Fla. Was recruited by then-head coach Mario Cristobal and Ron Turner honored the scholarship — Smith's only offer — when the new coach arrived. As a true freshman in 2013, started all 12 games and recorded 39 catches for 388 yards (9.9-yard average) and two touchdowns. In '14, led all college tight ends in receptions while setting FIU single-season marks receptions, receiving yards, and touchdowns by a tight end — started all 12 games, producing 61-710-8 (11.6). In '15, caught 36-397-4 (11.0) before suffering a season-ending torn left ACL injury against Old Dominion. Despite the injury, finished the game and totaled 10-183-2 on the day. Started all 11 games played in '16, and posted 42-506-4 (12.0). Sat out the Western Kentucky contest — suffered severe burns when his pregnant girlfriend intentionally poured boiling water on him. Attempted the 3-cone drill three times but did not record a time.

Strengths: Good muscularity. Experienced, four-year starter. Well built with very good athletic ability. Has a 38-inch vertical jump, indicative of exceptional lower-body explosion and leaping ability. Good run strength to break arm tackles after the catch. Tough and willing blocker. Efficient stalk blocker seals defenders at the second level. Very driven, motivated and diligent in his approach. Good weight-room worker. Solid football character.

Weaknesses: Measured the shortest of any tight end at the Combine with small, inconsistent hands that led to eight drops in 2016. Could stand to do a better job of setting up defenders as a route runner, sinking his hips and creating separation. Lacks ideal bulk to factor as an in-line blocker. Limited hip roll and strength at the point of attack. Has minimal special teams experience.

Future: Quick, athletic, undersized, short-to-intermediate target with enough grit and determination to contribute on special teams and earn a roster spot as a move-blocker.

Draft projection: Fourth- to fifth-round pick.

TE [Y] JEREMY SPRINKLE, #83 (Sr-5)

ARKANSAS ▶ GRADE: 5.38

Ht: 6-4 7/8 | Wt: 252 | 40: 4.68 | Arm: 34 1/2 | Hand: 10 3/4

History: Arkansas native. Receiver-tight end-defensive end also played basketball and baseball in high school. Offered scholarship by then-head coach Bobby Petrino's staff. Redshirted in 2012. Played all 12 games in '13, starting two, and caught four balls for 68 yards (13.8-yard average) and zero touchdowns. In '14, recorded 7-84-1 (12.0) in 13 appearances. Started 7-of-15 games played n '15, and caught 27-389-6 (14.4). Started 11-of-12 games played in '16, and totaled 33-380-4 (11.5). Was suspended for the Belk Bowl against Virginia Tech — as part of the Belk Bowl festivities each player received a $450 gift card to the Belk department store, but Sprinkle took additional items and was cited for unlawful concealment. His 11 career touchdowns are most by an Arkansas tight end. Finished his recreation and sport management degree. Did not bench press at the Combine because of a wrist injury or perform the shuttles as a result of having to catch flight.

Strengths: Very good size, with long arms, big hands, a giant wingspan and a wide catching radius. Works to sustain blocks and finish with a solid base and technique. Climbs to the second level and seals off linebackers. Versatile with alignments, seeing time at in-line, detached, at fullback and H-back. Has been a regular on special teams all four years. Good body control to adjust to poorly thrown balls — extends to pluck the ball out of the air. Very durable and has not missed any time due to injury.

Weaknesses: A bit high-cut and tight-hipped. Recorded a low 29-inch vertical jump, indicative of marginal lower-body explosion and leaping ability. Is not a natural-handed catcher. Needs to spend more time in the weight room, continue to fill out his big frame and improve his functional strength.

Future: A high-cut, thick-bodied, strong, tough in-line blocker with good receiving skills, Sprinkle is at his best attached as a blocker and could fill a similar role as Colts 2012 third-round pick and now Patriots TE Dwayne Allen as an ascending short-area receiver and solid, all-around performer. Has eventual starter potential.

Draft projection: Third- to fourth-round pick.

Scout's take: "Sprinkle is talented. He is the best blocking tight end I have seen this fall. He looks awkward bending at the waist, but he gets after guys and creates some movement (as a run blocker)."

TIGHT ENDS

OFFENSIVE LINE

UNIVERSITY OF ALABAMA

Nawrocki's TOP 10

1. **CAM ROBINSON**
2. **Ryan Ramczyk**
3. **Garett Bolles**
4. **Forrest Lamp**
5. **Pat Elflein**
6. **Dan Feeney**
7. **Ethan Pocic**
8. **Dorian Johnson**
9. **Dion Dawkins**
10. **Isaac Asiata**

OLG ISAAC ASIATA, #54 (Sr-6)

UTAH ▶ GRADE: 5.52

Ht: 6-3 1/8 | Wt: 323 | 40: 5.34 | Arm: 33 3/4 | Hand: 10 3/8

History: Married (Angelia). Cousin of Matt Asiata (Vikings). Utah native. Redshirted in 2011. Served an LDS mission in Tulsa, Okla. Returned to the field in '13 when he started 4-of-6 games played at right tackle. In '14, started all 13 games — seven at right guard, six at left guard. Started all 25 games OLG in 2015-16. Was flagged for seven penalties as a senior. Awarded the Morris Trophy (top Pac-12 offensive lineman as voted on by defensive linemen). Wore jersey No. 68 against Washington to honor injured teammate J.J. Dielman. Will be a 24-year-old rookie. Graduated with a degree in sociology. Was a medical exclusion from the Combine because of Lisfranc surgery on his right foot.

Strengths: Exceptional size and mass. Good straight-line power to maul defenders and create movement at the point of attack. Produced a Combine-best 35 bench-press reps and converts weight-room strength to the field. Plays with physicality. Very good finishing strength in the run game. Efficient cut blocker. Good anchor and strain to maintain the edge when locked up in pass protection, with recovery strength and adequate body control to adjust.

Weaknesses: Can be overaggressive lunging —overextends and falls off blocks. Recorded a 25 1/2-inch vertical jump, indicative of marginal lower-body explosion. Recorded the slowest 10-yard split (1.97 seconds) of any guard at the Combine, revealing average initial quickness climbing to the second level — late to arrive. Can be short-circuited against complex pressure packages. Eyes can be late scanning in pass protection and is at his best with simplified assignments. Could stand to be more disciplined and consistent getting off the ball, taking proper angles and playing under control. Weight has fluctuated throughout his career and will need to be monitored.

Future: A strong, physical run blocker with lapses in pass protection, Asiata has starter-quality traits for a power-blocking run team such as the Bills, Raiders or Chargers. Physically is capable of competing from Day One and bolstering a run game, but will take some time to adapt to handling NFL pressure packages. Will require a year to adapt to an offense featuring a complex playbook and will be best with streamlined blocking assignments.

Draft projection: Third- to fourth-round pick.

Scout's take: "(Asiata) has heavy hands. He's smarter than he plays when you talk to him. He's a lot better than (Titans' 2015 third round pick [66] Jeremiah) Poutasi who was already cut and is in Jacksonville now. (Poutasi)

OFFENSIVE LINE

just struggled to learn, and that's been part of the stain on Utah lineman. It won't be an issue with Asiata. He will be a good pro."

C-OLG **ERIK AUSTELL**, #76 (Sr-5)

CHARLESTON SOUTHERN ▶ GRADE: 5.16

Ht: 6-3 1/4 | Wt: 301 | 40: 5.24 | Arm: 32 | Hand: 9

History: Married (Taylor). Prepped in Georgia, where he played linebacker, defensive end, option quarterback, and running back. Was recruited as a 220-pound defensive lineman, redshirted in 2012, and had surgery to repair a torn right meniscus. Converted to left tackle in '13, and responded by starting all 12 games played. Did not play against VMI (stinger). Graded out at 82 percent with 74 knockdowns. Sat out the '14 season opener (illness) then started the next 11 at OLT. In '15, started the first nine games at left tackle before suffering a season-ending torn pectoral injury. Started all 10 games played at OLT in '16, grading out at 91.4 percent with 84 knockdowns in the Buccaneers' shotgun option offense. Was suspended against Florida State — was one of 32 players punished for a self-reported financial aid violation related to book purchases. Team captain earned his criminal justice degree. First CSU player invited to the Combine. Weight has went from 220 to 240 to 270 each year and played senior season in the 280's. Showed up at the Shrine game at 290 and weighed 301 at the Combine.

Strengths: Scrappy competitor. Plays hard with good effort. Gets off the ball quickly and into his blocks. Understands angles and leverage — gets good positioning to seal and wall off defenders. Efficient climbing to the second level and fitting on linebackers. Fine cut blocker. Recorded an 8'11" broad jump, indicative of good lower-body explosion. Very good football character — committed to the weight room, practices hard and is receptive to coaching. Good football intelligence and processing speed to adapt to movement and handle the blitz. Solid showing as a run blocker at the East-West Shrine game.

Weaknesses: Has a lean frame — not naturally big-boned and has been dinged up throughout his career. Measured the smallest hands and shortest arm length and wingspan (75 1/4 inches) of any offensive linemen at the Combine. Not stout or explosive at the point of attack and creates little movement in the run game. Will be overmatched by massive wide bodies and anchoring against top power. Has not regularly faced top competition.

Future: College left tackle lacking ideal length to handle the edges and the core strength

desired at guard in the pros. Is still adapting to playing at a higher weight and stumbled a bit through drills at the Combine carrying extra pounds. Projects most ideally as a center with swing backup versatility, though will require a few years to adjust to the NFL game and continue developing his core strength. Developmental project for a stretch-zone scheme.

Draft projection: Fifth- to sixth-round pick.

ORT **ZACH BANNER**, #73 (Sr-5)

USC ▶ GRADE: 5.47

Ht: 6-8 3/8 | Wt: 353 | 40: 5.59 | Arm: 34 7/8 | Hand: 10 3/4

History: Biological father is Pro Bowler Lincoln Kennedy, who played 11 years with the Falcons and Raiders (1993-2003). As a Washington prep, was a USA Today All-American, basketball state champion, and finalist for the Watkins Award, given to the nation's top African-American high school scholar athlete. Redshirted in 2012. Joined the USC basketball team following the season but did not see any action. Was a non-factor in '13 when he underwent hip impingement surgery on both hips. Started all 13 games at right tackle in '14. Started all 14 games in '15, including 12 at ORT and two at left tackle. Was the Trojans' OLT in '16 when he started all 11 games played. Sprained his left ankle against Utah, received a platelet-rich plasma injection, and sat out against Arizona State and Colorado. Totaled 25 penalties the last two seasons. Team captain graduated with a communication degree. Finalist for the Senior CLASS Award.

Strengths: Rare size, length and mass — is a $25 cab ride to get around and can collapse a line with down blocks and create wide running lanes. Excellent anchor strength — absorbs and controls defenders in pass protection and can shut down speed rushers once he gets his hands on them. Plays on his feet with surprising balance for as massive as he is. Can cover up linebackers at the second level. Versatile enough to play both sides and contribute as an emergency left tackle. Good football smarts. Has a charismatic personality and will add life to an NFL O-Line room.

Weaknesses: Tends to set too tall and is not a natural knee bender. Is late to redirect and adjust to speed, with average recovery quickness. Has some heaviness in his feet, recording among the slowest 10-yard split times (1.97 seconds) of any offensive tackle at the Combine. Also produced the slowest 20-yard shuttle time (5.27), indicative of limited flexibility and burst. Too undisciplined and frequently flagged for costly, inopportune penalties. Does not adjust well to moving targets.

Weight has fluctuated too much throughout his career, pushing 400 pounds and he was still the heaviest player (353) at the Combine, down seven pounds from the Senior Bowl, where he allowed two sacks in the game. Turned off some executives with excuse-making in the interview process. *Future:* Massive, big-bodied, long-limbed right tackle who could be blinded by the bright lights of the NFL and has yet to prove consistent. Has the physical tools to readily become a starting right tackle if he can control his weight and learn to play with more discipline. Long-term durability and weight concerns could affect his draft status. Rare size, fluctuating weight and lack of discipline profiles very similar to 49ers' 2015 seventh-round pick and starting ORT Trent Brown, though Banner is not as light on his feet. *Draft projection:* Second- to third-round pick. *Scout's take:* "He's an NFL starter at right tackle. He's better than (Rams' 2015 second-round pick) Rob Havenstein and a lot of guys that are playing right tackle right now."

OLT-OLG ADAM BISNOWATY, #69 (Sr-5)
PITTSBURGH ▶ GRADE: 5.27
Ht: 6-5 5/8 | Wt: 304 | 40: 5.24 | Arm: 33 7/8 | Hand: 11 3/8

History: Last name is pronounced "biz-NO-vah-tee." Pittsburgh native. Two-way lineman also competed in wrestling and track and field in high school. Redshirted in 2012. Manned left tackle for the Panthers. Started 8-of-9 games played in '13 before sitting out the final four contests because of a back strain. Started 10-of-11 games played in '14. Served a one game suspension against Virginia. Did not play against Syracuse and did not start against Miami because of a high left ankle sprain. Started all 12 games played in '15. Sat out against Akron (high left ankle sprain). Started all 13 games in '16. Team captain finished his communication degree. *Strengths:* Good size and length with a well-distributed frame, long torso and huge hands. Can bump and steer defenders seal off lanes in the run game. Experienced four-year starter with an efficient kick-slide to run rushers wide of the pocket. Enough anchor strength to withstand power. Tough and competitive. Good football intelligence and instincts. *Weaknesses:* Tends to play a bit tall, negating his leverage and power in the run game, and creating difficulty reaching second-level targets. Has some tightness in his lower body, is not a natural bender and appears mechanical in his lateral movement. Could do a better job of using his hands to lock out and create extension in pass protection. Limited recovery speed.

Struggled to match up with speed on the edges at the Senior Bowl in one-on-one drills and in the game — was beat off the ball by speed (Dawuane Smoot) and up-and-under by inside swim moves (Haason Reddick). Durability has been a nagging issue throughout his career. *Future:* Scrappy, college left tackle lacking ideal agility and hip flexibility for the left side in the pros and looked more comfortable on the interior at the Senior Bowl. Projects better as a right tackle in the pros and may find the most comfortable fit at left guard. Could emerge as a marginal starter and functional swing backup in a league short on linemen. *Draft projection:* Fourth- to fifth-round pick. *Scout's take:* "(Bisnowaty) is smart, tough and all those qualities you want, but I can't shake Senior Bowl one-on-one's from my head. He got beat every way you could in one-on-one's — he was cross-faced, run over and beat around the edge. You want to pull for him because of his intangibles. Smart and tough can go a long way in this league."

OLT GARETT BOLLES, #72 (Jr-5)
UTAH ▶ GRADE: 5.74
Ht: 6-5 | Wt: 297 | 40: 4.98 | Arm: 34 | Hand: 9 3/8

History: Bolles and his wife, Natalie, have a newborn son named Kingston. Utah native was a high school defensive tackle and lacrosse player. Bounced to five different schools as a teenager because of suspensions and/or expulsions. In a story on kutv.com, Bolles described himself as a troubled teen influenced by drugs, alcohol, and gangs. "You name it. I've done it," said Bolles, who acknowledged he was headed "down the wrong path to prison." Was arrested in 2010 for vandalizing a rival school's field, then kicked out of his father's house the following year. Turned his life around and refocused on football after he was taken in by his neighbor/lacrosse coach's family. Served an LDS mission in Colorado Springs in 2013. Resurfaced at Snow College (UT), where he played 2014-15 and was one of the most highly sought after JUCO recruits in the country. With the Utes in '16, started all 13 games at left tackle. Wore jersey No. 74 because he was inspired by the "Blind Side" story of Michael Oher (Panthers), whom Bolles considers a hero. Will be a 25-year-old rookie. Did not perform the bench-press test at the Combine because of a left pectoral strain. *Strengths:* Has a short trunk, long torso and ideal length. Very good athlete with agility, hip flexibility, balance and knee bend to sink, anchor and handle edge speed. Very good movement skill and explosion for a big man, confirmed by

87

best 10-yard split (1.68 seconds), 20-yard split (2.75), broad jump (9'7") and three-cone drill (7.29) of any offensive linemen. Flashes shock in his punch. Aggressive run blocker. Runs his feet on contact and drives defenders into the ground on the move. Plays with physicality and pinballs safeties at the second level. Can even work up to the third level and run the field effortlessly. Can be a nasty finisher when engaged and takes pride in burying defenders.

Weaknesses: Smooth-muscled and needs to spend more time in the weight room and improve his strength. Unrefined technician in pass protection — oversets and overextends, lunges and loses positioning on the edge. Takes some bad angles and gets out-leveraged at the second level. Underdeveloped eyes — late to diagnose and help pick up the blitz. Marginal personal and football character. Was penalized 17 times in 2016 — does not play with enough discipline and can be too grabby. Overaged.

Future: An athletic, college left tackle with the balance, bend and agility to step into a starting line-up at left tackle and compete readily from a physical standpoint. Technique, discipline and football IQ still have a long way to go before he is ready, and frequent mental mistakes could hinder his development and force a team to bring him along more slowly on the right side. Has some similarities to Rams 2014 second overall pick Greg Robinson, whose inconsistency has led to being benched and moved to the right side and who may never reach his ceiling.

Draft projection: Top-40 pick.

Scout's take: "If he were tough and smart, he would probably be a first-rounder. In this (weak) tackle class, who knows — maybe he still will be. Taking into consideration the full package with some of his limitations in football intelligence and football character, not to mention his age, he's a second-rounder. I graded him in the third. He won't get there, but that's what I think he'll play to in the league. He has a bust factor."

ORG BEN BRADEN, #71 (Sr-5)

MICHIGAN ▶ GRADE: 5.14

Ht: 6-6 1/2 | Wt: 329 | 40: 5.07 | Arm: 34 | Hand: 9 7/8

History: Michigan native grew up playing hockey. Was then-head coach Brady Hoke's first commitment. Redshirted in 2012. Made two appearances in '13. Started all 12 games at right tackle in '12. Shifted to left guard in '15, starting all 13 games. Sat out the '16 season opener versus Hawaii (minor injury/precautionary), but started 11-of-12 games played — seven at left, four at OLG. Did not start against

Rutgers (coach's decision). Graduated.

Strengths: Plays with intensity and competes every down. Battles and scraps for positioning in the run game. Can be effective mirroring his man in tight quarters in pass protection. Registered a 2.92 20-yard split at the Combine, indicative of sustained burst ideal for pulling. Smart, tough and physical. Measured 17% body fat at the Combine, indicative of strong endurance for an offensive lineman. Versatile and has played multiple positions. Very durable.

Weaknesses: Plays too top-heavy, narrow-based and straight-legged and consequently is stressed by speed in pass protection inside and even more at left tackle. Plays upright, bends at the waist and spends too much time on the ground. Very inconsistent sustaining blocks — too easily slips off. Does not generate movement in the run game.

Future: A tough, top-heavy waist-bender with too much stiffness in his body to sustain blocks. Will intrigue more on paper with measurables than he will with performance on the field. Could warrant interest as a multi-position backup in a power-blocking scheme such as the Chargers, Raiders or Lions.

Draft projection: Late draftable pick.

Scout's take: "(Braden) played left tackle, but I gave him a more positive grade as a guard. He is a better fit there. ...I didn't think he was good enough to play on our line. I don't think he is athletic enough for tackle or center. I thought he was a guard only. He ran better than I expected (at the Combine). It wouldn't surprise me if he went in the fifth (round) for the league."

C-ORT DANIEL BRUNSKILL, #71 (Sr-5)

SAN DIEGO STATE ▶ GRADE: 5.09

Ht: 6-5 1/8 | Wt: 273 | 40: 5.19 | Arm: 33 7/8 | Hand: 9 7/8

History: California native also competed in volleyball, lacrosse, and wrestling. Walked on at SDSU. Redshirted as a center in 2012. Moved to tight end and appeared in 13 games in '13 (no stats). Played all 13 games in '14, starting four, and tallied five receptions for 31 yards (6.2-yard average) and one touchdown. Started all 14 games in '15, collecting 10-112-2 (11.2). After being used as a blocking tight end, moved to right tackle in '16 — started all 14 games, and allowed one sack. On track to graduate with a civil engineering degree. Opted not to run the 40-yard dash at the Combine.

Strengths: Good agility and movement skill — light on his feet for a big man. Very quick to the second level cutting off linebackers. Smart, coachable and has a love of the game. Good football intelligence. Has lined up at tight end and ideal for tackle-eligible opportunities. Has

OFFENSIVE LINE

special teams experience.

Weaknesses: Lacks bulk strength, measuring the lightest of any offensive linemen at the Combine, and plays small. Not a natural knee-bender and plays too upright and flat-footed in pass protection, allowing defenders to get underneath his pads and walk him back. Lacks core functional strength to handle power in the pros and needs to improve lower-body strength.

Future: Converted blocking tight end who kicked inside to right tackle as a senior, yet looks more suited in the pros for the center position where he entered the program. Smart finesse, positional blocker with the agility and intelligence desired at the pivot, though must add bulk and learn to play bigger. Developmental project.

Draft projection: Priority free agent.

ORG-ORT COLLIN BUCHANAN, #72 (Sr-4)
MIAMI-OHIO ▶ GRADE: 5.17
Ht: 6-4 3/4 | Wt: 316 | 40: 5.35e | Arm: 32 3/8 | Hand: 10 1/2

History: Prepped in Michigan, where he also played basketball. As a true freshman in 2013, made 10 appearances in a reserve role. Took ownership of the right tackle position in '14 when he started all 12 games. Started all 11 games played in '15. Sat out against Wisconsin while nursing a high left ankle sprain. Broke his left wrist in the spring of '16. In the fall, started all 12 games played. Did not play against Buffalo (illness). Was a medical exclusion from running at the Combine because of a right hamstring injury and did not perform shuttles because of a right calf strain.

Strengths: Very good body mass and thickness for an interior blocker. Experienced, three-year starter. Has a solid anchor to stop a charge. Plays on his feet with good balance. Generates some initial movement in the run game when he gets his hands on defenders. Is alert to the blitz and solid mirroring base ends in pass protection.

Weaknesses: Lacks ideal body and arm length for the OT position. Has relatively thin ankles and wrists that invite injury. Heavy plodding mover — late to initiate contact at the second level and adjust to moving targets. Inconsistent pad level, which leads to falling off blocks (see Cincinnati). Frequently short sets to compensate for his lack of lateral agility, and uses more of a shuffle-and-slide technique than kick-slide, opening his shoulders quickly and leaving the inside susceptible to counter moves. Hands tend to shoot wide of the target — could stand to do a better job consistently recoiling Marginal grip strength. Needs to learn to become a more consistent finisher. Measured 30.6% body fat at the Combine, the highest of any offensive linemen and indicative of a lack of endurance.

Future: A big-bodied, phone-booth blocker most ideally suited for a move inside in the pros. The further he is asked to travel, the more stressed his technique becomes. A better pass protector than run blocker, Buchanan will be most optimally suited for a man-blocking scheme.

Draft projection: Late draftable pick.

Scout's take: "He has nice size, decent feet and balance. He's not strong or physical. He gets pushed back and knocked around too much. I was worried about his strength and power. I'd rather have him as a free agent."

OLT AVIANTE COLLINS, #69 (Sr-5)
TCU ▶ GRADE: 5.25
Ht: 6-4 1/8 | Wt: 295 | 40: 4.86 | Arm: 33 3/8 | Hand: 9 3/8

History: First name is pronounced "AH-vee-on." Father, Bill, was a standout sprinter at TCU. Houston native also lettered in track and field in high school. As a true freshman in 2012, started all 13 games — 10 at right tackle, three at left tackle. Drew 11 penalty flags. Started 9-of-12 games in '13 — six at ORT, three at OLT. Sat out the '14 season opener (foot sprain) before appearing in eight games, drawing just one start at OLT. Played three games in '15 before breaking his nose vs. Stephen Austin (out 7 weeks) and taking a redshirt. In '16, returned to start all 13 games at ORT. Was flagged for 11 penalties in 2016. Graduated. Did not perform shuttles or jumps at the Combine because of a left knee injury.

Strengths: Very fluid movement skills. Excellent feet, short-area burst and athletic ability for a 300-pounder. Recorded a Combine-best 4.81-second 40-yard time, best among offensive tackles and revealing outstanding long speed to climb to the second and third levels and run the field. Good balance, body control and recovery quickness — seldom on the ground. Locks on in pass protection and finishes (see Arkansas), flashing a mean streak. Bench-pressed 225 pounds 34 times at the Combine, tying for the most among tackles at the event. Versatile and has played four line positions (all but center).

Weaknesses: Has very small hands and short arms and can be too grabby when defenders gain an edge. More of a grabber than a puncher and needs to learn to keep his hands inside and bring his feet with him. Has a linear build and narrow waist lacking bulk and can be inverted by power. Tends to set tall and play too upright. Could stand to do a better job sustaining blocks and cut down on holding penalties.

Future: Underpowered, developmental zone

OFFENSIVE LINE

blocker with rare foot speed more ideally suited for the left side than the right where he spent most of his college career. Most of his flaws are correctable and has a lot of upside to be groomed as a swing tackle in a zone-blocking scheme with eventual starter potential. A poor man's version of Saints' 2013 second-round pick Terron Armstead, Collins should be able to start Year Two with continued physical development, though narrow bone structure could challenge him to stay healthy.

Draft projection: Fourth- to fifth-round pick.

ORG **ETHAN COOPER**, #59 (Sr-4)

INDIANA (PA.)   ▶ GRADE: 5.01
Ht: 6-2 1/2 | Wt: 322 | 40: 5.33 | Arm: 32 5/8 | Hand: 10 3/8

History: Pennsylvania native also competed in track and field in high school. Didn't have the grades to qualify for big-time college football. As a true freshman in 2013, saw action in six games, starting three of the final four at right guard. Shifted to left guard, and started all 23 games 2014-15. Started all 12 games at right tackle in '16 for the Division II Crimson Hawks. Played in a traditional, pro-style offense as an underclassman before transitioning to an up-tempo spread his last two seasons.

Strengths: Has a very thick frame with broad shoulders, tree-stump legs and well-distributed mass. Good upper-body strength and grip strength to latch on and ride defenders wide. Flashes pop in his punch. Solid base in pass pro. Is tough, competitive and has been very durable.

Weaknesses: Short and short-armed. Has some tightness in his hips and limited blocking range. Struggles to cut off linebackers. Functional lateral agility. Not a natural knee bender and does not roll his hips and generate power through his lower half. Has a 24 1/2-inch vertical jump, indicative of a lack of lower-body explosion. Regularly matched up against inferior competition and allowed two sacks during the NFLPA all-star game.

Future: Squatty, strong, square-cut, short-stepper was able to align at right tackle in the Pennsylvania Scholastic Athletic Conference, but projects as a backup guard only in the pros and more ideal on the right side where he began his college career. Will need to prove his mettle on a practice squad for a power-blocking team.

Draft projection: Priority free agent.

ORT **COLE CROSTON**, #64 (Sr-5)

IOWA   ▶ GRADE: 5.17
Ht: 6-5 3/4 | Wt: 306 | 40: 5.25e | Arm: 34 1/2 | Hand: 9 1/8

History: Father, Dave, was an Iowa lineman before he was drafted 61st overall by the Packers in 1987. Cole is an Iowa native who also lettered in basketball, baseball and golf in high school. Joined the Hawkeyes as a preferred walk-on. Bulked up 80-plus pounds over his time in Iowa City. Redshirted in 2012. Made two appearances in '13. Saw limited action in 13 games in a reserve role in '14. Injury opened the door for Croston to start 10-of-14 games in '15 — six at right tackle, four at left tackle. In '16, started 8-of-9 games played, including the first five at OLT and three more at ORT. Played hurt from Sept. 24 through the end of the regular season, coping with a stress fracture in his right shin that limited his effectiveness and sidelined him for four games.

Strengths: Has very long arms with broad shoulders and a sturdy frame to continue growing into. Solid technician with quick, active hands. Understands angles and positioning and climbs to the second level. Very good lateral agility. Effective cut blocker. Plays with great effort. Extremely smart and tough, playing through injury much of senior season. Very dependable and accountable. Versatile and has played both left- and right-handed and shown he can handle the edges. Has NFL pedigree and is a very quick learner.

Weaknesses: Needs to continue getting stronger and developing his core functional, football-playing strength to match up against NFL power. Has a soft anchor and can be walked back at times. More of a catcher than a puncher.

Future: Tough, smart, self-made developmental swing tackle with the competitiveness, work ethic and wiring to become a serviceable pro with continued development in an NFL strength program. Most ideally suited for a zone-blocking scheme.

Draft projection: Late draftable pick.

OLT **JULIEN DAVENPORT**, #70 (Sr-4)

BUCKNELL   ▶ GRADE: 5.34
Ht: 6-6 3/4 | Wt: 318 | 40: 5.46 | Arm: 36 1/2 | Hand: 10 1/2

History: Cousin, Michael Kidd-Gilchrist, plays for the Charlotte Hornets. Julien also played basketball as a New Jersey prep. Started all 44 games of his career at left tackle for the FCS Bison, who ran a pro-style offense. Blocked an overtime field goal attempt against VMI. Two-year captain earned a Senior Bowl invite.

Strengths: Rare arm length and huge wingspan (87 1/2 inches) measured the longest of any player at the Combine and allows him to control defenders. Efficient pass protector with good base, balance and body control. Good shuttle, slide and mirror. Recorded a 4.69-second short shuttle and 7.57-second 3-cone drill, indicative of good agility, flexibility and burst. Very smart and well-versed in a pro-style of-

OFFENSIVE LINE

fense. Has been extremely durable and never missed a practice in his career.

Weaknesses: Has a thin basketball build with little power in his core and needs to improve his functional strength and power step. Tends to play very upright and is often late to reach second-level targets. Has not regularly been challenged against better competition and struggled to match up with the speed of Carroll Phillips and Jordan Willis at the Senior Bowl.

Future: Very agile, long-limbed, rangy, small-school left tackle with rare length and the athletic frame to emerge as an eventual NFL starter with continued physical development.

Draft projection: Third- to fourth-round pick.

Scout's take: "(Davenport) has a long ways to go. I put him in the third (round) for us. It might be a little rich. He's not a plug-and-play starter, but there's going to be a run on offensive linemen once you get out of the first few rounds. There just aren't enough of them this year. A lot of them are going to be overdrafted."

OLT-OLG DION DAWKINS, #66 (Sr-5)

TEMPLE ▶ GRADE: 5.62

Ht: 6-3 7/8 | Wt: 314 | 40: 5.11 | Arm: 35 | Hand: 9 7/8

History: Two-way lineman from New Jersey. Attended Hargrave Military Academy (Va.) in 2012. Played the first five games in '13, starting one game at each tackle spot, before suffering a broken right foot and undergoing season-ending surgery. Started all 11 games played at left tackle in '14. Sat out against Central Florida while nursing a right ankle sprain. In March '15 was arrested and charged with aggravated assault for his involvement in a fight that left one student seriously injured. Ultimately, charges were dismissed, and Dawkins participated in a diversionary program. Had surgery to repair a torn right meniscus before the '15 season, but was able to start 13-of-14 games at OLT. Was benched for a series against SMU (minor rules violation). Started all 14 games at OLT in '16 and was flagged six times and allowed two sacks. Graduated with a criminal justice degree.

Strengths: Outstanding arm length. Good power in his body. Has functional football-playing strength to move defenders off the line. Plays heavy-handed. Flashes a mean streak in the run game and seeks to finish (see downfield pancake vs. Cincinnati). Aggressive working up to the second level and sealing linebackers and even fitting on defensive backs. Understands angles and leverage. Good grip and anchor strength in pass protection to sit down and stop a charge — locks down defenders once he gets his hands on them. Clocked the second-fastest 3-cone drill time (7.29 seconds) among

offensive tackles at the Combine, indicative of outstanding agility and change of direction.

Weaknesses: Soft-bodied and small-handed. Is a bit high-cut and tight in his hips and ankles. Often bends at the waist when he gets out of position and recovery quickness will be more exposed vs NFL pass rushers on an island. Unrefined hand use in pass pro — overaggressive punch. Stressed by speed on the edges (see Penn State). Was not regularly challenged against American Athletic Conference competition. Could be challenged to acclimate to a complex NFL playbook. Lack of discipline shows up on film (multiple penalties on same drive of third quarter vs. Penn State, including a TD-negating illegal block in the back). Looked uncomfortable adjusting to playing guard at the Senior Bowl. Has been slowed by foot, ankle and knee injuries and missed eight career games to injury.

Future: A big, strong, powerful, top-heavy blocker capable of creating a surge in the run game, Dawkins is adept enough in pass pro to lock on and wall off. Will require some patience adapting to the sophistication of the NFL, especially if he is moved inside where the game gets on top of guards faster. Size, strength, power and temperament appear most ideally suited for a role as a starting right tackle, though has good enough feet to remain on the left side if he can improve his pass-pro technique.

Draft projection: Second- to third-round pick.

Scout's take: "(Dawkins) needs more pass pro work. He probably will be better at right tackle (in the pros). If he gets thrown into the lineup too soon, he won't be ready. Trying to play him at left tackle out of the gate will be like Arizona trying to play D.J. Humphries right away. He needed a redshirt year. Dawkins is not as athletic, and I think you're going to need to start him on the right side. Eventually maybe he kicks back over (to left tackle)."

C-OG-ORT J.J. DIELMAN, #68 (Sr-5)

UTAH ▶ GRADE: 5.21

Ht: 6-4 7/8 | Wt: 309 | 40: 5.25e | Arm: 32 1/4 | Hand: 10

History: Full name is Jeffrey Joseph Dielman. Cousin, Kris, was a Pro Bowl offensive lineman for the Chargers (2003-11) before a severe concussion forced him to retire. Two-way lineman helped win an Arizona state championship at Desert Vista High. Redshirted in 2012 and appeared in one game in '13. Started all 26 games at right tackle 2014-15. Shifted to center in '16, starting the first five games, before suffering a season-ending injury to his right foot. Team captain. Graduated with a degree in economics. Was a medical exclusion from working out at the Combine (Lis-

OFFENSIVE LINE

franc surgery on right foot).

Strengths: Outstanding size for the center position. Very light on his feet and quick into his blocks. Good agility to reach and seal defenders and work up to the second level. Flashes some nastiness and seeks to finish. Has enough strength to absorb the blitz and stop a charge. Tough competitor with a scrappy football temperament. Versatile and has played inside and outside, with enough length and agility to fill in as an emergency tackle. Has a gritty NFL pedigree.

Weaknesses: Marginal arm length and functional football-playing strength. Can be over-aggressive lunging and wind up on the ground too much. Could stand to improve contact balance and sustain (pad level rises). Lacks core power in his body to roll his hips and move defenders off the ball.

Future: A tough, aggressive, agile movement center most ideally suited for a zone-blocking scheme. Capable of competing for a swing interior backup role immediately.

Draft projection: Late draftable pick.

Scout's take: "(Dielman) needs to get stronger and more powerful, but you can get bigger and stronger in the weight room. It's difficult to (become) more athletic. He has played all five positions. None of our (scouts) that went through there gave him much love, but he has a chance to become a player."

OLG JESSAMEN DUNKER, #66 (Sr-5)

TENNESSEE STATE　　▶ GRADE: 5.32

Ht: 6-4 1/4 | Wt: 318 | 40: 5.01 | Arm: 33 1/2 | Hand: 10

History: Moved from Georgia to Florida as a high school junior, the first year he played football. Parade All-American began his college career at Florida, where he redshirted in 2012. In January '13, was arrested and charged with grand theft of a motor vehicle — was pulled over while riding a scooter he had purchased for $600. As it turned out, the scooter was stolen and Dunker was driving on a suspended license. Transferred to FCS Tennessee State, where he started all 13 games at left tackle in '13. Started 11-of-12 games in '14 — seven at OLT, four at left guard. Did not start against Tennessee-Martin. Started 8-of-10 games in '15 (seven at OLG, one at right guard). Did not start against Austin Peay (back), and was held out the first series against Tennessee Tech. Dealt with a nagging back injury during '16 fall camp, and was not cleared until just before the season. Came off the bench in the season opener against Arkansas-Pine-Bluff, but started 10-of-11 games at OLT. Graduated. Invited to the Senior Bowl. Did not perform shuttles at the Combine because of a right hamstring injury.

Strengths: Has outstanding size with good body thickness. Takes good angles to seal and wall off. Very good athlete. Flashes power in his hands and delivers a nasty punch. Good agility and movement skill, as evidenced by clocking some sub-5-flat 40 times at the Combine along with a 1.71-second 10-yard dash, indicative of outstanding initial burst. Efficient in space reaching linebackers and maneuvering through traffic. Showed improvement in one-on-one pass-rush drills at the Senior Bowl. Versatile and has played inside and outside.

Weaknesses: Lacks ideal body and arm length for the edges. Has some tightness in his hips, will set tall and get out-leveraged in pass protection. Does not play with power and can struggle matching up against big bodies. Needs to improve his lower-body strength. Eyes, anticipation and blocking instincts could stand to improve. Marginal football character — does few extras and gets by coasting.

Future: Similar to Cowboys' 2015 third-round pick (91) Chaz Green, Dunker will take a few years before he is ready to enter a lineup, though he possesses intriguing physical tools, with the agility, athletic ability and recovery speed to compete for a starting OLG job if he learns to take the game more seriously, stops making excuses and improves life skills. Back injury requires closer scrutiny.

Draft projection: Fourth- to fifth-round pick.

Scout's take: "(Dunker) is big, long and athletic. He reminded me of some of the (University of) Florida guys in recent years. This kid plays with an edge. He has upside."

C-ORG PAT ELFLEIN, #65 (Sr-5)

OHIO STATE　　▶ GRADE: 5.76

Ht: 6-2 5/8 | Wt: 303 | 40: 5.29 | Arm: 33 1/4 | Hand: 9 3/4

History: Ohio native was a four-year letterman in football, track and field and wrestling (national qualifier). High school teammate of Michigan tight end Jake Butt. Was considered a 'Plan B' recruit, as he wasn't offered by OSU until the higher-rated Kyle Kalis de-committed — the result of Jim Tressel's departure. Redshirted in 2012 after a gangrene infection caused him to lose 30 pounds. In '13, served as the Buckeyes' sixth lineman, seeing action in all 14 games. Became a fixture in '14 when he started all 15 games — first three at left guard, final 12 at right guard. Started all 13 games at ORG in '15. Made a seamless transition to center in '16 — won the Rimington Trophy and Big Ten Offensive Lineman of the Year and was an Outland Trophy finalist after starting all 13 games. Two-time team captain graduated

OFFENSIVE LINE

with a communications degree.

Strengths: Has a thick, power base and good hip snap. Plays with good leverage and physicality. Very good awareness to see the blitz and switch off blocks. Good base and balance. Quick, active hands — good placement. Scrappy competitor — plays to the whistle and sometimes beyond. Good finishing strength. Tough, intense and passionate about the game. Exceptional worker, at practice, in the weight room and on game day. Assignment sound. Example leader and offensive tone-setter. Versatile and has played all three interior line positions. Outstanding personal and football character. Very motivated and driven to succeed. Extremely dependable and has been described as one of the best leaders in the history of the program.

Weaknesses: Undersized, tight-hipped and labors to get around the edge on short pulls. Can be challenged by gap penetrators. Has some heaviness in his movement and can be late to reach the second level and initiate contact on linebackers. Has a 23 1/2-inch vertical jump, the lowest of any interior offensive linemen in the draft, and indicative of marginal lower-body explosion.

Future: A very low-risk, high-floor, Day One starter with the wiring, leadership traits and toughness desired in an NFL pivot. Compensates for lack of elite athletic ability with gritty competitiveness. Still has room to improve in pass protection, yet has the tools to start at any interior O-Line position and make an impact readily, and could be a 10-year starter.

Draft projection: Top-50 pick.

Scout's take: "(Elflein) is still getting his footwork down at center, but he's the top center in the draft. He can play center or guard. He has all the intangibles. … I thought he was just okay at the Combine. He didn't run well. He did okay in the drill work. He gets a nod because of his versatility — he can play center or guard. I still think he is a third-rounder all day. I just didn't see him being much better than that. He stumbles a lot. He's not a smooth guy."

ORG JERMAINE ELUEMUNOR, #72 (Sr-5)

TEXAS A&M ▶ GRADE: 5.16

Ht: 6-3 7/8 | Wt: 332 | 40: 5.23 | Arm: 33 1/4 | Hand: 9 1/2

History: Last name is pronounced "eh-LOO-muh-nor." Born in England, and moved to New Jersey in 2009. Discovered football on TV and a subsequent Google search. Was a better wrestler than football player in high school (was not an all-conference football player). In '12, walked on at Lackawanna College (Pa.), where he played four positions along the line (all but center). In '13, played eight games at left guard and two at left tackle. Experienced concussion symptoms at one point during the season. Verbally committed to UCLA and Arkansas before signing with Texas A&M, where he redshirted in 2014. Was a reserve guard in '15, seeing action in all 13 games (started bowl game against Louisville). Became an American citizen before the '16 season. Started all 12 games played — eight at right tackle, four at right guard. Did not play against South Carolina (concussion symptoms). Was hurt on the first play versus UTSA, but did not miss a start. Graduated with a degree in recreation, parks and tourism sciences. Did not perform jumps or shuttles at the Combine because of a right hamstring injury.

Strengths: Is light on his feet with good movement skill for a 330-pounder. Very good body mass and natural strength. Tied for the most bench-press reps (34) among offensive tackles and has good weight-room strength. Solid in pass protection when he latches on. Battle-tested against top competition. Stout and athletic enough to serve as an emergency tackle. Has a big upside from late introduction to football.

Weaknesses: Has short arms and small hands. Only a one-year starter with limited football experience and it shows in his technique — takes short, choppy steps in pass pro, shuffles instead of kick-slides and hands tend to flail without intent, allowing defenders to work his edges. Is still learning to handle the speed and complexity of the game and can be overwhelmed by well-designed pressure packages (see Alabama). Not a natural knee bender. Appears to tire late in games in an up-tempo offense —registered 27.1% body fat at the Combine, indicative of a lack of endurance. Durability must be evaluated carefully given concussion history.

Future: Strong, powerful, thick-bodied, barrel-chested late bloomer with upside to continue blossoming into a potential starter with continued development. Lined up at both right tackle and guard but is most optimally suited to play on the inside in the pros. Has the mass, strength and feet to compete readily in the pros, though will require a few years of seasoning digesting the complexity of the NFL before he is ready to plug in.

Draft projection: Fifth- to sixth-round pick.

ORG-C DAN FEENEY, #67 (Sr-5)

INDIANA ▶ GRADE: 5.68

Ht: 6-3 7/8 | Wt: 305 | 40: 5.24 | Arm: 33 3/8 | Hand: 10 1/4

History: Two-way lineman also lettered in volleyball as a prep. Manned right guard exclusively his first three seasons. As a true freshman in 2012, started all 12 games, tallying 54 knockdowns. In '13, was sidelined by a Lisfranc fracture in his right foot (received medical hardship waiver). Returned to start all 12 games in '14, notching 80 knockdowns. In '15, piled up 102 knockdowns in 13 starts. Started all nine games played in '16 — five at right tackle, four at ORG — though he sustained a concussion in Week Two against Ball State, causing him to miss four games. Allowed just two sacks in 3,355 career snaps. Two-year captain graduated with an exercise science degree.

Strengths: Experienced, four-year starter in the Big Ten Conference. Rolls off the ball flatbacked, runs his feet on contact and washes defenders down the line. Flashes some shock in his punch and can create movement at the line. Plays with a good wide base and balance in pass protection. Has good anchor and grip strength to latch on and control defenders. Anticipates the blitz and stunts and has the recovery quickness to switch off and adapt to pressure. Versatile and has played inside and outside and even showed he can handle playing center at the Senior Bowl. Tough, focused, example leader. Has a gritty, old-school temperament and blue-collar approach to the game. Respected team leader.

Weaknesses: Slightly undersized for a guard. Has some tightness in his body and lacks fluidity in his movement. Pops up out of his stance too often and could play with more consistent leverage and knee bend. Is a bit top-heavy and will lunge at times, lose balance and get overextended. Hands will shoot wide of target.

Future: Tough, scrappy, competitive in-line blocker with the strength and movement skill to readily become an NFL starting right guard and enough versatility to play inside or outside and fit in any kind of blocking scheme. Similar football-playing talent to Rams' 2005 third-round pick and Bills Pro Bowl OLG Richie Incognito, though with stronger football character.

Draft projection: Second- to third-round pick.

Scout's take: "I graded him in the third round, but really wanted to put him in the fourth for us. He has a good skill set with versatility to play center. He upgrades our line as a backup, but I don't know that he can start for us. When anyone gets on his edges, he struggles. Being hurt has not helped him either. I could see him fitting into the second (round) if the medical is all clean. He's a good football player."

C KYLE FULLER, #55 (Sr-5)

BAYLOR ▶ GRADE: 5.23

Ht: 6-4 3/4 | Wt: 307 | 40: 5.24 | Arm: 34 1/8 | Hand: 10 1/4

History: Texas native. Redshirted in 2012. Was a reserve in '13, but still managed 22 knockdowns in 13 appearances. Took ownership of the center spot in '14 when he started all 13 games, grading out at 87.3 percent with 49 knockdowns. Started all 13 games in '15, and posted an 88.9 percent grade with 51 knockdowns. Graded out at 88.9 percent again in '16 when he started all 13 games, amassing 68 knockdowns. Best game was against Oklahoma State when he graded out at 93 percent with four knockdowns. Graduated with a degree in communication studies.

Strengths: Outstanding size with the longest arms and biggest hands of any center at the Combine. Has a frame to carry 320 pounds and the mass to cover up big bodies and handle size. Functional anchor strength once engaged. Plays alert with fine football intelligence. Has enough agility to re-direct and switch off blocks against stunts and blitzes.

Weaknesses: Plays too upright and straight-legged with marginal body control and falls off blocks. Marginal sustain and finishing strength. Spends too much time on the ground. Does not play strong and lacks explosive lower-body power, as confirmed by the lowest broad jump (7'8") of any center at the Combine. Seldom reaches the second level and is best in short-areas. Lacks desirable grit and toughness. Overwhelmed playing guard in Senior Bowl one-on-one's.

Future: Size prospect with enough savvy and agility to warrant developing. Position-sustain blocker needs to get stronger and learn to play with more fire in his belly to fend for a starting job. Has some similarities to 49ers' 2014 third-round pick and Browns C Marcus Martin when exiting USC.

Draft projection: Fourth- to fifth-round pick.

OLT ANTONIO GARCIA, #53 (Sr-5)

TROY ▶ GRADE: 5.31

Ht: 6-6 1/4 | Wt: 302 | 40: 5.12 | Arm: 33 3/8 | Hand: 9 7/8

History: Has a son named Owen. Atlanta native also played basketball in high school. Redshirted in 2012. In '13, started the first six games at left tackle — graded out at 72.7 percent with 10 1/2 knockdowns — before his season was cut short by a right knee injury which required microfracture surgery. Started all 12 games at OLT in '14 — graded out at 87 percent, allowed 2 1/2 sacks, and tallied 35 knockdowns. Started all 12 games at OLT in '15, and allowed three sacks while collecting 33 knockdowns. Started 12-of-13 games at OLT in '16 — accumulated 69 knockdowns, and did not allow a sack. Had 10 penalties. Was suspended for the first quarter of the season opener against

Austin Peay (violation team rules). Graduated with a degree in criminal justice.

Strengths: Has a strong trunk and very good body length with a lean, athletic frame. Natural knee bender with good recovery speed. Carries his weight very well. Very light on his feet and excels mirroring his man in pass protection. Led all offensive tackles with a 31-inch vertical jump, indicative of good lower-body explosion. Displays a mean streak and flashes nastiness in his play, with a bad-tempered football disposition that shows up through the whistle and in kick-slide drills at the Combine when he jarred a fellow participant with his punch in a non-contact drill. Plays angry and seeks to bury defenders. Rises to the occasion against better competition (see Clemson). Matched up well with speed at the Senior Bowl and flashed power.

Weaknesses: Thin-waisted and not naturally big-boned. Very inconsistent with technique and awareness — can be late off the ball, uses a narrow base and flat-out whiffs at times (see Ohio vs Tarrell Basham), stopping his feet. First move is too often straight up — plays tall and overly relies on his athletic talent too much. Overextends too often and could do a better job of keeping his feet underneath him and anchoring in pass protection. Will require some extra reps to assimilate a game plan.

Future: A lean, quick-footed left tackle with good finishing strength and an old-school football temperament that will resonate with NFL offensive line coaches. Has the athletic talent of a future all-pro if he could learn how to harness his aggression, play with consistent technique and steady his hot-and-cold performance. Has starter-quality feet, bend, balance and recovery speed and most of his flaws are correctable.

Draft projection: Fourth- to fifth-round pick.

Scout's take: "The kid from Troy has a chance. He's an athletic left tackle. He is a developmental guy but he's a really good developmental talent. He won't escape the fifth (round) and he could become a long-time starter if the light ever stays on."

ORT AVERY GENNESY, #65 (Sr-5)

TEXAS A&M   ▶ GRADE: 5.24

Ht: 6-3 1/2 | Wt: 318 | 40: 5.41 | Arm: 33 5/8 | Hand: 9 1/2

History: Last name is pronounced "JIN-ih-see." Was a late qualifier coming out of Mississippi, so he attended East Mississippi Community College, where he played left tackle 2012-13. Redshirted in '14. Started all 26 games at OLT 2015-16. Was flagged eight

times in '16. Graduated with a degree in agricultural leadership and development.

Strengths: Very good body mass and thickness. Hands are very active. Good base and balance and is seldom on the ground. Plays under control and is functional mirroring defenders in pass protection. Has enough agility to reach and seal the edge and climb to the second level and fit on linebackers.

Weaknesses: Lacks ideal height for the edges. Very limited hip flexibility, negating his power and leverage. Plays upright and struggles to generate a surge in the run game or anchor and stop a charge. Registered a Combine-low 20-inch vertical jump among all participants, indicative of a marginal explosion and lower-body strength. Measured 28.5% body fat at the Combine and could stand to lean up and improve endurance.

Future: Finesse, upright, round-bodied college left tackle lacking ideal length and flexibility to handle NFL edge speed. Is most ideally suited to play on the right side. Inability to unlock his hips and play with power could restrict his chances of moving inside or earning a starting job. Best fit could come as a swing backup tackle.

Draft projection: Fifth- to sixth-round pick.

Scout's take: "(Gennesy) has very tight ankles when you see him in person. He cannot bend. His only chance is in a zone scheme. He'll be a marginal starter at best, and if he is starting for you, you're probably in trouble."

OLG-C SEAN HARLOW, #77 (Sr-4)

OREGON STATE   ▶ GRADE: 5.12

Ht: 6-4 1/8 | Wt: 303 | 40: 5.19 | Arm: 32 | Hand: 9 1/2

History: Father, Pat, was the 11th overall pick in the 1991 draft, and had an eight-year career with the Patriots and Raiders (1991-98) and is a head football coach at JSerra (CA) HS. Sean is a two-way lineman from California. Was slated to redshirt in 2013, but was needed to start the final nine games at right tackle. Started all 12 games in '14 — first five at ORT, final seven at left tackle. Played through back spasms against Hawaii. In '15, started the first seven games at OLT before suffering a season-ending broken right ankle, coupled with a left shoulder injury suffered in August that he played through all season. Required two surgeries, and wasn't cleared for football activities until the following July. Was healthy enough to return in Week Four of the '16 season, and he started the final nine games at OLT. Team captain graduated with a degree in human development and family sciences.

Strengths: Has enough agility to reach and

OFFENSIVE LINE

seal lanes. Anticipates angles and can win at the snap with quickness in the run game. Recorded a 30 1/2-inch vertical jump at the Combine, indicative of good lower-body explosion. Very tough to battle and play through multiple injuries. Scrappy competitor — flashes a mean streak. Very intelligent, quick learner. Vocal, respected team leader known for having a tough, old-school approach to the game. Versatile and has played on both edges. Has NFL pedigree.

Weaknesses: Has very short arms, tied for the shortest among offensive linemen at the Combine, and is not big-boned. Plays upright, bends at the waist too much and slides off blocks. Soft anchor — plays small, gives up too much ground and is pushed around too much in pass protection. Opens up his hips and leaves the inside susceptible to counter moves. Long-term durability is a concern given injury history and body type.

Future: Short-armed, college left tackle most ideally suited for a move inside in the pros. Has the athletic ability, feet, football IQ and toughness that could project best to center. Fits best as an interior backup, with some upside as a developmental center.

Draft projection: Late draftable pick.

ORT **WILL HOLDEN**, #74 (Sr-5)

VANDERBILT   ▶ GRADE: 5.01

Ht: 6-7 1/2 | Wt: 311 | 40: 5.49 | Arm: 33 1/4 | Hand: 10 1/8

History: Father, Kevin, is a 30-year Navy veteran. Will also lettered in track and field as a Florida prep. Redshirted in 2012. Saw action as a reserve in all 13 games in '13. Started 10-of-12 games at right tackle in '14. The Commodores' left tackle was injured before the season, so Holden was moved to the blind side where he started all 25 games 2015-16. Allowed seven sacks as a senior. Graduated with a degree in Human and Organizational Development. Will be a 24-year-old rookie.

Strengths: Good size. Has played left- and right-handed. Flashes some strength in his hands. Understands angles and can get positioning and wall off defenders in the run game. Very intelligent. Highly durable. Strong personal character.

Weaknesses: Plays too tall and upright, negating his leverage, strength and power. Plays on skates in pass protection and loses his base (see Tennessee). Lacks lower-body, anchor strength. Struggles to handle edge speed and lacks the foot quickness desired on the left side in the pros. Overextends and spends too much time on the ground. Struggles reaching and fitting on linebackers at the second level.

Future: Long-framed, sleigh-backed, right tackle only with limited agility to earn a starting nod. Lacks versatility desired in a backup. Size and smarts are redeeming qualities and will allow him to have more success off the field than on it.

Draft projection: Priority free agent.

Scout's take: "I think he's a free agent. I was surprised he was invited to the Combine. I didn't think his play warranted it."

ORG **DANNY ISIDORA**, #63 (Sr-5)

MIAMI (FLA.)   ▶ GRADE: 5.37

Ht: 6-3 3/8 | Wt: 306 | 40: 5.07 | Arm: 33 | Hand: 9 7/8

History: Florida native. Redshirted in 2012. Saw limited action in two games in '13, as he missed the first 10 games of the season because of a broken left foot (required surgery). Started all 39 games at right guard 2014-16. Played through a torn left meniscus suffered at the start of the season as a junior. Team captain graduated with criminology degree.

Strengths: Thickly built with a strong trunk, powerful legs and a big bubble butt. Recorded the fastest 10-yard split (1.72 seconds) of any guard at the Combine, indicative of outstanding initial burst off the line. Rolls his hips on contact and seeks to finish blocks. Plays with urgency and is quick climbing to the second level to cut off linebackers. Patient and measured in pass protection. Good grip strength to lock up and control defenders in pass pro. Good football IQ and awareness to stunts and line games — keeps his head on a swivel and looks to help. Tough and will play through injuries.

Weaknesses: Has a compact frame with below-average body and arm length and at times lets defenders up and under his pads, gives some ground in pass pro and slips off blocks in the run game. Could stand to improve strike in his hands and sustain better against moving targets. Would benefit from improving hip flexibility — overextends on the move, bending at the waist and negating some second-level power. Is stressed when gap shooters get outside his cylinder.

Future: Tough, scrappy, compact brawler with the competitiveness and toughness to contribute readily in the pros. Quality pass protector at his best in tight quarters where he can mash defenders in the run game and would fit most ideally in a man-blocking scheme.

Draft projection: Fourth- to fifth-round pick.

Scout's take: "(Isadora) is just small. That's my biggest concern."

OLG-OLT DORIAN JOHNSON, #53 (Sr-4)

PITTSBURGH ▶ GRADE: 5.65

Ht: 6-4 7/8 | Wt: 300 | 40: 5.29 | Arm: 35 1/4 | Hand: 10 7/8

History: Pennsylvania native also competed in track and field in high school. Was one of the most highly sought after linemen in the country, and chose Pittsburgh over offers from Penn State, Alabama, Ohio State, and Notre Dame, amongst others. As a true freshman in 2013, made 12 appearances, including three starts — two at left tackle, one at right guard. Took ownership of the left guard position, and started all 39 games 2014-16. Has been flagged for a total of three penalties the last three years. First Pittsburgh first-team All-American offensive lineman since Ruben Brown 22 years earlier. Sprained his ankle in his final game (Pinstripe Bowl against Northwestern) and did not participate in the Senior Bowl.

Strengths: Excellent size, with the body and arm length desired on the outside and has filled in as an emergency left tackle. Can create a surge in the run game and is trusted to clear the line in short-yardage situations. Understands angles, leverage and positioning. Extremely assignment-sound and diligent in his approach. Very competitive. Measured a lean 17.2% body fat and is well-conditioned for an offensive lineman. Outstanding work habits in all phases. Very focused, determined achiever. Extremely business-like in his approach.

Weaknesses: Tends to play too upright in pass protection, negating his agility. Catches too much and could stand to play with more hip snap and hand shock. Bench-pressed 225 pounds only 21 times and needs to get stronger up top. Short-stepping puller at times struggles to connect with moving targets downfield and out wide on screens. Recorded the second-slowest 3-cone drill time (8.41 seconds) and 20-yard short shuttle (5.12) among guards at the Combine, indicative of marginal lateral agility and hip flexibility that does not play as well without help on both sides. Could require extra time to acclimate to a complex playbook.

Future: Lean, efficient, smart, dependable plug-and-play starter at left guard with the length to contribute on the outside in a pinch. Could require some initial patience to adapt to the complexities of the NFL, though has the physical talent to compete readily.

Draft projection: Second- to third-round pick.

Scout's take: "(Johnson) grows on you the more you watch him. I didn't like his tape at first. He's extremely smart, professional and takes the game very seriously. That's why he will make it. He's a third-round talent."

OLT RODERICK JOHNSON, #77 (Jr-3)

FLORIDA STATE ▶ GRADE: 5.20

Ht: 6-6 3/4 | Wt: 298 | 40: 5.40e | Arm: 36 | Hand: 10 3/4

History: Also competed in track and field as a Missouri prep. Played eight games as a true freshman in 2014 — started the final five at left tackle, and graded out at 82.2 percent. Started all 26 games at OLT 2015-16, and took home the Jacobs Trophy (Atlantic Coast Conference top blocker) both years. Team captain. Was a medical exclusion at the Combine because of a pectoral strain and was battling the flu that caused him to lose weight.

Strengths: Excellent length with vines for arms, huge hands and an enormous wingspan (86 3/8 inches). Can get positioning and secure good fits in the run game to seal lanes. Functional pass protector that wins with length and can ride pass rushers up the field. Plays on his feet with good balance.

Weaknesses: Plays upright. Lacks core strength and gets knocked back easily (see Michigan) — will struggle to handle NFL power given his high hips and short torso that allows pass rushers to easily get underneath his pads. Segmented mover that does not play under control and often overextends. Lacks shock in his punch and hand use is sloppy. Soft finisher that leaks the edges too much. Gets rocked handling speed-to-power moves.

Future: Underpowered, developmental left tackle most ideally suited for a zone-slide protection scheme. Still growing into his body and needs to get stronger and improve functional strength. Lacks ideal feet for the left side and core strength for the right and could fit best as a swing backup tackle. Might have some value as a jumbo blocking tight end.

Draft projection: Fifth- to sixth-round pick.

Scout's take: "(Johnson) gets beat all the time. The offensive line is bad, and he is a part of it — it's a big reason why they have been losing. He's a waist-bender who gets out of position a lot. He's not very strong. He's a basketball player trying to play football. Seattle seems to like ex-basketball players. Maybe they'll take a flier on him late. I wouldn't draft him."

ORG KYLE KALIS, #67 (Sr-5)

MICHIGAN ▶ GRADE: 4.99

Ht: 6-4 1/8 | Wt: 303 | 40: 5.15e | Arm: 33 1/8 | Hand: 10 1/8

History: Prepped in Ohio, where he won a state championship and garnered Parade and U.S. Army All-American honors. Redshirted in 2012. Started 9-of-12 games played at right guard in '13. Was benched at one point during the season; dealt with a right ankle injury that sidelined him against Northwestern; and was hampered by back pain. A back issue flared up again during '14 fall camp, but he was able to play all 12 games and start the final eight at ORG. Started all 26 games at ORG 2015-16. Desires to be a WWE wrestler following football career.

Strengths: Big-boned with functional length. Experienced four-year starter in the Big Ten conference. Plays on his feet with good balance. Intense and competitive. Can control defenders in the run game when he latches on. Alert in pass protection and has enough movement skills to mirror defenders. Good weight-room strength and work habits. Exposed by speed in the Orange Bowl vs. Florida State and struggled at the Senior Bowl.

Weaknesses: Has too much stiffness in his body and is a lumbering plodder. Plays too straight-legged and narrow-based, negating his power — first move is up. Does not strike with any explosion at the second level. Has a history of back injuries and durability needs to be examined closely.

Future: Good-sized, barrel-chested, stiff-bodied plodder with a back injury history that causes pause for concern at a position that requires a lot of bending and core strength. Camp body.

Draft projection: Priority free agent.

Scout's take: "(Kalis) is stiff from the hips down. He does a decent job in a short area. As soon as he gets extended, the game becomes a struggle for him."

OLG-C FORREST LAMP, #76 (Sr-5)
WESTERN KENTUCKY ▶ GRADE: 5.81
Ht: 6-3 5/8 | Wt: 309 | 40: 5.01 | Arm: 32 1/4 | Hand: 10 5/8

History: Two-way lineman from Florida. Redshirted in 2012. Became a fixture in '13 when he started all 12 games — first three at right guard, final nine at left tackle. Started all 27 games at OLT 2014-15. Started all 12 games played at OLT in '16, though he sat out against Vanderbilt and Houston Baptist because of knee bruise/MCL sprain. Had a nine-yard touchdown reception against Memphis in the Boca Raton Bowl to cap his career. Allowed three sacks the last three years. Two-time team captain and first-team All-Conference USA selection. Sustained a high ankle sprain during Senior Bowl practice and departed after a day.

Strengths: Experienced four-year starter. Good base and balance to handle speed in pass protection. Has hip flexibility to run the field and connect on linebackers in space. Bench-pressed 225 pounds 34 times at the Combine, tied for the best among offensive tackles and indicative of good strength. Solid anchor. Recorded a good 20-yard short shuttle time (4.62 seconds) and 3-cone-drill time (7.55) at the Combine, indicative of good lateral agility, bend and burst. Also ran a 1.70-second 10-yard split that ranks tops among guards at the Combine. Efficient movement skill. Very smart. Understands leverage and angles. Is tough and will battle through injuries. Blue-collar grinder. Film junkie with strong preparation habits. Matched up well against Alabama and LSU the last two years and showed he could handle better competition.

Weaknesses: Lacks ideal body and arm length to function on the edges in the pros, with arms that measured among the shortest of all offensive linemen at the Combine, and a frame that looks maxed out. Allows defenders into his frame and gives some ground in pass protection. Does not play with consistent power or move defenders off the ball. Limited finishing strength. Has a history of wrist injuries and wears braces on both hands.

Future: A college left tackle with the length of an NFL guard or center, Lamp has been a very dependable, 51-game starter and could contribute readily for an outside, stretch-zone running game. Could be best at the center position if it's not too much strain on his wrists to snap-and-step.

Draft projection: Top-50 pick.

Scout's take: "I might be a little harsh, but I don't think he is the first-round talent he has been talked up as being. I had him sitting in the fifth (round) during the fall on my school (visit). That was the consensus around the league. He was 292 (pounds) when I was there. He is intriguing. If he can play center, maybe I'll move him into the fourth, but there's no proof he can do it. I was disappointed he left the Senior Bowl after one day. He'll wind up in the first few rounds because there are no tackles, and he worked out well. He fits what we do on our line, and I wanted to like him more. I just think he'll play to a third- or fourth-round level and has to be inside. I still struggle with his lack of length and power."

OLT JAVARIUS LEAMON, #52 (Sr-5)
SOUTH CAROLINA STATE ▶ GRADE: 5.10
Ht: 6-7 1/8 | Wt: 332 | 40: 5.30e | Arm: 35 1/4 | Hand: 9 5/8

History: South Carolina native was committed to Clemson, but failed to qualify academically. Signed with FCS South Carolina State, where he redshirted in 2012. Manned left tackle for the FCS Bulldogs. Played 11

OFFENSIVE LINE

games in '13, starting the final three. Sat out two games (coach's decision). Served a four-game academic suspension to open the '14 season before returning to start six of the final eight games. Was ejected from the season finale against Norfolk State for his role in an on-field brawl. Started all 22 games 2015-16. Graded out at 90 percent as a senior. Will be a 24-year-old rookie. Did not work out at the Combine because of a right foot injury.

Strengths: Has rare body and arm length with an 83 1/8-inch wingspan that measured the fourth longest among tackles at the Combine. Functional pass protector — gains depth in pass sets. Athletic enough to get positioning and lean on/wall off defenders in the run game.

Weaknesses: Plays too tall, bends at the waist and falls off blocks. Not a natural knee-bender and does not show much hip snap. Carries his hands too low. Can be beaten off the ball and struggle to handle speed (see Clemson). Uses a shuffle technique instead of kick-sliding and footwork will require refinement. Needs to improve core strength and learn to process movement more quickly. Recorded a 23 1/2-inch vertical jump at the Combine, among the lowest of any offensive tackles and indicative of marginal lower-body explosion. Could stand to cut high 28.4% body-fat percentage.

Future: Very long-limbed, underdeveloped, upright left tackle with very desirable length and enough movement skill to warrant developing. Ability to absorb NFL complexities will dictate his future. Developmental project likely to need time on a practice squad.

Draft projection: Late draftable pick.

Scout's take: "To me, (Leamon) is not a 'football player.' He's a long ways away."

ORT **CAMERON LEE**, #78 (Sr-4)

ILLINOIS STATE ▶ GRADE: 5.26
Ht: 6-4 3/4 | Wt: 312 | 40: 5.44 | Arm: 33 7/8 | Hand: 10 7/8

History: Illinois native also played basketball and baseball in high school. Joined FCS Redbirds as a walk-on. Redshirted in 2013. Was a reserve in '14 (13 appearances). Started all 13 games at right guard in '15. Started all 12 games in '16 — six at ORG, five at right tackle — and graded out 95 percent or better 12 times. Racked up 75 knockdowns, and allowed one sack.

Strengths: Good size. Fairly stout and consistent in pass protection — keeps battling for position. Shuffles, mirrors and works to sustain blocks. Alert to see stunts and loops and switches off blocks. Flashes some aggression in the run game. Assignment-sound and dependable. Fared well against better competition (see Northwestern). Very intelligent and

football smart. Good football character — has not missed a practice in two years.

Weaknesses: Average arm length for the edges. Tends to pop up out of his stance and play too upright, leading to too much waist-bending. Bench-pressed 225 pounds only 18 times at the Combine, the lowest of any interior offensive linemen, and needs to learn to strike with more violence in his punch instead of allowing defenders inside his frame and leading with his head. Catches too much. Did not regularly match up against top competition.

Future: Smart, competitive position-sustain blocker with the size, smarts and enough anchor strength to function readily in pass protection in the pros. Has room to improve as a run blocker and would benefit a great deal if he could learn to unlock his hips and tap the potential in his punch. Developmental prospect with many correctable flaws and would benefit from a few years in an NFL strength program.

Draft projection: Late draftable pick.

Scout's take: "(Lee) plays on his toes too much. That usually doesn't translate well to our level. He has some intriguing developmental qualities though."

OLG **COREY LEVIN**, #62 (Sr-5)

TENNESSEE-CHATTANOOGA ▶ GRADE: 5.10
Ht: 6-3 7/8 | Wt: 307 | 40: 5.19 | Arm: 33 1/2 | Hand: 10 7/8

History: Engaged (Anna Beth). Prepped in Georgia. Redshirted in 2012. Started 11-of-12 games at left tackle in '13. Started all 14 games in '14 — first three at OLT, final 11 at left guard. Was the Southern Conference's top blocker for the second straight season in '15 after starting all 13 games — first seven at OLT, final six at OLG. Started all 13 games in '16 — 12 at OLG, one (Furman) at right tackle. Graduated with a degree in health and human performance.

Strengths: Good size with big hands. Experienced, 51-game starter. Quick into blocks. Shuffles and slides and shows awareness to the loops and stunts. Recorded the second-best 20-yard shuttle (4.73 seconds) and 3-cone drill time (7.55) of guards at the Combine, and it translates pulling around the corner. Blue-collar worker. Versatile and has played multiple positions. Smart and dependable. Has been very durable. Strong personal and football character.

Weaknesses: Lacks ideal length for the edges and plays short-armed. Not explosive at the point of attack. Could improve anchor strength — gets walked back. Does not play big and is too easily controlled. Struggles sustaining blocks in space after initial contact.

Future: Good-sized, top-heavy, tough, gritty blocker with enough agility to project to center,

OFFENSIVE LINE

though looks most optimally suited for a swing interior backup role.

Draft projection: Late draftable pick.

Scout's take: "I gave (Levin) a free-agent grade. He's not strong or physical. He does have some athletic skill. I didn't see a great football player to give him a draftable grade."

ORG DAMIEN MAMA, #51 (Jr-3)

USC   ▶ GRADE: 5.28

Ht: 6-3 1/2 | Wt: 334 | 40: 5.87 | Arm: 35 | Hand: 11

History: California native won a state championship, and garnered Parade and USA Today All-American honors. Weighed nearly 400 pounds entering USC. Played 12 games as a true freshman in 2014, drawing four starts — first two at right guard, last two at left guard. Sat out against Washington State (knee). Started 13-of-14 games at left guard in '15. Did not start against UCLA (violation team rule). Had an ankle sprain during '16 fall camp then split snaps with Chris Brown in the season opener against Alabama (non-start). On the season, started 13-of-14 games at OLG without allowing a sack. Suffered a stinger in practice leading up to Arizona State. Had a cyst in his knee drained before the Washington contest. Did not bench press at the Combine because of a left pectoral strain.

Strengths: Very good mass with exceptional arm length and huge hands, the biggest mitts of any interior lineman. Physical at the point of attack. Adequate balance for a big man. Recorded a functional 1.90-second 10-yard split and is surprisingly explosive off the ball in short areas to root defenders out of the hole. Good anchor to stop a charge and grip strength to control and steer.

Weaknesses: Bad-bodied with too much fleshy mass and heaviness in his movement. Not a natural knee-bender. Weight has fluctuated greatly throughout his career and needs to be monitored. Has sluggish feet, as evidenced running the slowest 20-yard split (3.35 seconds) and 40-yard time (5.93) of any player at the Combine. Also recorded the slowest 3-cone drill time (8.55 seconds), indicative of very marginal agility that shows up letting defenders work his edges. Marginal recovery quickness. Plays a bit narrow-based, struggles unlocking his hips in space and whiffs at the second level. Marginal awareness and blocking instincts — late to see twists and stunts. Pass protection production benefitted heavily from playing behind sensational sophomore QB Sam Darnold.

Future: Big, strong, powerful guard that plays more efficiently than he tests and could compete for a job in a power-blocking scheme and eventually crack a starting lineup if he

learns to play with more discipline and smarts.

Draft projection: Fourth- to fifth-round pick.

Scout's take: "There was a buzz on (Mama) in the fall (as being a mid-round talent). He is so inconsistent — he looks like a different player from one play to the next. One snap he's driving guys off the ball. The next he is the last one to move and letting nose tackles run by him."

OLT CONOR McDERMOTT, #68 (Sr-5)

UCLA   ▶ GRADE: 5.25

Ht: 6-8 1/8 | Wt: 307 | 40: 5.17 | Arm: 34 3/4 | Hand: 11

History: Brother, Kevin, is the Vikings' long snapper. Tennessee prep won state championship in football and basketball, and was awarded Mr. Basketball. Suffered a dislocated shoulder in his final basketball game. Delayed enrollment (attended a boarding school in Connecticut). Redshirted in 2012. Sustained a concussion during '13 spring practice. Made one appearance in '13 when he had surgery to repair a separated left shoulder. Started the final seven games in '14, including one as a blocking tight end and seven at left tackle. Started all 12 games played at OLT in '15, missing just the California contest because of a right knee sprain. Started all 12 games at OLT in '16. Turns 25 in October. Did not bench at the Combine because of a left shoulder injury.

Strengths: Excellent body and arm length with huge hands. Solid technician — efficient mover with clean feet and a fluid kick-slide to take away edge speed. Understands leverage and positioning and keeps working to seal lanes. Recorded among the best 20-yard shuttle (4.58 seconds) and 3-cone drill (7.52) times among tackles at the Combine, indicative of good hip flexibility, balance, bend and burst. Strong personal and football character. Quick study. Takes pride in his craft.

Weaknesses: Very thin-legged with minimal lower-body strength and power, very noticeable in deceleration on bags at the Combine and in his inability to generate movement in the run game. Too tall for the position. Long-term durability is a concern given narrow bone structure and lack of strength. Overaged.

Future: Angular, long-limbed, thin-legged, wall-off blocker with movement skill to attract the interest of zone-stretch O-Line coaches. A much better pass protector than run blocker, McDermott needs to play in a slide-protection scheme to have a chance of sticking on a roster.

Draft projection: Fourth- to fifth-round pick.

Scout's take: "(McDermott) is a non-athletic overachiever. You can't get away being as stiff and up and down at tackle as you can inside. He's long and tough, but he is linear and

OFFENSIVE LINE

stiff. There's no girth to him. He looks like a basketball player without pads on. I don't see any upside to draft and develop him, but someone will."

OLG JORDAN MORGAN, #67 (Sr-5)

KUTZTOWN (PA.) ▶ GRADE: 5.35

Ht: 6-2 5/8 | Wt: 309 | 40: 5.39 | Arm: 34 5/8 | Hand: 10

History: Philadelphia native. Arrived as a 235-pound walk-on. Redshirted in 2012. Manned left tackle for the Golden Bears. Started all 11 games in '13. Started all 10 games played in '14. Did not play against Lock Haven (injury). Started all 22 games 2015-16. Gene Upshaw Award winner as the top Division II lineman. Two-year captain graduated with a degree in leisure and sport studies. Earned invitation to the Senior Bowl and Combine.

Strengths: Has a strong lower body with a thick frame and very good arm length. Plays heavy-handed. Washes defenders down the line and can re-establish the line of scrimmage. Good football-playing temperament and finishing strength. Flashes pop in his punch. Athletic enough to lead up through a hole, pull and connect on a moving target. Functional anchor strength. Good football character.

Weaknesses: Has tight ankles and lacks ideal body length and foot speed to handle the edges in the pros. Needs to learn to play with better knee bend — overextends and lunges too much. Regularly overmatched ordinary competition and struggled to anchor against power (USC DT Stevie Tu'lkolovatu) and handle inside moves (Michigan DT Ryan Glasgow) in one-on-one drills at the Senior Bowl.

Future: High-hipped, thick-bodied, Division II standout ideally suited to move from left tackle to guard in the pros for a power-blocking run game. Senior Bowl struggles clearly showed the need for a year of seasoning, though has upside to continue developing and work habits to fend for a starting job in Year 3.

Draft projection: Fourth- to fifth-round pick.

Coach's take: "(Morgan) is a great kid. He's a hard worker. He's one of those guys who is going to lead by example. He goes about his business in a workmanlike manner, and he does a ton of work when no one is watching."
—Jim Clements, Kutztown Football Coach

ORG-ORT TAYLOR MOTON, #72 (Sr-5)

WESTERN MICHIGAN ▶ GRADE: 5.48

Ht: 6-5 1/4 | Wt: 319 | 40: 5.21 | Arm: 34 1/8 | Hand: 10 5/8

History: Also competed in basketball and track and field as a Michigan prep. Redshirted in 2012. Started all 25 games at right tackle 2013-14. Shifted to right guard in '15, starting all 13 games. Moved back to ORT in '16, and started all 14 games for the Cotton Bowl participants. His 52 starts are most in school history. Allowed only two sacks the last three years. Team captain earned his business degree.

Strengths: Physically imposing human being with a very thick build and looks every bit the part. Outstanding point-of-attack strength. Moves well for as big as he is, as evidenced by superb 4.63-second 20-yard shuttle and 7.73-second 3-cone drill, displaying very good agility. Climbs to the second level and takes out linebackers. Outstanding grip strength — when he gets his hands on defenders, it's over. Good jolt in his hands to shock defenders (see Wisconsin vs. T.J. Watt). Matched up favorably against better competition (see Illinois and Northwestern). Plays with good awareness. Recorded a 30 1/2-inch vertical jump, indicative of very good lower-body explosion. Experienced, four-year starter. Very strong personal and football character. Respected, team leader. Extremely durable.

Weaknesses: A bit duck-footed and tight-hipped and could stand to do a better job of unlocking his hips to avoid lunging and over-extending. Hands need to be retrained to punch instead of shooting from underneath. Gets stressed by speed on his edges and struggles sustaining when the pocket moves or when he is in space.

Future: A massive, big-bodied, right tackle with the contact balance and agility ideally desired in a zone-blocking scheme. Has good enough feet and length to remain outside, but most optimally will fit on the inside in the pros.

Draft projection: Third- to fourth-round pick.

Scout's take: "He has a big body and good balance. I see him moving to guard, where he played in 2015. He's strong and powerful. You see more limitations when an area expands on him. ...He looked pretty good at the Senior Bowl and did a number on (Dawuane) Smoot on Illinois. Our (scouts) had late grades on him during the fall — in the fourth, fifth and seventh. I think he'll wind up in the third (round)."

C TYLER ORLOSKY, #65 (Sr-5)

WEST VIRGINIA ▶ GRADE: 5.36

Ht: 6-3 3/8 | Wt: 298 | 40: 5.30e | Arm: 32 1/4 | Hand: 9 3/4

History: Redshirted in 2012. Manned the center spot for the Mountaineers. Played 11 games in '13 — started three of the first four, but gave way to a fifth-year senior. Took ownership of the position as a sophomore, and started all 39 games 2014-16, allowing only one sack

OFFENSIVE LINE

during that stretch. Was a Rimington Trophy finalist, as well as a finalist for the Senior CLASS Award. Two-year captain graduated with a degree in sport and exercise psychology. Was a medical exclusion from working out at the Combine because of a right hamstring injury.

Strengths: Plays on his feet with good balance and consistently sustains with very good inside hand placement. Sound technician — works his hands and feet in unison. Very good awareness to ward off incoming pressure — continuously scans. Grades out highly in pass protection. Tough competitor. Outstanding weight-room worker. High football IQ — makes the line calls and sets protection. Very good practice habits. Tough and will push through injuries. Vigilante leadership traits — is accountable and demands accountability, serving as a coach on the field. Smart and articulate.

Weaknesses: Lacks ideal mass. Has short arms and small hands, negating his ability to adjust and recover when defenders get on his cylinder. Sets a bit tall at times and could struggle with the bull rush from massive wide bodies (see walked back in Senior Bowl one-on-one's vs. USC NT Stevie Tu'Ikolovatu). Does not play with power or knock defenders off the ball. Lacks top finishing strength. Small frame could be more prone to injury.

Future: Quick, zone-blocking center with the eyes, instincts, awareness, contact balance and leadership traits highly desired in an NFL starter. What he lacks in size and length he compensates for with base, technique and toughness and could emerge as a very efficient performer in a slide-protection scheme.

Draft projection: Fourth- to fifth-round pick.

C-ORT **ETHAN POCIC**, #77 (Sr-4)

LSU ▶ GRADE: 5.67

Ht: 6-6 | Wt: 310 | 40: 5.14 | Arm: 33 1/8 | Hand: 10 1/8

History: Last name is pronounced "po-sick." Consensus All-American. Appeared in six games as a true freshman in 2013, drawing one start at center as an injury replacement. Started all 12 games played in '14 — nine at right guard, three at center. Sat out against Louisiana-Monroe (right ankle). Started all 12 games at center in '15, racking up 132 knockdowns. Started all 12 games in '16, including 11 at center and one (Southern Miss) at right tackle. Did not allow a sack, and paced Tiger linemen with 106 knockdowns and 38 'great effort' plays. Team captain graduated with a sports administration degree.

Strengths: Outstanding body length for a tackle, with very good feet and agility. Good snap-and-step quickness. Understands angles,

leverage and positioning and works to maintain it. Climbs to the second level very quickly and can seal off and finish linebackers. Extremely tough. Gritty football temperament and seeks to finish blocks. Very versatile and could play every position on the line.

Weaknesses: At times appears too tall for the center position, getting out-leveraged at the point (see Auburn, Texas A&M) and appearing overly grabby. Was challenged by the speed of Auburn DT Montravius Adams. Struggled to anchor and was knocked back too much at the Senior Bowl. Not well built to withstand power and could stand to improve his core, functional, football-playing strength.

Future: A very intelligent, versatile, five-tool player proficient in pass protection and tenacious in the run game. Has immediate starter potential inside and outside and could prove to be a better right tackle than NFL center.

Draft projection: Second-round pick.

Scout's take: "(Pocic) has no power. He's flat-assed, long and tall. He's a steer guy. He's probably more of a tackle than a center."

OLT **RYAN RAMCZYK**, #65 (Jr-4)

WISCONSIN ▶ GRADE: 6.26

Ht: 6-5 5/8 | Wt: 310 | 40: 5.20e | Arm: 33 3/4 | Hand: 10 7/8

History: Last name is pronounced "RAM-check." Stevens Point, Wis. native. Was offered a scholarship — by then-head coach Paul Chryst — to Pittsburgh, but did not want to go that far from home. Signed with Division II Winona State, but did not enroll, opting instead for technical school. When his high school coach took a job at Division III Wisconsin-Stevens Point, Ramczyk returned to football. Started all 22 games at left tackle 2013-14. Wanting another chance at the FBS level, reached out to Wisconsin, where he was offered a preferred walk-on spot by Chryst. Was put on scholarship during his '15 redshirt season. In '16, stepped into the lineup and started all 14 games at left tackle. Had post-season surgery to repair a torn labrum in his right hip that kept him from working out at the Combine as a medical exclusion.

Strengths: Has very good feet and movement skill and attacks defenders in the run game. Pulls very efficiently and reaches the second level with urgency to spring open holes (see first TD vs. Nebraska). Very good eyes to locate blockers and create leverage at the point of attack. At times looks dominant pancaking defenders (see Purdue) and flashes an explosive jolt in his hands as a run blocker. Excellent playing range. Maneuvers in space with great body control and can run the field, climbing to the second and third level — makes the game look easy. Sound technician with a smooth, effortless kick-slide — keeps his shoulders squared and absorbs a charge without giving ground. Played in a pro-style offense. Tough competitor.

Weaknesses: Has an underdeveloped frame and could benefit from more time in the weight room. Has average arm length, at times plays short-armed and can be troubled by power and length— see vs. Michigan's Taco Charlton and Michigan State's Malik McDowell. Durability needs to be carefully evaluated following hip surgery.

Future: Athletic, technique-sound, plug-and-play starter with the feet, athletic ability and body control to become a 10-year starter on the left side. Draft standing and NFL future could be affected by medical evaluations.

Draft projection: First-round pick.

Scout's take: "The one-year wonder. He is talented. He is just not a powerful guy. Nowadays, the pass rush comes in waves with guys rotating on each side looking for the best matchups. You would like to have a guy with a little more power. I'm not sure he wouldn't be a better guard."

OLT CAM ROBINSON, #74 (Jr-3)

ALABAMA ▶ GRADE: 6.35
Ht: 6-6 1/4 | Wt: 322 | 40: 5.16 | Arm: 35 1/2 | Hand: 10 1/2

History: Father is former Chargers ILB Steve Foley. Louisiana prep was a consensus All-American and the consensus No. 1 tackle recruit in the nation. Made an immediate impact for the Crimson Tide — started all 43 games 2014-16. Allowed 10 sacks in three seasons, though only one in '16, while amassing 115 knockdowns during career. Won the Outland Trophy, and twice was voted top blocker in the Southeastern Conference. Team captain. In May '16, was arrested in his hometown of Monroe, La. for possession of a controlled substance, illegal possession of a firearm and possession of a stolen gun. Even though the district attorney declined to prosecute, citing insufficient evidence, the school imposed urine tests, drug counseling, mental health consultation, gun safety/ownership education, community service, and ride-alongs with local police. Did not bench at the Combine because of two shoulder issues.

Strengths: Very well-built with broad shoulders, a thick trunk, rare arm length and well-distributed mass. Rolls off the ball flat-backed and drives defenders backward in the run game (see LSU and Texas). Good core strength. Recorded one of the top-5 10-yard splits (1.77 seconds) for offensive tackles at the Combine and is deceptively quick initially getting into blocks. Very fluid in his movement with fine

recovery speed. Appeared quick-hipped in Combine drills. Strikes with pop in his hands and good inside placement. Light on his feet for a big man and can pull and cover up defenders in the run game. Regularly matched up with some of the best pass rushers in the country and held his ground. Plays with confidence. Good competitor.

Weaknesses: Plays down to the level of competition (see Arkansas). Allows defenders to cross his face and could stand to improve his awareness. Vulnerable to quick inside counters. Does not always bring his feet with him and gets overextended and falls off some blocks. Takes some questionable angles. Could improve pop and power in his hands. Has been flagged too much (23 penalties the last two years) and could stand to play with more discipline. Shoulders must be evaluated carefully for long-term durability.

Future: Massive, long-limbed, three-year starter in the Southeastern Conference that might be more suited for the right side than the left in the pros given his body power and ability to generate a surge. Has enough length, agility and competitiveness to stick on the left side and showed gradual improvement throughout his career, though he will need to be challenged to eliminate the inconsistencies in his game.

Draft projection: Top-15 pick.

Scout's take: "Robinson has had some issues with his shoulders so his strength is down. He is a big body, and he can really bend. I'm not worried about his character. He was immature and hanging with the wrong people. His mom will kick his butt if he falls out of line again. It was a one-time, out-of-character incident."

C-OLG CHASE ROULLIER, #73 (Sr-5)

WYOMING ▶ GRADE: 5.22
Ht: 6-3 5/8 | Wt: 312 | 40: 5.56 | Arm: 32 1/4 | Hand: 9 1/2

History: Name is pronounced "ROO-lee-ay." Two-way lineman who also played basketball as a Minnesota prep. Redshirted in 2012. Played 10 games in '13, starting four (three at left guard, one at center). Started all 24 games at OLG 2014-15. Shifted to center in '16, and started all 14 games, grading out at 93.7 percent with 65 knockdowns and allowing one sack, one QB hit, four QB hurries and recording one penalty. Two-year captain graduated with a mechanical engineering degree (3.2 GPA). Will be a 24-year-old rookie.

Strengths: Outstanding size. Extremely intelligent. Very good football intelligence to set protection and make line calls. Good short-area burst and balance to climb to the second level and fit on linebackers, as confirmed by

OFFENSIVE LINE

4.47-second 20-yard shuttle at the Combine, the best among all offensive linemen. Very durable — has not missed any time to injury. Versatile and has experience at guard and center.

Weaknesses: Not a natural bender and tends to play tall. Could stand to do a better job finishing blocks — marginal sustain. Late to reach the block point on short pulls and can be beaten to easily to the spot. Did not regularly match up against top competition and struggled with the quickness of Ronald Blair against Appalachian State (2015) from the OLG position. Footwork has room for improvement.

Future: Very football-smart, assignment-sound, finesse, positional blocker lacking finishing strength. Could warrant interest as a swing interior backup.

Draft projection: Late draftable pick.

ORT JUSTIN SENIOR, #58 (Sr-6)

MISSISSIPPI STATE   ▶ GRADE: 5.23

Ht: 6-4 5/8 | Wt: 331 | 40: 5.59 | Arm: 34 | Hand: 10 1/4

History: Born to Jamaican parents, and grew up in Montreal. Attended Hargrave Military Academy (Va.) in 2011. Redshirted in '12. Appeared in 11 games in '13, starting one at left tackle. Started all 13 games at right tackle in '14. Started all 12 games at ORT in '15, missing just the Arkansas contest (left ankle). Started all 13 games at ORT in '16, and tallied 33 knockdowns. Graduated in three years with a sociology degree. The top-rated prospect for the Canadian Football League draft, according to the league's scouting bureau. Was a medical exclusion from the bench-press test at the Combine because of a right shoulder injury.

Strengths: Outstanding size and overall mass to cover up bodies in the run game. Short sets in pass pro and has the anchor strength to hold up. Flashes some pop in his punch. Good grip strength and inside hand placement to latch on and control defenders. Regularly matched up against Southeastern Conference competition and showed gradual improvement during his three years as a starter.

Weaknesses: Was the only offensive lineman at the Combine to register a 2.0-second 10-yard split, revealing poor initial quickness. Lacks physicality and point-of-attack strength. Soft football-playing temperament. Opens his shoulders too quickly in his kick-slide, leaving the inside vulnerable. Overly analytical thinker — slow processor with marginal blocking instincts.

Future: Stiff, high-hipped, heavy-legged big body lacking the agility, flexibility and initial quickness to survive the rigors of the NFL's trenches. Could require time on a practice squad

and likely have to prove himself in the CFL.

Draft projection: Fifth- to sixth-round pick.

Scout's take: "(Senior) is not a finisher. He's a big guy that doesn't really show you much. He'll be a backup and be out of the league in three years, one of those type(s) of guys. His redeeming quality is his size."

ORT DAVID SHARPE, #78 (Jr-3)

FLORIDA   ▶ GRADE: 5.46

Ht: 6-6 1/4 | Wt: 343 | 40: 5.49 | Arm: 35 3/8 | Hand: 10

History: Florida native also played basketball in high school. Sustained a high ankle sprain during 2014 fall camp. On the season, appeared in six games while providing depth at tackle. Started 13-of-14 games at left tackle in '15. Non-start was Vanderbilt when he was dealing with a foot injury. Started all 13 games at OLT in '16. Allowed seven sacks the last two seasons and was flagged for 12 penalties. Sprained his right ankle against South Carolina.

Strengths: Has an enormous frame with an 87-inch wingspan the size of a small aircraft carrier — effective steering speed wide of the pocket. Has a thick, power base and good anchor strength to stop a charge. Carries his weight well for a big man and is functional sliding and mirroring in pass protection (See Missouri). Walls off and seals lanes. Recorded a quick 20-yard shuttle (4.78 seconds) and 3-cone drill (7.87) times for the second heaviest offensive lineman at the Combine and has enough agility and balance to match up with NFL speed rushers.

Weaknesses: Heavy-bodied, waist-bender — lunges, overextends and falls off blocks. Recorded a 7'4" broad jump, the lowest among all participants at the Combine and indicative of marginal lower-body strength and explosion. Frequently shoft sets and opens his shoulders too early. Too often relies on natural talent rather than technique. Not a puncher and does not consistently use his long arms to create extension. Bench-pressed 225 pounds only 19 times and noticeably lacks upper-body development.

Future: Exceptional-sized, long-limbed flash player who will tease with his sheer mass and rare length and will have to prove he has enough grit, toughness and desire to survive the everyday grind of the NFL's trenches. Underpowered for the right side and has enough athletic ability for the left and could minimally develop into a solid backup swing tackle, with the physical tools to emerge as a starter with a year in an NFL strength program.

Draft projection: Third- to fourth-round pick.

Scout's take: "Sharpe kind of reminds me of (Bills 2011 second-round pick [41]) Cordy

OFFENSIVE LINE

Glenn. (Sharpe) is very talented. He's just a classic underachiever. He probably will be a swing right tackle. He has good enough feet to be a left tackle. There are a lot worse starting around the league than him."

OLG NICO SIRAGUSA, #56 (Sr-5)

SAN DIEGO STATE   ▶ GRADE: 5.42

Ht: 6-4 1/4 | Wt: 319 | 40: 5.39 | Arm: 33 1/2 | Hand: 10 5/8

History: California native and Mater Dei High product. Redshirted in 2012. Appeared in all 13 games in '13, drawing one start at right guard. As a sophomore, became a stalwart at left guard, where he started all 41 games 2014-16. Tore his right labrum vs. Hawaii in mid-October of '14 and finished the season with it. Sprained his right ankle against South Alabama in 2015 and played through the rest of the season with it. Team captain. Suffered a dislocated thumb during Senior Bowl practice. Allowed four sacks in three seasons as a starter.

Strengths: Outstanding size with a powerful base. Good core strength and ankle flexion to generate movement at the line of scrimmage. Solid anchor. Controlled mover. Recorded a 32-inch vertical jump, the best of all offensive linemen at the Combine and indicative of outstanding lower-body strength. Also recorded the quickest 20-yard short shuttle (4.56 seconds) of any guard at the Combine, revealing surprisingly nimble feet for a 320-pounder. Very tough and will battle through injuries, as he did much of his sophomore and junior seasons. Very personable and will spark an O-Line room.

Weaknesses: Below-average arm length. Does not consistently strike with his hands and could play with more violence in his punch. Needs to learn how to gauge the natural power in his body and unlock the power in his hips. Catches and absorbs too much instead of punching and replacing his hands. Is late to reach the second level and struggles initiating contact with linebackers. Could be more stressed by speed on his edges in the pros than he was in the Mountain West Conference.

Future: Big, naturally strong, barrel-chested blocker ideally suited for a power running game. Has the size, strength and sheer mass to maul defenders and create lanes in the running game, though will require an adjustment period to acclimate to handling speed in pass protection. Ideally will have a year to be groomed before being thrust into a starting lineup at either guard position.

Draft projection: Third- to fourth- round pick.

Scout's take: "Siragusa does not have much pop. He's not a grinder. He struggles in space. There was a big grade on him coming into the season. I was expecting to see a more dominant player."

ORT DAN SKIPPER, #70 (Sr-4)

ARKANSAS   ▶ GRADE: 4.97

Ht: 6-9 5/8 | Wt: 309 | 40: 5.43 | Arm: 33 3/8 | Hand: 10 1/2

History: Engaged to be married (Mackenzie) on March 25. Prepped in Colorado, where he blocked in a wing-T offense. As a true freshman in 2013, played all 12 games, starting the final eight at guard. Added a school-record three blocked field goal attempts. Started all 13 games at left tackle in '14. Unhappy with Skipper's overaggressive play and costly penalties early in the season, head coach Bret Bielema worried Skipper would be a "marked man" in the eyes of officials. Consequently, he suggested Skipper change his jersey number from 76 to 63, signifying a "rebirth." Eventually changed again to No. 70. Started all 13 games at right tackle in '15, grading out at 83 percent. Back at left tackle in '16, started all 13 games, including a career-best effort against Mississippi State (97 percent grade). Notched seven career blocked field goals. Team captain has a biology degree. Opted not to perform the bench-press test at the Combine.

Strengths: Rare height. Is tough, smart and competitive. Plays aggressively with very good effort and goes hard to the whistle. Played in a pro-style offense. Three-year starter on both edges in the Southeastern Conference.

Weaknesses: Has very short arms that combined with long frame create natural leverage issues. Very stiff and upright with limited knee bend. Plays narrow-based and labors to cut off edge speed. Lumbers in space and struggles to adjust to moving targets. Too grabby — flagged for 12 penalties in 2016. Tended to wear down as the season went on.

Future: Very lean, long-limbed, tight-hipped right tackle only lacking ideal length and bulk to earn a starter job. Will need to prove he could become a serviceable backup on both sides to fend for a roster spot. Greatest value could be his length to block kicks on special teams.

Draft projection: Late draftable pick.

ORT SAM TEVI, #52 (Sr-3)

UTAH   ▶ GRADE: 5.12

Ht: 6-5 3/8 | Wt: 311 | 40: 5.29 | Arm: 34 | Hand: 10 1/8

History: Last name is pronounced "Tevv-ee." Also lettered in basketball and track and field as a Texas prep. Was recruited as a defensive lineman — recorded nine tackles, two tackles for loss, and one sack in 11 appear-

OFFENSIVE LINE

ances. Converted to the offensive line in '14, and saw limited action in 13 games. Started all 13 games at left tackle in '15. Started all 10 games played at right tackle in '16. Did not play against San Jose State (back). Had his right leg rolled up on four plays into the Washington game, and did not play the following week against Arizona State. Graduated with a degree in sociology.

Strengths: Functional foot athlete with enough lateral agility to hook and seal defensive ends and win with quickness. Light on his feet — quick into blocks and working up to the second level. Plays with good base and balance and is seldom on the ground.

Weaknesses: Plays short-armed with limited extensions and is too often late to shoot and replace his hands. Is not a glass-eater and shows little consistency sustaining blocks — often one hit and falls off. Allows defenders to cross his face (see UCLA vs. Takkarist McKinley) and is late sliding to cut off the edge. Could require extra time to acclimate to an NFL playbook and be overwhelmed by complex pressure packages. Bench-pressed 225 pounds only 15 times at the Combine, tied for the fewest among offensive linemen and needs to get stronger.

Future: Converted defensive tackle still adapting to the offensive line and refining his technique. Has the athletic ability, base and contact balance ideally sought in a zone-stretch blocking scheme and does his best work on the move.

Draft projection: Late draftable pick.

ORG-ORT **NATE THEAKER**, #72 (Sr-6)

WAYNE STATE (MICH.)　　▶ GRADE: 5.11

Ht: 6-4 3/4 | Wt: 315 | 40: 5.48 | Arm: 32 5/8 | Hand: 9 5/8

History: Michigan native. Suffered a cracked tibia in high school. Redshirted in 2011. Was the backup right tackle in '12 when he saw action in all 10 games, drawing two starts. Started 10-of-11 games in '13 — nine at right guard, one at ORT. Sat out the '14 season opener (left ankle), but started all 10 games played — first five ORG, last five ORT. Missed the '15 season after having a herniated disc surgically repaired. Returned to start all 11 games at left tackle in '16 and was named the Great Lakes Intercollegiate Conference Offensive Lineman of the Year. Team captain graduated with a criminal justice degree and is pursuing his master's degree. Turns 24 in October.

Strengths: Good size. Intense, scrappy competitor plays with a chip on his shoulder. Flashes pop in his hands and controls defend-

ers. Adequate anchor strength. Plays hard and goes to the whistle. Versatile and has played inside and out and on both sides. Has long-snapping experience.

Weaknesses: Has very short arms and small hands. Short-stepper with heavy feet. Tends to play too narrow-based. Overmatched marginal competition and did not distinguish himself against post-season all-star competition. Inconsistent footwork and technique — hands shoot wide of the target. Takes questionable angles working to the second level.

Future: A bump-and-steer blocker who must make significant strides with his technique and pad level to earn a roster spot. Versatility could help carve out a niche as an interior backup. Offers additional value as an emergency long snapper.

Draft projection: Late draftable pick.

Scout's take: "I gave (Theaker) a late-round grade, pushing him from tackle to guard. He's smart enough and has enough skill. He really didn't do much at (the NFLPA) all-star game."

C **JON TOTH**, #72 (Sr-5)

KENTUCKY　　▶ GRADE: 5.29

Ht: 6-4 7/8 | Wt: 307 | 40: 5.54 | Arm: 33 5/8 | Hand: 10

History: Indianapolis native also competed in track and field (throws), basketball and lacrosse in high school. Redshirted in 2012. Played all 12 games in '13, and started the final 11. Started all 37 games 2014-16. Team captain graduated with a mechanical engineering degree.

Strengths: Outstanding size and body thickness. Good base and balance in a phone booth and matches up well against power. Smart to see the blitz. Has a love of the game and is committed and dedicated to his craft. Film junkie. Smart and articulate. Tough and competitive. Great weight-room worker. Very durable and has been the bell cow of the Wildcats' offensive line. Experienced, four-year starter in the Southeastern Conference.

Weaknesses: Average athlete. The further he is asked to travel, the more his mechanics break down. Limited blocking range — struggles to adjust to moving targets and fit on linebackers at the second level. Recorded the slowest 3-cone drill time (8.09 seconds) of any center at the Combine, indicative of limited agility and change of direction. Relies too much on his upper-body strength.

Future: Big-bodied, blue-collar, top-heavy, left-handed pivot with the girth, mass and in-line power to match up well against massive wide bodies. A short-area blocker most ideally suited for a man-blocking scheme. Could overcome his athletic limitations and eventually earn a starting job with his professional approach and love of the game.

Draft projection: Fourth- to fifth-round pick.

Scout's take: "(Toth) has really good size, and he is a four-year starter. He looks really good when you see him in person and has great weight-room numbers, but it doesn't translate to the football field. You put on the tape and it is very (ordinary). I was shocked when I saw him in person. He reminded me of (Bengals 2014 fourth-round pick) Russell Bodine, all rocked up with muscle, but underwhelming on the field."

ORT JERRY UGOKWE, #78 (Sr-5)

WILLIAM & MARY   ▶ GRADE: 5.17

Ht: 6-7 3/8 | Wt: 321 | 40: 5.63 | Arm: 35 3/8 | Hand: 10 3/8

History: Last name is pronounced "you-go-kway." Parents are Nigerian immigrants. Played only two years of high school football at Georgetown Prep in Maryland. Joined William & Mary as a preferred walk-on. Redshirted in 2012. In '13, started 7-of-8 games played at left tackle before suffering a season-ending left patella injury. Started all 11 games played at right tackle in '14. Suffered a broken right ankle against Towson, and missed the season finale against Richmond. Started all 24 games at ORT 2015-16. On track to complete his economics degree.

Strengths: Looks every bit the part. Outstanding size with very long arms and big hands to smother defenders once he has his hands on them. Plays with a bit of an edge and seeks to finish. Works at his craft and has a nice kick-slide. Has played right- and left-handed with experience on both edges.

Weaknesses: Is a bit high-cut with limited hip flexibility and explosion in the run game. Struggles to get off the track and adjust on the second level, as confirmed by recording the slowest 3-cone drill time (8.36 seconds) of any tackle in the draft. Tends to play tall, negating his leverage and recovery speed in pass protection, and will give up the edge (see North Carolina State). Technique is not consistent — hands too often shoot wide of target, pad level rises and plays too segmented. Did not regularly match up against top competition.

Future: Big-bodied, tight-legged, upright, seal-off blocker with upside to continue molding. Many of his issues are correctable, and he has the physical talent to emerge as an eventual starter with continued refinement. Developmental swing backup tackle.

Draft projection: Late draftable pick.

OLT CHAD WHEELER, #79 (Sr-5)

USC   ▶ GRADE: 5.26

Ht: 6-7 | Wt: 306 | 40: 5.49 | Arm: 33 1/8 | Hand: 9 ½

History: Santa Monica, Calif. native. Had a shoulder surgery as a high school senior in 2011. Redshirted in '12. Hurt his knee during '13 spring practice, but started all 14 games at left tackle. In '14, started the first eight games at OLT before suffering a season-ending torn right ACL injury. Returned to start 12 games in '15. Did not play against Notre Dame (concussion). Also missed the Holiday Bowl against Wisconsin after an altercation with police at his apartment — NBC News reported police responded at 8:45 a.m., and encountered Wheeler "possibly under the influence of drugs or alcohol, punching walls and windows, and injuring his hands..." Wheeler did not cooperate, and was hit with bean bag rounds. He was taken to the hospital and placed under protective custody for psychiatric evaluation. Did not start the first two games of the '16 season while dealing with plantar fasciitis, but started the final 11 at OLT. Has a non-governmental organizations degree. Was stopped from performing the 3-cone drill after third attempt because of a right ankle injury.

Strengths: Outstanding body length. Plays on his feet and is seldom on the ground. Competitive and effortful. Is quick into blocks and works up to the second level efficiently. Plays with strong hands and latches on and controls defenders in pass protection. Solid technician — understands angles and positioning. Experienced, four-year starter at left tackle. The game is important to him.

Weaknesses: Has short arms and small hands. Tends to play too upright and allows quick ends cross his face too easily. Can be late to adjust to movement. Appeared plodding and too deliberate in his movement through Combine drills. Not explosive off the line and does not generate movement off the ball. Bench-pressed 225 pounds only 15 times at the Combine as a result of shoulder injuries and needs to continue improving his strength. Has been nagged by injuries and long-term durability is a concern.

Future: A good-sized, soft-spoken, left tackle whose performance has dipped since early in his career as a result of an assortment of injuries and off-field issues. Has mid-round athletic talent, though concerns about wiring could knock him down a round or two and affect his draft status.

Draft projection: Fourth- to fifth-round pick.

Scout's take: "He's a talented foot athlete, but we have him turned upside down on our board. He makes some character guys look like gems."

OFFENSIVE LINE

DEFENSIVE LINE

DEFENSIVE LINE

TEXAS A&M ATHLETICS

Nawrocki's TOP 10

1. **MYLES GARRETT**
2. **Jonathan Allen**
3. **Solomon Thomas**
4. **Charles Harris**
5. **Takkarist McKinley**
6. **Taco Charlton**
7. **Jordan Willis**
8. **Chris Wormley**
9. **Tim Williams**
10. **Malik McDowell**

3T MONTRAVIUS ADAMS, #1 (Sr-4)

AUBURN   ▶ GRADE: 5.46

Ht: 6-3 5/8 | Wt: 304 | 40: 4.86 | Arm: 32 3/4 | Hand: 9 1/4

History: Pronounced "mon-TRAY-vee-us." Highly recruited out of Georgia. Manned the nose tackle for the Tigers. As a true freshman in 2013, recorded 20 tackles, 1 1/2 for loss and one sack in 13 appearances. Sat out against Western Carolina (left MCL sprain). Started 10-of-13 games in '14, and produced 43-8-3 with one interception. Started all 26 games the next two seasons — totaled 44-3-2 1/2 with one batted pass and two forced fumbles in '15; and 44-8 1/2-4 1/2 with two batted passes, one interception and one forced fumble in '16. Team MVP. Graduated.

Strengths: Very quick off the ball when he fires off and plays low. Capable of piercing gaps and creating penetration at the snap, troubling LSU's Ethan Pocic with initial quickness. Looked unblockable at times at the Senior Bowl in one-on-one drills.

Weaknesses: Has small hands and short arms and often plays short-armed. Tends to pop up out of his stance and play too tall and narrow-based, and consequently gets washed easily by double teams. Average eyes and diagnostic ability. Tepid intensity level — could use more glass in his diet. Plays out of control and misses tackles, struggling to break down in space. Average hand use to disengage. Pad level fluctuates. Bland pass rusher.

Future: A very quick, one-gap penetrator who needs to have an angle to be effective. Inconsistent interior defender with enough strength, athletic ability and quickness to contribute in a rotational role where he can stay fresh and concentrate on winning at the snap.

Draft projection: Second- to third-round pick.

Scout's take: "I was disappointed with Adams. He has no production to back up the speed he has shown in workouts. He's not strong or physical. I was underwhelmed by his tape."

3T-NT-5T JONATHAN ALLEN, #93 (Sr-4)

ALABAMA   ▶ GRADE: 7.40

Ht: 6-2 5/8 | Wt: 286 | 40: 4.99 | Arm: 33 5/8 | Hand: 9 3/8

History: Father, Richard, is an Army veteran. Prepped in Virginia, where he was a consensus All-American and the state's Gatorade Player of the Year. Played defensive end in the Crimson Tide's 3-4 front. As a true freshman in 2013, moved up the depth chart when Dalvin Tomlinson was lost to injury. Played 13 games, and notched 16 tackles, three for loss and one-half sack with one forced fumble. Started 12-of-14 games in '14, and produced 33-11 1/2-5 1/2 with one batted pass. Also blocked a PAT against Arkansas (14-13 win). Experienced severe cramping against Texas A&M. Had rotator cuff surgery. In '15, started 11-of-15 games, and totaled 36-14 1/2-12 with four batted passes and two forced fumbles. Sat out the second half of the Louisiana-Monroe contest with a left shoulder injury (underwent post-season labrum surgery). In '16, took home the Nagurski, Bednarik, Hendricks, and Lombardi Awards. Was the Southeastern Conference Defensive Player of the Year after racking up 69-16-10 1/2 with two batted passes, one blocked field goal attempt, and two fumble recovery scores in 15 starts. His 28 1/2 career sack ranks second in Alabama history behind Derrick Thomas. Team captain. Graduated in 3 1/2 years with a degree in financial planning and consumer affairs. Declined invitation to Senior Bowl.

Strengths: Extremely strong at the point of attack and can press off blocks and set the edge with ease. Outstanding awareness and football instincts — locates the ball instantly and has a pass-rush plan to beat blockers. Strong and effortful to flatten down the line and make plays in pursuit. Very good initial quickness off the ball to pierce gaps. Can convert speed to power and bull blockers into the backfield with leverage. Excellent career sack (28 1/2) production is a tribute to his motor and initial burst. Registered a very low 1.69-second, 10-yard split at the Combine that ranks tied for second among defensive tackles and indicates outstanding initial quickness to disrupt gaps. His 7.49-second 3-cone drill ranked best among all defensive tackles at the event and is indicative of exceptional lateral agility. Uses his hands with violence and plays heavy-handed. Displays a variety of pass-rush moves (swim, dip, club and stutter step). Consistently productive, three-year starter in the Southeastern Conference. Very smart and football smart and will represent a community with class. Scheme-diverse and can play the piano across the defensive line.

Weaknesses: Lacks ideal arm length for an end in an odd front and at times will give some ground vs. double teams. Is not a dynamic-hipped, creative pass rusher. Bench-pressed 225 pounds only 21 times and is still recovering his strength. Was surrounded by an extremely talented two-deep rotation that keeps the defensive line unusually fresh. Durability needs to be evaluated carefully following shoulder surgeries on both sides earlier in his college career.

Future: A very good football player with the versatility, football character and toughness to make an immediate impact rushing the passer. Is most ideally suited for a role inside as a one-gapping "under" tackle in a "40" front, though he has the base strength to stack the line, read and react in a two-gapping "30" front. Has a similar skill set to Buccaneers' 2010 third overall pick Gerald McCoy, with the quickness, instincts and pass-rush skill to become a perennial Pro Bowl player in a Tampa-2 defense.

Draft projection: Top-10 cinch.

Scout's take: "Allen is so valuable because

he can rush the passer and play inside or out. He can obviously be a three-technique, but he could also be a base end if needed. He has position flex to play in an even or odd front and anywhere on the line. There are not many guys smart, strong and quick enough to do it. He's a franchise building block."

DLE **TARELL BASHAM**, #93 (Sr-5)

OHIO ▶ GRADE: 5.45

Ht: 6-3 3/4 | Wt: 269 | 40: 4.76 | Arm: 34 1/4 | Hand: 10 1/4

History: Prepped in Virginia then spent 2012 at Hargrave Military Academy (Va.). Was a 4-3 defensive end his first three seasons. As a true freshman in '13, recorded 32 tackles, 9 1/2 for loss and 7 1/2 sacks with one batted pass and two forced fumbles in 13 games (five starts). Started 7-of-12 games in '14, and had 33-6-5 with two batted passes and one forced fumble. Had his left meniscus repaired prior to his junior season. Started 11-of-12 games in '15, and produced 43-10-5 1/2 with one batted pass and two forced fumbles. In '16, was the Mid-American Conference Defensive Player of the Year — registered 50-16-11 1/2 with two batted passes in 14 starts. Ohio's all-time sacks leader (29 1/2). Graduated with a degree in marketing and communications.

Strengths: Has outstanding size with very long arms and a frame to continue growing into. Plays with good balance and is seldom on the ground. Very quick off the ball, flashing an explosive burst to run by blockers (see Troy). Flashes power in his hands. Mismatches tight ends with speed and burst and flashes the ability to convert speed into power. Competes hard and chases down the line. Has functional anchor strength to hold ground and defend the run.

Weaknesses: Has some tightness in his body and struggles to bend the edge. Bench-pressed 225 pounds only 15 times at the Combine and needs to continue getting stronger. Could benefit from learning how to use his hands better at the top of the rush. Has not developed a diverse, pass-rush arsenal and must refine his repertoire to compete against more nuanced NFL big bodies.

Future: Long-legged, high-hipped, developmental pass rusher with a high ceiling. Shows big-time flashes of becoming a legit NFL sack artist, but is still a year away and must continue honing his craft and becoming more consistent on a down-to-down basis. Would highly benefit from spending time with a veteran pass rush coach who can teach him the nuance of rushing the passer. Still growing into his body and needs to get stronger to handle an every-down role in the pros.

Draft projection: Third- to fourth-round pick.

Scout's take: "Our coaches really like him. I

DEFENSIVE LINE

don't think he can be a linebacker after watching him work out (at the Combine). He needs to have his hand in the dirt and be coming forward. That's how he is going to make his living."

DLE-OLB TASHAWN BOWER, #46 (Sr-4)
LSU ▶ GRADE: 5.02
Ht: 6-4 3/4 | Wt: 250 | 40: 4.83 | Arm: 33 3/8 | Hand: 9 7/8

History: Prepped in New Jersey. Provided depth at defensive end his first two seasons in Baton Rouge. As a true freshman in 2013, notched three tackles, zero for loss and zero sacks in six appearances. Played all 13 games in '14, tallying 16-2 1/2-0. Played nine games in '15, drawing three starts at DE, and contributed 18-4-1 1/2 with one batted pass and one forced fumble. Missed two October contests (high left ankle sprain), and did not see action against Arkansas. Transitioned to a hybrid DE/linebacker role in '16 when he played all 12 games, starting four in base defense, and totaled 23-5 1/2-4 with one batted pass and one forced fumble. Came off the field in sub-packages.

Strengths: Functional size and strength with good arm length. Very good weight-room worker. Plays hard and competes. Chases hard and pursues to the ball. Very determined achiever. The game is important to him.

Weaknesses: Limited athlete. Extremely tight-hipped and plays too tall with limited knee bend. Was the only defensive linemen to measure a single-digit (6%) body-fat percentage at the Combine and appears overly lean and muscular for the position and more prone to injury, with very marginal hip flexibility or armor to help protect from injury. Was never a full-time starter. Marginal career sack production (5 1/2 sacks). Appeared to stiff in LB drills at the Combine to play on his feet.

Future: Stiff base end who filled an early-down, run-plugging role in seven career starts and lacks the hip flexibility and bend to be cut loose to rush the passer. Appears to be more of a body-builder than football player. Teased scouts with a three-sack performance in the Citrus Bowl against Louisville in his final game and has the work ethic and love of the game for a patient, veteran coaching staff to attempt bringing along slowly on a practice squad for a role as a base left end.

Draft projection: Priority free agent.

3T CALEB BRANTLEY, #57 (Jr-4)
FLORIDA ▶ GRADE: 5.65
Ht: 6-2 5/8 | Wt: 307 | 40: 5.14 | Arm: 32 | Hand: 9 3/4

History: Has a daughter, Caleigh. Florida native was raised by his mother and grandmother, as his father was in and out of prison. Red-shirted in 2013 (Most Valuable Offensive Scout Team Award). Played all 12 games in '14, starting the bowl game against East Carolina, and recorded 21 tackles, four for loss and zero sacks with two forced fumbles. Was cited in July '15 for skipping out on a $90 tab at a local bowling alley. Played three-technique and nose in the fall when he started 10-of-13 games, and produced 29-6 1/2-3. Did not play against Florida Atlantic (groin/abdomen). In '16, started 11-of-13 games at the three-technique, and totaled 31-9 1/2-2 1/2 with one forced fumble. Did not start against Missouri or Georgia while dealing with a left hand injury.

Strengths: Good athlete. Quick and sudden off the ball with the agility to slice gaps and disrupt the backfield. Good closing burst to the quarterback. Has quick hands to swat and come underneath blockers. Has a good feel for blocking pressure and flattens down the line to find the ball. Secure tackler. Finished the regular season strong against LSU and Florida State and matched up well against better competition. Has enough strength to stack the point on the nose.

Weaknesses: Has short arms and small hands with a lot of smooth muscle and lacks bulk. Tends to rise up out of his stance too much when he tires. Only played in 47 percent of snaps the last two years as a starter and has never been an every-down bell cow. Marginal career sack production (5 1/2). Is not stout taking on and shedding blocks and loses gap integrity, swimming off and trying to disengage. Lacks the anchor to neutralize the double team.

Future: A quick, high-hipped, rotational, gap shooter with the balance, bend and closing speed to pressure the passer from the inside. Is at his best working in gaps for a single-gap scheme and has the athletic tools to contribute readily and emerge as a very solid starter. Could be best in a deep rotation that allows him to stay fresh as he was utilized in college.

Draft projection: Second- to third-round pick.

Scout's take: "Brantley is sitting in the fourth round for us. I think he is underrated as an 'under' tackle. His production is not great, but the movement skill is there. Against some of the best competition late in the season, he played very well."

DLE FADOL BROWN, #6 (Sr-6)
MISSISSIPPI ▶ GRADE: 5.24
Ht: 6-3 3/4 | Wt: 273 | 40: 4.91 | Arm: 35 | Hand: 10 1/4

History: Prepped in South Carolina. Attended North Carolina Tech prep school in 2011. Began his college career at Florida International in '12 — recorded eight tackles, two for

DEFENSIVE LINE

loss and 1 1/2 sacks with one batted pass in 10 games (three starts at defensive tackle). Sought a transfer when head coach Mario Cristobal was fired. Sat out '13 per NCAA transfer rules. With Ole Miss in '14, started 9-of-13 games, and produced 38-5 1/2-1/2. Started 8-of-11 games played in '15, managing 32-4 1/2-1, though he was a non-factor the last four games of the season because of a stress fracture in his left foot. Had surgery in December, but the pain lingered throughout the '16 season when he put up 39-6-2 1/2 in eight games (four starts). Graduated with a general studies degree. Will be a 24-year-old rookie.

Strengths: Exceptional size and arm length with a frame to carry 300 pounds. Possesses explosive power in his body (though often does not use it). Flashes strength and power to drive blockers into the backfield. Plays on his feet with good balance. Will battle through injuries.

Weaknesses: Limited instincts. Late to diagnose and locate the ball. Marginal sack production. Has a thin lower body with some tightness in his movement and tends to play too tall with bad technique. Inconsistent effort and motor. Lacks variety as a pass rusher and does not know how to use his hands as weapons to come free. Will require patience adapting to NFL concepts. Overaged. Durability must be evaluated closely given the stress fracture in his foot that lingered since 2015.

Future: A top-heavy, high-hipped pass rusher who possesses the size, frame and base to be considered as a developmental five-technique for a "30" front. Does not consistently utilize his natural talents and gets by coasting too much. Raw, developmental project with upside.

Draft projection: Fifth- to sixth-round pick.

Scout's take: "Brown is a fast riser. He was a FIU transfer that never played and transferred when they tried to move him to nose tackle. He went to a JUCO and Mississippi was right up the street. He was not at the junior college two weeks before Mississippi saw him and decided to take him in. After the starter dislocated his ankle, Brown got his chance and started leading the team in sacks and TFL's. He has a lot of talent, but he was not on the radar coming into the season and a lot of scouts overlooked him."

DLE **TACO CHARLTON**, #33 (Sr-4)

MICHIGAN ▶ GRADE: 5.86

Ht: 6-5 5/8 | Wt: 277 | 40: 4.94 | Arm: 34 1/4 | Hand: 9 3/4

History: Also played basketball in high school. Was a reserve/special teams player as a true freshman in 2013, collecting two tackles, one-half of loss and zero sacks in 10 appearances. Played all 12 games in '14, drawing one

start at defensive end, and recorded 19-5 1/2-3 1/2. In '15, contributed 30-8 1/2-5 1/2 with one forced fumble in 13 games (three starts). Broke out in '16 when he led the Big Ten in sacks — registered 43-13-9 1/2 with two batted passes in 11 starts on the weak side. Missed September contests against Central Florida and Colorado because of an ankle injury. Graduated.

Strengths: Looks every bit the part of a star NFL pass rusher, with a prototypical build, outstanding body length, fluid movement skills and very good athletic ability. Good edge-setting, point-of-attack strength. Covers ground in a hurry when he opens his stride. Very good closing speed was reflected in 20-yard split (2.71 seconds), among the fastest of defensive ends at the Combine. Secure tackler with long arms to corral ball-carriers. Has the length to disrupt passing lanes. Proved he could produce on big stages, as he did with his 2 1/2-sack signature performance against Ohio State.

Weaknesses: Unpolished and inconsistent, and career has been marked by underachiever tendencies. Needs to refine his hand use and learn how to create a pass-rush plan. Motor idles too much, and he does not play with consistent intensity, disappearing for stretches. Can be late to find the ball. Ordinary 1.71-second, 10-yard split for a pass rusher, indicating average initial get-off speed. Tends to play too upright. Overly analytical processor who does not trust his eyes and plays slow. Only a one-year starter. Benefitted from being surrounded by a very talented supporting cast that created more one-on-one situations.

Future: Exceptional-sized, thick-bodied, long-limbed base end with the scheme flexibility to fit into a "30" or "40" front. Took time to put it all together, and remains one of the most polarizing prospects in this year's draft. Made his senior season his best and is on a path to become a very solid starter, and potential star, though can be expected to take another three seasons before he emerges as the type of unique talent he is capable of becoming. May always be challenged to avoid complacency and to sustain a level of excellence, and is likely to be motivated by contract years.

Draft projection: Top-50 pick.

Scout's take: "Taco didn't wow me at the Combine, and he didn't wow me on tape. You hear prognosticators and even people in our own building talking about him as a great defensive end — I just haven't bought in. He'll (be drafted) highly just off his sheer physical traits. I will stand by my grade (in the third round) and see how his career plays out. I know what I saw, and I can only grade what I see."

DEFENSIVE LINE

DT CHUNKY CLEMENTS, #11 (Sr-4)

ILLINOIS ▶ GRADE: 4.97

Ht: 6-2 3/8 | Wt: 301 | 40: 5.10e | Arm: 32 7/8 | Hand: 10 3/8

History: Ohio prep missed the first half of his senior football season because of a right ACL tear. Provided defensive line depth as a true freshman in 2013, and was credited with four tackles, one for loss and zero sacks in 10 appearances. Played all 13 games in '14, drawing three starts, and recorded 24-6-2 with three batted passes and one forced fumble. Switched from jersey No. 99 to No. 11. Started 10-of-12 games in '15, and produced 35-11 1/2-1/2 with one batted pass and two forced fumbles. Added six hurries. In April '16, was charged with misdemeanor battery after he was accused of punching a man at a party in March. Pleaded not guilty in June, and entered a second-chance agreement which required 20 community service hours. Was not suspended. Started 7-of-11 games in '16, and collected 36-7-3 1/2 with one batted pass and one forced fumble. Was hurt against Iowa, and did not play against Northwestern. Was a medical exclusion from the Combine with a right foot injury. Suffered a left shoulder injury at his pro day and did not finish benching or working out.

Strengths: Looks the part with a solid build and good athletic ability. Flashes quickness off the snap to penetrate gaps and knife into the backfield. Has enough strength to hold the point and play off blocks. Solid career production.

Weaknesses: Tight-hipped and takes choppy steps. Tends to play too tall. Inconsistent pad level. Has a limited playing range and seldom makes plays outside the box. Motor runs too hot and cold.

Future: Adequate-sized, athletic, rotational three-technique with enough quickness to contribute in a rotation if he can learn to be more consistent in his approach.

Draft projection: Priority free agent.

Scout's take: "You see flashes, but there's too much inconsistency in his game. That's why there was a lack of playing time. I thought he was more of a two-gap, anchor type than a gap penetrator, but he's versatile enough to play both spots."

DLE-LOLB BRYAN COX, #94 (Sr-5)

FLORIDA ▶ GRADE: 5.18

Ht: 6-2 7/8 | Wt: 265 | 40: 4.92 | Arm: 33 3/4 | Hand: 9 1/2

History: Son of Bryan Sr., a Pro Bowl linebacker who played 12 years in the NFL (1991-2002), most notably with the Dolphins, and spent the last three years coaching defensive line for the Falcons. Bryan Jr. is a Fort Lauderdale (Fla.) St. Thomas Aquinas product. Missed half of his senior season because of torn left wrist ligaments. Redshirted in 2012. Made eight appearances in '13, recording five tackles, two for loss and two sacks. With Donte Fowler playing the "Buck," Cox started 10-of-11 games played at defensive end in '14, contributing 29-6-4. Sat out the bowl game against East Carolina (hip surgery). Started 13-of-14 games in '15 — 11 at DE, two at rush end — and produced 45-10 1/2-3 1/2 with one batted pass and two forced fumbles. In '16, played the left side, his natural position, and totaled 19-2 1/2-1/2 with one forced fumble in 10 games (five starts). Was dealing with an ankle sprain and knee tendinitis then hurt his thumb during Missouri pre-game warm-ups — was a non-factor against Missouri and Georgia. Two weeks later, sprained his right ankle against South Carolina — sat out against LSU and Florida State, and did not record any stats against Alabama or Iowa at the end of the season.

Strengths: Has functional anchor strength to dig his heels in the dirt and set a hard edge. Good competitor. Flashes power in his hands. Versatile and has played many techniques, lining up on both sides and also operating out of two-point stance in even and odd fronts. Experienced, three-year starter in the Southeastern Conference. Has NFL pedigree. Has contributed as a tight end in short-yardage situations.

Weaknesses: Plays tall with too much heaviness in his movement and is not a natural knee bender. Bench-pressed 225 pounds only 16 times at the Combine and needs to improve strength. Recorded a 26-inch vertical jump at the Combine, the lowest of any defensive end at the event and indicative of marginal athletic ability and lower-body explosion. Durability has been an issue throughout his career. Minimal career sack production (10).

Future: A high-hipped, smooth-muscled, base left end ideally suited for a "40" front, Cox could also warrant some late developmental interest as an outside linebacker in a "30" front. Struggled battling through injuries as a senior but showed enough toughness and effort in 2015 to receive a chance to compete for a backup job.

Draft projection: Late draftable pick.

DLE KEIONTA DAVIS, #93 (Sr-5)

TENNESSEE-CHATTANOOGA ▶ GRADE: 5.23

Ht: 6-3 | Wt: 271 | 40: 4.86 | Arm: 34 | Hand: 9 1/2

History: Pronounced "kee-OHN-tay." Chattanooga native also competed in basketball and track and field in high school. Suffered a torn right ACL during his senior football season in

2011. Redshirted in '12. Played 11 games n '13, starting four, and recorded 21 tackles, four for loss and 11/2 sacks. Did not play against Furman (hyperextended left knee). Was hampered by a high right ankle sprain at the beginning of the '14 season (sat out against Jacksonville State) — 28-10 1/2-5 1/2 with five batted passes, one interception and four blocked kicks in 13 games (one start). Started all 13 games at right end in '15, and notched 39-17-13 1/2 with six batted passes and one forced fumble. Was the Southern Conference Defensive Player of the Year in '16 after registering 44-11 1/2-10 1/2 with seven batted passes, three forced fumbles and one blocked kick in 13 starts at RDE. Team captain graduated with a business degree. Invited to the Senior Bowl. Was a medical exclusion from working out at the Combine because of injury (cervical spine).

Strengths: Has a frame to easily carry 290 pounds, inviting the ability to kick inside and mismatch guards on third down. Plays with good balance and body control. Good hand-eye coordination and awareness to bat down 18 passes in his career. Uses his feet well to set up blocks. Notched a sack and four tackles in the Senior Bowl and showed well against better competition. Very good career sack production (31).

Weaknesses: Has some noticeable tightness in his body and is not a natural bender. Overwhelmed by the double team and gets moved off spots. Struggles tackling in the open field. Lacks ideal foot speed to race the corner. Has no special-teams experience. Was not regularly challenged against lesser competition.

Future: Stocky, strong, long-armed, productive pass rusher with a knack for disrupting passing lanes. Has enough size, length and athletic ability to warrant developing as a pass rusher. Injury history will need to be vetted carefully, and medical evaluations could affect his draft status.

Draft projection: Late draftable pick.

Scout's take: "I graded (Davis) as a PFA. I didn't think he was as good as (Saints 2015 fifth-round pick) Davis Tull, who has since been cut for injuries."

DRE-ROLB DYLAN DONAHUE, #49 (Sr-6)

WEST GEORGIA ▶ GRADE: 5.05

Ht: 6-2 5/8 | Wt: 248 | 40: 4.79 | Arm: 30 1/4 | Hand: 9

History: Father, Mitch, played 31 games with the 49ers and Broncos (1991-94). Prepped in Montana. Tore his left labrum as a high school junior. Redshirted at NAIA Montana Western in 2011. Did not play football in '12. Went the junior college route, and played two years at Palomar College (Calif.). Started all 10 games in '13,

and posted 67 tackles, 13 1/2 for loss and 8 1/2 sacks. Started all 10 games in '14, and notched 64-22-10 1/2 with one batted pass, one forced fumble and one blocked kick. Transferred to Division II West Georgia, and was used primarily as a weak-side defensive end. Started 11-of-12 games in '15, and produced 53-17 1/2-12 with two forced fumbles. In September, missed two games and came off the bench in another because of an MCL sprain. Was the Gulf South Conference Defensive Player of the Year in '16 after racking up 67-20-13 1/2 with one batted pass and one blocked kick. Team captain. Will be a 25-year-old rookie.

Strengths: Competitiveness shows up heavily on tape in relentless pursuit effort. Plays hard and leaves everything on the field in practice and games. Plays with leverage and flashes pop in his hands. Has a passion for the game. Is tough and will battle through injuries. Outstanding weight-room worker.

Weaknesses: Modest size with deficient arm length. Tied for the smallest hands (9 inches) and possesses the shortest arms (30 1/4) and wingspan (74 1/8) of any defensive linemen at the Combine. Recorded a low 29 1/2-inch vertical jump. Was a bit overwhelmed by performing on a big stage at the Combine and several times needed to be corrected about performing drills properly. Could stand to play with more discipline and may require some extra reps to assimilate a complex game plan. Production was inflated vs. ordinary competition. Not fluid dropping into coverage. Overaged.

Future: Tough, scrappy, overachieving, small school college defensive end lacking the length and discipline needed to secure a roster spot. Could warrant some looks as a leverage rush linebacker from an aggressive "30" front, though lack of length could be too much of a hindrance to overcome. Has the tenacity desired to become a fixture on special teams with continued focus.

Draft projection: Priority free agent.

DLe-ROLB KEN EKANEM, #4 (Sr-5)

VIRGINIA TECH ▶ GRADE: 5.09

Ht: 6-2 3/4 | Wt: 257 | 40: 4.89 | Arm: 32 | Hand: 10 ½

History: Last name is pronounced "ee-CAN-um." Virginia native tore his right ACL and meniscus in the state championship in 2011. Redshirted in '12. Was primarily a special-teams player in '13 when he tallied three tackles, zero for loss and zero sacks in 11 appearances. Impact right defensive end for the Hokies. Stepped into the lineup in '14, and produced 53-14 1/2-9 1/2 with one batted pass and one forced fumble in 13 starts. Had off-season surgery to repair a torn left rotator cuff. Started all 13 games in

DEFENSIVE LINE

'15, and totaled 39-9 1/2-4 1/2 with three batted passes and two forced fumbles. Started all 13 games played in '16, and logged 36-10-7 1/2 with two batted passes. Suffered a slight tear to his right pectoral muscle against Syracuse — did not play against Miami (right arm), and played through it the rest of the season. Had 36 hurries in three seasons as a starter. Graduated with a management degree. Opted not to bench press at the Combine.

Strengths: Times the snap well and has a quick first step to rip past blockers, using his hands and feet in unison and showing a pass-rush plan. Efficient hand usage to work off blocks — shows quick slaps, swat, club and arm-over moves that allow him to beat blockers off the edge and play faster than his timed speed would suggest. Experienced, three-year starter with solid sack production.

Weaknesses: Has short arms and a small 77-inch wingspan. Is not stout against the run or initially explosive off the edge. Catches and gets driven back as a tackler. Recorded an ordinary 30 1/2-inch vertical jump, indicative of limited lower-body explosiveness. Notched a 4.63-second 20-yard short-shuttle that was among the slowest of defensive ends at the Combine, revealing a lack of hip flexibility and burst.

Future: Deceptively athletic end with enough of an arsenal as a pass rusher to contribute in a rotation. Lack of length may suit him best for a role in a "30" front as a "bandit" linebacker.

Draft projection: Late draftable pick.

DRE-ROLB MYLES GARRETT, #15 (Jr-3)
TEXAS A&M　　▶ GRADE: 7.90
Ht: 6-4 1/2 | Wt: 272 | 40: 4.66 | Arm: 35 1/4 | Hand: 10 1/4

History: Texas native was a Parade All-American and the state's 5A Defensive Player of the Year. Made an immediate impact in 2014, as he broke Jadeveon Clowney's Southeastern Conference record for sacks by a freshman. Was the Aggies' Defensive MVP after posting 53 tackles, 14 for loss and 11 1/2 sacks with one batted pass and one blocked field goal attempt in 12 games (eight starts at rush end). Sat out against Missouri (concussion). In '15, led the SEC in sacks and tackles for loss while deployed as a rush end in defensive coordinator John Chavis' upfield scheme — registered 59-19 1/2-12 1/2 with three batted passes, one interception, five force fumbles and a blocked punt in 13 starts. Had his wisdom teeth pulled less than a week before the Nevada game. Started 9-of-11 games played in '16, and managed 33-15-8 1/2 with one batted pass, two forced fumbles and a blocked field goal attempt. Sustained a high left ankle sprain against Arkansas — sat out against South Carolina and New Mexico State; was hobbled in mid-season contests, including non-starts against Tennessee and Mississippi State; and did not feel healthy until Nov. 19 against UTSA. Team MVP and captain. Was a Bednarik Award finalist and two-time Lombardi Award finalist. Garrett's 32 1/2 sacks were No. 1 in the country 2014-16. Does not turn 22 until after Dec. 29. Did not run the shuttles at the Combine because of a tight hamstring.

Strengths: Has exceptional arm length and overall size. Extremely strong — bench-pressed 225 pounds 33 times at the Combine. Outstanding lower-body acceleration and take-off speed, confirmed by notching a 1.58-second 10-yard split at the Combine. Has a long second step and can trim the edge. Exceptional hip flexibility for a 272-pound man. Very strong core. Explosive drive-thru, tackler. Has exceptional career sack production (32 1/2). Recorded a 41-inch vertical jump, tops among all defensive linemen at the Combine, and has rare spring in his legs. Consistently matched up against the best competition in the Southeastern Conference. Versatile and scheme-diverse, capable of fitting into a "30" or "40" front and lining up as a hand-in-the-dirt end or outside linebacker from a two-point stance. Played thru an ankle injury much of the season and showed he will battle through injuries.

Weaknesses: Motor does not always rev on tape, and he leaves some production on the field. Plays in spurts and is not as consistently dominant as his physical talents suggest he should be. Still learning how to develop a pass-rush arsenal. Complacency too often appears to settle in after initially being stalled and needs to develop more counter moves. Does not consistently flatten down the line and pursue with top effort. Much of his production came outside the Southeastern Conference against ordinary competition, with 16 sacks being recorded against Lamar, Rice, Louisiana-Monroe, Nevada and UTSA and only 12 being tallied against SEC opponents.

Future: Consistently drew extra attention from opponents and was forced to deal with double- and even triple-teams, yet still found a way to create consistent pressure as a marked man. Has a unique combination of balance, bend, burst and power to become an impact NFL pass rusher. A dynamic game-changer with rare explosive traits, Garrett stands to become one of the league's most elite pass rushers and possesses one of the most extraordinary skill sets to enter the league since Julius Peppers was selected second overall in 2002.

Draft projection: Top-10 cinch.

Scout's take: "I worried about him taking

plays off and some of the concerns our (scouts) expressed about toughness until I went to the school and saw how often he was being chipped and seeing two and three extra blockers coming his way. You have to gameplan for him. He is going to free up his teammates to make a lot of plays.

DT-3T RYAN GLASGOW, #96 (Sr-5)

MICHIGAN ▶ GRADE: 5.28
Ht: 6-2 7/8 | Wt: 302 | 40: 5.14 | Arm: 33 3/8 | Hand: 9 5/8

History: Last name is pronounced "GLASS-go." Brother, Graham, is a guard for the Lions. Ryan also played basketball as an Illinois prep. Joined the team as a preferred walk-on. Redshirted in 2012. Was a depth player in '13, scratching two tackles, zero for loss and zero sacks in 11 appearances. Manned the nose tackle for the Wolverines. Started 11-of-12 games in '14, and recorded 22-4-0 with one forced fumble. Earned a scholarship prior to the '15 season when he totaled 25-5-1 in nine starts, though he missed the final four games because of a torn left pectoral muscle. Started all 13 games in '16, and amassed 42-9 1/2-4 with one forced fumble and one batted pass. Graduated with economics degree. Will be a 24-year-old rookie.

Strengths: Extremely competitive and keeps working to the ball in pursuit. Plays hard with very good energy and much of his production comes from second effort. Goes to the whistle. Strong tackler. Alert to screens setting up and reacts quickly. Football is very important to him. Respected, vocal team leader. Has NFL pedigree.

Weaknesses: Limited body control. Plays a bit tall and can be knocked off the spot and struggle to split double teams. Bench-pressed 225 pounds only 20 times at the Combine and needs to continue improving his strength. Too often leads with his chest and could stand to do a better job of using his hands to disengage from blocks.

Future: Try-hard overachiever who has lined up as a three-technique and nose tackle in college and is more ideally suited for a role on the nose in the pros. Could provide depth in a rotation.

Draft projection: Fifth- to sixth-round pick.

Scout's take: "Glasgow is a later-round, lunch-pail type of guy. He's not a great athlete — he just plays his (butt) off and has enough ability to create some upfield penetration."

DRE-NT DAVON GODCHAUX, #57 (Jr-3)

LSU ▶ GRADE: 5.38
Ht: 6-3 3/8 | Wt: 310 | 40: 5.19 | Arm: 32 3/8 | Hand: 10 1/4

History: Overcame a challenging upbringing in Louisiana that included his father being in jail when he was born, his home being shot up when people came to kill his brother, and health issues of his mother, all of which he still draws motivation from. Has a son, Davon II. Suffered a torn ACL and LCL during his senior season as a Louisiana prep. Also played basketball. In July 2014, was cited for criminal mischief — as a prank, he threw firecrackers into an apartment unit. Took over the right defensive tackle job a month into his freshman season —started 10-of-13 games, and produced 42 tackles, 11 1/2 for loss and zero sacks with one forced fumble. Started all 12 games in '15, and notched 41-9-6 with one batted pass and one forced fumble. In '16, was deployed as a right defensive end in new defensive coordinator Dave Aranda's 3-4 scheme — started all 12 games, and totaled 62-8 1/2-6 1/2 with one batted pass. Was arrested in late September, and charged with false imprisonment and domestic abuse battery/child endangerment (both misdemeanors). Charges were dropped days later, and Godchaux returned to the team without missing game action. At the end of the year, received team award for performance, leadership and commitment. Did not finish workout at the Combine after suffering a left hamstring injury during his 40-yard dash.

Strengths: Has a well-distributed frame and carries his weight well. Good functional strength to stack the point and work off blocks. Versatile enough to play anywhere along LSU's "30" front. Flashes short-area burst closing on the ball. Experienced, three-year starter in the Southeastern Conference with 14 career sacks.

Weaknesses: Has short arms and gets stuck on blocks. Bench-pressed 225 pounds only 18 times at the Combine and needs to improve his strength and develop more pass-rush moves. Needs to do a better job of feeling blocking pressure and anticipating. Limited anchor strength to dig his heels in the dirt vs. the double team. Measured 27% body fat at the Combine and has room to improve stamina and conditioning.

Future: A big-bodied, short-limbed, developmental five-technique with enough strength and quickness to play on the nose or kick over the guard and shoot gaps from the three-technique. Has continued to improve since the time he has arrived on campus and overcome a great deal of adversity in his life.

Draft projection: Third- to fourth-round pick.

DLE-LOLB DAESHON HALL, #10 (Sr-4)

TEXAS A&M ▶ GRADE: 5.66
Ht: 6-5 1/4 | Wt: 266 | 40: 4.79 | Arm: 35 | Hand: 9 5/8

History: Moved from Washington to Texas in high school. Played basketball, and was Texas' 4A Defensive Player of the Year. Had

DEFENSIVE LINE

both labrums surgically repaired after the season. Bulked up 60 pounds during his time at A&M. Thrown into the fire prematurely as a true freshman in 2013 — tallied 29 tackles, three for loss and zero sacks with one interception in 13 games (one start). Was ejected for throwing a punch against Rice. Played all 13 games in '14, and collected 29-6-4 1/2. Playing opposite Myles Garrett, started all 26 games the next two seasons — totaled 54-14 1/2-7 with two batted passes and two forced fumbles in '15; and 50-13-4 1/2 with one batted pass, two forced fumbles and 12 hurries in '16.

Strengths: Outstanding size and arm length. Looks the part with a big frame with plenty of growth potential. Competes hard and battles at the point of attack. Good instincts to locate the ball, anticipate blocking pressure and play off blocks. Has a 36-inch vertical jump, indicative of good athletic ability and lower-body explosion. Versatile and has played a number of techniques along the line throughout his career, showing he can play up from a two-point stance or set an edge. Strong personal and football character.

Weaknesses: Does not play to his size and gets pushed around too much. Bench-pressed 225 pounds only 18 times at the Combine and needs to improve strength. Needs to improve his base, anchor strength and learn how to use his hands better and lock out and set a hard edge. Inconsistent pad level. A lot of production was flushed to him playing opposite Myles Garrett. Needs to develop a better pass-rush plan.

Future: An intriguing, athletic pass rusher with unique versatility to play up or down in multiple fronts. One of the few prospects in the draft with the size, frame and enough athletic ability to be utilized as an outside linebacker or 5-technique in an odd front or as an end in an even front, and versatility could drive up his value.

Draft projection: Second- to third-round pick.

Scout's take: "(Hall) is really a 4-3 base end. He has a big frame but not the strength. He's stiff and mechanical."

DRE-ROLB **CHARLES HARRIS**, #91 (Jr-4)

MISSOURI ▶ GRADE: 6.18
Ht: 6-2 3/4 | Wt: 253 | 40: 4.81 | Arm: 32 3/8 | Hand: 9 5/8

History: Two-way player who also starred on the hardwood as a Kansas City, Mo. prep (did not play football until junior season). Recruited to Missouri by then-head coach Gary Pinkel. Redshirted in 2013. Was behind Shane Ray (Broncos) and Markus Golden (Cardinals) in '14, but contributed 19 tackles, four for loss and two sacks with two batted passes and one forced fumble in 14 games (one start). Inherited the right end spot in '15, and responded

with 56-18 1/2-7 with one batted pass and two forced fumbles in 12 starts. Sat out '16 spring practice after having his right labrum surgically repaired. As a redshirt junior, adapted to a new scheme which called for the lineman to play more of a read-and-react, gap-control style compared to the simpler, upfield scheme of previous years. Started all 12 games in the fall, and registered 61-12-9 with two batted passes and two forced fumbles. On track to graduate with a degree in health science. Had both labrums surgically repaired while at Missouri.

Strengths: Outstanding athlete with great initial quickness, bend and burst off the edge. Beats blockers to the spot in the run game slicing gaps and knifing into the backfield, using his quickness and stutter steps to stunt inside. Works a variety of pass-rush moves to come free, deploying a dip/rip, spin, bull and inside-counter moves. Is able to convert speed to power. Has outstanding closing speed to track down backs to the perimeter. The game is important to him and he works at it.

Weaknesses: Lacks ideal bulk and needs to continue getting stronger to handle double teams. Can be late to shed and locate the ball at times. Recorded the slowest 60-yard shuttle (12.53 seconds) of any player at the Combine, indicative of limited hip flexibility and endurance. Has an average 32-inch vertical jump and 9'1" broad jump, indicative of a lack of lower-body explosion. Needs to continue developing his pass-rush repertoire.

Future: A long, lean, high-hipped, athletic, natural bender with the short-area burst and explosion to pressure the edges and creatively harass quarterbacks. Was more impactful in 2015 in a defense better designed to maximize his pass-rushing talents. Very productive, high-effort, creative sack artist with the length, athletic ability and short-area burst to be effective as "Jack"/"Bandit" pass rusher in a "30" front or ripping off the edge in a 4-3 front, and has the athletic tools to become a regular double-digit sack producer in the pros.

Draft projection: First-round pick.

Scout's take: "I was surprised he didn't test better (at the Combine). He didn't run or jump particularly well. I was expecting to see a more explosive athlete based on the way he plays."

DRE-ROLB **TREY HENDERICKSON**, #11 (Sr-4)

FLORIDA ATLANTIC ▶ GRADE: 5.32
Ht: 6-4 | Wt: 266 | 40: 4.62 | Arm: 32 | Hand: 9 7/8

History: Florida native won a state championship as a defensive end-tight end. Was a backup/special teams player as a true freshman in 2013 (wore jersey No. 19), recording nine tackles, 2 1/2 for loss and 1 1/2 sacks in 12 appearances. Was deployed at right defensive end. Started 9-of-12 games in '14 (wore jersey No. 14), and posted 32-10-5 with one batted pass, two forced fumbles. Started 11-of-12 games in '15 (wore jersey No. 9), and recorded 39-15-13 1/2 with five forced fumbles. Started all 12 games in '16, and registered 51-15-9 1/2 with two batted passes, one forced fumble and four blocked kicks. Added 20 hurries in three seasons as a starter. Team captain and Conference USA Defensive Player of the Year is FAU's all-time leader in sacks (29 1/2), tackles for loss (42 1/2) and forced fumbles (eight). Was a medical exclusion from bench-pressing at the Combine because of a left hand injury.

Strengths: Very good size and size potential with a frame to easily hold 275 pounds. Outstanding pass-rushing production with relentless effort in pursuit, as evidenced by eight forced fumbles. Good initial quickness and burst. Recorded the fastest 60-yard shuttle (11.43 seconds) of any defensive lineman at the Combine, indicative of exceptional stamina. Very competitive and keeps working to come free. Disruptive and effortful pass rusher. Solid East-West Shrine Bowl showing — consistently won one-on-one battles. Practices very hard and brings it every snap.

Weaknesses: Has short arms and small hands. Tight-hipped and struggles to dip and bend. Has an underdeveloped lower body and could struggle setting the edge. Does not play big or powerful in the run game. Can be abrasive in the locker room and grate on teammates.

Future: Highly productive, very effortful edge rusher who must continue to get stronger and play the run with more strength to become a complete every-down player in the pros. Has drawn comparisons to Raiders' 2016 undrafted free agent James Cowser and must prove he can overcome his lack of arm length in the pros.

Draft projection: Fourth- to fifth-round pick.

Scout's take: "He flashed at the East-West Shrine game against a bunch of bad offensive lineman. I wish he were more powerful. I didn't think he set the edge well on tape. He is a (pass rush) specialist to me."

NT TREYVON HESTER, #91 (Sr-5)

TOLEDO ▶ GRADE: 5.25

Ht: 6-2 3/8 | Wt: 300 | 40: 5.12 | Arm: 32 | Hand: 9 ¾

History: Pittsburgh native. Greyshirted in 2012. Played all 12 games in '13, starting the final 10, and recorded 39 tackles, 7 1/2 for loss and 3 1/2 sacks with one batted pass. Started 11-of-13 games in '14, and tallied 49-9 1/2-2 with one batted pass and two forced fumbles.

Stepped into the lineup in Week Two when the starter was lost for the year. Had off-season surgery to repair a torn left labrum. Returned to start all 12 games in '15, and recorded 34-6 1/2-2 1/2 with one batted pass and one forced fumble. Shed 20 pounds in preparation for his senior season. Started all 10 games played in '16, and posted 39-8-5 with one pass breakup and one forced fumble. Tore his right labrum against Ohio — sat out against Akron and Northern Illinois in early November then had surgery, knocking him out of the bowl game against Appalachian State, as well as the East-West Shrine Game. Team captain. Was a medical exclusion from the bench-press test at the Combine because of right shoulder injury.

Strengths: Experienced, four-year starter. Solid anchor strength. Good athlete who plays on his feet and flattens down the line. Can be disruptive working in gaps. Feels blocking pressure instinctively and is alert to find the ball. Has an effective swim move and consistently beats defenders into gaps and knows how to work the edge with rips, swats and hand slaps.

Weaknesses: Has short arms and small hands and has been nagged by shoulder injuries that will need to be cleared medically. Tends to rise out of his stance in search of the ball and pad level could stand to become more consistent.

Future: A quick, athletic, movement nose tackle who consistently showed improvement throughout his career and has enough get-off speed to be disruptive playing in gaps. Has enough inside pass-rush ability to contribute in a rotation for an even or odd front and has eventual starter potential.

Draft projection: Fourth- to fifth-round pick.

NT JALEEL JOHNSON, #67 (Sr-5)

IOWA ▶ GRADE: 5.50

Ht: 6-2 5/8 | Wt: 316 | 40: 5.31 | Arm: 33 1/4 | Hand: 9 5/8

History: Also wrestled as a prep in Illinois, where he won a state championship at Montini Catholic. Redshirted in 2012. Saw very limited action in seven games in '13. Was a backup in '14 when he recorded 11 tackles, 2 1/2 for loss and one sack in 13 appearances. Started all 27 games as a 4-3 defensive tackle the next two seasons — totaled 45-5 1/2-3 1/2 with one batted pass in '15; and 56-10-7 1/2 with two batted passes and a safety in '16.

Strengths: Good hand strength to control blockers and jolt blockers with a powerful six-inch punch. Good power in his body to gore through blockers and push the pocket. Keeps working to the quarterback and wears down blockers with his heavy hands and hand-fighting

DEFENSIVE LINE

techniques. Solid showing at the Senior Bowl.

Weaknesses: Has a tendency to pop up out of his stance and play too upright. Inconsistent get-off. Bench-pressed only 19 reps at the Combine (2 not counted), the fewest of any defensive tackle at the Combine and needs to continue getting stronger. Has some heaviness in his movement and can be late to arrive at the ball. Struggles to split the double team.

Future: Big, round-bodied, tight-hipped, upright power player with a set of the most violent hands in the draft to win battles in tight quarters. Is most ideally suited to play on a shade, though has enough lateral agility to be effective as a three-technique. Became more consistent as a senior and has eventual starter potential.

Draft projection: Third- to fourth-round pick.

NT **D.J. JONES**, #93 (Sr-4)

MISSISSIPPI ▶ GRADE: 5.32

Ht: 6-0 5/8 | Wt: 319 | 40: 5.03 | Arm: 32 1/2 | Hand: 10 1/4

History: Also played basketball and threw shot and discus as a South Carolina prep. Committed to Oklahoma State out of high school, but failed to qualify academically, and spent two years at East Mississippi Community College. Started all 12 games in 2013, and posted 49 tackles, 13 for loss and eight sacks with one forced fumble. Started all 12 games in '14, and had 29-12 1/2-4 with two forced fumbles. Won a pair of NJCAA national championships. Verbaled to Florida State before changing his mind. With Ole Miss in '15, contributed 40-5 1/2-4 with one forced fumble in 13 games (three starts). Dealt with a concussion leading up to the Memphis game. Also dealt with concussion symptoms during '16 fall camp. On the season, started all 12 games at nose tackle, notching 30-3-2 with one batted pass and one interception.

Strengths: Plays with natural leverage and power and is not easily moved off spots. Outstanding weight-room strength and functional football-playing strength. Recorded the best 10-yard split time (1.65 seconds) of any defensive tackle at the Combine, indicative of outstanding short-area quickness he often shows disrupting gaps and working edges.

Weaknesses: Not naturally big or big-framed. Is short and short-armed and allows blockers to get inside his frame. Too easily stalled against double teams. Can be a tad late off the ball. Needs to become more consistent using his hands. Small frame and concussion history raise questions about ability to handle the rigors of a 16-game season.

Future: Squatty nose tackle that plays with leverage, power and quickness and has very

good movement skill for a big man to play multiple interior techniques. Is most ideally suited for a role as a movement nose tackle in an even or odd front and would be best in a rotation.

Draft projection: Fourth- to fifth-round pick.

5T-1T **JARRON JONES**, #94 (Sr-5)

NOTRE DAME ▶ GRADE: 5.24

Ht: 6-5 3/4 | Wt: 316 | 40: 5.41 | Arm: 35 1/2 | Hand: 10 1/2

History: Prepped in New York, where he won a state championship and played basketball. Redshirted in 2012. Was part of the rotation in '13 when he recorded 20 tackles, one for loss and one sack with one forced fumble and two blocked kicks in 12 games (one start). Did not play against Michigan. In '14, started the first 11 games at nose tackle, and managed 40-7 1/2-1 1/2 with one batted pass and one forced fumble. Suffered a Lisfranc fracture to his left foot against Louisville, and missed the last two games. Tore his right MCL during '15 fall camp — missed the entire regular season before returning for the Fiesta Bowl against Ohio State (did not record any stats). Started 6-of-12 games at NT in '16, and totaled 45-11-2 with three batted passes, one interception and one forced fumble. Had a career game against Miami (six tackles for loss) then played just 12 snaps against Navy's triple-option. Graduated with a sociology degree. Did not run shuttles at the Combine because of injury to knees.

Strengths: Has rare size, with the longest wingspan (85 3/8 inches) of any defensive lineman at the Combine and vines for arms. Good power to work through blocks and power his way into the backfield (see Miami). Has the strength to press the pocket and walk blockers back. Good athlete who shows flashes of dominance. Rare length could be an asset on block teams.

Weaknesses: Motor idles too much. Registered the slowest 10-yard split (1.98 seconds) of any player at the Combine, indicative of marginal short-area burst and acceleration. Recorded the lowest vertical jump (20 1/2 inches) of any defensive linemen at the event, displaying marginal lower-body explosion. Registered 24.6% body fat at the Combine. Was not a full-time starter as a senior. Too heavy and non-explosive. Needs to adopt a more professional approach to the game. Questionable football passion and competitiveness. Takes plays off and loafs too much. Not an easily coachable, team player.

Future: A big-framed, long-armed, naturally big-boned underachiever lacking the desire, competitiveness and toughness needed to survive the rigors of the NFL's trenches. Has the

DEFENSIVE LINE

skill set to line up anywhere along a "30" front and could warrant interest as a developmental 3-4 defensive end for a team with a strong support programs able to develop his life skills. Has a lot of untapped athletic potential if the light ever comes on.

Draft projection: Fifth- to sixth-round pick.

Scout's take: "He plays very stiff and erect. He's a rotational guy that doesn't even play the whole game. After I saw him in person, I was disappointed with his body type. He looks like a defensive end with long arms and a skinny, linear frame, but he doesn't have the twitch. He plays nose and shade for them and that's kind of how he moves around, like a nose tackle."

5T **NAZAIR JONES**, #90 (Jr-4)

NORTH CAROLINA ▶ GRADE: 5.24

Ht: 6-5 1/8 | Wt: 304 | 40: 5.11 | Arm: 34 5/8 | Hand: 10 7/8

History: First name is pronounced "nah-ZAYHR" (goes by "Naz"). Two-way lineman from North Carolina. At age 16, was diagnosed with complex regional pain syndrome — experienced lower-body paralysis and weight dropped to 215 pounds. Receives weekly injection of Enbrel (anti-inflammatory medication). Redshirted in 2013. Played all 13 games in '14, and was credited with 35 tackles, 7 1/2 for loss and 2 1/2 sacks with four batted passes, one interception and one forced fumble. Started all 10 games played at the three-technique in '15, and posted 40-4-0 with three batted passes, one interception and one forced fumble. Suffered a left leg injury when he was high-lowed by a pair of Georgia Tech offensive linemen. Missed three October games. Also missed the bowl game against Baylor (concussion). Started all 12 games played at nose tackle in '16, and amassed 70-9 1/2-2 1/2 with three batted passes and one forced fumble. Sat out against James Madison (concussion).

Strengths: Very good size and arm length that he uses well to disrupt passing lanes. Good strength at the point of attack to stack the run and two-gap. Plays with physicality, competes hard and runs to the ball.

Weaknesses: Tends to play too tall and narrow-based. Leggy and lacks twitch. Green eyes and instincts. Recorded the slowest 3-cone drill (7.89 seconds) of all defensive linemen at the Combine, indicating a lack of lateral agility. Has a low 24-inch vertical jump, among the lowest of all defensive tackles at the Combine and indicative of limited lower-body explosion. Marginal career sack production (5).

Future: Outstanding-sized, long-framed, slow-twitch, power player with enough size, length and play strength to be groomed as a developmental five-technique for a "30" front.

Draft projection: Fourth- to fifth-round pick.

DLE-3T **TANOH KPASSAGNON**, #92 (Sr-5)

VILLANOVA ▶ GRADE: 5.44

Ht: 6-6 3/4 | Wt: 289 | 40: 4.82 | Arm: 35 5/8 | Hand: 10 5/8

History: Name is pronounced "tawn-o pass-N-yo." Pennsylvania native. Competed in basketball and track in high school, and didn't play football until his junior year. Redshirted in 2012 for the FCS Wildcats. Appeared in 11 games in '13, and recorded 15 tackles, 1 1/2 for loss and one sack. In '14, managed 12-5-3 1/2 with two forced fumbles in six games, but missed eight because of a torn right MCL and meniscus. Started all 11 games as a 3-4 defensive end in '15, and produced 33-9 1/2-6 1/2 with one interception and one blocked kick. In '16, was the Colonial Athletic Association Defensive Player of the Year after registering 45-21 1/2-11 with one batted pass, one forced fumble and one blocked kick in 13 starts at DE. Team captain earned a Senior Bowl invitation. Completed degrees in finance and accounting.

Strengths: Exceptional size, frame and growth potential with a body that looks like it was sculpted out of granite. Measured the tallest and tied for the longest arms (35 5/8 inches) of any defensive linemen at the Combine and uses it well to corral ball carriers. Easily beat Western Kentucky OL Forest Lamp in one-on-one drills at the Senior Bowl and turned in a solid Senior Bowl showing. Flashes ability to split the double team. Good closing burst to the quarterback. Tough and will battle through injuries. Very smart. Rare length can become a factor on kick-block teams.

Weaknesses: Too leggy, tight-hipped and rigid in his movement. Plays too narrow-based with limited body power and will struggle to anchor against NFL blockers. Not a strong, drive-thru tackler. Instincts are still developing — is not always quick to sort out the run and trust what he sees. Late to feel double teams. Production was racked up against ordinary competition. Not a glass-eater. Recorded a 7.49-second 3-cone drill time indicative of limited lateral agility and change of direction.

Future: Rare physical specimen still growing into his body and figuring out the game and will require several years of development before he is NFL ready, yet possesses very unique moldable traits and intelligence to continue developing.

Draft projection: Third- to fourth-round pick.

Scout's take: "He's body beautiful. You couldn't draw one up to look any better. He was a 'wow' guy at Senior Bowl weigh-ins."

DEFENSIVE LINE

DLE-LOLB CARL LAWSON, #55 (Jr-4)

AUBURN　　　　　　　▶ GRADE: 5.52

Ht: 6-1 3/4 | Wt: 261 | 40: 4.74 | Arm: 31 1/2 | Hand: 10 3/8

History: Blue chipper out of Georgia. As a true freshman in 2013, recorded 20 tackles, 7 1/2 for loss and four sacks with two forced fumbles for the national runners-up. Missed the '14 season after tearing his left ACL in April. Manned the Tigers' "Buck" position his final two seasons. Started all seven games played in '15, and managed 17-3-1, though he suffered a cracked hip in the opener against Louisville, and missed six games. Started all 13 games in '16, and notched 30-13 1/2-9 with one forced fumble. Added 42 career hurries. Two-year captain will be a 21-year-old rookie.

Strengths: Outstanding motor. Resilient working the edge — creates a lot of production from second effort. Extremely strong and tied for the most bench-press reps (35) of any player at the Combine. Very good grip strength to control and rip off blockers and flashes violence in his hands. Ran a 1.58-second 10-yard split at the Combine, indicative of exceptional initial burst. Can convert speed to power and walk offensive tackles back to the quarterback. Strong, physical tackler.

Weaknesses: Extremely stiff, as reflected in 7.46-second 3-cone drill that ranked last among outside linebackers at the Combine. Gets hung up on stunts and inside loops and struggles to clear his shoulders through small creases. Does not play off blocks easily once engaged and has a limited range inside the box, seldom producing far outside of it. At times loses sight of the ball rushing hard upfield and allows blockers to run him wide. Has short 31 1/2-inch flappers. Lacks the hip flexibility to match up with tight ends or backs in man coverage and got beat up by the ball in LB drills at the Combine. Durability has been an issue throughout his career — has been slowed by hip, knee and ankle injuries — and could continue to be an issue given body stiffness.

Future: Very rigid, straight-line power rusher who compensates for a lack of dynamic pass-rush moves with relentless effort that consistently creates pressure and moves quarterbacks off spots. Projects to an "elephant" role in a "40" front and could warrant consideration as a left outside linebacker in a "30" front such as the Steelers.

Draft projection: Second- to third-round pick.

Scout's take: "Lawson is a walking china doll. He looks like an undersized tin man. With all due respect, he plays his (butt) off. He's so stiff though, there's no way he can be an end."

3T JEREMIAH LEDBETTER, #55 (Sr-5)

ARKANSAS　　　　　　▶ GRADE: 5.10

Ht: 6-3 1/8 | Wt: 280 | 40: 4.86 | Arm: 34 1/4 | Hand: 10

History: Father, Sheldon, was a Buccaneers 1983 seventh-rounder; and cousin, Isaac Byrd, played parts of six years with the Panthers and Titans/Oilers (1997-2002). Also played basketball and baseball in high school (moved from Georgia to Florida). Spent three years at Hutchinson (Kan.) Community College. Redshirted in 2012. Played 11 games in '13, and posted 64 tackles, 10 for loss and seven sacks with three batted passes, one interception and one forced fumble. Played in 12 games in '14, and recorded 72-23 1/2-16 with two blocked kicks. Was used as a defensive end by the Razorbacks in '15 when he played all 13 games, starting the final 12, and produced 55-7 1/2-2 with one batted pass. In '16, started all 13 games — first eight at defensive tackle, final five at DLE — and collected 49-7 1/2-5 1/2 with two batted passes and one forced fumble.

Strengths: Good arm length and overall size. Very athletic big man with the balance to do a standing backflip. Carries his weight well. Flashes pop in his hands and strength at the point of attack. Bench-pressed 225 pounds 29 times at the Combine and recorded a DT-best 32 1/2-inch vertical jump — clearly has explosive power in his body. The game is important to him. Has NFL pedigree.

Weaknesses: Plays too tall and pad level consistently rises at the snap, allowing blockers to neutralize his first move. Does not have a pass-rush plan. Lacks the base strength to handle double teams and could stand to add bulk and get stronger. Only a one-year starter with developing eyes and instincts.

Future: High-cut, long-limbed, developmental base end with intriguing size, length, athletic ability and explosive movement skill to warrant developing as a rotational three-technique. Appears most comfortable working on the edges, though has experience inside and outside and could provide some backup versatility.

Draft projection: Late draftable pick.

DLE-DT MALIK McDOWELL, #4 (Jr-3)

MICHIGAN STATE　　　　▶ GRADE: 5.70

HT: 6-6 1/4 | WT: 295 | 40: 4.89 | ARM: 34 3/4 | HAND: 10 1/2

History: Highly recruited out of Detroit. As a true freshman in 2014, recorded 15 tackles, 4 1/2 for loss and 11/2 sacks in 13 appearances. Stepped into the lineup in '15 when he started all 14 games at nose tackle, and produced 41-13-4 1/2 with one interception, two forced fumbles and one blocked punt. Started 8-of-9 games — five at NT, three at defensive end —

DEFENSIVE LINE

and managed 34-7-1 1/2 in '16. Was suspended for the first half against BYU after being ejected for targeting against Indiana. Hurt his ribs against Northwestern then suffered a season-ending left ankle sprain against Illinois. Will be a 21-year-old rookie.

Strengths: Great size and movement skill for a near-300-pounder, with loose ankles, good body control and a strong power base. Versatile and can play anywhere along the line. Flashes the ability to penetrate gaps and disrupt the backfield (see Notre Dame). Has good strength to press off blockers, lock out and anchor. Capable of converting speed to power. Very long arms to corral ball-carriers. Flashes a second gear to track down backs and close to the ball.

Weaknesses: Tends to play very tall and narrow-based. Does not play with gap integrity and freelances too much. Motor does not consistently run, and he leaves a lot of production on the field. Very sporadic down-to-down effort. Lacks the grit and toughness desired for a two-gap, read-and-react role on the inside. Very immature with a sense of entitlement that has stunted his growth and development as a person and player.

Future: A very athletically gifted, inconsistent, enigmatic underachiever who has warranted comparisons from scouts to Falcons' 2014 second-round pick (37th overall) Ra'Shede Hageman and could wind up fitting as a one-gapping, interior disruptor. However, McDowell could be most optimally suited for a Michael Bennett-like role in a Tampa-2 defense, kicking inside in nickel situations to mismatch guards with his quickness and setting the edge on run downs. Could thrive in a culture such as the Seahawks or Panthers that embraces individual personalities within the team concept. A high-ceiling, low-floor talent who is more likely to succeed the lower he is drafted and could provide the greatest return with a new team on his second contract.

Draft projection: Second- to third-round pick.

Scout's take: "(McDowell's) interview was one of the most difficult to sit through. There was a lot of blame for everyone else. It was very self-centered. It confirmed what you see on tape. He is a boom-or-bust guy — there is no in-between. …How far does he slide before someone says this guy is too big, too long and too athletic not to draft? Some coach will be pounding the table saying, 'I know I can change him.' I'm just glad it won't be us."

DRE-ROLB TAKKARIST McKINLEY, #98 (Sr-4)

UCLA ▶ GRADE: 5.92
Ht: 6-2 | Wt: 250 | 40: 4.61 | Arm: 34 3/4 | Hand: 9 3/4

History: First name is pronounced "tuh-CAR-ist." Grew up without a father, and was

abandoned by his mother. Also ran track as a California prep (10.58-second 100 meters). Originally committed to Cal, but didn't qualify academically. Played at Contra Costa Community College (Calif.) in 2013, and posted 33 tackles, 18 for loss and 16 sacks. Would have spent another year there if not for a UCLA assistant who discovered a clerical error on McKinley's transcript. Was ruled eligible, and immediately transferred to UCLA. Joined the team in September, and chipped in 6-3 1/2-2 1/2 with one forced fumble in 10 games (one start). In '15, started 12-of-13 games at defensive end — produced 35-7 1/2-4 1/2 with four batted passes, two forced fumbles and one blocked kick. Started all 10 games played in '16, and totaled 50-18-10 with three forced fumbles in 10 starts. Suffered a groin injury in the season opener against Texas, and did not play against UNLV. Withdrew from the Senior Bowl because of a torn right labrum.

Strengths: Has very long arms. Outstanding initial take-off speed, as evidenced producing among the fastest 10-yard splits (1.55 seconds) of any defensive end at the Combine. Consistently beats blockers off the ball at the snap and creates a disruptive backfield presence. Keeps working to come free and plays hard and competes.

Weaknesses: Lacks ideal height and plays too upright. Not a natural bender, and stiffness was very evident in the 20-yard shuttle (4.62 seconds) and 3-cone drill (7.54) that ranked the slowest among edge rushers at the Combine. Needs to learn how to develop more of a pass-rush plan. Eyes and instincts are still developing. Average anchor strength to set an edge. Sack production is inflated against ordinary competition.

Future: A compact, disruptive, speed rusher lacking ideal balance and bend to peel the edge of a "40" front and could warrant the most consideration in a speed-rushing role that allows him to concentrate on crashing the corner for an odd front such as those run in Pittsburgh and Baltimore. Concerns about his ankle flexion, hip flexibility and contact balance could affect how good of a pro he becomes.

Draft projection: Top-50 pick.

Scout's take: "He is stiff, stiff, stiff. He's a straight-line speed guy that falls down when he tries to bend. Two-thirds of his production comes when he is unblocked vs. bad competition. He will get way overdrafted."

DLE-LOLB AVERY MOSS, #9 (Sr-5)

YOUNGSTOWN ▶ GRADE: 5.24
Ht: 6-3 3/8 | Wt: 264 | 40: 4.86 | Arm: 34 1/2 | Hand: 10 3/8

History: Born and raised in Compton, Calif. before moving to Arizona in sixth grade. Played just two years of football, and didn't get serious about it until his senior year when he realized his basketball ceiling would be lower Division I (was part of state championship basketball team). Missed half of his junior football season with a broken wrist then missed 10 basketball games senior year because of a shoulder injury. Began his college career at Nebraska (recruited by then-head coach Bo Pelini). As a true freshman in 2012 (wore jersey No. 94), collected four tackles, zero for loss and zero sacks in three appearances before he was shelved by a right labrum tear. In '13, split snaps at defensive end with Randy Gregory — played 12 games, starting three, and tallied 36-8-4 1/2 with one batted pass and a 25-yard interception touchdown. Did not accompany the Cornhuskers to the Gator Bowl against Georgia; a month later, was banned from the campus, a punishment stemming from a 2012 incident in which he was convicted of public indecency (exposed himself — twice — to a 22-year-old student worker inside a residence hall convenience store). When his appeal was denied, Moss followed Pelini to FCS Youngstown State. Played 10 games in '15, starting two at RDE, and recorded 25-4 1/2-3 with two batted passes and one forced fumble. Was suspended against Robert Morris (violation of team rules). Put together a full season in '16 when he and Derek Rivers formed the most talented defensive end duo in the FCS — registered 59-17 1/2-11 with three batted passes and four forced fumbles for the national runners-up in 15 games.

Strengths: Good size and arm length. Has quick feet and is athletic moving in space with the quickness, agility and balance to bend the end. Good chase speed to flush the pocket and string out backs to the perimeter. Is competitive and around the football a lot. Solid wrap tackler.

Weaknesses: Lacks strength at the point of attack and does not play to his size. Benchpressed 225 pounds only 14 times at the Combine, the fewest of any defensive end, and does not lock out or play with strength and physicality. Developing eyes and anticipation — is a tick late to diagnose and stays locked up too long. Only a one-year starter. Did not catch the ball naturally at the Combine in LB drills. Character requires closer scrutiny and should require additional player programs support.

Future: An underdeveloped edge rusher with intriguing length and athletic ability to be groomed as a weak-side rusher, Moss could fit in either an even or odd front and has the pass-rush skills to evolve as a second-wave rusher.

Draft projection: Fifth- to sixth-round pick.

Scout's take: "The off-field issues are going

to affect (Moss). He's a size player with upside potential, but he's more of a rotational player."

DRE AL-QUADIN MUHAMMAD, #8 (Jr-4)

EX-MIAMI (FLA.)   ▶ GRADE: 5.01

Ht: 6-3 1/2 | Wt: 253 | 40: 4.89 | Arm: 33 1/4 | Hand: 9 3/8

History: Highly recruited Don Bosco Prep (N.J.) product. Was a reserve in '13 when he had eight tackles, two for loss and two sacks in 13 appearances. After the '14 spring game, got into a fight with a former teammate. The incident was reported to police as an aggravated battery, but he was not charged. Was reinstated in time for '15 spring practice. Committed a separation violation, and was suspended for the season opener against Bethune-Cookman. Deployed as a hybrid rusher, started 7-of-12 games played, and totaled 54-8 1/2-5 with one batted pass and one forced fumble. Was dismissed from the team a week before the '16 season for receiving impermissible benefits in the form of majorly discounted luxury cars. Additionally, the Miami Herald reported Muhammad was not forthcoming, a factor which also influenced the dismissal decision. Reportedly was set to transfer to Hampton, but did not play in '16.

Strengths: Looked comfortable in LB drills at the Combine and showed enough confidence flipping his hips to transition to linebacker, where his size could be best suited. Flashes some power off the edge.

Weaknesses: Very limited play history with only a half-season as a starter. Has some tightness in his body and appears overly muscled in his movement to be fluid redirecting in coverage. Comes off the ball too upright and gives up his chest. Will need to learn an array of pass-rush moves. Production was largely racked up against tight ends.

Future: Thin-legged, top-heavy, high-hipped edge rusher who will be forced to take a long road back to redemption after repeated mistakes left him suspended for two of the last three seasons. Could warrant some interest as a 3-4 outside linebacker after showing well in LB drills at the Combine.

Draft projection: Priority free agent.

DLE-LOLB NOBLE NWACHUKWU, #97 (Sr-5)

WEST VIRGINIA   ▶ GRADE: 5.14

Ht: 6-1 3/8 | Wt: 268 | 40: 4.84 | Arm: 33 1/8 | Hand: 9

History: History: Last name is pronounced "wah-Chew-coo." Born to Nigerian parents. Prepped in Texas, though he didn't play football until his junior year of high school (also competed in basketball and track and field). Redshirted n 2012. Saw limited action in nine games in '13, and was credited with five tack-

DEFENSIVE LINE

les one for loss and one sack. Sprained his right MCL prior to the Week-Two contest at Oklahoma. A defensive end in the Mountaineers' 3-3-5 scheme, started all 13 games in '14, and produced 34-82-2 with four batted passes. Started all 13 games in '15, and logged 47-13-8 1/2 with one batted pass and one forced fumble. Sat out against Texas (leg). Notched 40-7 1/2-4, including two batted passes, one forced and recovered fumble in 12 games in '16. Team captain graduated with a degree in multidisciplinary studies.

Strengths: Fine grip strength to control blockers. Bench-pressed 225 pounds 27 times, indicative of outstanding upper-body strength. Solid run defender. Hustles, chases and competes. Has a quick, disruptive, inside counter move. Athletic enough to fall back into coverage. Experienced, three-year starter. Strong personal and football character. Committed weight-room worker.

Weaknesses: Lacks ideal height. Tied for the smallest hands (9 inches) of any defensive linemen at the Combine. Gets hung up in traffic and stuck on blocks. Is not an accomplished handsfighter and could stand to add more variety to his pass-rush arsenal. Limited special-teams experience.

Future: Thick-bodied, developmental, power-leverage rusher with noticeable strength in his hands and desirable effort to develop into a functional wave role contributor, if he proves he can factor on special teams.

Draft projection: Late draftable pick.

DRE-PRS IFEADI ODENIGBO, #7 (Sr-5)

NORTHWESTERN ▶ GRADE: 5.13
Ht: 6-3 | Wt: 258 | 40: 4.68 | Arm: 32 5/8 | Hand: 10 1/2

History: Name is pronounced "if-AH-dee-o-DEN-uh-bo." Born to Nigerian parents. Ohio prep also competed in track. One of the top-rated recruits in NU history — chose the Wildcats over offers from Alabama, Ohio State, Michigan, and Notre Dame, amongst others. Played one game as a true freshman in 2012 before suffering a season-ending right labrum tear (granted medical hardship). Was deployed as a pass-rush specialist/rotational player throughout his career. In '13, tallied nine tackles, 6 1/2 for loss and 5 1/2 sacks with one batted pass in 12 appearances. Played 12 games in '14, and collected 11-3-3 with three forced fumbles. Played 12 games in '15, and tallied 19-5-5. Sat out against Nebraska while nursing a high left ankle sprain. Played all 12 games in '16, starting five, and notched 22-12-10 with two forced fumbles, including a four-sack performance against Iowa.

Strengths: Good get off and initial quickness. Uses power and leverage to create exten-

sion and lock out. Can convert speed to power and walk blockers back to the quarterback (see Ohio State). Uses an effective two-hand swipe and long-arm-stab to torque blockers and displays a small assortment of finesse hand moves to change up his approach and rip free. Good closing burst. Recorded a 10'8" broad jump, indicative of exceptional lower-body explosion.

Weaknesses: Lacks base strength ideally suited to anchor vs. the run and has never been a full-time starter. Developing eyes and instincts. Takes short, choppy steps and does not open his stride off the edge. Has a history of shoulder and ankle injuries, and durability must be evaluated. Appeared upright and stiff through LB drills at the Combine. Lacks special-teams experience.

Future: Athletic, thin-waisted, situational pass rusher with the athletic traits to earn a role as a nickel pressure player in the pros. Inability to contribute on special teams and anchor vs. the run will limit his draft value, yet has enough tools to develop.

Draft projection: Late draftable pick.

NT LARRY OGUNJOBI, #65 (Sr-5)

UNC CHARLOTTE ▶ GRADE: 5.31
Ht: 6-2 5/8 | Wt: 305 | 40: 5.03 | Arm: 32 5/8 | Hand: 10

History: Last name is pronounced "Oh-UN-joe-bee." Born to Nigerian immigrants. North Carolina native. Weighed 350 pounds as a high school sophomore before shedding nearly 100 once he dedicated himself to football. Signed as part of Charlotte's first recruiting class. Redshirted in 2012. A 3-4 nose tackle, Ogunjobi started all 44 games of his career spanning 2013-16 — recorded 42 tackles, 9 1/2 for loss and 2 1/2 sacks with two batted passes in '13; 48-11 1/2-5 with two batted passes in '14; 62-14 1/2-2 1/2 with one blocked kick in '15; and 65-13 1/2-3 with two batted passes in '16. Added 33 career hurries. Had his left labrum surgically repaired after his freshman season, and had the right labrum done after his junior season. Graduated with degrees in computer science and biology, and has aspirations of attending medical school.

Strengths: Very quick off the ball shooting into gaps and disrupting the backfield. Is a good athlete and plays on his feet, clearing them through traffic and running to the ball. Flashes power in his punch. Locates the ball quickly. Experienced four-year starter.

Weaknesses: Has small hands and short arms and plays short-armed, letting defenders inside his frame and falling off some tackles. Has a tendency to play upright. Needs to learn how to use his hands better to separate from blockers and work the edges. Was not regularly chal-

DEFENSIVE LINE

lenged by top competition, struggled against Louisville and showed little at the Senior Bowl.

Future: Very thick-bodied, high-hipped, competitive, one-gapping nose tackle who plays too small, though he does possess desirable quickness to generate some pressure if slanted, stunted and allowed to play in gaps. Will intrigue more as a height-weight-speed prospect than football player.

Draft projection: Third- to fourth-round pick.

PRS-ROLB **EJUAN PRICE**, #5 (Sr-6)

PITTSBURGH · ▶ GRADE: 5.15

Ht: 5-11 3/8 | Wt: 241 | 40: 4.83 | Arm: 32 3/4 | Hand: 10

History: Linebacker-tight end from Pittsburgh Woodland Hills High. As a true freshman in 2011, started 5-of-13 games at "Will" linebacker, contributing 27 tackles, 6 1/2 for loss and four sacks. Missed the '12 season because of a torn pectoral muscle. Was used as a hybrid LB/defensive end in '13 when he started 4-of-6 games, and managed 23-4-1 with one batted pass before suffering a season-ending back injury. Sat out the '14 season with another torn pectoral. Was healthy his final two seasons when he was used as a 4-3 DE. Started all 13 games in '15, and produced 48-19 1/2-11 1/2 with one batted pass, one forced fumble, a 32-yard fumble recovery touchdown and one blocked PAT. Was a Hendricks Award finalist in '16 after finishing second nationally in tackles for loss — registered 45-23-13 with one batted pass, three forced fumbles, a safety and one blocked PAT in 13 starts. Team captain graduated with communication degree. Will be a 24-year-old rookie. Opted not to run the 3-cone drill at the Combine.

Strengths: Times the snap well and beats blockers off the ball with excellent anticipation and suddenness. Feasts on tight ends — consistently wins with natural leverage and an assortment of jab steps and hand slaps. Very good career sack production (29 1/2). Aggressive closing speed — accelerates through contact.

Weaknesses: Is small-framed and injury-prone, and long-term durability must be a consideration given that he missed two full seasons in college as a result of pectoral injuries. Average lateral agility and change of direction. Can be engulfed once blockers get their hands on him. Overaged.

Future: Very stocky, quick-hipped, power-leverage rusher who compensates for his lack of length with a strong base, an explosive punch and good balance working the edges. Could carve a niche as a situational pass rusher in the pros and warrant some interest as a 3-4 outside linebacker.

Draft projection: Fifth- to sixth-round pick.

NT **ELIJAH QUALLS**, #11 (Jr-4)

WASHINGTON ▶ GRADE: 5.29

Ht: 6-0 5/8 | Wt: 313 | 40: 5.17 | Arm: 30 5/8 | Hand: 9 3/8

History: Also wrestled as a prep in California, where his gridiron exploits included playing defensive tackle and running back (at 285 pounds). Redshirted in 2013. Was a depth player in '14 when he recorded 13 tackles, two for loss and zero sacks in 14 appearances. Played all 13 games in '15, starting the first eight at nose tackle, and was credited with 23-4 1/2-2 with one batted pass. Sprained his left ankle against Arizona — sat out the next three games, and ceded starts to Greg Gaines in the final two. Played alongside Gaines in '16 when he tallied 35-5-3 in 14 games (11 starts). Non-starts went to up-and-comer Vita Vea.

Strengths: Plays low to the ground and is surprisingly stout at the point of attack to handle double teams. Bench-pressed 225 pounds 33 times at the Combine, more than any other defensive tackle at the event and indicative of outstanding strength. Flashes power in his hands. Recorded a 1.69-second 10-yard split, one of the quickest times among defensive tackles and indicative of outstanding quickness to work the edge. Lined up from a two-point stance rushing from the edge at times.

Weaknesses: Does not look the part, with extremely short arms (30 5/8 inches) and a dumpy-looking physique that leaves him velcroed to blocks too long. Wingspan (74 inches) measured the shortest of any defensive linemen at the Combine, smaller than most receivers. Measured 28.2% body fat at the Combine and needs to improve conditioning and stamina. Marginal career sack production (5).

Future: A thick-bodied, small-framed, strong-handed, movement nose tackle at his best when he is slanting, stunting and on the move. Needs to keep his weight in check to be more than a part-time, rotational wave player and has the agility, similar to Falcons 2015 5th-round pick Grady Jarrett, to exceed his draft expectations, though Qualls needs to show he can control his weight and find a peak condition.

Draft projection: Fourth- to fifth-round pick.

DRE-ROLB **DEREK RIVERS**, #11 (Sr-5)

YOUNGSTOWN ▶ GRADE: 5.38

Ht: 6-3 5/8 | Wt: 248 | 40: 4.63 | Arm: 32 3/4 | Hand: 9 3/8

History: Attended Fork Union (Va.) Military Academy in 2012. As a reserve in '13 (wore jersey No. 27), was credited with 13 tackles, 4 1/2 for loss and 2 1/2 sacks in 10 appearances. Did not play against Morehead State (left quad strain) or South Dakota. Played left and right

DEFENSIVE LINE

for the FCS Penguins. Played all 12 games in '14, starting the final 11, and produced 50-17-13 with one forced fumble. Started all 11 games in '15, and registered 52-15 1/2-8 with one forced fumble. The Penguins went to the national championship in '16 when Rivers racked up 58-19 1/2-14 with one batted pass and one forced fumble in 16 starts at LDE. Added 45 hurries the last three seasons. Team captain owns YSU career sacks record (41). Earned an invitation to the Senior Bowl.

Strengths: Good balance to clear his feet through traffic and run to the ball. Bench-pressed 225 pounds 35 times at the Combine and has very good weight-room strength. Recorded a 2.53-second 20-yard split at the Combine, tops among defensive linemen and indicative of the sustained burst often required to flush the pocket. Flashed at the Senior Bowl in one-on-one drills. Very productive.

Weaknesses: Has short arms and stays blocked too long. Tight-hipped and needs to do a better job anchoring against the run. Does not play strong or physical. Gets knocked off the ball and pinned inside and outside. Instincts are just adequate locating the ball and can be short-circuited by a complex game plan. Not a natural bender able to dip and bend the edge and does not have a pass-rush plan. Production came in clumps vs. bad opponents.

Future: Strong, straight-line fast, edge rusher with the speed more typically seen on the right side than the left end in which he played and has the tools to make a living converting speed to power in pass-rush situations. Inconsistencies against the run have been glaring and he does not play with the same strength and power that his Combine workout might indicate.

Draft projection: Fourth- to fifth-round pick.
Scout's take: "There were games he was just standing around and not going hard. He has short arms. He's not good against the run. His hand use is marginal at best. He could have had 20 sacks if he didn't take plays off, especially at that level. I wish he were tougher."

DLE ISAAC ROCHELL, #90 (Sr-4)
NOTRE DAME ▶ GRADE: 5.36
Ht: 6-4 1/4 | Wt: 280 | 40: 4.91 | Arm: 32 3/4 | Hand: 9 3/4

History: Two-way lineman from Georgia, where he won Class A private state championship. Broke his left hand at the beginning of his senior season. As a true freshman in 2013, had 10 tackles, zero for loss and zero sacks in 11 appearances. Played mostly strong-side defensive end for the Irish. Started all 13 games in '14, and produced 39-7 1/2-2 1/2 with three batted passes. In '15, started all 13 games — 10 at DE,

and three of the final four at defensive tackle when Daniel Cage was out — and logged 63-7 1/2-1 with two batted passes. During his pre-season press conference, ND head coach Brian Kelly revealed Rochell was less than 100 percent in previous years: "He's had some back issues since he's been here...This is the first time in two years he's been able to squat heavy, do all the leg lifts, do all the things necessary to be explosive." Started all 12 games in '16, and totaled 55-7-1 with one batted pass. Team captain graduated with a political science degree. Did not perform shuttles at the Combine after pulling his hamstring during the 40-yard dash.

Strengths: Functional athlete with good size and length. Plays with good strength to lock out and set the edge and can walk tackles back. Versatile and has played inside and outside and has enough girth to line up anywhere along a "30" front. Plays hard and competes. Tough and willing to play through injury and has been dependable as a starter.

Weaknesses: Minimal career sack production (4 1/2) and is not a creative pass rusher — does not have a plan or show a second gear. Limited closing burst to finish. Is not a quick shedder and stays blocked too long. Does not show the burst to penetrate gaps and could do a better job of discarding blockers.

Future: A rotational five-technique ideally suited for a backup role who can get a team through a game or two if thrust into the lineup as a starter, but is not talented enough to win with as a regular starter. Is most ideally suited for a "30" front.

Draft projection: Fourth- to fifth-round pick.
Scout's take: "(Rochell) is a backup. He can play the five-technique. He is a decent athlete. He doesn't have much sack production. He will generate more pressures than sacks. Every once in a while he will beat his guy off the mark. He can be a dependable backup."

DLE-LOLB GARRETT SICKELS, #90 (Jr-4)
PENN STATE ▶ GRADE: 5.21
Ht: 6-3 1/2 | Wt: 261 | 40: 4.93 | Arm: 32 1/8 | Hand: 9 1/2

History: Also played lacrosse as a prep in New Jersey, where he was a U.S. Army All-American. Redshirted in 2013. A reserve/special teams player in '14, recorded 11 tackles, three for loss and two sacks in 13 games. In '15, lined up opposite Carl Nassib (Browns) — started all 12 games played, and produced 35-5-3 with one batted pass and one forced fumble. Did not play against Michigan State (injured). Was the Nittany Lions' Defensive MVP in '16 — started 12-of-14 games, and totaled 47-12 1/2-6, including 9-3 1/2-2 1/2 in an upset of

DEFENSIVE LINE

Ohio State despite being suspended for the first half. Explained head coach James Franklin: "Garrett's been a model citizen for us for three years. We just had a situation where we had a bye week and some guys wanted to get home early for the long weekend. He ended up not going to a class." Punishment ended after he sat the first series against Purdue.

Strengths: Very good energy and consistent effort. Feels blocking pressure and is quick to locate the ball. Very active hands with good placement to control, shed and work down the line and chase in backside pursuit. Adequate point-of-attack strength to hold the edge. Good contact balance. Solid tackler. Played big on the brightest stage against Ohio State and consistently generated pressure. Has a blue-collar approach, works hard in the weight room and is an unselfish, team player.

Weaknesses: Has short arms and small hands. Comes off the ball too upright and stays engaged too long. Lacks ideal foot speed to take the edge or pierce gaps. Seldom wins at the snap with quickness or burst. Not a strong, knockback tackler and does not generate a lot of force through his lower half. Segmented in his rush plan and could do a better job of using his hands and feet in unison. Limited special teams experience.

Future: Gritty, high-effort, overachieving college 4-3 end who is more ideally suited for the left side in the pros than the right on which he most often played, lacking ideal burst, bend and hip flexibility to creatively beat left tackles. Profiles as a functional base end with enough athletic traits to warrant standing up as an outside linebacker in a "30" front. Could use another year in an NFL strength program to continue developing his lower-body power and compete for a starting job in Year Three. Has solid backup potential.

Draft projection: Fifth- to sixth-round pick.

3T TANZEL SMART, #77 (Sr-4)

TULANE ▶ GRADE: 5.22

Ht: 6-0 5/8 | Wt: 296 | 40: 5.21 | Arm: 32 7/8 | Hand: 9 5/8

History: Baton Rouge, La. native. Played 12 games as a true freshman in 2013, collecting 14 tackles, one-half for loss and zero sacks with one batted pass. Manned the three-technique, and started all 36 games the next three seasons — totaled 47-6 1/2-2 with one batted pass and one forced fumble in '14; 62-15-2 with one forced fumble in '15; and 67-18 1/2-5 1/2 with one forced fumble in '16. Team captain graduated with a degree in applied computing.

Strengths: Good instincts to feel blocks unfolding. Plays hard and chases the ball. Plays

with natural leverage and anchors surprisingly well for his lack of size. Has active hands and works the edges efficiently in unison with his feet. Recorded the fastest 3-cone drill (7.53 seconds) and among the fastest 20-yard short shuttles (4.57) of any defensive tackle at the Combine, indicative of very good lateral agility and change of direction. Experienced, three-year starter. Has been very durable and not missed any time due to injury.

Weaknesses: Very undersized with marginal length in his body and arms and can be engulfed when defenders get their hands on him, as he was locked down by LSU's Ethan Pocic in one-on-one drills at the Senior Bowl practices and consistently . Lacks ideal bulk and gets washed by the double team at times. Could stand to do a better job of coming to balance in space.

Future: Quick, active, one-gap penetrator who needs to play in gaps to be effective. Has enough quickness and athletic ability to contribute in a wave role.

Draft projection: Fifth- to sixth-round pick.

DLE-LOLB DAWUANE SMOOT, #91 (Sr-4)

ILLINOIS ▶ GRADE: 5.56

Ht: 6-3 1/8 | Wt: 264 | 40: 4.81 | Arm: 33 1/4 | Hand: 9 1/4

History: First name is pronounced "duh-WON." Also was a standout track and field athlete, including hurdles, as an Ohio prep. Played seven games as a true freshman in 2013, and notched eight tackles, one for loss and sack. Tore a ligament in his left elbow during '14 spring practice. Bulked up 40 pounds for his sophomore season. Backed up at the Leo in '14, and recorded 33-7 1/2-2 1/2 with two batted passes. Started all 12 games at the Leo in '15, and produced 40-15-8 with two batted passes and three forced fumbles. Head coach Lovie Smith and defensive coordinator Hardy Nickerson arrived in '16, and Smoot produced 56-15-5 with one batted pass, two forced fumbles, and a safety in 12 starts at defensive end. Added 10 hurries. Team captain. Was a medical exclusion from the bench-press test because of a left pectoral injury.

Strengths: Very quick, active hands. Plays on his feet with good balance and bend and has a good closing burst to the ball. Good functional play strength to invert the line of scrimmage and work off blocks. Strong tackler. Flashes ability to convert speed to power (though it showed more often in 2015). Plays with good discipline and understands defensive concepts. Solid football intelligence.

Weaknesses: Has very small hands and a body that appeared underdeveloped at the Combine. Just adequate take-off speed and

126

could improve close at the top of his rush. Has a 29 1/2-inch vertical jump, indicative of below-average lower-body explosion and overall athletic ability. Lacks elite closing burst to take the corner consistently and win with speed. Struggled matching up with the power of Western Michigan's Taylor Moton. Appeared too upright and uncomfortable playing on his feet in LB drills at the Combine.

Future: A strong, base, 4-3 end with the strength to stack the corner and enough agility and pass-rush skill to generate some edge pressure and move the pocket. Left evaluators consistently desiring more after a sensational junior season that placed him in the first-round conversation, though has athletic tools to work with and eventual starter traits.

Draft projection: Second- to third-round pick.

Scout's take: "(Smoot) lacks consistency and production. He plays hard and leverages blocks and makes run plays on a consistent basis, but I didn't see a talented pass rusher. I thought he peaked (in 2015) and played a little better. I was expecting to see him dominate this year, and it didn't happen. Is that because he didn't have (Raiders 2016 second-round pick) Jihad Ward next to him — it's difficult to say."

NT VINCENT TAYLOR, #96 (Jr-4)

OKLAHOMA STATE ▶ GRADE: 5.09

Ht: 6-2 5/8 | Wt: 304 | 40: 5.09 | Arm: 34 3/8 | Hand: 10 1/8

History: Born and raised in New Orleans, but moved to San Antonio, Tex. after Hurricane Katrina. Redshirted in 2013. Played 10 games in '14, and recorded 13 tackles, one for loss and zero sacks. A 4-3 defensive tackle for the Cowboys, Taylor started all 13 games in '15, and produced 48-8 1/2-5. Started all 13 games in '16, and registered 51-13-7 with one batted pass and two forced fumbles. Blocked five kicks in his career, a school record. Team captain. On track to graduate in May.

Strengths: Good upper-body strength with long arms that he has used well on special teams to knock down kicks (5). Can press off blocks and push the pocket with physicality. Plays hard and competes. Has an effective swim move and uses his hands to disengage. Very solid sack production (12) from the inside the last two years.

Weaknesses: Plays tall and narrow-based with too much stiffness in his lower half, and consequently labors to change direction, flatten laterally or loop and stunt with precision. Overly reliant on his upper-body strength — needs to play wider-based and improve his anchor. Short-stepper with limited playing range.

Future: Top-heavy, high-hipped, movement nose tackle lacking ideal base, balance and bend desired in the trenches. Could fend for a role as a short-area clogger.

Draft projection: Late draftable pick.

DLE-3T SOLOMON THOMAS, #90 (Soph-3)

STANFORD ▶ GRADE: 6.37

Ht: 6-2 5/8 | Wt: 273 | 40: 4.69 | Arm: 33 | Hand: 9 3/8

History: Born in Chicago, and lived in Australia for five years before prepping in Texas. Highly recruited USA Today and U.S. Army All-American honors. Redshirted in 2014. Played all 14 games in '15, and recorded 39 tackles, 10 1/2 for loss and 3 1/2 sacks with a 34-yard fumble recovery touchdown. In '16, was the Morris Trophy winner (top Pac-12 defensive lineman) and Stanford's leading tackler — started all 13 games in the Cardinal's 3-4 — nine at defensive tackle, four at defensive end — and registered 62-15-8 with one forced fumble, a safety and a 42-yard fumble recovery touchdown. Notched 12 tackles and 1 1/2 sacks against Notre Dame, and was MVP of the Sun Bowl against North Carolina. Added 13 hurries over two seasons. Team captain. Turns 22 in December.

Strengths: Very urgent football-playing temperament. Outstanding initial quickness to cross the face of blockers and pierce gaps. Plays with heavy hands and very good functional, football-playing strength, as he confirmed bench-pressing 225 pounds 30 times at the Combine. Is very stout at the point of attack, with a frame to potentially bulk up and play the five-technique. Also recorded a 1.56-second 10-yard split at the Combine, indicative of exceptional short-area acceleration and closing speed. Has a 35-inch vertical jump and good lower-body explosion. Extremely tough and competitive. Versatile and plays inside and outside, kicking inside to mismatch guards with his exceptional quickness as he did at the end of the Sun Bowl on the game-clinching sack. Extremely smart and understands football concepts. Outstanding personal and football character and has alpha-male leadership qualities. Is a vocal, emotional, team leader.

Weaknesses: Has small hands and is undersized by NFL standards for a 3-4 defensive end and lacks ideal fluidity to play on his feet in coverage. Is overly muscular and has a very tight stride. Can be turned by the double team. Combine grunter who strained to finish drills.

Future: Very-strong, explosive, top-heavy power rusher most optimally suited as a base end in a "40" front, with the agility to kick inside in nickel situations. Compares similarly to Rams' 2008 second overall selection Chris

DEFENSIVE LINE

Long exiting Virginia, though Thomas is not as nuanced of a hands-fighter and has even more power in his body. Is wired for success and has exceptional leadership qualities to make an impact wherever he lines up.

Draft projection: Top-15 pick.

Scout's take: "Coaches are going to fall in love with (Thomas') makeup. They love him in our place. He is not a natural pass rusher. He had lot of sack production, but it was complementary, not created on his own."

NT DALVIN TOMLINSON, #54 (Sr-5)

ALABAMA ▶ GRADE: 5.58

Ht: 6-2 7/8 | Wt: 310 | 40: 5.13 | Arm: 33 1/2 | Hand: 10 1/8

History: Father, Gleaton, died of lung cancer when Dalvin was six, and mother, Melinda, died of diabetes while Dalvin was in high school. He was the first wrestler in Georgia history to win three state heavyweight championships (169-2 career record). In the spring of '12 — before arriving at Alabama — tore his left ACL playing soccer. Redshirted that year. Made his debut against Virginia Tech in '13, but tore his right ACL. A rotational player in '14, recorded 22 tackles, 5 1/2 for loss and two sacks in 14 games. Played all 15 games for the national champs in '15, and contributed 34-1/2-0 with six batted passes. Was deployed as a defensive end and defensive tackle in Jeremy Pruitt's aggressive, multiple-front scheme. Started all 15 games in '16, and registered 62-5 1/2-3 with four batted passes and four forced fumbles. Earned two degrees, finance and financial planning. Did not perform bench-press test at the Combine because of left pectoral strain.

Strengths: Extremely tough. Plays with a good base and balance. Outstanding strength at the point of attack and can handle the double team. Strong, forceful tackler. Recorded a 4.59-second 20-yard shuttle at the Combine, indicative of very good short-area burst. Received consistently high marks from executives at the Combine for his exceptional football intelligence and understanding of the game. A coaches' favorite known for annually claiming the team's Iron Man award in the weight room annually since he entered the program.

Weaknesses: Has some heaviness in his movement, and much of his production is schemed for him and flushed from a very talented front. Marginal career sack production (5) and was not often asked to work edges and turn the corner. Only a one-year starter. Durability must be evaluated.

Future: Big, strong, square-cut, power rusher with the football intelligence and passion for the game to control gaps and factor readily as a movement nose tackle. Was asked to stack-and-shed from a read-and-react role more than attack gaps, yet possesses enough power and quickness to be more productive than he was as a senior.

Draft projection: Second- to third-round pick.

Scout's take: "(Tomlinson) is not just an anchor guy. He can play a little tackle to tackle. He will be drafted more highly than people expect because he can push the pocket."

NT STEVIE TU'LKOLOVATU, #96 (Sr-6)

USC ▶ GRADE: 5.21

Ht: 6-1 1/8 | Wt: 331 | 40: 5.42 | Arm: 33 | Hand: 10 1/4

History: Last name is pronounced "TOO-ee-koe-loe-VAH-too." Married (Kalo). Uncle, Sione Pouha, was a defensive tackle for the Jets (2005-12). Stevie prepped in Utah. Was part of Utah's 2009 recruiting class (redshirted) then went on an LDS mission to the Philippines 2010-12. Returned to the Utes in '13, but missed the season because of a Lisfranc fracture in his right foot. Got back on the field in '14, scratching eight tackles, one for loss and zero sacks in 12 appearances. Played 13 games in '15, starting three of the final four at right DT, and tallied 28-6-2 with two batted passes and a 37-yard fumble recovery touchdown. Lived out of his car for nearly a month and a half while the paperwork for his graduate transfer to USC was finalized. Started 12-of-13 games at nose tackle in '16, and posted 53-2-1/2 with one batted pass. Yielded the start against Arizona to Josh Fatu (coach's decision), though Stevie played 33 snaps. Sprained his left PCL against Oregon. Will be a 26-year-old rookie.

Strengths: Measured the heaviest (331 pounds) of any defensive lineman at the Combine and is extremely stout, with natural leverage and power to collapse the pocket. Dominated one-on-one drills at the Combine with bulldozer power and consistently walked back centers to the quarterback. Outstanding anchor strength.

Weaknesses: Very heavy-footed and lacks bend, burst and agility to penetrate gaps. Recorded a high 31.4% body-fat percentage at the Combine, indicative of marginal stamina. Recorded the slowest 20-yard shuttle (4.19 seconds) and broad jump (7'7") of any defensive linemen at the event, indicating marginal short-area burst and explosion. Overaged.

Future: Strong, physical, wide-bodied, power-rusher capable of cementing the middle of a defense and pushing the pocket. Dominated in the run game in college and could readily fill a rotational, two-down, run-stuffing role in the pros.

Draft projection: Late draftable pick.

DEFENSIVE LINE

NT-5T EDDIE VANDERDOES, #47 (Jr-4)

UCLA ▶ GRADE: 5.23

Ht: 6-3 1/8 | Wt: 305 | 40: 4.99 | Arm: 33 1/8 | Hand: 10 5/8

History: Last name is pronounced "van-der-DOZE." California native garnered USA Today and U.S. Army All-American honors, and was rated the No. 1 defensive tackle recruit in the nation by multiple recruiting services. Signed with Notre Dame, but had a change of heart between February and fall camp, as he wanted to stay closer to home, in part, because his grandmother had breast cancer. Notre Dame head coach Brian Kelly fought the release, and it took two appeals before the NCAA granted immediately eligibility. Played 3-4 defensive end his first two seasons. As a true freshman in 2013, recorded 39 tackles, 4 1/2 for loss and one-half sack with one forced fumble in 13 games (seven starts). Broke his foot during '14 spring practice. Started 12-of-13 games in the fall, and produced 50-5 1/2-2 with one forced fumble. Did not start against Cal a week after he was caught throwing a punch against Oregon. In '15, tallied 8-2-0 in the season opener against Virginia before suffering a season-ending torn left ACL injury. Was a 4-3 nose tackle in '16 when he totaled 27-1 1/2-1 1/2 in 12 starts. Strained his right knee against UNLV then sprained his right ankle prior to the Colorado contest. Also had two career receptions for 36 yards (18.0-yard average), as well as two one-yard rushing touchdowns.

Strengths: Outstanding size. Flashes the ability to control blockers at the point of attack. Has strong hands to press and jerk blockers. Surprisingly light on his feet and fights through double teams. Functional two-gap ability to man the nose. Has seen some time on offense and contributed in short-yardage and goalline situations.

Weaknesses: Takes plays off and does not run hard to the ball. Tires easily and often can be seen loafing in the fourth quarter. Has a round body that looks like it has not seen a weight room. Has 26% body fat that reveals a lack of stamina resulting from the torn ACL he suffered in 2015 from which he still does not appear to have recovered. Marginal career sack production (4). Scouts say he reads his own press clippings too much and has a sense of entitlement.

Future: Has not fully recovered from the knee injury upon return in 2016, yet possesses enough athletic ability and burst to become a disruptive presence if he ever recovers, though his underachiever tendencies and sense of entitlement could hinder his chances.

Draft projection: Fourth- to fifth-round pick.

Scout's take: "Vanderdoes was overweight and out of shape when I passed through the program. He had more quickness and strength before his knee injury. When coaches see his body, they'll have a hard time warming up to him. He's a middle rounder at best. I put a late grade on him."

3T CHARLES WALKER, #97 (Jr-4)

OKLAHOMA ▶ GRADE: 5.12

Ht: 6-1 7/8 | Wt: 310 | 40: 4.96 | Arm: 33 3/4 | Hand: 9 5/8

History: Has a daughter. Prepped in Texas. Redshirted in 2013. Appeared in eight games in '14, and recorded 10 tackles, one for loss and one-half sack. Sprained his left knee against Tulsa, and missed five games. Played 12 games in '15, and logged 36-10-6 with one batted pass and one forced fumble. Sat out the semifinal against Clemson (concussion). In '16, started the first four games as a 3-4 defensive end — managed 7-2-0 with four batted passes before succumbing to a season-ending concussion. Left the Sooners in mid-November to prepare for the draft.

Strengths: Has the quickness to be effective slanting and working in gaps as he did early in his career. Has proven he can be disruptive in the backfield working the edges of blockers. Good enough strength to anchor against the run.

Weaknesses: Short. Has small hands. Recorded the slowest 3-cone drill (7.89 seconds) and 20-yard shuttles (4.96) of any defensive end at the Combine, indicative of marginal lateral agility. Durability is a concern given multiple concussions that forced him to leave his team prematurely. Was called out by his coaching staff and the scouting community for a lack of commitment after what some perceived to be "quitting" on the team.

Future: High-cut, quick-footed, one-gap penetrator who looked sorely out of place lined up in a stack-and-shed five-technique role in 2016. Is most ideally suited for a three-technique role in a "40" front where he excelled in 2015.

Draft projection: Priority free agent.

Scout's take: "The concussions are going to spook a lot of teams. He's off our board already."

DLE-OLB DeMARCUS WALKER, #44 (Sr-4)

FLORIDA STATE ▶ GRADE:

Ht: 6-3 5/8 | Wt: 280 | 40: NA | Arm: 33 | Hand: 10 1/2

History: Florida native. Chose FSU over Alabama. As a true freshman in 2013, recorded 18 tackles, two for loss and one sack in 12 games (three early-season starts at right end in place of injured Mario Edwards). Was a 3-4 Sam in '14 when he started 11-of-14 games, and produced 38-6-1 with one forced fumble. Yielded three October starts to Lorenzo Featherston. Played with his hand on the ground his last two sea-

DEFENSIVE LINE

sons. Was the team's defensive MVP in '15 after registering 58-15 1/2-10 1/2 with five batted passes one interception, four forced fumbles and one blocked field goal in 13 starts. Was a Hendricks Award finalist and the Atlantic Coast Conference Defensive Player of the Year (AP) in '16 when he was second nationally in sacks — totaled 68-21 1/2-16 with two batted passes, three forced fumbles and one blocked PAT. Joined Peter Boulware and Reinard Wilson as the only Seminole pass rushers with multiple 10-sack seasons. Two-year captain graduated with a social science degree. Sat out the Senior Bowl because of a left foot injury that also kept him out of Combine workouts.

Strengths: Good length. Has a big frame with well-distributed mass throughout. Effective looping and stunting and has a very quick, efficient inside counter move (see Florida vs. David Sharpe). Very good closing speed to the quarterback and accelerates through contact — smells blood. Spins off blocks and keeps working to flush the pocket. Good hand technician and displays a nice array of moves. Competes hard and racks up production with outstanding effort. Strong tackler. Has a knack for tomahawking the ball. Good career sack production (27 1/2). Vocal leader. Has played tight end in goalline situations.

Weaknesses: Tight-hipped and is not a natural bender who sinks his hips and bends the edge. Tends to play tall. Lacks explosiveness off the ball. Struggles to split double teams. Bench-pressed 225 pounds only 18 times at the Combine and needs to get stronger. Still developing positional instincts. A lot of his production is schemed for him.

Future: Similar to Panthers' 2014 second-round pick (60th) and Patriots DE Kony Ealy, Walker lines up on both sides and can kick inside and be disruptive mismatching guards in nickel situations.

Draft projection: Late second-round pick.

Scout's take: "How he got all those sacks baffles me. I didn't think he was a very good player."

NT CARLOS WATKINS, #94 (Sr-5)

CLEMSON ▶ GRADE: 5.47
Ht: 6-3 1/4 | Wt: 309 | 40: 5.01 | Arm: 34 5/8 | Hand: 10 3/8

History: Also played basketball as a North Carolina prep. Made nine appearances in '12, and recorded 16 tackles, one for loss and zero sacks. In '13, collected 11-1 1/2-0 in three games (one start) before his season was derailed by a car accident which killed one of his high school teammates. Watkins was a passenger in a car that hydroplaned and struck an electrical pole. Backed up Grady Jarrett (Fal-

cons) in '14, and was credited with 13-2-0 in 11 games. Sat out the Florida State game as punishment (minor violation team rules) then was suspended against Wake Forest for a violation of team rules. Started all 15 games in '15, and produced 59-8-3 1/2 with a 15-yard interception return score against Appalachian State. Despite breaking a bone in his hand at the end of '16 fall camp, Watkins totaled 82-13 1/2-10 1/2 with four batted passes and a blocked PAT. Set a school single-season record for sacks by a defensive tackle, as the Tigers won the national championship. Team captain graduated with sociology degree.

Strengths: Very good size with outstanding arm length. Good body mass and base strength to stack the point. Has the short-area burst to beat blockers off the ball and into gaps. Plays hard and chases the ball. Flashes some pop in his hands. Physically tough to battle through injuries. Versatile and has played multiple techniques, as a three-technique and on the nose. Registered 14 sacks the past two years from the inside.

Weaknesses: Hip tightness shows up in his consistently high pad level. Slow to redirect with marginal lateral agility, as confirmed in slow 20-yard shuttle (4.89 seconds) and 3-cone drill (7.89) at his pro day, which both would have ranked near the bottom of defensive tackles at the Combine. Struggles splitting the double team. Needs to learn how to use his hands better to disengage from blocks and expand his pass-rush repertoire. Benefitted from a strong supporting cast that consistently flushed the pocket. Registered 24.5% body fat at the Combine, indicative of a lack of endurance, and noticeably tires late in games.

Future: Big, strong, wide-bodied, interior pass rusher with the eye-popping sack production from the inside to grab the attention of evaluators. At his best when he's firing off the ball low and slanting into gaps and will be most optimal working in a wave role.

Draft projection: Third- to fourth-round pick.

DRE-ROLB-PRS TIM WILLIAMS, #56 (Sr-4)

ALABAMA ▶ GRADE: 5.72
Ht: 6-2 7/8 | Wt: 244 | 40: 4.66 | Arm: 32 3/4 | Hand: 9 1/4

History: Has a daughter (Chantis). Recruited out of LSU's backyard in Baton Rouge, La. Saw limited action in seven games as a true freshman in 2013, scratching three tackles, one for loss and zero sacks. Was suspended for the '14 opener against West Virginia (violation team rules). On the season, tallied 5-1 1/2-1 1/2 in 12 appearances. A backup "Jack" linebacker/pass-rush specialist for the Crimson Tide, Williams played all 15 games in '15, and chipped in 19-12 1/2-10 1/2 with one batted pass. Played all 15 games in '16, starting two, and posted 31-16-9 with two batted passes, two forced fumbles and a 23-yard fumble return touchdown against Arkansas. Added 12 hurries. Was arrested in late September to carrying a pistol without a permit (suspended first half versus Kentucky). Turns 24 in November. Was a medical exclusion from the bench-press test at the Combine because of a right shoulder injury. Admitted at the Combine to failing multiple drug tests during his time at Alabama.

Strengths: Explosive, quick-twitch athlete with outstanding burst and hip flexibility to scream off the edge and generate pressure. Can convert speed to power and has very good closing speed. Beats blockers out of their stance and wins with leverage. Has a nice spin move and developed some hand slaps to swat away the hands of blockers. Displays violence in his punch to press thru blocks. Explosive, drive-thru tackler.

Weaknesses: Lacks bulk and strength to set the edge and defend the run and can be covered up by big bodies — limited football-playing awareness and instincts. Needs assignments to be streamlined so that he can be turned loose. Has never been a full-time starter. Needs to continue improving his lower-body strength. Recorded a slow 4.59-second 20-yard shuttle and 7.39-second 3-cone drill, indicative of marginal lateral agility. Questionable personal character creates continual distractions. Marginal weight-room strength.

Future: A sleek-framed, sudden edge rusher with better size and athletic ability than Seahawks' 2012 first-round pick (15th) and Raiders LB Bruce Irvin. Can be ideally suited for the wide-nine technique deployed in defenses such as those in Philadelphia, Detroit and Miami. Must prove to teams during interviews and private visits that he loves football.

Draft projection: Second-round pick.

Scout's take: "The most underrated talent at Alabama is No. 56. He has first-round talent, but his character is going to knock him down. He played close to 260 (in 2015) and was down to 238 (in 2016). He doesn't look that big when you see him on the field because he is surrounded by so many giants. He has some issues, but the coaches love him there."

DLE-LOLB JORDAN WILLIS, #75 (Sr-4)

KANSAS STATE ▶ GRADE: 5.88

Ht: 6-3 3/4 | Wt: 255 | 40: 4.57 | Arm: 33 1/2 | Hand: 9 7/8

History: Prepped in Missouri, where he won a state championship as a sophomore. Tore his right meniscus before joining the Wildcats. As a true freshman in 2013, had one sack in nine appearances. Dealt with a torn left meniscus in the offseason. Started all 13 games at right end in '14, and recorded 25 tackles, 6 1/2 for loss and four sacks with one batted pass. Played with a torn right thumb ligament in the Alamo Bowl against UCLA. Moved to the left side in '15, and produced 36-15 1/2-4 with three batted passes, three forced fumbles and a blocked field goal. Was the Big 12 Defensive Player of the Year in '16 — started all 13 games, and registered 52-17 1/2-11 1/2 with three batted passes and three forced fumbles. Team captain. Graduated. Was named the South team's Most Outstanding Player at the Senior Bowl after notching two sacks.

Strengths: Well-built and looks the part, with a striated musculature and huge, trapezoid muscles. Produced the most explosive 10-yard split (1.53 seconds) and 3-cone drill (6.85) of any defensive linemen at the Combine, showing rare take-off speed, initial burst and balance. Has strong hands and uses them to control and rip off blocks. Plays with good leverage. Very active, energetic and competitive and consistently brings pressure and flushes the pocket. Recorded a 39-inch vertical jump, indicative of outstanding lower-body explosion. Practices and prepares like a seasoned pro and is committed to his craft. Film junkie.

Weaknesses: Has tightness in his body and lacks the hip flexibility to be a dynamic edge rusher. Can continue developing a better pass-rush plan and learn how to change gears and string moves together. Hands and feet do not consistently work in unison to set up blockers. Not a natural bender and too often relies on pure straight-line power. A lot of his production was clearview where he was unblocked and overmatching tight ends. Was beat up by the ball in LB drills at the Combine and struggles to catch cleanly.

Future: Strong, powerful, energetic, college base end with the motor, relentlessness, work ethic and preparation habits to consistently generate pressure and disrupt backfields. Though he is not a natural bender with dynamic pass-rush skill, Willis will be an extremely productive pro because of how hard he works at his craft. A power rusher with Day One plug-and-play potential, Willis will fit best as a left base end in a "40" front and is wired to become a consistent double-digit sack producer within a few years.

Draft projection: Top-50 pick.

Coach's take: "Jordan is the epitome of what our program is all about. He comes to practice exactly the same way he goes to a ballgame. If

DEFENSIVE LINE

you were unaware of the setting, you couldn't tell the difference between what he does on the practice field and what does on the game field. … He gives you his very best of every second of every minute of every hour of every day of every week. He is going to be a highly successful young guy in a lot of ways, because he is that committed to doing the best that he can." — *Kansas State Head Coach Bill Snyder*

DLE **DEATRICH WISE**, #48 (Sr-5)
ARKANSAS　　　　　　　▶ GRADE: 5.32
Ht: 6-5 1/4 | Wt: 274 | 40: 4.96 | Arm: 35 5/8 | Hand: 10 1/2

History: First name is pronounced "DEE-trich." Father, Deatrich Sr., was drafted by the Seahawks in 1988. Prepped in Texas. Redshirted in 2012 — played against Jacksonville State, notching a sack, but suffered a hand injury which sidelined him the rest of the season. Played all 12 games in '13, and recorded 17 tackles, three for loss and two sacks. Had a left knee injury during '14 fall camp (sat out Week Two versus Nicholls State) before collecting 13-3-2 in 10 games (one start). Did not play the final two regular season games. A pass-rush specialist in '15, Wise played less than half of the Razorbacks' defensive snaps, but produced 31-10 1/2-8 with three batted passes and three forced fumbles in 13 games. Despite breaking his right hand in the '16 season opener against Louisiana Tech, played all 13 games — starting the first eight — and totaled 49-5 1/2-3 1/2 with three batted passes and one forced fumble. Had a reduced role after separating his shoulder against Auburn. Team captain graduated with kinesiology degree.

Strengths: Has exceptional length — tied for the longest arms (35 5/8 inches) of any defensive linemen at the Combine. Uses his length well to disrupt the vision of quarterbacks with good leaping ability and hand-eye coordination to bat down passes. Corrals ball-carriers with his long arms. Opens his stride in space and can cover ground. Is tough and will battle through injuries. Scheme-diverse.

Weaknesses: Average speed to the perimeter and can be outflanked and lose contain vs. speed (see Alabama). Has some heaviness in his movement and is not sudden redirecting — limited playing range. Plays too tall and can be uprooted against the double team. Raw technician — does not play to his size. Only a one-year starter. Durability has been an issue throughout his career and needs to be examined.

Future: Tough, lanky, upright, strong-side defensive end battled through injuries as a senior did not produce the way he is capable, yet possesses the size, length and athletic ability to

warrant developing. Could be best in a wave role. Durability considerations could affect his draft status.

Draft projection: Fourth- to fifth-round pick.

5T-3T **CHRIS WORMLEY**, #43 (Sr-5)
MICHIGAN　　　　　　　▶ GRADE: 5.78
Ht: 6-5 1/8 | Wt: 298 | 40: 4.86 | Arm: 34 1/8 | Hand: 10 1/2

History: Prepped in Ohio, where he also competed in basketball and track and field. Recruited to Michigan by then-head coach Brady Hoke. Redshirted in 2012 after tearing his ACL in August. Played all 13 games in '13, and recorded 19 tackles, 4 1/2 for loss and 2 1/2 sacks with one batted pass. Played all 12 games in '14, starting the final six in place of the injured Willie Henry, and chipped in 21-5-3. Primarily a 3-4 defensive end in '15, started 11-of-13 games, and logged 43-14 1/2-6 1/2 with one batted pass and one forced fumble. A 4-3 DE in '16, totaled 40-9-6 in 13 starts. Team captain was named the Wolverines' top defensive lineman his last two seasons.

Strengths: Exceptional size and arm length. Plays on his feet with very good balance and outstanding strength to set the edge. Wins with leverage and technique — plays square to the line, uses his long arms to lock out and burrows vs. the double team. Flashes shock in his punch and has a healthy pass-rush repertoire with an efficient arm-over, rip, swat, club, swim and up-and-under moves. Has the bulk strength to walk blockers back to the quarterback. Strong, forceful tackler. Versatile and scheme-diverse — has played inside and outside and for even and odd fronts. Experienced, three-year starter. Very solid personal and football character. Good career sack production (18).

Weaknesses: Not explosive off the ball. Does not always sacrifice his body around piles and sell out pursuing down the line. Will let his pads rise too consistently locating the ball and could do a better job shooting his hands to disengage. Did not dominate the way a man with his physical traits could in '16.

Future: A rare-sized, athletic big man that could bring the most value to a scheme-diverse defense that deploys multiple fronts. Has the size and strength to stack the corner for a "30" front and enough quickness to pierce gaps inside for a "40" front. Was at his best in an odd front in '15 and future could be brightest there.

Draft projection: Second- to third-round pick.

Scout's take: "Wormley in my opinion will be a good three-technique. I don't think he is quick or fast enough as a defensive end to play outside. I don't think he has anything special on the edge other than some strength vs. the run."

DEFENSIVE LINE

LINEBACKERS

Nawrocki's TOP 10

◄ 1. **REUBEN FOSTER**
2. **Derek Barnett**
3. **Haason Reddick**
4. **Jarrad Davis**
5. **Zach Cunningham**
6. **Ryan Anderson**
7. **Raekwon McMillan**
8. **T.J. Watt**
9. **Kendell Beckwith**
10. **Duke Riley**

LINEBACKERS

LOLB-LDE RYAN ANDERSON, #22 (Sr-5)

ALABAMA ▶ GRADE: 5.88

Ht: 6-2 | Wt: 253 | 40: 4.82 | Arm: 31 1/2 | Hand: 9 3/8

History: Won a state championship as an Alabama prep. Redshirted in 2012. Played all 13 games in '13, and recorded five tackles, 1 1/2 for loss and 1 1/2 sacks in 13 games. Played all 14 games in '14, and tallied 25-8-3. Had his left labrum surgically repaired in the offseason. Was arrested in January '15 for misdemeanor third-degree domestic violence, criminal mischief. According to a police release, Anderson and a female student engaged in an argument and damaged each other's vehicles. An impactful reserve in the fall, collected 37-11 1/2-6 with two forced fumbles in 15 games for the national champs. Stepped into the lineup in '16 when he started all 15 games at "Sam" linebacker, and registered 61-19-9 with three pass breakups, one interception (26-yard TD) and four forced fumbles. Added 28 hurries the last three seasons. Injured his thumb during Senior Bowl practice. Already graduated. Did not perform bench-press test at the Combine because of a left thumb injury and opted out of the shuttles and jumps.

Strengths: Outstanding motor and field energy. Very good base, balance and point-of-attack strength to control blockers and set the edge with force. Is a 500-pound bench-presser with a low center of gravity. Jolts big bodies with his punch and plays bigger than his size. Can convert speed to power. Strong, knockback tackler who consistently tries to tomahawk and jar the ball loose. Extremely tough. Competitive and physical. The game is important to him and he commands respect with his business-like approach and alpha-male leadership. Holds his teammates accountable.

Weaknesses: Lacks ideal length and has short arms with a frame that looks maxed out. Shows some tightness in his hips redirecting and lacks initial burst off spots, as confirmed at the Combine running a 1.82-second 10-yard split, the slowest among any linebackers. Could stand to do a better job of using his hands at the top of his rush. Only a one-year, full-time starter. Registered 17.4 percent body fat at the Combine, the second-highest among linebackers and indicative of a lack of endurance. Limited cover skills — will be challenged by speed backs and sleek tight ends in man coverage and has limited experience zone-dropping. Not fluid changing direction. Plays a bit recklessly in space, flying like a runaway train and struggling to come to balance and consequently will miss some tackles.

Future: A short, compact, power-leverage rusher in similar mold as Cardinals 2015 second-round pick (58th overall) Markus Golden. Possesses the football temperament to contribute readily with his hand in the dirt and become a disruptive edge presence in a 30-front. Looks destined for a team like the Steelers.

Draft projection: Top 50-pick.

Scout's take: "Anderson has a weird build with little calves and 31-inch arms. He has to go to (a team running a 3-4 defense.) He's not quite as accomplished as a pass rusher as (Ravens 2016 second-round pick [42nd] Kamalei) Correa, but he plays like him."

WLB-ILB **ALEX ANZALONE**, #34 (Jr-4)

FLORIDA ▶ GRADE: 5.37

Ht: 6-2 7/8 | Wt: 241 | 40: 4.64 | Arm: 32 1/8 | Hand: 9 1/8

History: Last name is pronounced "Anzah-LOAN-eee." Linebacker-fullback won a Pennsylvania state championship and was the Class AA Player of the Year. Joined the Gators for 2013 spring practice, but tore his right labrum (required surgery). Saw limited action in the fall, scratching two tackles, zero for loss and zero sacks in 10 appearances. Sat out against LSU (ankle) then dislocated his shoulder against Georgia Southern, and missed the season finale against Florida State. Was a backup/special teams player in '14, recording 14-1-0 in 12 appearances. In '15, was considered the "quarterback of the defense" by teammates, but managed 6-0-0 in two starts at weak-side linebacker before suffering a season-ending right shoulder injury. Started the first eight games of the '16 season at WLB, and totaled 53-4-3 with two pass breakups before suffering a season-ending broken left forearm injury.

Strengths: Outstanding size. Good athlete. Moves fluidly with urgency down the line in pursuit of the ball and can string out ball-carriers to the sideline. Plays square to the line of scrimmage and does not cross over his feet. Good length to match up with tight ends. Very active and energetic. Has special teams' experience.

Weaknesses: Durability is a serious concern given history of shoulder injuries, and strength is noticeably down — bench-pressed 225 only 16 times at the Combine. Lacks ideal take-on strength and knockback power in his body. Measured a 30 1/2-inch vertical jump at the Combine, revealing marginal lower-body explosion. Has missed playing time every year because of injury.

Future: Big, fast, athletic linebacker who

must shake his china-doll reputation to become an NFL starter. May never be durable enough to be trusted as a starter, and injury history could relegate him to a role as a three-position backup in a "40" front. Has some similarities to Cowboys' 2006 first-round pick (18th overall) Bobby Carpenter, who played for five teams during his 8-year NFL career and always struggled to make it through a full season healthy despite intriguing athletic tools.

Draft projection: Third- to fourth-round pick.

Scout's take: "(Anzalone) might fit better as a 'Sam' in a 3-4 (defense) than as a true 'Sam' in a 4-3. For a big guy, he's not a killer around the line of scrimmage. He is big and long and moves around well enough to get looks in the (third round)."

ROLB-DRE **DEREK BARNETT**, #9 (Jr-3)

TENNESSEE ▶ GRADE: 6.17

Ht: 6-3 | Wt: 259 | 40: 4.86 | Arm: 32 1/8 | Hand: 10

History: Prepped at Brentwood Academy in Tennessee. Set school records for tackles for loss and sacks by a true freshman — started 10-of-13 games in '14, and racked up 72 tackles, 20 1/2 for loss and 10 sacks. Had off-season shoulder surgery. Started all 13 games at RDE in '15, and produced 69-12 1/2-10 with one pass breakup and one forced fumble. Started all 13 games at RDE in '16, and registered 56-19-13 with five pass breakups, one interception and two forced fumbles. Added 31 hurries in three seasons. Bested Reggie White for Tennessee's all-time career sacks record (33), and his 52 career tackles for loss ranks second behind Leonard Little. Will be a 21-year-old rookie. Opted to complete a full workout at the Combine with exception of the bench-press test despite battling illness.

Strengths: Outstanding motor, energy and effort — keeps working to come free. Times the snap very well and has very good take-off speed. Feels blocking pressure and understands how to work edges and how to set up inside, spin moves. Regularly whips tight ends in one-on-one situations. Very quick hands with refined technique as a rusher. Strong edge-setter vs. the run. Extremely competitive and rises to the occasion in critical situations. Recorded among the fastest 3-cone drill times (6.96 seconds) of any pass rusher at the Combine, indicative of outstanding agility and change of direction. Has a relentless football temperament and gets energized in the fourth quarter when the going gets tough. Record-setting career sack production (33), with the majority of it (29) coming against SEC competition. Outstanding football character — extremely motivated, studies a lot of film and takes a very business-like approach to the game.

Weaknesses: Has some stiffness in his body and is not an elite athlete with natural bend to trim the corner. Could learn to play with more power and to develop a stronger bull-rush move. A bit straight-linish and tight in the hips and does not have elite take-off speed, burst or acceleration to win one-on-one matchups with athletic talent alone. Has limited coverage experience to drop into zones and lacks long speed to cover tight ends or match up with backs on wheel routes. Has an ordinary 31-inch vertical jump and average weight-room strength — could stand to improve lower-body power.

Future: Motor, disruptiveness and hand slaps are reminiscent of Tamba Hali exiting Penn State. What Barnett lacks in pure athletic ability he can be counted on to compensate for with tremendous effort, energy and relentlessness. Is scheme-diverse and can fit in both even and odd fronts, though his lack of length and elite athletic traits could play best in a "30" front. A better football player than tester.

Draft projection: First-round pick.

Scout's take: "(Barnett) is really, really good. I think you can put 20 pounds on him and make him a helluva three-technique. He has not even begun to fill out his body. He looks fleshy when you see him up close. …He's a stiff, strong, straight-line burst guy. I think those qualities play better inside."

MLB KENDELL BECKWITH, #52 (Sr-4)

LSU ▶ GRADE: 5.52

HT: 6-2 1/4 | WT: 243 | 40: 4.80E | ARM: 33 | HAND: 9 1/2

History: Louisiana native was the state's 3A Defensive MVP (also played quarterback). As a true freshman in 2013, recorded 11 tackles, one for loss and one sack with one forced fumble in 12 games. In '14, overtook D.J. Welter at "Mike" linebacker — played all 13 games, starting the final seven, and contributed 77 tackles, 7 1/2 for loss and two sacks with three pass breakups and one interception (29-yard TD against New Mexico State). Also had a five-yard gain on a successful fake punt against Wisconsin. Started all 12 games at MLB in '15, and produced 84-10-3 1/2 with one pass breakup and two forced fumbles, including 8-4-2 1/2 against Texas Tech in the Texas Bowl. Sprained his left LCL during '16 spring practice. In the fall, played the "Mack" linebacker position in new defensive coordinator Dave Aranda's 3-4 scheme — totaled 91-6-1 with four pass breakups in 10 starts before tearing his left ACL against Florida. Butkus Award finalist. Was a medical exclusion from the Combine because of knee injury.

Strengths: Exceptional size with broad shoulders, a big bubble butt and well-distributed thickness throughout his frame. Plays the run with physicality and hits with thump — can catapult backs on impact (see Jacksonville State and Missouri). Keeps his feet through traffic. Triggers fast and knifes into the backfield. Attacks downhill and bows up near the goalline (see Auburn). Quick eyes to sort out pullers and beat blockers to a spot. Plays with good hand usage and controls blockers at the point of attack.

Weaknesses: Lacks top-end speed, and tackling mechanics begin to break down outside the box, where he can be overextended and miss some open-field opportunities. Does not get great depth in zone drops and has just adequate coverage range. Makes few plays on the ball and could stand to improve eyes looking up crossers and anticipating routes unfolding. Needs to do a better job making himself skinny as a blitzer and fitting through gaps. Did not handle defensive checks and calls until senior season and may require some time to acclimate to play-calling role in the pros. Scouts have raised the question about how much he loves football. Durability must be carefully evaluated.

Future: Big, physical thumper with the size, toughness and instincts to earn a starting job in the middle of a "30" or "40" front when healthy. Knee injury could knock down his draft value a round, though appears well on his road to recovery and could be active during his rookie season.

Draft projection: Second- to third-round pick.

Scout's take: "Beckwith is a dual-scheme fit linebacker. He can play in any front. He has gotten better each year. I don't think he would be as good in a 3-4 (front) with guards coming out on him on a consistent basis. He's a good football player."

LOLB-SLB VINCE BIEGEL, #47 (Sr-5)

WISCONSIN ▶ GRADE: 5.44

HT: 6-3 1/4 | Wt: 246 | 40: 4.68 | Arm: 32 3/8 | Hand: 9 1/8

History: Engaged to be married to Sarah on July 1. Grew up on a cranberry farm. Also competed in hockey and track and field as a prep in Wisconsin, where he was a consensus All-American and the state's Gatorade Player of the Year. Was forced to redshirt in 2012 because of a broken right foot. Played 13 games in '13, starting two, and tallied 25 tackles, three for loss and two sacks with two pass breakups. An outside linebacker for the Badgers, he started 13-of-14 games in '14, and produced 56-16 1/2-7 1/2 with two pass breakups and two forced fumbles. In '15, amassed 66-14-8 in 13 starts at OLB. Started all 12 games played at OLB in '16, and logged 44-6-4 with one pass breakup. Did not play against Michigan or Ohio State after having surgery to repair a broken left foot. Added 16 hurries the last two seasons. Team captain graduated with a degree in life sciences communication.

Strengths: Outstanding size with good length to lock out and create extension. Strong at the point of attack and can leverage the edge. Good hand technician — rips, swats, jerks and flashes violence in his hands to disengage. Relentless pursuit effort moves quarterbacks off a spot and generates a lot of tackle production. Good football IQ. Intense competitor with alpha-leader qualities. The game is important to him.

Weaknesses: Too upright in coverage with very choppy steps in reverse — seldom asked to cover and can be challenged to cover speed backs and tight ends. Average change of direction, as confirmed by 4.33-second 20-yard shuttle time at the Combine. Modest sack production — is often a step late to arrive and struggles to finish. Ordinary initial get-off and explosion off the edge.

Future: A strong-side, 3-4 outside linebacker primarily used to rush the passer, Biegel has some similarities to Texans 2011 second-round pick (42nd) and Falcons LDE Brooks Reed. Could warrant some interest in a 4-3 front as a strong-side linebacker or left defensive end if he bulks up, though is at his best moving forward and ideally suited for a 3-4 front. Very dependable, high-energy overachiever who can be trusted to play hard every snap and affect the game with his effort. A high-floor, low-ceiling pass-rusher. Also warranting looks as a three-position linebacker for teams running "40" fronts.

Draft projection: Third- to fourth-round pick.

Scout's take: "(Biegel) looked a little stiff. That's how he appeared to me when he was at practice and when I saw him live during the fall. He did not have a natural bend to him. I know some other teams (running 4-3 defenses) think he could stand on his feet and be a three-position (linebacker). I didn't see the lateral quickness to play on his feet as a linebacker."

MLB BEN BOULWARE, #10 (Sr-4)

CLEMSON ▶ GRADE: 5.01

Ht: 6-0 | Wt: 238 | 40: 4.86 | Arm: 30 1/2 | Hand: 10

History: Suffered a compound fracture to his left arm racing dirt bikes as a kid. Highly recruited South Carolinian also was an all-state baseball player. Sustained a concussion in 2011. As true freshman in '13, played 11 games, and recorded 25 tackles (seven on special teams), 1 1/2 for loss and zero sacks. Missed three October games because of a left knee injury. Was ejected for targeting against Georgia Tech. Played all 13 games in '14, starting two, and logged 58-5-1 with one pass breakup and a 47-yard interception touchdown. Had nine tackles on special teams. Started on the weak side in '15 when he produced 82-8-3 1/2 with seven pass breakups, two interceptions and three forced fumbles. Bruised his left shoulder against Wake Forest, and played hurt the last three games of the regular season. In '16, was the national champs' leading tackler — started all 14 games at WLB, and produced 116-11 1/2-4 with two pass breakups, one interception and three forced fumbles. Did not play against South Carolina State (right ankle). Added 22 pressures the last two seasons. Team captain graduated with a sociology degree. Opted not to run the 40-yard dash at the Combine.

Strengths: Good eyes and anticipation. Active and energetic and is around the ball a lot. Plays on his feet with good balance and has a knack for slipping blocks. Keys the QB in coverage, sniffs out screens and has a feel for receivers passing through his zones. Capable of carrying backs in man coverage. Has excelled in special teams' coverage. Vocal team leader very motivated to disprove critics and has a giant chip on his shoulder.

Weaknesses: Short and short-armed and struggles to disengage when he gets locked up. Bounces off some tackles (limited wrap) and too much of production comes down the field. Can be pinballed and pancaked (see national championship vs Cam Robinson). Tied for having the lowest vertical jump (29 1/2 inches) of any linebacker at the Combine, indicative of marginal lower-body explosion. Struggles to get skinny and time up the blitz. Not an explosive tackler. Recorded the slowest 60-yard shuttle time (12.16 seconds) of any linebacker at the Combine, indicative of a lack of endurance. Notorious for his dirty play — see neck choke vs Louisville and dirty antics explained after Ohio State game.

Future: Stocky, short-armed, scrappy inside linebacker with the toughness and tackling skills to readily make a mark on special teams. Plays the game with a chip on his shoulder, but does not have the frame, feet or athletic ability desired to become more than a backup 'Mike' linebacker.

Draft projection: Late draftable pick.

ROLB-PRS TYUS BOWSER, #81 (Sr-4)

HOUSTON ▶ GRADE: 5.46

Ht: 6-2 5/8 | Wt: 247 | 40: 4.68 | Arm: 33 1/4 | Hand: 10 1/8

History: Texas native prepped at John Tyler High, where he also drew a Division I basketball scholarship. High school teammate of Greg Ward. As a true freshman in 2013, recorded 26 tackles, 5 1/2 for loss and five sacks with two pass breakups, one interception and one forced fumble in 13 games (one start at defensive end). Played all 13 games in '14, and tallied 13-3 1/2-3 in 13 games (one start at DE). Was deployed as a 3-4 outside linebacker in '15 — started all 14 games, and produced 50-6 1/2-5 1/2 with three pass breakups, one interceptions and one forced fumble. Started all eight games played at OLB in '16, and totaled 47-12-8 1/2 with three pass breakups, one forced fumble and one safety. Missed five mid-season games after suffering an orbital fracture in what head coach Tom Herman described as a "freak accident" with teammate and fellow starting MLB Matthew Adams that resulted from an "over competitive" situation. Graduated.

Strengths: Limber, flexible athlete with loose hips. Produced the most explosive vertical jump (37 1/2 inches) of any linebacker at the Combine, indicative of outstanding lower-body explosion, that, combined with long arms, results in disrupting passing lanes. Flashed pass-rush skill against Louisville. Light on his feet and can match up well with tight ends in man coverage. Showed gradual improvement every season and has upside to continue developing.

Weaknesses: Will benefit from spending more time in the weight room and getting stronger. Average career sack production — still learning how to develop a pass-rush plan and could stand to add variety to his rush repertoire. Does not appear to play with confidence. Can be locked down when big bodies get their hands on him and needs to develop more counter moves and learn to play with more strength. Inconsistent run defender lacking the anchor strength to match up against NFL big bodies.

Future: A solid-framed, athletic, ascending pass rusher with the lower-body explosion, athletic ability and burst to emerge as a disruptive edge rusher with a year of development in an NFL strength and conditioning program to add bulk and improve his strength. Still very much a work in progress and will require patience in the pros.

Draft projection: Third- to fourth-round pick.

Scout's take: "(Bowser) is kind of raw. His instincts are not great. He has some bend and speed, but his motor runs hot and cold too much watching him on tape."

WLB BLAIR BROWN, #33 (Sr-4)

OHIO ▶ GRADE: 5.25

Ht: 5-11 1/2 | Wt: 238 | 40: 4.64 | Arm: 31 1/4 | Hand: 9 3/8

History: Prepped in California. Redshirted in 2012. Played seven games in '13, and recorded 17 tackles, one for loss and zero sacks. Did not play the last six games. Was a weak-side linebacker for the Bobcats. Started 8-of-11 games played in '14, and tallied 55 tackles, four for loss and one sack with two pass breakups and one forced fumble. Did not play against Akron (right ankle), and was ejected against Northern Illinois (targeting). Started all 11 games played in '15, and produced 65-4 1/2-0. Sat out two November contests (ankle). Was the team's leading tackler in '16 when he piled up 128-15-4 1/2 with one forced fumble. Hurt his knee against Kent State. Graduated. Recorded 12 penalties the last three years. Did not perform bench-press test at the Combine because of a pectoral strain.

Strengths: Good lateral pursuit and speed to the perimeter. Exceptional 20-yard short shuttle time (4.18 seconds), indicative of outstanding short-area burst and explosion. Paced all inside linebackers with a 37-inch vertical jump, indicative of very good athletic ability. Chases hard to the sideline and plays with urgency moving downhill. Effective shooting gaps as a blitzer (gets skinny). Has the movement skill to match up with backs in man coverage.

Weaknesses: Has short arms and lacks point-of-attack strength to take on blocks. Lacks ball skills and awareness in zone coverage and has minimal production on the ball. Was beat up by the ball during catching drills at the Combine. Needs to spend more time in the weight room and continue to improve strength. Needs to learn to control his emotions better and avoid taking foolish penalties.

Future: Sleek, athletic, run-and-hit linebacker with the speed, balance and burst to make an immediate impact as a core special teams performer and be groomed into a greater role as a weak-side linebacker in a "40" front. Has enough bulk to function at all three linebacker spots for defenses seeking three interchangeable linebackers, such as the Panthers, Cowboys and Seahawks.

Draft projection: Fifth- to sixth-round pick.

Scout's take: "I graded him as a free agent in the fall and thought he was stiff on tape. After seeing him move around (at the Combine), I was wrong. He is a draftable talent and will be a good core (special) teams' player."

LINEBACKERS

NLB **JAYON BROWN**, #12 (Sr-4)

UCLA ▶ GRADE: 5.14

Ht: 6-0 | Wt: 231 | 40: 4.73 | Arm: 31 3/8 | Hand: 9 5/8

History: Long Beach (Calif.) Poly product. As a true freshman in 2013, was the Bruins' Rookie of the Year on special teams after collecting six tackles, zero for loss and zero sacks with one forced fumble in 13 games. Made 12 appearances in '14, and notched 2-0-0. Saw more playing time in '15 after Myles Jack's injury. Started 9-of-12 games — five at 3-4 outside linebacker, four at "Mike" linebacker — and led the Bruins with 93-2-1/2 and six pass breakups. Missed the Arizona State contest while nursing a back injury. A 4-3 weak-side linebacker in '16, Brown was the Pacific-12's leading tackler — racked up 119-7-21/2 with six pass breakups and three interceptions in 12 starts. Graduated in the fall of 2016. Opted not to run shuttles at the Combine.

Strengths: Outstanding motor and effort production. Quick to sort out traffic and slip and avoid blockers. Good speed to chase down backs to the perimeter. Good coverage instincts and ball skills. Fluid hips to carry backs in man coverage. Tied with Florida's Alex Anzalone for having the best 10-yard split (1.57 seconds) of any inside linebacker at the Combine, indicative of exceptional burst. Loves football, is a very diligent worker and unselfish team player. Smart and articulate. Very good personal and football character.

Weaknesses: Marginal size with the body and frame of a safety. Has short arms and is too easily engulfed by big bodies. Dragdown tackler lacking strength, pop and explosion on contact — gets carried for extra yardage and plays small.

Future: An excellent college football player with the build of an NFL strong safety, Brown could carve a niche as a pure core special teams' contributor, with the production, instincts and makeup to earn a roster spot. Could warrant consideration as a rotational weak-side nickel or dime linebacker in a "40" front, though greatest impact will come as a core special-teams contributor.

Draft projection: Late draftable pick.

Scout's take: "If he were a little bigger, I would have given him a draftable grade. He's very instinctive and highly productive, but he's small, slow and weak. I wanted to like him. He just doesn't have the body type to hold up. After I saw him in practice, I knew he was not big enough to play for us."

MLB-FB **RILEY BULLOUGH**, #30 (Sr-5)

MICHIGAN STATE ▶ GRADE: 5.04

Ht: 6-1 5/8 | Wt: 226 | 40: 4.73 | Arm: 31 1/4 | Hand: 9 7/8

History: Third-generation Spartan with several relatives who played at MSU, including brother, Max (Texans). Michigan native played linebacker, safety and quarterback in high school. Suffered a broken collarbone in Week Five of his senior season. Redshirted in 2012. Had a shoulder injury during '13 fall camp, preceding a move from running back to fullback. On the season, notched three special-teams tackles in 14 games. Moved to linebacker in '14 when he recorded 29 tackles, four for loss and 3 1/2 sacks with two interceptions in 13 games (one start). Was the Spartans' leading tackler in '15 after starting 13-of-14 at "Mike" linebacker and producing 106-7 1/2-4 with two pass breakups, two interceptions (TD) and two forced fumbles. Was ejected for targeting against Air Force (suspended the first half against Central Michigan). Started all nine games played at "Mike" in '16, and posted 76-6 1/2-0 despite missing games against Wisconsin, Indiana and BYU because of a right shoulder injury. Against Maryland, accumulated three personal fouls, the last of which was a targeting flag which got him ejected. Team captain graduated with a degree in media and information. Did not run the 40-yard dash or perform shuttles at the Combine because of a left hamstring injury.

Strengths: Good intensity and effort. Active and energetic. Very competitive filling downhill and will sacrifice his body taking on isolation-lead blocks. Measured the lowest body-fat percentage (7.7%) of any linebacker at the Combine, indicative of exceptional endurance and conditioning. Solid production. Has deep football bloodlines.

Weaknesses: Tight-hipped and limited athletically. Lacks bulk and strength at the point of attack and gets velcroed to blocks and struggles to disengage. Recorded a 31 1/2-inch vertical jump indicative of limited lower-body explosion and striking power. Limited coverage skills.

Future: Undersized, inside linebacker with few redeeming physical traits. Could be tried as a fullback, where he spent time early in his college career, and will need to prove himself on special teams to stick on a roster.

Draft projection: Priority free agent.

ROLB-DRE **JOSH CARRAWAY**, #93 (Sr-5)

TCU ▶ GRADE: 5.26

Ht: 6-3 | Wt: 242 | 40: 4.74 | Arm: 34 1/4 | Hand: 9 1/4

History: Texas native. Had three meniscus scopes his first two years. As a true freshman in 2012, notched four tackles, zero for loss and zero sacks in four appearances. Redshirted in 2013. Played all 13 games in '14, starting seven of the first eight at left end, and tallied 33-5-2 with a 33-yard interception return touchdown and one forced fumble. Started all 13 games at LDE in '15, and totaled 47-1 1/2-9 with two pass breakups and one forced fumble. Also had a fumble recovery touchdown. Moved to right end in '16, and produced 49-11-8 with one forced fumble. Hurt his right ankle against Iowa State, and played the next three weeks at 80 percent health, according to head coach Gary Patterson. Graduated.

Strengths: Very good arm length. Good athlete. Displays some natural bend, burst and suddenness off the edge, flashing an effective inside move. Has the speed to stretch plays to the perimeter.

Weaknesses: Has small hands. Lacks point-of-attack strength and can be run at. Inconsistent effort. Average instincts locating the ball. Needs to learn how to use his hands better to dip, rip and swim past blockers. Did not look comfortable opening his hips or dropping during LB drills at the Combine. Recorded a 29 1/2-inch vertical jump, indicative of limited lower-body explosion. Has a history of multiple right knee injuries, and long-term durability must be considered carefully.

Future: Thin-framed, high-hipped, narrow-based, undersized college pass rusher who lacks bulk for an every-down role. Plays too small to be effective on early downs defending the run, though could warrant some interest as a pass-rush specialist on third downs and might need to prove he can play on his feet as a "Will" linebacker to find a true every-down home.

Draft projection: Fifth- to sixth-round pick.

WLB-ILB ZACH CUNNINGHAM, #41 (Jr-4)

VANDERBILT ▶ GRADE: 5.90

Ht: 6-3 1/2 | Wt: 234 | 40: 4.67 | Arm: 34 3/8 | Hand: 9 1/4

History: Also competed in basketball and track as a prep in Alabama, where he was named the state's 5A Lineman of the Year. Signed with Vanderbilt and then-head coach James Franklin over offers from Auburn, Ole Miss, Miami and Oregon, amongst others. Redshirted in 2013. Played 11 games in '14, starting the final five at 3-4 inside linebacker, and recorded 67 tackles, seven for loss and two sacks with two pass breakups and one forced fumble. Was suspended for the Charleston Southern contest. Was the Commodores' leading tackler in '15 after starting 9-of-12 games at ILB and producing 103-16 1/2-4 1/2 with three pass breakups and four forced fumbles. Had 19 tackles against Georgia. Was the Southeastern Conference's leading tackler for the second straight season in '16 when he racked up 125-16 1/2-0 with three pass breakups, two forced fumbles and a blocked field goal attempt.

Strengths: Excellent size and length with a frame to grow into. Had the longest arms (34 3/8 inches) and wingspan (81 5/8 inches) of any linebacker at the Combine. Plays on his feet with good balance for as long limbed as he is. Consistently productive vs. the run and has a knack for slipping blockers and using his excellent length to corral ball carriers. Recorded a low 1.58-second 10-yard split at the Combine, revealing outstanding short-area burst and closing speed. Has a 35-inch vertical jump and 10'5" broad jump that reveal good explosiveness and were among the best measures of linebackers at the Combine. Impressed executives with football intelligence and recall at the Combine despite being quiet-natured and reserved. Coachable, unselfish, team player.

Weaknesses: Has a very lean frame. Bench-pressed 225 pounds only 15 times at the Combine and needs to spend more time in the weight room and get stronger. Can be overwhelmed at the point of attack and could stand to do a better job using his hands to shed blocks. Drag-down tackler lacking physicality and will miss a few each game not securely wrapping or coming to balance in space. Inefficient blitzer lacking the body power to gore through a hole — gets hung up too much. Did not record an interception in four years during college and hands looked like skillets at times during cover drills at the Combine.

Future: A lean, long-framed, high-cut, athletic linebacker capable of playing multiple positions, Cunningham is reminiscent of Cardinals 2004 second-round pick (33rd overall) Karlos Dansby and would be best suited on the weak side in a "40" front where he is covered up and free to roam. Most of his flaws are correctable with continued physical development and could prove to be a Pro Bowl-caliber performer when he fills out his frame and improves his strength.

Draft projection: Top-50 pick.

Scout's take: "(Cunningham) looks like he can add 20 pounds because he is so tall and lean. He's not a physical smashmouth hitter. He does make some athletic plays. He lines up as a 3-4 'Mike' because he is athletic enough to turn and run and get outside. He has some coverage ability, but he's not a very fluid guy. You can't put him at 'Will.' I don't know if his hands are good enough to put him at 'Sam' though it's becoming a lost art in college football. You don't

LINEBACKERS

see many linebackers shooting their hands when they get engaged to keep extension. It's more dip, rip and avoid than shed. It's part of the trend with spread offenses — few (college) teams are power blocking."

WLB-ILB JARRAD DAVIS, #40 (Sr-4)

FLORIDA   ▶ GRADE: 6.13

Ht: 6-1 3/8 | Wt: 238 | 40: 4.65e | Arm: 33 1/2 | Hand: 9 3/4

History: First name is pronounced "Jared." Had knee and ankle injuries as a Georgia prep. As a true freshman in 2013, was the Gators' Most Valuable Special Teams Player after recording 24 tackles, two for loss and zero sacks with one pass breakup and one forced fumble in 12 games (one start). In '14, collected 23-1-0 in nine games (one start) before tearing his meniscus against South Carolina. Played all 15 games in '15, and started the final 12 at weakside linebacker when Alex Anzalone was lost for the season — produced 98-11-3 1/2 with four pass breakups, one interception and one forced fumble. Started all nine games played at the "Mike" linebacker in '16, and posted 60-6-2 with four pass breakups. Had 15 tackles against Vanderbilt. Sprained his left ankle against Missouri then sprained his left ankle against Arkansas — played hurt against Alabama, but sat out four of the final five games. Opted not to work out or participate in on-field drills at the Combine.

Strengths: Very good instincts with an aggressive football-playing temperament. Plays the game like his hair is on fire and flies to the ball. Good hip roll through contact — has knockback power in his body when he strikes. Explosive blitzer — good timing and pierces gaps. Extremely tough and competitive and it consistently shows up in pursuit. Tied with UCLA's Jayon Brown for having the best 10-yard split (1.57 seconds) of any inside linebacker at the Combine, indicative of exceptional burst. Good awareness to sniff out screens and react to the thrown ball in front of him in zone coverage. Outstanding personal and football character — always seeking ways to improve.

Weaknesses: Misses some tackles in space overrunning the ball and not coming to balance. Has some tightness in his hips that can be exposed in man coverage by quick-footed backs — loses a step in transition. At times can be engaged by big-bodied blockers. Has a nagging history of lower-body injuries (knee and ankle) that may not disappear given the urgency with which he plays.

Future: An explosive, every-down linebacker with playmaking ability, Davis has the instincts, range, competitiveness and coverage ability to plug into a starting lineup readily and show up big on special teams coverage. The ability to survive a 16-game season is the greatest question mark facing Davis, and medical grades could dictate where he is drafted.

Draft projection: Top-40 pick.

Scout's take: "(Davis) can play all three (linebacker) spots. He's sitting right on the bubble of the first- and second(-round) for us. The injuries are what spook you about him."

MLB KEVIN DAVIS, #33 (Sr-5)

COLORADO STATE   ▶ GRADE: 5.11

Ht: 6-1 7/8 | Wt: 235 | 40: 4.89 | Arm: 32 3/8 | Hand: 10 1/4

History: Father, Keith, is a retired Army drill instructor and sergeant major. Kevin grew up on a military base, and lived in Germany for eight years. Parade All-American finished his high school years in Colorado, where he also played hockey. As a true freshman in 2012, recorded 23 tackles, zero for loss and zero sacks in eight appearances before tearing his left ACL. Tried to return in '13, but wasn't fully rehabilitated and shut it down after four games (granted medical hardship). In '14, tallied 22-2 1/2-1 in 11 games (one start). Sat out two September contests because of a right shoulder injury. Was the Rams' leading tackler from his weak-side linebacker position the last two seasons, as he started all 26 games — totaled 101-14-3 with two pass breakups and one interception in 15; and 110-10 1/2-3 with two pass breakups, one interception and four forced fumbles in '16. Team captain has degrees in sociology and interdisciplinary studies.

Strengths: Good size. Fine instincts — is active and around the ball a lot. Trusts his eyes and locates the ball quickly. Secure, wrap tackler. Is tough and will battle through injuries. Caught the ball well in drills in the Combine. Outstanding practice habits. Good football smarts.

Weaknesses: Plays small and narrow-based with no knockback power and catches contact too much. Bench-pressed the fewest reps (11) of any linebacker at the Combine, indicative of marginal strength. Ran the slowest 20-yard split (2.89 seconds) and produced the lowest broad jump (9'0") of any linebacker at the Combine, revealing marginal explosion. Late to get out of breaks in coverage and react to the thrown ball. Long-term durability is a concern given history of shoulder and knee injuries.

Future: A tough, try-hard "Mike" linebacker ideally suited for a backup role. Has the desire and football smarts ideally suited for a role on special teams.

Draft projection: Priority free agent.

MLB **BROOKS ELLIS**, #51 (Sr-4)

ARKANSAS ▶ GRADE: 5.12

Ht: 6-1 7/8 | Wt: 240 | 40: 4.78 | Arm: 31 3/4 | Hand: 9 3/4

History: Prepped at Fayetteville (Ark.) High, where he won a pair of state championships and was recognized as the state's Defensive Player of the Year twice. Dislocated his left kneecap in September of his senior year. As a true freshman in 2013, recorded 33 tackles, two for loss and one-half sack with one pass breakup in 12 games (started final four at middle linebacker). Started all 11 games played at MLB in '14, and produced 72-5 1/2-2 with five pass breakups, two interceptions and two forced fumbles. Sustained a concussion against Northern Illinois. Sat out two October contests (left leg bone bruise). Started all 13 games in '15 — first two at weak-side linebacker, final 11 at MLB — and totaled 102-8-1 1/2 with three pass breakups and one interception. Was the Razorbacks' leading tackler in '16 when he notched 83-7-1 with five pass breakups and a 47-yard interception return touchdown against TCU. Team captain graduated with a degree in pre-professional exercise science. Campbell Trophy finalist.

Strengths: Good size and carries his weight well. Good awareness and football smarts. Led all inside linebackers with a 6.81-second 3-cone drill time and 11.28-second 60-yard shuttle at the Combine, revealing very good balance and endurance. Solid career production. Very intelligent. Takes the game seriously and works at his craft. Has special teams experience.

Weaknesses: Tight-hipped and plays upright consequently, lacks point-of-attack strength. Tied for having the lowest vertical jump (29 1/2 inches) of any linebacker at the Combine, indicative of marginal lower-body explosion. Is often late to arrive at the perimeter and struggles to reach the perimeter, getting out-leveraged by speed. Limited cover skills.

Future: Tough, smart, hard-working overachiever lacking the hip flexibility and foot speed desired to earn a starting role. Has the intelligence to fend for a job as a backup and try earning his ticket on special teams.

Draft projection: Late draftable pick.

ROLB **DEVONTE' FIELDS**, #92 (Sr-5)

LOUISVILLE ▶ GRADE: 5.27

Ht: 6-2 1/2 | Wt: 236 | 40: 4.71 | Arm: 32 3/8 | Hand: 9

History: Prepped in Texas. Began his college career at TCU. Two weeks after signing in 2012, was arrested for marijuana possession. Made an immediate impact in the fall — started all 13 games at right end, and racked up 53 tackles, 18 1/2 for loss and 10 sacks with four pass breakups, one interception and two forced fumbles, earning Big 12 Freshman of the Year honors. Was suspended a game-and-a-half to open the '13 season. Managed 4-2-0 in three games before suffering a season-ending broken right foot injury. In January '14, was attacked and robbed at his home (school residency policy requires freshmen and sophomores to live on campus, but Fields was an exception thanks to 'extenuating circumstances'). Did not consent to a police search of his residence, and did not want to press charges against his attackers. Was suspended from the team in May when he was the suspect of a domestic disturbance with his then-girlfriend of two years. According to the police report, Fields was accused of punching the woman in the head and threatening her with a gun. The woman told police that before Fields entered the home, he punched out a window. Charges were eventually dismissed upon his completion of anger management courses, but he was permanently suspended by TCU. Played at Trinity Valley College (Tex.) in the fall, recording 61-6-6 1/2 with seven pass breakups and two forced fumbles in 12 starts. In '15, joined Bobby Petrino's Louisville team — was the Cardinals' defensive player of the year after producing 64-22 1/2-11 with three pass breakups and two forced fumbles in 13 starts at the "Mo" linebacker. Played through a torn right labrum the last nine games (required post-season surgery). In '16, played the left end in defensive coordinator Todd Grantham's hybrid 3-4 — started 11-of-12 games played, and put up 45-9-6 with three pass breakups and one interception. Hurt his shoulder against NC State, and did not play against Virginia. Was a medical exclusion from the bench-press test at the Combine because of a left shoulder injury.

Strengths: Flashes timing, anticipation and burst to beat blockers off the ball with natural bend. Good closing burst to the quarterback. Has an understanding of leverage and how to set up blockers. Has showed he could be a disruptive backfield presence early in his career.

Weaknesses: Lacks ideal bulk and length and is not naturally big-boned. Tied for having the smallest hands (9 inches) of any linebacker at the Combine. Will not be able to hold up against the run in the pros without adding considerable mass. Registered the slowest 3-cone drill time (7.41 seconds) and 20-yard shuttle (4.55 seconds) of any outside linebacker at the Combine, indicative of a lack of agility and balance. Inconsistent effort — throttles hot and cold and does not consistently compete. Personal character is a concern and will re-

LINEBACKERS

quire considerable extra maintenance.

Future: A lean, athletic, open-side end with enough pass-rush talent to warrant late consideration for a team with a strong locker room. Has limited bulk to defend the run and needs to get stronger to compete for more than a third-down pass-rush role. Fields' lack of consistency and past transgressions could force him to earn a spot as an undrafted free agent.

Draft projection: Late draftable pick.

Scout's take: "Fields is a talented player, but he is a character reject for us. I stacked him in the fourth round as a player. He looks like a 3-4 (outside) linebacker. He has some intriguing traits."

WLB-ILB REUBEN FOSTER, #10 (Sr-4)
ALABAMA ▶ GRADE: 6.32
Ht: 6-0 | Wt: 229 | 40: 4.65e | Arm: 32 3/8 | Hand: 10 1/4

History: At 18 months old, was being held by his mother when his father shot her. She survived, while Reuben was wounded in the back. His father, Danny, was arrested in Florida in 2013 after being on the run for 16 years. Reuben has an eight-year-old daughter (A'Zyia). Alabama native. USA Today All-American, state Defensive Player of the Year and consensus top-rated inside linebacker in America. Injured his hamstring during a recruiting combine in July 2012. Was a special teams player and backup "Mike" linebacker as a true freshman in '13 when he tallied 12 tackles, one for loss and zero sacks in nine appearances. Sustained a concussion during the '14 spring game. Played 11 games in the fall (started season opener against West Virginia at MLB in place of suspended Trey DePriest), and collected 22-2-1. Did not play against Tennessee (injured), and missed November contests against Auburn and Missouri (neck). Incurred multiple stingers his first two years at Alabama, an issue coaches attributed to poor tackling technique. Started 8-of-15 games at the "Will" in '15, and recorded 73-8-2 with nine pass breakups. Was leaner as a senior, trimming down from 240 pounds to 225. In '16, won the Butkus Award after leading the Crimson Tide with 115-13-5 and two pass breakups in 15 starts at WLB on the inside of a 3-4 front. Was carted off the field against Ole Miss because of cramping. Sustained a concussion against Arkansas. Chipped a bone on his left hand against Mississippi State then re-injured the hand against Chattanooga. Team captain. Graduated. Declined invitation to Senior Bowl, and was a medical exclusion at the Combine after having his right rotator cuff surgically repaired. Was sent home from the Com-

bine after an argument with a hospital worker.

Strengths: Flies fast to the ball and arrives with intent seeking to deliver high-impact collisions. Natural knee bender with explosive striking force. Physical, drive-through tackler and fearless striker with outstanding playing speed to the perimeter to chase down ball-carriers. Very good lateral pursuit — goes hunting sideline-to-sideline and sets the tone with violent hits. Triggers quickly and has good agility to slip blocks. Plays bigger than his size and will take on linemen. Good hip flexibility to flip and turn — covers a lot of ground in zone drops. Invokes fear in receivers crossing the middle with physical presence and is alert to jump routes developing in front of him. Has the agility to blanket tight ends and run with backs in man coverage. Outstanding weight-room strength. Extremely tough and will battle through injuries. Impact special teams' performer early in career. Extremely competitive and breathes football.

Weaknesses: Lacks ideal height and bulk and long-term durability must be evaluated given history of injuries. Has thin wrists and bone structure could be more susceptible to injury — played with cast on his left hand in 2016. Can be overaggressive and get out of position not coming to balance in space. Plays a bit recklessly and out of control and could stand to become a more secure tackler. Marginal hands — tends to play the receiver more than the ball (in anticipation of a bit hit). Is at his best with simple assignments.

Future: An extremely passionate, highly athletic, explosive, run-and-hit playmaker with the competitiveness, natural knee bend and football passion to become a perennial Pro Bowl performer. Size, speed, instincts and striking ability are ideally suited for a role as a weak-side linebacker in an even or odd front. Distractions have followed Foster most of his life, and though he has overcome a ton of adversity to accomplish what he has, his NFL future will be hinged heavily upon his ability to manage people around him and stay focused, and the team that drafts him would be wise to wrap him with a strong support system upon his arrival and embrace all his flaws. Has a special linebacking temperament and was born to play the game.

Draft projection: Top-15 pick.

Scout's take: "Foster is an impact player. He is just beat to (expletive). He has had a lot of injuries. He is distracted easily. And he just started calling the defense after years in the system. He is not coming in and lining people up (in the pros). With all the personnel groupings today, the game has become basketball on grass, and you better be able to get guys aligned in the middle."

ILB **BEN GEDEON**, #42 (Sr-4)

MICHIGAN ▶ GRADE: 5.27

Ht: 6-1 3/4 | Wt: 244 | 40: 4.78 | Arm: 32 5/8 | Hand: 10

History: Brother, Alex, played football at Harvard; brother, Sam, played rugby at Navy. Ben played linebacker-running back from Ohio. As a true freshman in 2013, was credited with 19 tackles, one for loss and zero sacks in 13 appearances. Played all 13 games in '14, and tallied 17-1 1/2-1. Played 12 games in '15, drawing one start as the "Will" linebacker in a 3-4 defense, and accumulated 34-3-0. Did not play against Rutgers (left ankle). Had a bone spur removed from his left ankle prior to his senior season. Stepped into the lineup full time at inside linebacker in '16 — was the Wolverines' leading tackler with 106-15 1/2-4 1/2 and two pass breakups. Earned his economics degree.

Strengths: Outstanding size. Is aggressive attacking downhill, understands where he fits in the defense and fills properly with urgency. Very dependable tackler inside the box. Sacrifices his body and plays with good energy. Produced the lowest 20-yard short shuttle time (4.13 seconds) of any linebacker at the Combine with the exception of teammate Jabrill Peppers, indicative of outstanding short-area burst. Bench-pressed 225 pounds 27 times at the Combine, tops among all linebackers, and it translates to good functional play strength. Intensely competitive and business-like in his approach. Was a three-year, core special teams' contributor. Impressed scouts with professionalism during the Senior Bowl.

Weaknesses: Lacks ideal foot speed to the perimeter and can be outflanked to the edges by speed backs. Struggles to match up with backs in man coverage (see bowl game vs. Florida State). Limited coverage instincts and production. At times dips his heads as a tackler and misses in the open field. Could benefit from playing with more shock in his hands. Only a one-year starter.

Future: Classic overachiever with the toughness, grit and football character desired in the middle of a defense. Is most ideally suited for a two-down role as a throwback "Mike" in a 3-4 front. Minimally contributes readily as a 4-phase core special teamer and provides backup depth.

Draft projection: Fourth- to fifth-round pick.

Scout's take: "I kind of liked (Gedeon). He is a true 'Mike' (linebacker). He is a late-round

talent. He is smart and instinctive. I think he is a two-down player."

MLB **CONNOR HARRIS**, #16 (Sr-5)

LINDENWOOD (MO.) ▶ GRADE: 5.23

Ht: 5-11 1/8 | Wt: 242 | 40: 4.71 | Arm: 30 1/8 | Hand: 9 3/8

History: Married (Marissa). High school safety was named Missouri 6A Defensive Player of the Year en route to a state championship. Started all 48 games of his career at middle linebacker, and set the NCAA career tackles record (633). As a true freshman in 2012, produced 126 tackles, eight for loss and one sack with four pass breakups and one forced fumble in 12 games. Also had 12 carries for 22 yards (1.8-yard average) and zero touchdowns. In '13, managed 33-1/2-0 with two pass breakups in three games before a right shoulder injury required season-ending surgery — suffered a grade 3 AC joint (three torn ligaments). Returned to play 11 games in '14, and racked up 152-4 1/2-2 with two interceptions. Also carried 11-188-4 (17.1). Was the Mid-America Intercollegiate Athletics Association Defensive Player of the Year in '15 — amassed 184-12 1/2-4 1/2 with seven pass breakups, two interceptions and one forced fumble in 11 games. Also ran 26-121-3 (4.7). Was the National Defensive Player of the Year in '16 after registering 138-8 1/2-1 with one pass breakup, two interceptions (TD) and one forced fumble. Also punted 19 times for 738 yards (38.6-yard average) with six inside the 20-yard line. Was a team captain 2013-16. Graduated with criminal justice degree. Earned invitations to the Senior Bowl and Combine. Will be a 24-year-old rookie.

Strengths: Has a low center of gravity and very good balance and knee bend and a powerful base. Keen eyes and instincts with a terrific nose for the ball. Highly anticipatory — and noticeably a film junkie. Fills downhill with urgency and flows well laterally. Loves to play the game and it shows. Rare tackling production as an experienced, four-year starter. Exceptional personal and football character and is always seeking ways to improve. Could serve as an emergency punter.

Weaknesses: Had the shortest arms (30 1/8 inches) of any linebacker at the Combine and could struggle disengaging against NFL big-bodied blockers. Can be hung up on blocks and at times plays small. Bench-pressed 225 pounds only 18 times and needs to get stronger. Regularly chewed on Division II competition.

Future: An extremely competitive tackling machine with the instincts, toughness and aggression to overcome his lack of height and es-

LINEBACKERS

tablish himself as an immediate special-teams contributor. Will push for playing time and could emerge as a dependable starter.

Draft projection: Fourth- to fifth-round pick.

MLB KEITH KELSEY, #55 (Sr-4)

LOUISVILLE   ▶ GRADE: 4.97

Ht: 6-0 3/8 | Wt: 233 | 40: 4.94 | Arm: 31 3/8 | Hand: 10 1/8

History: Father, Keith Sr., was a standout linebacker at the University of Florida. As a true freshman in 2013, Keith Jr. recorded 24 tackles, one for loss and zero sacks with two pass breakups in 12 games. Did not play against Houston. Started all 39 games in the Cardinals' 3-4 scheme the next three seasons. Played "Mike" in '14, and produced 87-7-6 with three pass breakups. Played "Sam" in '15, and registered 107-12-3 1/2 with three pass breakups and one forced fumble. Exited the Kentucky game with a right ankle sprain. Was the leading tackler for the second straight year in '16 when he played inside linebacker, and totaled 93-5 1/2-1 with two pass breakups and three forced fumbles. Team captain graduated with criminal justice degree.

Strengths: Football smart and instinctive. Is around the ball a lot. Plays hard and competes. Strong on-field leadership traits. Makes checks and lines up the defense.

Weaknesses: Short, short-armed and undersized with very stiff hips and too much heaviness in his movement. Needs to learn to use his hands better to shed blocks. Marginal speed to reach the perimeter. Tied for having the lowest vertical jump (29 1/2 inches) of any linebacker at the Combine, indicative of marginal lower-body explosion. Registered the slowest 20-yard shuttle time (4.59 seconds) of any linebacker at the Combine, indicative of marginal flexibility and burst. Slowed to transition and catch during cover drills at the Combine.

Future: Undersized, instinctive, two-down "Mike" linebacker with limited speed to factor on special teams. Camp body.

Draft projection: Priority free agent.

Scout's take: "(Kelsay) can't run. He's a true 'Mike'. He doesn't play with his hands and gets covered up (by blockers) way too often. He looks and plays like a free agent."

MLB-OLB HARVEY LANGI, #21 (Sr-6)

BYU   ▶ GRADE: 5.25

Ht: 6-1 7/8 | Wt: 251 | 40: 4.70e | Arm: 32 7/8 | Hand: 9 1/8

History: Last name is pronounced "long-ee." High school running back from Utah, where he won a pair of state championships. Was suspended for a playoff game his senior season af-

ter he was charged with trespassing (was hanging out at a house under construction). Began his college career at Utah. As a true freshman in 2011 (wore jersey No. 21), carried 13 times for 70 yards (5.4-yard average) and zero touchdowns with two receptions for six yards (3.0-yard average) and zero touchdowns. Served an LDS mission in Florida 2012-13. Influenced and inspired by the church, transferred to BYU wanting to live according to the school's mission and honor code. An inside linebacker with the Cougars, sat out the '14 season opener against Connecticut (left MCL sprain) before collecting 14 tackles, zero for loss and zero sacks in 12 games (one start). Started all 11 games played at "Mike" in '15, and produced 68-6 1/2-4 1/2 with one pass breakup and two interceptions. Missed two October contests (left MCL sprain). The Cougars switched to a 4-3 scheme in '16, and Langi started 12-of-13 games — eight at defensive end, four at middle linebacker — and totaled 57-5-2 with two pass breakups and one forced fumble. Did not start against Massachusetts, as he was used at RB in place of the injured Jamaal Williams. Was MVP of the Poinsettia Bowl against Wyoming thanks to 16-tackle performance. At BYU, had 25-102-2 (4.1) rushing with four kickoff returns for 73 yards (18.3-yard average). Team captain will be a 25-year-old rookie. Opted not to run at the Combine.

Strengths: Outstanding size and thickness. Steps downhill aggressively and fills fast. Plays hard with good effort and flies around the field. Sacrifices his body and can smash isolation-lead blockers. Physical taking on blockers and quick to press off them. Versatile and has played inside and on the edges and has intriguing athletic tools that also could project well to fullback. Respected team leader and tonesetter. Productive tackler in the Senior Bowl.

Weaknesses: Has very small hands. Plays too narrow-based and crosses his feet in the phone booth. Technique and footwork will require refinement. Needs to become a more secure tackler. Has some tightness in his hips and struggles to unlock them and transition cleanly moving in reverse. Very out of control in wave drills at the Combine, stumbling changing direction and plays a bit recklessly and out of control. Overaged.

Future: A high-effort athlete who has bounced between multiple positions in college and projects ideally to inside linebacker in the pros, though has enough athletic ability to come off the edge as he did much of senior season and could provide a flexible mismatch piece to a creative coordinator. Has the size,

LINEBACKERS

toughness and energy to make an impact on special teams.

Draft projection: Fourth- to fifth-round pick.

WLB ELIJAH LEE, #9 (Jr-3)

KANSAS STATE ▶ GRADE: 5.22

Ht: 6-2 1/2 | Wt: 229 | 40: 4.72 | Arm: 31 1/2 | Hand: 9

History: Missouri's 6A Defensive Player of the Year (defensive end) also played basketball in high school. As a true freshman in 2014, recorded 19 tackles, 4 1/2 for loss and 4 1/2 sacks with one pass breakup and one forced fumble. Started all 13 games at weak-side linebacker in '15, and produced 80-7 1/2-5 with one pass breakup, three interceptions and one forced fumble. Was the Wildcats' leading tackler for the second straight year in '16 when he amassed 110-6 1/2-1 1/2 with three pass breakups, two interceptions and one forced fumble. Did not garner a Combine invite. Will be a 21-year-old rookie.

Strengths: Very good athlete. Has good closing speed to track down backs to the perimeter and very good overall playing range to close distances quickly. Registered a 38-inch vertical jump at his pro day, which would have been the best among linebackers at the Combine, and indicative of explosiveness. Good hip flexibility to get depth in coverage. Very good production. Is still growing into his body and has upside.

Weaknesses: Has small hands and short arms. Developing eyes and instincts. Bench-pressed 225 pounds only 18 times and noticeably lacks functional football-playing strength on contact. Lacks bulk and power in his body and does not strike with power. Can be too overaggressive pursuing the ball and run himself out of plays.

Future: A fast-flowing, undersized, developing, weak-side linebacker with the range and hip flexibility to fit a nickel coverage and special teams' role. Has athletic traits to be molded.

Draft projection: Fifth- to sixth-round pick.

Scout's take: "I gave him a draftable grade for the league. I don't think he makes us any better. He's not very big. I don't know how well he'll hold up."

MLB MARQUEL LEE, #8 (Sr-4)

WAKE FOREST ▶ GRADE: 5.17

Ht: 6-3 1/4 | Wt: 235 | 40: 4.78 | Arm: 32 1/2 | Hand: 9 1/2

History: First name is pronounced "mar-KELL." As a true freshman in 2013, recorded 14 tackles (team-high on special teams), zero for loss and zero sacks in 11 games. Sat out against Miami (right knee bruise). Took ownership of the "Mike" linebacker spot as a sopho-

more, and started all 37 games the next three seasons — totaled 101-12-4 with one pass breakup and one forced fumble in '14 despite a concussion against Florida State; 71-10-3 with three pass breakups in '15; and team-high 105-20-7 1/2 with three forced fumbles in '16. Two-time team captain. Did not play in the East-West Shrine Game (foot). Opted not to run the 40-yard dash or shuttles at the Combine.

Strengths: Outstanding size and growth potential with a frame to easily be 250 pounds. Measured the second-lowest body-fat percentage (8.3%) of any linebacker at the Combine, indicative of exceptional endurance. Bench-pressed 225 pounds 25 times to lead all outside linebackers at the event and has good weight-room strength. Flashes closing speed as a blitzer and has good career sack production (14 1/2). Has special teams experience.

Weaknesses: Tight-hipped and a bit straight-linish — plays too upright and slow. Not a natural knee-bender and does not strike with explosion. Athletic limitations show up in the open field and in coverage, lacking the foot speed to keep stride with backs and fluidity to match up with tight ends. Is late to react to the thrown ball, with zero career interceptions (in 37 starts). Has a tendency to freelance too much.

Future: High-cut, upright, straight-line middle 'backer with two-down, run-stopping potential. Is a liability in coverage and lacks discipline desired on the front lines. High production does not match average instincts. Has some physical tools to be developed and fend for a spot on special teams.

Draft projection: Fifth- to sixth-round pick.

SLB-DLE JoJo MATHIS, #5 (Sr-4)

WASHINGTON ▶ GRADE: 5.12

Ht: 6-1 5/8 | Wt: 266 | 40: 4.90e | Arm: 33 | Hand: 9

History: Married (Savitri) with a son (Mathis IV). Prepped in California. Played defensive end for the Huskies. As a true freshman in 2013, tallied seven tackles, zero for loss and zero sacks in 12 games. Played 11 games in '14, and collected 16-2-2. Missed two September contests to be with his mother, who was diagnosed with lupus. Did not play against Arizona State. Started 7-of-11 games played in '15, and contributed 30-6-2 with two forced fumbles. Sat out against Oregon and Stanford (lower leg injury). In '16, started 5-of-7 games played before his season was derailed by a torn toe ligament (required surgery). Was a medical exclusion from working out at the Combine because of right foot injury.

Strengths: Has good upper-body strength

LINEBACKERS

and flashes pop in his punch to jolt defenders and continue working the edge. Solid base strength to anchor against the run. Has a strong bull-rush move and can generate a push with natural leverage. Versatile enough to have lined up in multiple techniques along the line, inside and outside, as well as standing up, and creates some plays with effort.

Weaknesses: Lacks ideal height. Heavy-bodied with minimal length and tight hips. Tied for having the smallest hands (9 inches) of any linebacker at the Combine and measured the heaviest (266), while also measuring the highest body-fat percentage (22.5%) in line with many offensive linemen. Average athlete. Lacks variety of pass-rush moves. Marginal production. Durability has been an issue.

Future: Lacks ideal burst and bend to be an effective edge rusher, though could warrant an opportunity as a power-leverage rusher in a 3-4 defense such as the Steelers or Ravens once he recovers from injury.

Draft projection: Priority free agent.

ILB RAEKWON McMILLAN, #5 (Jr-3)

OHIO STATE ▶ GRADE: 5.68

Ht: 6-1 7/8 | Wt: 240 | 40: 4.64 | Arm: 33 | Hand: 9 3/4

History: Prepped in Georgia. High school Butkus Award winner, consensus All-American and consensus No. 1 inside linebacker recruit in the country. As a true freshman in 2014, played 13 games for the national champs, and totaled 54 tackles, 6 1/2 for loss and 2 1/2 sacks with one pass breakup and one interception. Did not play against Navy or Alabama (coach's decisions). Started all 26 games at middle linebacker the next two seasons (leading tackler in both) — registered 119-4-1 1/2 with four pass breakups in '15; and 102-7-2 with four pass breakups and two forced fumbles in '16. Team captain. Turns 21 on Nov. 17.

Strengths: Outstanding size, with the biggest hands of any linebacker at the Combine. Good body power and functional play strength. Instinctive locating the ball. Strong at the point of attack taking on blocks and hits on the rise. Physical tackler. Fills with the proper shoulder and takes good angles. Plays very hard with good effort. Aggressive blitzer capable of winning with power and savvy. Matches up well against tight ends in coverage. Good football intelligence to line up the defense. Finished the season strongly.

Weaknesses: Lacks ideal foot quickness to always reach the perimeter. Overaggressively bites on some play-action and misdirection. Shows some heaviness moving in reverse and is not fluid opening up his hips or explo-

sive playing the ball. Limited coverage range, which showed up during Combine drills with small distances he was covering in the wave drill, and can be outflanked by backs in man coverage and late to close on thrown balls in front of him in zone coverage.

Future: A tough, instinctive middle linebacker in a similar mold as Chargers 2013 second-round pick (38th) Manti Te'o and Falcons 2008 second-round pick (37th) Curtis Lofton, McMillan made an immediate impact upon his arrival and has been a tackling machine for the Buckeyes since he arrived on campus. Profiles as an immediate run-stopping specialist on early downs where he excelled in college and must improve coverage skills to stay on the field every down in a pass-first league.

Draft projection: Top-50 pick.

Scout's take: "(McMillan) is instinctive but not a flashy playmaker. He's just steady and consistent. He does not get knocked around, but he is not a true downhill thumper that smashes blocks. He has average coverage skills and is not a good blitzer. ... He ran fast (at the Combine) just like (Saints' 2015 first-round pick [31st] Stephone Anthony) and someone is going to get enamored with the speed and over-draft (McMillan). I don't see any pop, and he (doesn't) play (as fast as) the way he ran (at the Combine)."

WLB-SS MATT MILANO, #28 (Sr-4)

BOSTON COLLEGE ▶ GRADE: 5.24

Ht: 6-0 1/2 | Wt: 223 | 40: 4.71 | Arm: 32 | Hand: 9 3/8

History: As a true freshman in 2013, notched five tackles, zero for loss and zero sacks in 13 games. Played 12 games in '14, and tallied 18-3-1 with one pass breakup. Did not play against Maine. Started all 12 games at "Sam" linebacker, and produced 60-17 1/2-6 1/2 with three pass breakups, two forced fumbles and two blocked punts. Started all 13 games at SLB in '16, and totaled 58-11-6 1/2 with two pass breakups, a 19-yard interception return touchdown against Connecticut and a blocked punt. Has 24 career special teams tackles. Scheduled to graduate in May. Strained his left hamstring running the 40 at the Combine and did not perform shuttles.

Strengths: Takes good angles to the ball and is aggressive filling. Forceful striker. Very good body control coming to balance in the open field and securing tackles. Good eyes and instincts. Plays with outstanding energy and effort. Times up the blitz very well. Smart, disciplined and tough. Assignment-sound. Very prideful special teams' contributor (see three blocked punts).

Weaknesses: Lacks ideal size for an every-down linebacker. Does not have the foot speed ideally desired to match up with slot receivers and gives up way too much size against tight ends in man coverage. Marginal career ball production. Has some tightness in transition. Uses a shuffle technique and is not natural backpedaling in reverse.

Future: A modern, hybrid-type defender lacking ideal cover skills to match up with NFL receivers, yet possessing enough quickness, size and toughness to function as a sub-package linebacker. Will offer the most value in the pros as a special teams' kamikaze covering kicks and taking punts off the toe as he repeatedly has done so well in college.

Draft projection: Fourth- to fifth-round pick.

MLB **HARDY NICKERSON**, #10 (Sr-5)
ILLINOIS ▶ GRADE: 5.20
Ht: 5-11 5/8 | Wt: 232 | 40: 4.81 | Arm: 32 | Hand: 10

History: Father, Hardy Sr., was an All-Pro linebacker who played 16 years with the Steelers, Buccaneers, Jaguars and Packers (1987-2002), and currently serves as Illinois' defensive coordinator. Attended eight different schools growing up. Prepped in California. Began his college career at Cal. Redshirted in 2012. Played "Mike" linebacker all four years. Started 8-of-10 games played in '13, and recorded 64 tackles, five for loss and one sack with one pass breakup and one forced fumble. Suffered a Lisfranc fracture in his left foot against USC, sidelining him the final two games. Played all 12 games in '14, starting the final six, and contributed 70-2-0 with one pass breakup and one forced fumble. Was a captain and the Bears' leading tackler in '15 when he started all 13 games, and registered 112-2-1. Joined U of I as a graduate transfer in '16. Playing for his father — and head coach Lovie Smith, Nickerson led the Illini by posting 107-5 1/2-2 with two interceptions and one forced fumble. Team captain.

Strengths: Very good eyes and instincts and is clearly well-coached. Uses his hands well to play off blocks. Exceptional personal and football character, serving as a team captain in multiple programs. Film junkie. Lines up the defense. Has a passion for the game. Plays hard and competes. Outstanding football intelligence. Very good production. Solid East-West Shrine game showing. Has NFL pedigree.

Weaknesses: Lacks ideal size to take on blocks and fight through traffic. Minimal coverage production throughout his career and could be challenged to match up with the length of NFL tight ends in man coverage. Has some tightness in his hips that can be limiting

in zone coverage. Can be late to reach the perimeter and needs to continue working to open up his stride.

Future: Thickly built, short, compact, instinctive "Mike" linebacker with the football smarts and leadership traits to earn a roster spot as a backup and special teams' contributor.

Draft projection: Fifth- to sixth-round pick.

Scout's take: "Nickerson is your typical coach's son. He's supersmart and very instinctive. He is small though. He almost looks like a strong safety. He does a good job in the box, but he really has to labor to get to the sideline. I do love the way he plays."

ROLB-DRE-PRS **CARROLL PHILLIPS**, #6 (Sr-6)
ILLINOIS ▶ GRADE: 5.38
Ht: 6-3 1/4 | Wt: 242 | 40: 4.63 | Arm: 33 | Hand: 9 3/4

History: Cousin of Luther Campbell. Won a state championship at Miami Central High. Was supposed to be part of Cincinnati's 2011 recruiting class, but failed to qualify academically. Resurfaced in '13 at Copiah-Lincoln Community College (Miss.), where he recorded 50 tackles, eight for loss and four sacks with three pass breakups and one interception (TD) in eight games. With the Illini in '14, notched 6-1-1 in seven games before he was sidelined by a neck injury. Played all 12 games in '15, starting three at defensive end, and chipped in 26-4 1/2-2 with two pass breakups. Started 11-of-12 games at DE in '16, and produced 56-20-9 with one forced fumble, including 6-2 1/2-2 against Western Michigan. Was ejected for targeting against Purdue (suspended for the first half against Rutgers). Graduated with sociology degree. Will be a 25-year-old rookie.

Strengths: Has the frame to easily add another 10 pounds. Good hip flexibility. Quick hands. Explosive off the edge and times the snap well to beat blockers off the spot. Can dip, bend and trim the corner and consistently beat offensive tackles in one-on-one matchups. Recorded the best 20-yard split (2.53 seconds) of any pass rusher at the Combine, indicative of exceptional sustained burst that often comes into play running the arc, flushing the pocket and closing on quarterbacks. Good pursuit effort flattening down the line.

Weaknesses: Limited anchor strength to set the edge. Has not yet developed a full pass-rush arsenal and needs to learn more counter moves to avoid getting controlled at the top of his rush. Recorded a 30-inch vertical jump, indicative of a lack of lower-body strength. Only a one-year starter. Overaged.

Future: A lean, explosive edge rusher with the speed, burst and hip flexibility to take the

LINEBACKERS

corner. Very dynamic bending the edge and could develop into an impactful pass-rush specialist and warrant serious looks as a "Jack" linebacker in a 3-4 front such as New Orleans.

Draft projection: Fourth- to fifth-round pick.

Scout's take: "Phillips is a juco transfer that almost got lost in the shuffle. They move him around a bit. He was not natural playing 'Mike' (linebacker), so they put him on the edge. He looks like a 3-4 outside linebacker, but if you ask him to stand up, it could be an issue. He is explosive moving forward. He looked like a small 'elephant' end to me."

ROLB-WLB-RDE HAASON REDDICK, #7 (Sr-5)

TEMPLE ▶ GRADE: 6.15

Ht: 6-1 1/2 | Wt: 237 | 40: 4.52 | Arm: 32 3/4 | Hand: 10 1/8

History: Safety-running back from New Jersey. Missed his junior season because of a fractured femur. Was limited to three games as a senior because of a torn meniscus. Joined the Owls as a 185-pound, preferred walk-on defensive back. Redshirted in 2012. Played nine games in '13, drawing one start at defensive end, and recorded 14 tackles, four for loss and one sack with one pass breakup. Played nine games in '14, starting two, and tallied 23-7-1 1/2 with one pass breakup. Did not play the final two games (injured). In March '15, was arrested and charged with aggravated assault stemming from an off-campus fight. Ultimately avoided trial by participating in a diversionary program. In the fall, started 12-of-14 games at DE, and produced 45-12 1/2-5 with one pass breakup and one forced fumble. Did not start against SMU or Connecticut. Broke out in '16 when he racked up 65-22 1/2-10 1/2 with four pass breakups and three forced fumbles in 14 starts. Graduated with criminal justice degree. Formerly wore No. 58 prior to earning a single digit for being one of the team's toughest players.

Strengths: Great instincts. Very quick off the ball with outstanding acceleration and closing burst. Knows how to get skinny and fit through gaps on inside stunts and pressure packages. Very disruptive backfield presence that continually flushes the pocket and makes plays behind the line. Tough and competitive. Showed steady improvement. Very versatile and can play multiple positions, with the speed to run with receivers and zone eyes to sniff out screens and buzz the flats.

Weaknesses: Lacks ideal length and needs to add some bulk for a pass rushing role. A bit tight in the hips and straight-linish and will miss tackles in space playing out of control. Could stand to develop more variety of pass-rush moves. Is not a refined hand fighter.

Future: An undersized, power-leverage rusher who drew comparisons from scouts to Bills 2010 sixth-round pick and Steelers LOLB Athur Moats before a monster senior season jettisoned Reddick up draft boards. Has continued his ascent in the post-season and has the explosive rush ability to factor readily as a pass rusher. Enhanced his value playing on his feet at the Senior Bowl, and his versatility will drive up his value. Strong all-star game production followed by an even stronger Combine showing and quality interviews could push Reddick from preseason scouting unknown into the first round.

Draft projection: Top-40 pick.

Scout's take: "(Reddick) is an undersized end that really needs to be a 3-4 rush guy. He wasn't on the map coming into the season. I put him in the fifth (round) for us in the fall. He showed well at the Senior Bowl, but I didn't see instincts on his feet (as a bubble linebacker). He'll learn it quickly though. I still think he'll be best rushing. He's an explosive player and runs well. Every time you see him, he keeps inching up (his draft value)."

WLB JALEN REEVES-MAYBIN, #21 (Sr-4)

TENNESSEE ▶ GRADE: 5.28

Ht: 6-0 3/8 | Wt: 230 | 40: 4.65e | Arm: 32 1/4 | Hand: 9 5/8

History: Has a daughter (Alivia). Tennessee native played linebacker, running back and quarterback in high school. Tore his right labrum during senior season, and missed his first spring practice at Tennessee while recovering from surgery. As a true freshman in 2013, collected 14 tackles (team-best 11 on special teams), zero for loss and zero sacks, with one blocked punt in 11 games. In May '14, was at a party in his hometown when he was grazed on the arm by a bullet. Started all 13 games at "Will" linebacker in the fall, and produced 101-11-2 with one interception. Was the Vols' leading tackler for the second straight year in '15 — started all 13 games at WLB, and registered 105-14-6 with four pass breakups and two forced fumbles. Tore his left labrum during '16 spring practice (required surgery). In the fall, managed 20-2-0 in four starts at WLB, though he injured his left shoulder again versus Ohio. Tried to play through the pain against Florida then opted for season-ending surgery to repair a biceps subluxation. Was ejected from the season opener versus Appalachian State for targeting. Team captain graduated with a degree in recreation and sports management. Opted not to work out at the Combine and was a medical exclusion from the bench-press test because of bicep injury.

Strengths: Flies to the ball with very good burst and closing speed. Sniffs out screens and beats blockers to the ball. Aggressive knifing into the backfield when he sees it. Has enough hip flexibility to buzz deep zones and shadow backs and tight ends in man coverage. Covers a lot of ground and has outstanding playing range. Measured the third-lowest body-fat percentage (9.2%) of any linebacker at the Combine, indicative of good endurance. Respected, team leader. Proven producer at an early age against top Southeastern Conference competition. Has special teams' coverage production.

Weaknesses: Has a thin, tapered frame lacking girth of an NFL linebacker. Lacks point-of-attack strength and can be pinballed when blockers get to him. Gives too much ground to run around blocks. Not a strong, drive-thru tackler — shoots low. Durability has been a consistent issue throughout his career.

Future: Maybin-Reeves must prove that he can stay healthy in a big man's game, and his draft value is likely to drop a round or two because of durability concerns. Has proven special teams' coverage ability, and best chance to stay healthy in the pros could be in a more limited special teams' role.

Draft projection: Fifth- to sixth-round pick.

Scout's take: "I liked (Maybin-Reeves) even though he will be on the small size. He looks more like a 3-4 'Will' than a 4-3 'Will.' I thought he was a see-ball, get-ball type. He reminded me of (Vikings' 2014 7th round [223] pick Brandon Watts)."

WLB DUKE RILEY, #40 (Sr-4)
LSU   ▶ GRADE: 5.48
Ht: 6-0 1/2 | Wt: 232 | 40: 4.58 | Arm: 32 | Hand: 9 1/4

History: Has a son (Elijah). Louisiana native won a pair of state championships at John Curtis Christian High. As a true freshman in 2013, was credited with seven tackles, one-half for loss and zero sacks in 13 appearances as a backup/special teams player. Played all 13 games in '14, drawing one start at "Sam" linebacker, and tallied 20-0-0. Played all 12 games in '15, and recorded 24-1/2-0. In '16, made the most of his only season atop the depth chart — was the Tigers' MVP after producing 93-9-1 1/2 with one pass breakup and one interception in 12 starts as a 3-4 inside linebacker. Wore jersey No. 4 in the Citrus Bowl against Louisville as tribute to the late Joe McKnight.

Strengths: Outstanding athlete. Good field energy and lateral pursuit to track down ball-carriers to the sideline. Plays with bounce in his feet and very good movement skill. Fills fast and attacks gaps. Flashes pop as a tackler playing with natural knee bend. Covers a lot of ground in zone coverage and has the agility and speed to match up with backs and tight ends in man coverage. Showed gradual improvement. Solid special teams cover man. Quick learner. Good football character.

Weaknesses: Lacks bulk and bulk strength and can be overmatched at the point of attack. Can be engulfed by second-level blockers and rooted out of the hole. Only a one-year starter (playing behind NFL starting linebackers Deion Jones and Kwan Alexander). Was still feeling his way and played a bit passively triggering and taking on blocks. Gave up some plays overpursuing and allowing the cutback.

Future: A fast-flowing, run-and-hit, weakside linebacker ideally suited for a 4-3 front, Riley follows in a long line of talented LSU linebackers who often have had to wait their turn for an opportunity. Made the most of it as a senior and profiles as an immediate impact special teams performer and first-year NFL starter.

Draft projection: Second- to third-round pick.

Scout's take: "He's not as straight-linish as (Tampa Bay Buccaneers' 2015 fourth-round pick [124th] Kwan) Alexander, and he's a better overall football player and more instinctive. I think he has a better LB skill set than (Falcons second-round pick [52] Deion Jones). (Riley) will be a trained assassin on special teams. He's played on all of them. He'll get looks in the second (round)."

SLB-DRE PITA TAUMOEPENU, #50 (Sr-4)
UTAH   ▶ GRADE: 5.18
Ht: 6-1 1/4 | Wt: 243 | 40: 4.68 | Arm: 32 3/8 | Hand: 9 7/8

History: Name is pronounced "peet-tuh tao-mo-eh-pen-new." Born in Texas, raised in Tonga (played rugby) and moved to Utah at age 17 — won a state championship at Timpview High, registering 25 sacks in his only season of high school football (also competed in track). Was deployed as a pass-rush specialist by the Utes. As a true freshman in 2013, saw limited action in seven games, and recorded six tackles, two for loss and one sack. Played all 13 games in '14, drawing one start at left end in the bowl game against Colorado State, and chipped in 17-5 1/2-5 1/2. Played all 13 games in '15, and logged 9-6-6. Played all 13 games in '16, starting five at right end, and produced 41-12-9 with three forced fumbles.

Strengths: Good movement skill and get-off speed to time the snap and beat blockers with quickness. Flashes an inside spin move. Great motor and effort — plays hard every down. Re-corded a 6.91-second 3-cone drill time, indicating very good balance and burst, and it translates to the edge.

Weaknesses: Lacks bulk and functional play strength to anchor and can be run at. Too much of a one-trick pony — lacks variety in his pass-rush arsenal and can be stalled and engulfed if he does not win with speed at the snap. Has some hip tightness that limits ability to drop into coverage. Has a low 28 1/2-inch vertical jump and is lacking lower-body explosion. Plays out of control and is not a strong, secure tackler. Average career production. English is his second language and is still learning how to communicate and understand football terminology.

Future: An undersized, college edge rusher utilized most optimally as a pass-rush specialist. Lacks the bulk needed to be an every-down factor and projects best to a 3-4 rush role. Is at his best with simple assignments where he could be cut loose to rush the passer on third down and will require a patient position coach and need some time to acclimate to the complexity of the NFL. Would benefit from a strong support system that could help him adjust to a new city.

Draft projection: Late draftable pick.

ILB-SS TANNER VALLEJO, #20 (Sr-4)

BOISE STATE   ▶ GRADE: 5.16

Ht: 6-1 1/4 | Wt: 228 | 40: 4.68 | Arm: 30 1/2 | Hand: 9 5/8

History: Pronounced "vuh-LAY-ho." Piled up 419 tackles his last three years as a California prep. As a true freshman in 2013, played 11 games, including starts as a 3-4 "Mike" in six of the final seven — recorded 51 tackles, 5 1/2 for loss and one-half sack with three pass breakups. Played MLB and nickel in a 4-2-5 the next two seasons. Was the Broncos' leading tackler in '14 when he started all 14 games, and produced 100-16 1/2-3 with four pass break-ups, 63-yard interception return touchdown against Fresno State in the Mountain West championship and a 31-yard fumble return score against Connecticut. Was the Fiesta Bowl Defensive MVP. Started all 10 games played in '15, and recorded 57-8-1 with two forced fumbles. Sustained a high left ankle sprain in Week Four — nagged him until he sat the last two games in October. Was suspended for the Poinsettia Bowl against Northern Illinois (violation team rules). A 4-3 "Sam" in '16, started all nine games played, and managed 69-6-1. Tore ligaments in his right wrist against Washington State — sat out against Utah State and played through the injury (as well as a sprained

left hand) until having season-ending surgery in November. Played for three different defensive coordinators. Was a medical exclusion from the bench-press test at the Combine and did not perform the 3-cone drill because of a groin injury.

Strengths: Active, energetic and competitive. Efficient slipping blocks. Good balance and hip flexibility to break down in the open field. Gains good depth in zone coverage and sees the quarterback and routes developing in front of him. Has a blue-collar approach to the game. Film junkie. Unselfish, team player. Is tough and will battle through injuries. Experienced four-year starter. Versatile and has played inside and out.

Weaknesses: Marginal size with very short arms. Lacks tackling strength and power. Struggles disengaging when blockers get their hands on him. Could do a better job of securing tackles, and his ability to wrap appeared affected by injury as a senior. Played a bit recklessly and out of control. Has a narrow build and is not built to withstand the physicality of the NFL game.

Future: Undersized, run-and-hit linebacker who continued to battle through injury as a senior and has the toughness and anticipation to become a factor on special teams. Is most ideally suited for a weak-side role in the pros or playing nickel linebacker and will need to prove his worth on special teams to earn a roster spot.

Draft projection: Sixth- to seventh-round pick.

Scout's take: "(Vallejo) was always playing displaced over (the) No. 2 (receiver in 2016). He's not physical in coverage or run support. He's too little for us. "

ILB ANTHONY WALKER, #1 (Jr-4)

NORTHWESTERN   ▶ GRADE: 5.39

Ht: 6-0 5/8 | Wt: 238 | 40: 4.66 | Arm: 30 3/8 | Hand: 9 1/2

History: Miami native was raised by his father, a high school coach. Northwestern offered based on Walker's speed and athleticism, but between high school and his 2013 redshirt year, he got overly muscular and stiff — went from 195 pounds to 240. Worked to improve his flexibility in order to get on the field. In '14, started 7-of-12 games — including the final six — at middle linebacker, and contributed 51 tackles, nine for loss and 1 1/2 sacks with three pass breakups, two interceptions ("pick-six" of Christian Hackenberg) and one forced fumble. Was the Wildcats' leading tackler in '15 when he started all 13 games at MLB, and racked up 122-20 1/2-4 with four pass breakups, one interception, one forced fumble and a fumble recovery touchdown. Wore No. 18 prior to junior season. Missed two weeks of '16 fall camp because of a knee injury that caused him to get off to a slow start in September. On the season, started all 13 games at MLB, and totaled 105-10-2 with five pass breakups, one interception and four forced fumbles. Team captain. On pace to complete his degree in learning and organizational change.

Strengths: Outstanding size with a strong lower body and thick trunk. Experienced, three-year starter in the Big Ten. Very active vs. the run and gets good run fits. Clocked the fastest 40-yard dash time of any inside linebacker at the Combine. Alert in zone coverage and plays the ball well in front of him. Times up the blitz well. Excellent weight-room worker. Strong leadership traits — holds teammates accountable.

Weaknesses: Overly muscular with limited hip flexibility and knee bend, correlating to too much heaviness in his movement and a lack of fluidity changing direction. Takes questionable angles and gets outflanked. Too easily lured by play-action and fooled by misdirection. Gets stuck on blocks and struggles to disengage, showing little pop playing downhill. Is not a true thumper and seeks to slip blocks before he stacks. Missed too many tackles on the perimeter given short arms and limited knee bend coming to balance.

Future: An active, upright, run-around, inside 'backer who looked more like a bodybuilder than football player in 2016 following a sensational sophomore season when he played at a significantly sleeker weight. Bulked up too much and did not play as fast or disciplined and production fell off.

Draft projection: Third- to fourth-round pick.

Scout's take: "(Walker) looked (too heavy and muscled up) when I went through the school. I thought he was better playing at a lighter weight (in 2015) and winning with his athleticism and speed."

ROLB-DRE T.J. WATT, #42 (Jr-4)

WISCONSIN   ▶ GRADE: 5.62

Ht: 6-4 1/2 | Wt: 252 | 40: 4.67 | Arm: 33 1/8 | Hand: 11

History: Full name is Trent Jordan. Brother of Texans All-Pro and Defensive Player of the Year J.J. Watt, as well as Derek, a fullback for the Chargers. Wisconsin native also lettered in track and field in addition to playing linebacker, tight end and quarterback. Redshirted in 2013. Sat out the '14 season after suffering a right patella subluxation. Suffered the same injury to the left knee during '15 spring practice. Both knees were surgically repaired.

Switched from tight end to linebacker. In the fall, played all 13 games, and recorded eight tackles, 1 1/2 for loss and zero sacks with three pass breakups. In '16, stepped into the lineup as a 3-4 outside linebacker — started all 14 games, and produced 63-151/2-11 1/2 with four pass breakups, a 17-yard interception touchdown and two forced fumbles. Played through pain after hurting his left shoulder against Nebraska.

Strengths: Outstanding body length and growth potential with a frame that looks like it could carry 260 pounds. Very good motor — chases, pursues and has a good closing burst. Strings out plays to the sideline. Has a fine club and jerk move. Plays with high energy and can be disruptive. Competes and plays hard. Presses off blocks and pushes the pocket. Flashes strength in his hands. Has NFL pedigree. Has a love of the game and transitioned quickly to defense. Produced the most explosive broad jump (10'8") of linebackers at the Combine along with a 37-inch vertical jump, indicative of exceptional lower-body explosion.

Weaknesses: Lacks body power and plays too small — gets pinballed by the double team. Plays upright and lacks desirable hip flexibility to move in reverse. Limited coverage experience and struggles to carry backs in man coverage (see mismatched on wheel route for TD in fourth quarter vs Penn State in Big Ten championship game). Inconsistent hand usage. Lacks variety as a pass rusher and will get stuck on blocks without a plan. Only a one-year starter. Durability has been an issue.

Future: Excellent-sized, high-motor, converted tight end displayed flashes of becoming an impact player in his first season as a starter and has drawn comparisons to Packers 2009 first-round pick Clay Matthews with comparable one-year production, pedigree and upside potential. Is still very much a developmental player that stands to be overdrafted based on his last name, however, and plays more similar to Bears 2012 first-round pick (19th overall) and Patriots SLB Shea McClellin with a narrow base and limited power, yet could still evolve into a very dependable, productive pro if used to accentuate his strengths the way McClellin is in New England.

Draft projection: Second- to third-round pick.

Scout's take: "T.J. Watt has some upside. I just left Wisconsin. He's probably a third (rounder) for us. He reminds me of (Redskins' 2014 second-round pick [47th] Trent Murphy). (Watt) is another better-football-player-than-athlete type. He has to be a 3-4 rush (linebacker)."

LINEBACKERS

DEFENSIVE BACKS

OHIO STATE ATHLETICS

Nawrocki's TOP 10

◀ **1. MARSHON LATTIMORE**
2. **Jamal Adams**
3. **Gareon Conley**
4. **Malik Hooker**
5. **Jabrill Peppers**
6. **Tre'Davious White**
7. **Adoree' Jackson**
8. **Marlon Humphrey**
9. **Marcus Williams**
10. **Justin Evans**

SS JAMAL ADAMS, #33 (Jr-3)

LSU ▶ GRADE: 6.27

Ht: 5-11 3/4 | Wt: 214 | 40: 4.56 | Arm: 33 3/8 | Hand: 9 1/4

History: Father, George, starred as a running back at Kentucky before he was picked 19th overall by the Giants in 1985. Highly recruited out of Texas. The Tigers' nickel back as a true freshman in 2014, Adams logged 66 tackles, five pass breakups and zero interceptions with five tackles for loss and one sack in 13 games (two starts). Started all 24 games at strong safety the next two seasons — totaled 67-6-4 with five tackles for loss and one forced fumble in '15; and 76-4-1 with 7 1/2 tackles for loss and one sack in '16. Team captain.

Strengths: Outstanding size and functional strength. Plays with superb eye discipline and has an intricate understanding of defensive concepts and where everyone lines up. Very good reactive quickness. Plays with a sense of urgency and strikes with authority. Will separate receivers from the ball and invoke fear with presence. Flies to the ball and is extremely physical in the box with explosive striking power. Good zone eyes and awareness to sort out what he sees. Drives hard on the thrown ball and is aggressive playing it in the air. Exceptional football intelligence and football character. Very strong back-end communicator and vocal team leader. Makes calls and adjustments and lines up the secondary, as he very noticeably can be seen doing. Film junkie. Alpha-male leadership qualities. Excels as a jammer on punt return and gunner on punt coverage and is very physical.

Weaknesses: Has a 31 1/2-inch vertical jump, indicative of below-average lower-body explosion. Just adequate long speed, revealing average speed to play deep middle coverage. At times will trust his instincts too much, and get caught peaking and bite on routes. Could have some struggles matching up with long-bodied tight ends and receivers in man coverage, with limited leaping ability to climb the ladder. Produced only five career interceptions, with just one in 2016 (playing more in the box).

Future: A tough, physical, in-the-box hammer with enough back-end coverage ability to function in centerfield, though always will be best suited in the box playing a mini-linebacker role, taking away the run game and trading wits

DEFENSIVE BACKS

matching audibles with savvy quarterbacks. Instant impact Day One starter with perennial Pro Bowl potential.

Draft projection: Top-15 pick.

Scout's take: "(Adams) is an awesome football player, and I love the player. Saying that, I still struggle with how highly he is going to get drafted. Where we are picking (in the top 16), I don't know if I could draft a box safety with 4.6 speed. The last time it happened with Mark Barron, he got converted to a linebacker. It's a passing league now. You have to be able to match up and cover. I don't see him being able to cover Jimmy Graham and Rob Gronkowski."

RCB BRIAN ALLEN, #14 (Sr-5)

UTAH ▶ GRADE: 5.21

Ht: 6-3 1/8 | Wt: 215 | 40: 4.52 | Arm: 34 | Hand: 10

History: Married (Paula) with a daughter (A'mya). Played receiver as a prep in Texas, where he also played basketball. Redshirted in 2012. Saw very limited action in 10 games in '13. Saw limited action in six games in '14 before he was shelved by a right knee fracture. Switched from receiver to cornerback in '15 when he recorded 26 tackles, three pass breakups and one interception with one forced fumble in 13 games (three starts). In '16, started 9-of-13 games (six at right cornerback, three at left cornerback), and posted 35-6-0 with 9 1/2 tackles for loss, 1 1/2 sacks and two forced fumbles. Graduated with two degrees: human development and family studies and economics.

Strengths: Rare body and arm length to match up with big receivers. Flashes striking ability to blow up screens (see San Jose State), support the run and separate receivers from the ball. Exceptional 3-cone drill time (6.64 seconds), indicative of outstanding lateral agility. Responsible and mature.

Weaknesses: Undisciplined eyes that get caught peeking in the backfield too much. A bit too grabby down the field. Not fluid in transition out of breaks, gathers too much and appeared tight and mechanical in his movement through Combine drills. Too tall and leggy, and footwork is choppy. Recorded among the highest 20-yard short shuttles at the Combine (4.37 seconds), indicating a lack of hip flexibility that shows up allowing too much separation on crossing routes. Not a natural catcher. Needs to become a more secure tackler (missed 11 in 2016).

Future: Rare-sized, converted receiver still learning how to play in reverse and read patterns instead of running them. Likes to use a shuffle-and-bail technique and is still very un-

derdeveloped as a cover man, though has shown ability to produce in press man coverage taking away short zones and showed improvement as a senior supporting the run. Looks ideally equipped for a developmental project in Seattle or Pittsburgh.

Draft projection: Late draftable pick.

LCB-FS CHIDOBE AWUZIE, #4 (Sr-4)

COLORADO ▶ GRADE: 5.82

Ht: 5-11 7/8 | Wt: 202 | 40: 4.46 | Arm: 30 5/8 | Hand: 8 1/2

History: Pronounced "chih-DOE-bey / ah-WOOZ-yeh." Cornerback-running back from California, where he also lettered in basketball and track. Dealt with a turf toe injury as a senior. Started 7-of-12 games as a true freshman in 2013 — six at nickel, one at left corner — and recorded 59 tackles, four pass breakups and zero interceptions with five tackles for loss, one sack and two forced fumbles. In '14, notched 64-8-0 with two tackles for loss in nine starts before a lacerated kidney ended his season. Was the leading tackler in '15, as he played LCB and NB and put up 84-7-2 with 12 tackles for loss, four sacks and one forced fumble. Was CU's Defensive MVP in '16 after starting all 14 games at LCB and producing 65-12-1 with six tackles for loss, four sacks, two forced fumbles and a blocked field goal attempt. Tried to play through a turf toe injury in the Alamo Bowl against Oklahoma State before he was forced out of the game. His 10 career sacks are most in school history by a defensive back. Completed his business (management) degree in three years.

Strengths: Understands zone concepts. Keys the quarterback and plays the ball well in front of him. Drives on slants and is aggressive striking. Recorded a 1.50-second 10-yard split, indicative of exceptional short-area burst and acceleration. Also notched a 11'0" broad jump revealing exceptional lower-body explosion. Good, secure tackler who flashes some pop on contact. Versatile and has played all over the secondary, at corner on the inside and outside and as a safety. Effective blitzer with great closing speed (see Michigan). Experienced, three-year starter. Football smart. Effective laying out to block field goals (see UCLA).

Weaknesses: Very small hands and short arms. Average twitch and burst to handle slot receivers, showing some tightness in his hips that allows separation in transition. Could be overmatched by the physicality of NFL big-bodied receivers in man coverage. Marginal interception production for a three-plus-year starter (3).

Future: An aggressive, tough, versatile corner with physicality that appears most ideally suited for the safety position in the pros. Versatility, toughness and intelligence could drive up his value.

Draft projection: Top-50 pick.

Scout's take: "We debated (in draft meetings) whether to move him to safety. He ran better at the Combine than we expected. He's still stacked as a corner right now. It's a plus that he can play both."

FS-NCB BUDDA BAKER, #32 (Jr-3)

WASHINGTON ▶ GRADE: 5.68

Ht: 5-9 5/8 | Wt: 195 | 40: 4.49 | Arm: 30 3/4 | Hand: 9

History: Washington native keyed three state championships, earning all-state honors as a safety and running back. Also starred as a sprinter, capturing a state title in the 100 meters (10.77 seconds). U.S. Army All-American was the state's top recruit. Was an impact free safety for the Huskies. As a true freshman in 2014, started all 14 games, and posted 80 tackles, six pass breakups and one interception with two tackles for loss, one sack and two forced fumbles. Started all 12 games in '15, and logged 49-7-2 with 1 1/2 tackles for loss. Sprained his left ankle against Utah State, and sat out against Cal. Sustained a concussion against Utah. Was the leading tackler in '16 when he totaled 71-6-2 with 10 tackles for loss, three sacks and one forced fumble in 14 starts.

Strengths: Experienced three-year starter. Is fluid flipping his hips and transitioning out of his breaks. Has NFL cornerback movement skills at the free safety position. Alert to read route combinations. Competes for the ball in the air and is more instinctive in coverage than his ball production would suggest. Aggressive playing the run and plays bigger than his size. Can drop from high to low and secure open-field tackles.

Weaknesses: Marginal height and bulk with a body that has taken a beating. Measured 13.2% body fat at the Combine, among the highest of defensive backs and indicative of lack of endurance. Notched the lowest vertical jump (32 1/2 inches) of any free safety at the Combine, revealing subpar lower-body explosion. Average tackling power — gnatty, ankle biter often shoots low. Has only five career interceptions.

Future: An instinctive, nickel safety in a similar mold as Cardinals' 2013 third-round pick Tyrann Mathieu (69th), though not the same instinctive playmaking ballhawk. Could carve out a niche manning slot receivers in nickel situations and roaming the back end on run downs. Greatest concern is ability to stay healthy given

his narrow frame.

Draft projection: Second- to third-round pick.

Scout's take: "I think he has to be a nickel. He is too small to be anything else. "

SS JAMAL CARTER, #31 (Sr-4)

MIAMI (FLA.) ▶ GRADE: 5.08

Ht: 6-0 7/8 | Wt: 218 | 40: 4.66 | Arm: 31 | Hand: 9 3/8

History: Has a son (Carter Jr.). Florida native. Played special teams as a true freshman in 2013, scratching six tackles, zero pass breakups and zero interceptions in 12 appearances. Played all 13 games in '14, drawing two starts in place of Deon Bush (Bears), and recorded 26 tackles, five pass breakups and one interception. Played 12 games in '15, starting one, and collected 48-2-1 with one forced fumble. Was ejected for targeting against Nebraska. Was rehabbing a hamstring injury when he was suspended for the bowl game against Washington State (violation team rules). Started 12-of-13 games at strong safety in '16, and totaled 85-3-0 with one tackle for loss. Was ejected for targeting against Florida State, and was suspended for the first half of the North Carolina contest. Did not run the shuttles at the Combine because of hamstring tightness.

Strengths: Active run defender will drop down in the box and attack ball-carriers. Good strength, as indicated by 19 bench-press reps of 225 pounds at the Combine. Has a feel for zone coverage and is alert to receivers passing through his zone and will jump routes in front of him. Has been a functional special teams contributor.

Weaknesses: Extremely tight-hipped and plays too upright with marginal transitional quickness. Recorded the slowest 40-yard dash (4.81 seconds) of any defensive back at the Combine, indicative of poor long speed and range. Labors through transition and movement is very strained. Only a one-year starter with two career interceptions. Marginal ball skills. Got beat up by the ball in the gauntlet drill at the Combine.

Future: An overly muscled, rocked-up, slow-twitch, box safety who looks like he has weaned on a weight-lifting machine. Looks like more of a bodybuilder than a football player. Will deliver some slobber-knockers when he has a clear lane and doesn't have to get off a straight-line track. Will have to prove he can bend and change direction well enough to factor on special teams to earn a roster spot.

Draft projection: Priority free agent.

Scout's take: "(Carter) is stiff as a board. He is a free agent all day."

DEFENSIVE BACKS

FS CHUCK CLARK, #19 (Sr-4)

VIRGINIA TECH ▶ GRADE: 5.90

Ht: 6-0 | Wt: 208 | 40: 4.54 | Arm: 32 1/4 | Hand: 9

History: Virginia native also played basketball and ran track in high school. As a true freshman in 2013, tallied 22 tackles, zero pass breakups and zero interceptions in 12 games, including two starts at nickel. Sat out against Miami (right ankle). Started 11-of-13 games in '14 — four at nickel, final seven at cornerback — and produced 73-11-1 with 8 1/2 tackles for loss and 1 1/2 sacks. Started all 13 games at corner in '15, and piled up 107-8-1 with three tackles for loss and one sack. Also had a 20-yard fumble recovery touchdown against Purdue. Moved to free safety in '16, and registered 94-2-0 with 2 1/2 tackles for loss and one forced fumble in 14 starts.

Strengths: Very good size. Fills hard and drops the hammer in run support. Is tough and aggressive. Great competitor. Recorded the lowest 20-yard short shuttle (4.07 seconds) of any free safety at the Combine, indicative of very good lateral agility. Experienced, three-year starter. The game is important to him. Plays with emotion. Very durable.

Weaknesses: Has small hands. Lacks awareness with his back to the ball in man coverage and is not a sophisticated coverage player. Marginal ball skills. False steps in his pedal, too often loses positioning downfield and plays the man instead of the ball. Only has one career interception.

Future: A good-sized, run-support player lacking the coverage skills desired on the back end, and profiles best in the box closer to the line of scrimmage. Lacks the ball skills and play-making ability desired in a starter, though he is serviceable and could become a barely adequate starter that teams are always seeking to upgrade. Minimally offers very good depth and contributions on special teams.

Draft projection: Fifth- to sixth-round pick.

CB JEREMY CLARK, #34 (Sr-5)

MICHIGAN ▶ GRADE: 5.06

Ht: 6-3 3/8 | Wt: 220 | 40: 4.60e | Arm: 32 7/8 | Hand: 9 3/8

History: Also lettered in track and field as a Kentucky prep. Recruited by then-head coach Brady Hoke. Redshirted in 2012. Played seven games in '13 without recording stats. Played all 12 games in '14, starting the first six at strong safety, and recorded 18 tackles, one pass breakup and zero interceptions. Suffered a right shoulder injury in Week Six at Rutgers. In '15, started 7-of-13 games — five at cornerback, two at nickel — and tallied 21-3-3. Started 3-of-4 games played at CB in '16, and was credited

with 10-3-0 before suffering a season-ending torn right ACL injury. Graduated. Was denied a sixth year of eligibility. Was invited to the Combine, but was a medical exclusion from running and jumping at the Combine because of a right knee injury. Played around 205 pounds and showed up at the Combine 15 pounds heavier.

Strengths: Rare size and body length to match up with and wear down big receivers. Bench-pressed 225 pounds 20 times, among the top cornerbacks at the Combine, and has good upper-body strength to jam receivers at the line. Physical tackler.

Weaknesses: Lacks foot speed for the edges and too often is overextended and stressed by speed if he cannot get his hands on receivers to disrupt their release. Marginal hip flexibility to transition cleanly out of breaks. Green eyes and anticipation. Does not appear confident in his technique and can be too grabby down the field. Not a natural catcher. Has never been a full-time starter.

Future: A big, strong, physical press corner who added 15 pounds and looked more like a safety than a cornerback at the Combine. Adds an enforcer element to the secondary, though durability could always be a concern given the heaviness in his movement. Could be tried as a developmental box safety and special teams contributor.

Draft projection: Priority free agent.

Scout's take: "(Clark) filled in nicely for (Jourdan) Lewis. I still gave him a free-agent grade."

LCB GAREON CONLEY, #8 (Jr-3)

OHIO STATE ▶ GRADE: 6.26

Ht: 6-0 | Wt: 195 | 40: 4.46 | Arm: 33 | Hand: 9 1/2

History: Ohio native also played basketball in high school. As a true freshman in 2014, tallied 16 tackles, two pass breakups and zero interceptions in 15 appearances. Started all 26 games the next two seasons — totaled 49-5-2 with one tackle for loss and one blocked kick in '15; and 26-8-4 in '16. Suffered a stinger against Oklahoma. Graduated.

Strengths: Very good long speed to keep stride with speedy, vertical receivers and has good recovery speed to catch up if he loses positioning. Has a 37-inch vertical jump and outstanding lower-body explosion. Excellent athlete with very long arms to disrupt receivers at the line and help recover. Outstanding top-end speed. Plays with awareness and has a feel for route concepts. Versatile and has lined up inside and outside and played to both sides and appears comfortable and confident in all phases. Good football intelligence and leadership traits.

Weaknesses: A bit leggy and tight-hipped when receivers close his cushion and loses

DEFENSIVE BACKS

some ground in transition on short, quick-hitting routes. Is late to open up on crossing routes. Could improve zone awareness — seeing the quarterback and his man and breaking on the ball more quickly. Bench-pressed 225 pounds only 11 times at the Combine and could stand to continue improving strength.

Future: A lean, long-limbed, athletic, smart, press corner with the length, long speed and confidence to match up against big, No. 1 receivers. Could stand to improve his strength as a tackler and continue developing physically, yet possesses all the tools to step into a starting lineup readily and compete from Day One and eventually emerge as a No. 1 corner. Strong leadership traits bring an added value.

Draft projection: First-round pick.

Scout's take: "(Conley) looked really good (at the Combine). He has a little hip tightness that you see in his transition sometimes and better long speed than short speed. You know I'm a hard grader. He keeps pushing his way up for me."

RCB TRESTON DeCOUD, #14 (Sr-5)

OREGON STATE ▶ GRADE: 5.22

Ht: 6-1 7/8 | Wt: 206 | 40: 4.63 | Arm: 33 | Hand: 9 1/4

History: Pronounced "day-kood." Cousin, Thomas, was a safety who played seven years with the Falcons and Panthers (2008-14). Also was a standout sprinter as a Louisiana prep. A partial qualifier, DeCoud began his college career at Division II Chadron State, where he redshirted in 2012. Saw limited action in '13, scratching four tackles, one pass breakup and zero interceptions in 10 appearances. Transferred to Nicholls State in order to be close to his mother, Chandrika, who was diagnosed with breast cancer. However, he was not granted immediate eligibility, so he played at Northwest Mississippi Community College in '14 — recorded 38-7-6 with one forced fumble and two blocked kicks in 10 games. With the Beavers in '15, started 9-of-10 games played at left corner, and chipped in 50-5-0 with 3 1/2 tackles for loss and one sack. Sustained a concussion against Colorado, and did not play against Utah. Started all 12 games in '16, and totaled 58-10-2 (75-yard TD against Idaho State), with eight penalties. Will be a 24-year-old rookie. Did not perform shuttles at the Combine because of a right hamstring injury.

Strengths: Exceptional body and arm length. Uses his length well at the line to disrupt and jam. Solid production on the ball. Willing, improved tackler. Has NFL pedigree. Confident and competitive. Experienced, three-year starter. Has some gunner experience.

Weaknesses: Average foot speed. Gathers to cut and labors a bit in transition. Plays narrow-

based and tends to rise in his pedal. Has a 31-inch vertical jump, tied for the lowest among cornerbacks at the Combine and indicative of limited lower-body explosion. Has a history of shoulder and concussion injuries, and long-term durability must be considered carefully. Could require a little extra time to acclimate to complex game plans. Overaged.

Future: Tall, long-limbed, press corner with intriguing length and ball skills to warrant developing. Will need to prove his wares on special teams to earn a role. Durability concerns could affect draft value.

Draft projection: Late draftable pick.

RCB RASUL DOUGLAS, #13 (Sr-5)

WEST VIRGINIA ▶ GRADE: 5.37

Ht: 6-1 5/8 | Wt: 209 | 40: 4.66 | Arm: 32 3/8 | Hand: 9 1/4

History: Also played basketball as a New Jersey prep. Spent three years at Nassau Community College (N.J.). Redshirted in 2012. Played 10 games in '13, and recorded 40 tackles, three pass breakups and three interceptions with one forced fumble. Played eight games in '14, and posted 43-15-2 with 7 1/2 tackles for loss, one sack, one forced fumble and two blocked kicks. Was a backup for the Mountaineers in '15 when he was credited with 8-1-1 and one forced fumble in 11 games. In '16, tied for the most interceptions in the country. Moved into the lineup at boundary corner in Week Two — logged 70-8-8 (TD) with 3 1/2 tackles for loss, one sack and one forced fumble in 13 games (12 starts).

Strengths: Outstanding length, ball skills and hands, which helped him tie for the nation's lead in interceptions. Fine zone instincts and anticipation. Sees routes unfolding and competes for the ball in the air like a receiver. Solid, secure tackler.

Weaknesses: Has below-average foot speed and struggles in man coverage. Plays into the boundary with less ground to cover. Rises in his pedal and can be late to transition out of breaks and challenged to keep stride with vertical receivers down the field. Limited burst out of his breaks. Marginal recovery quickness. Does not play to his size in the run game. Is not a natural catcher. Average Senior Bowl showing.

Future: Tall, high-hipped, press corner with intriguing ball skills ideally suited for a defense deploying a lot of press coverage such as the Seahawks, Panthers or Redskins.

Draft projection: Fourth- to fifth-round pick.

NCB-RS CORN ELDER, #29 (Sr-4)

MIAMI (FLA.) ▶ GRADE: 5.31

Ht: 5-9 7/8 | Wt: 183 | 40: 4.54 | Arm: 31 1/4 | Hand: 8 3/4

History: Decorated Tennessee running back — won three state football championships, three state basketball championships and competed in track. Appeared in 10 games as a true freshman in 2013, tallying seven tackles, zero pass break-ups and zero interceptions. Missed the final two games after tearing his right meniscus. Played all 13 games in '14, drawing one start, and recorded 34-4-0 with three tackles for loss and one sack. Played all 13 games in '15, starting the final seven, and contributed 41-11-2 with four tackles for loss and two sacks. Also returned 11 punts for 152 yards (13.8-yard average), including a 72-yard score against Bethune-Cookman. In '16, was the Hurricanes' Defensive Player of the Year — started all 13 games at LCB, and produced 76-12-1 with 4 1/2 tackles for loss, three sacks and one forced fumble. Suffered a thumb injury against Notre Dame. Returned 12 career kickoffs for 333 yards (27.8-yard average), including a 75-yard score — after eight laterals — against Duke as time expired as a junior. Team captain. Did not bench press at the Combine because of back tightness and finish shuttles after an injury running the 40-yard dash.

Strengths: Has loose hips and appears to play faster than his timed speed because of his fluidity. Good competitive playing speed. Versatile and aligns all over the field, inside and outside and on both the left and right. Carries a swagger and plays with confidence. Aggressive tackler for his size. Football smart. Has return ability.

Weaknesses: Lacks ideal size with short limbs and thin frame. Struggles to hem receivers at the line. Recorded a 1.64-second 10-yard split at the Combine, indicative of below-average short-area burst — and it shows up by allowing separation vs. top speed. Limited twitch and long speed. Has a bit of a riverboat gambler mentality and tends to bite on double moves.

Future: Short, thin-framed, competitive, nickel corner with the agility and confidence to compete for a job inside and seek to fill a punt-return role. A solid football player.

Draft projection: Fourth- to fifth-round pick.

Scout's take: "He's little — that's his problem. Someone might take a chance in the third (round). I thought he had to be a nickel and saw him as more of a fourth(-rounder)."

SS-CB-KR JUSTIN EVANS, #14 (Sr-4)
TEXAS A&M ▶ GRADE: 5.88
Ht: 5-11 5/8 | Wt: 199 | 40: 4.50e | Arm: 32 | Hand: 9 3/4

History: Played all over the field as a South Mississippi prep. Spent two years at Mississippi Gulf Coast College, where his exposure soared. Played 10 games in 2013, and recorded 47 tackles, seven pass breakups and five interceptions with three tackles for loss and two forced fumbles. Played 10 games in '14, and tallied

39-6-1. With the Aggies in '15, started all 12 games played at strong safety, and produced 78-3-1 with one tackle for loss. Sat out against Western Carolina (injury). Started all 13 games at free safety in '16, and registered 87-8-4 with five tackles for loss and one blocked kick. Was knocked out of the Arkansas game with a shoulder injury. Shared Aggies' defensive MVP with Myles Garrett. Added 17 career kickoff returns for 474 yards (27.9-yard average). Was a medical exclusion from working out at the Combine because of a right quadriceps injury.

Strengths: Excellent eyes to sort out the run and pass and work downhill quickly. Very athletic with loose hips, clean feet and urgency in his play. Accelerates through contact at full speed and drops the hammer (see Alabama). Plays with physicality and is a defensive tone-setter. Fearless in traffic and nifty negotiating through it. Good ball skills. Plays the ball like a receiver. Fine pattern recognition. Lines up in the slot and is quick to feel and jump routes. Has enough range to play on the back end. Measured only 4.6% body fat at the Combine, tied for the lowest among defensive backs and indicative of exceptional conditioning and stamina. Very tough and competitive. Smart.

Weaknesses: Lacks the size and frame for his body to withstand the punishment it delivers and durability could become a significant issue in a short time. Can be overaggressive and bite hard on play-action. Needs to do a better job wrapping up and securing tackles, and consequently could improve his open-field tackling. Had 23 missed tackles in 2016 in large part from flying into the pile at top speed with poor tackling form seeking big hits, playing too recklessly.

Future: A strong, impactful hitter with the toughness, competitiveness and physicality to make his presence felt readily in the run game, though he needs to become more secure of a tackler. Has the hips, feet and ball skills to match up in coverage and can make an impact readily as an interchangeable safety, though concerns about playing too big for his body require conversation.

Draft projection: Top-50 pick.

Scout's take: "Evans is smaller than (Falcons' 2016 17th overall pick) Keanu Neal and he can cover better. I love (Evans). He is athletic, has cover skills, and he is a hammer. He triggers really fast. His instincts are awesome."

SS-NCB-KR RUDY FORD, #23 (Sr-5)
AUBURN ▶ GRADE:
Ht: 5-11 1/8 | Wt: 205 | 40: 4.39 | Arm: 30 | Hand: 8 7/8

History: Alabama native and high school running back. Was asked to move to cornerback as a true freshman in 2013. Played all 14

DEFENSIVE BACKS

games, and was credited with five tackles, one pass breakup and zero interceptions. Also had six carries for 73 yards (12.2-yard average) and one touchdown. In October, Ford's mother, Terrie, suffered cardiac arrest and permanent brain damage. Was the Tigers' boundary safety in '14 when he secured 93-1-3 with 2 1/2 tackles for loss, one-half sack and one forced fumble in 13 starts. Led the team in tackles for the second straight season in '15 — started 11-of-13 games (six at safety, five at nickel), and totaled 118-2-2 with 3 1/2 tackles for loss, one sack and two forced fumbles. In '16, started 10-of-12 games — six at safety, four at nickel — and totaled 59-7-0 with 5 1/2 tackles for loss. Injured his right ankle against Alabama — did not play in the Sugar Bowl or Senior Bowl. Graduated.

Strengths: Aggressive run defender. Takes good angles. Tied for the most bench-press reps (20) among all strong safeties at the Combine and hits with physicality. Displayed exceptional straight-line speed (4.39 seconds) at his pro day workout and can recover when he loses positioning. Functional range on the back end (see Arkansas). Very good tackle production as an experienced, three-year starter in the Southeastern Conference.

Weaknesses: Has short arms and small hands. Lacks ideal hip flexibility to redirect easily and has limitations in man coverage against quick-breaking routes. Sticks in his transition. Average cover skills and ball awareness, and does not consistently play to his speed.

Future: Box safety better moving forward attacking the line of scrimmage than reversing and might fit best as a nickel cornerback. Has the speed and aggressiveness to be effective playing downhill in the box and blanketing short areas.

Draft projection: Fourth- to fifth-round pick.

Scout's take: "(Ford) ran like a Ferrari (at his pro day). We debated whether to stack him as a safety or as a nickel cornerback. It's a question we'll have to revisit again after the way he ran."

SS NATE GERRY, #25 (Sr-4)
NEBRASKA ▶ GRADE: 5.23
Ht: 6-1 7/8 | Wt: 218 | 40: 4.58 | Arm: 31 1/4 | Hand: 9 1/4

History: Last name is pronounced "GARY." Safety-receiver from South Dakota, where he won a state football championship and captured state track championships in the 100 meters and 200 meters (back-to-back). Broke his wrist as a high school underclassman then played his senior football season with a torn meniscus. Played 13 games as a true freshman in 2013, starting three at "Will" linebacker, and recorded 32 tackles (seven on special teams), zero pass

breakups and zero interceptions with two tackles for loss. Started all 13 games at free safety in '14, and produced 88-4-5 with seven tackles for loss, one-half sack and two forced fumbles. Tore his left meniscus during '15 spring practice. Was the Cornhuskers' leading tackler in the fall after registering 79-7-4 with three tackles for loss, one sack and one forced fumble in 13 starts at FS. Was ejected for targeting in the final two games of the season. Was suspended for the '16 season opener against Fresno State (violation team rules), but started all 11 games at strong safety, and totaled 74-8-4 with seven tackles for loss and one-half sack. Was suspended for the Music City Bowl against Tennessee for an academic violation — missed part of a group project and was three credits short in an online class. His 273 career tackles rank second in school history among defensive backs (Mike Brown). Team captain. Did not run the 3-cone drill at the Combine because of a groin injury.

Strengths: Exceptional size with good musculature. Fills fast, takes good angles and understands where he fits within the framework of the defense. Very good zone eyes and awareness to break on balls in front of him, recording 13 career interceptions. Experienced, core special teams performer with the effort to earn a spot. Has experience playing high and low and offers interchangeability. Excellent career tackle production. Outstanding weight-room worker. Has been very durable.

Weaknesses: Has small hands. Limited lateral agility. Marginal recovery quickness. Recorded a 31 1/2-inch vertical jump, the lowest among all safeties at the Combine and indicative of limited lower-body power and athletic ability. Overaggressive seeking out big hits, overextends and leaves his feet. Struggles coming to balance in the open field and misses too open-field tackles. Not a strong, drive-through tackler.

Future: Excellent-sized, tight-hipped, zone safety best in confined spaces. Has the football intelligence and toughness desired on special teams and could earn his way into a more regular role.

Draft projection: Fourth- to fifth-round pick.

Scout's take: "He ran for state titles in track (in high school), but I didn't see it in his play speed. I thought he struggled in coverage at the Senior Bowl."

LCB-FS SHAQUILL GRIFFIN, #10 (Sr-4)
CENTRAL FLORIDA ▶ GRADE: 5.50
Ht: 6-0 1/8 | Wt: 194 | 40: 4.37 | Arm: 32 3/8 | Hand: 8 3/4

History: Twin brother, Shaquem, was a linebacker for the Knights. Florida native also competed in track in high school. As a true freshman in 2013, notched eight tackles, one pass breakup and zero interceptions in eight appearances (one start). Played all 13 games in '14, drawing two starts, and tallied 17-0-1. Started 11-of-12 games in '15 — nine at cornerback, two at free safety — and produced 50-13-2 (TD) with one-half tackle for loss. Started all 13 games at corner in '16, and logged 50-15-4 (TD) with three tackles for loss and one blocked kick. Led the American Athletic Conference in passes defended (19).

Strengths: Looks the part. Outstanding size with exceptional speed. Excellent ball production — 28 pass breakups the last two years. Looked like a receiver highpointing and plucking the ball at the Combine. Very good instincts and awareness to sort out routes and pattern read. Aggressive playing the ball. Very natural locating and tracking the ball and climbing the ladder to catch. Has a 38 1/2-inch vertical jump and uses all of it. Is aggressive to fill in the run game. Has slot experience. Also lines up as the gunner and jammer on special teams.

Weaknesses: Has small hands. Shows some tightness in his hips and allows too much separation at break points. Is a bit upright in his pedal and narrow-based. Could stand to be more aggressive filling in run support and tends to shoot low. Could require some extra time to acclimate to complexities of NFL coverage. Did not consistently match up against elite competition.

Future: A lean, long-limbed, speedy cornerback who entered the Combine with little fanfare and blew the doors off the gym with his exceptional speed, agility and ball skills. Has NFL starter length, speed, athletic ability, ball skills and hands and could compete for a job readily, though some scouts will maintain he is a gold medalist only in the underwear Olympics.

Draft projection: Third- to fourth-round pick.

Scout's take: "I thought (Griffin) was a straight-line, speed guy. We had him stacked late on our board. I was impressed by what he did at the Combine. He caught my eye. He looked loose going up to grab the ball. A lot of times, these (defensive backs) cannot catch."

RCB NATE HAIRSTON, #15 (Sr-5)
TEMPLE ▶ GRADE:
Ht: 5-11 7/8 | Wt: 196 | 40: 4.57 | Arm: 31 | Hand: 9 1/2

History: Also ran track as a Maryland prep. Was recruited as a receiver. Redshirted in 2012. Played eight games in '13 (wore No. 85), and caught seven balls for 62 yards (8.9-yard average) and zero touchdowns. Missed four

games because of a left ankle injury. Played seven games in '14, and grabbed 13-88-0 (6.8). Switched to cornerback in '15, and tallied 11 tackles, one pass breakup and zero interceptions in 14 appearances. Started all 14 games at corner in '16, and produced 27-3-2 with three tackles for loss. Was limited in the Military Bowl against Wake Forest by a groin injury. Graduated with a degree in strategic communications.

Strengths: Good length. Has a strong trunk. Aggressive in run support and will come up to fill when he sees it. Can keep stride with receivers in man coverage and has gained a better understanding of zone concepts.

Weaknesses: Very narrow frame. Only a one-year starter. Still learning how to pedal and transition moving in reverse and movement appeared very segmented and out of sync during drills at the Combine, as he repeatedly stumbled, tripped and somersaulted and spent too much time on the ground. Struggles with his back to the ball. Average long speed.

Future: Good-sized, converted receiver who profiles as a green, developmental project. Has the size, aggressiveness, ball skills and toughness to ideally fit a "Tampa-2" defense such as San Diego, Seattle or San Francisco.

Draft projection: Priority free agent.

SS JOSH HARVEY-CLEMONS, #25 (Sr-4)
LOUISVILLE ▶ GRADE: 5.26
Ht: 6-4 1/4 | Wt: 217 | 40: 4.60e | Arm: 35 3/8 | Hand: 10 3/8

History: Lost both his parents by the time he entered his teenage years. Has a son. Highly recruited out of Georgia. Began his college career at the University of Georgia in 2012 when he recorded 14 tackles, one pass breakup and zero interceptions with one tackle for loss in 14 games. Was suspended for the '13 season opener (marijuana use). On the season, started all 11 games played at strong safety, and produced 66-5-1 with 5 1/2 tackles for loss and two forced fumbles. Was suspended four games — beginning with Gator Bowl against Nebraska — for a second failed drug test. Was dismissed in February '14. Followed defensive coordinator Todd Grantham to Louisville, and sat out the season per NCAA transfer rules. Started all 13 games at SS in '15, and produced 88-3-3 with two tackles for loss, one sack and one forced fumble. Started all 10 games played in '16, and totaled 61-2-0 with four tackles for loss and two sacks. Did not play against Wake Forest, Houston or LSU because of a hamstring injury. Was deployed as a SS in base 3-4, and morphed into a "star" (hybrid linebacker-safety) in sub-packages. Graduated with criminal justice degree. Did not perform most drills at the Combine because of a left hamstring injury.

Strengths: Measured the longest arms (35 3/8 inches) of any defensive back at the Combine and has rare length to match up with tight ends in man coverage. Fills fast downhill and is a willing, face-up tackler. Good zone awareness to play the ball in front of him. Flashes some ball skills in 50-50 situations. Solid competitor.

Weaknesses: Average functional speed. Too leggy and tall in his pedal with too much wasted motion in transition to handle slot receivers. Gets mismatched trying to cover quickness. Is not quick off spots and often late to arrive at the ball. Limited special teams experience.

Future: Rare-sized, high-hipped, long-levered interchangeable safety warranting interest as a dime linebacker. Has drawn comparisons to Vikings' 2016 seventh-round pick Jayron Kearse.

Draft projection: Fourth- to fifth-round pick.

Scout's take: "He's a big, long safety who is not that productive in either phase. He's not great in run support to project to (playing) 'Will' and he is not great in coverage. He doesn't get his hands on many balls. I wanted to make him a (weak-side) linebacker for us. A lot of them are (utilized) like strong safeties."

SS DELANO HILL, #44 (Sr-4)

MICHIGAN ▶ GRADE: 5.25

Ht: 6-0 3/4 | Wt: 216 | 40: 4.46 | Arm: 32 1/8 | Hand: 9 3/8

History: First name is pronounced "Duh-LAY-no." Detroit Cass Tech product won a pair of state titles. As a true freshman in 2013, saw very limited action in 13 games, and was credited with one tackle, zero for loss and zero sacks. Started 5-of-7 games played in '14 — three at strong safety, two at free safety — and recorded 20-0-0. Missed the season opener (broken jaw); missed four mid-season games (left leg); and was suspended against Maryland. Started 8-of-13 games in '15 — six at nickel, two at FS — and totaled 46-2-0 with 2 1/2 tackles for loss. Started all 13 games at SS in '16, and secured 52-3-3 (TD) with 4 1/2 tackles for loss and one forced fumble.

Strengths: Outstanding size. Tough and aggressive attacking downhill. Strong, secure tackler. Has exceptional timed speed and range to fly around the field and buzz the flats. Good balance in his feet and caught every ball through the gauntlet in front of him. Versatile and has lined up all over the field.

Weaknesses: Has some tightness in his hips and is a bit straight-linish, rising in his backpedal. Hands were shaky moving in reverse at the Combine — struggled tracking the ball over his head. Only a one-year, full-time starter.

Future: A very fast, versatile college defensive back who entered the season as a relative unknown and quickly began distinguishing himself on the scouting trails. Has the speed and athletic ability to factor on special teams immediately and has upside to be groomed as a defensive mismatch piece to cover backs, tight ends and even slot receivers.

Draft projection: Fourth- to fifth-round pick.

Scout's take: "Some scouts think he is strictly a free agent. Some people in the program think Hill is more fluid than (Jabrill) Peppers. (Hill) was listed as a free safety. I think he has to play in the box. He has something to him. I don't know that he can beat out anyone on our team, but I think he will make a team and surprise someone."

FS MALIK HOOKER, #24 (Soph-3)

OHIO STATE ▶ GRADE: 6.24 (X)

Ht: 6-1 | Wt: 206 | 40: 4.45e | Arm: 32 1/4 | Hand: 10 3/4

History: Grade would have been a point higher (7.24) if not for injuries. Prepped in Pennsylvania, where he was an outstanding basketball player — won two state championships. Didn't play football until his junior year. Redshirted in 2014. Was a reserve/special teams player in '15, scratching 10 tackles, zero pass breakups and zero interceptions. Broke out in '16 — registered 74-4-7 with 5 1/2 tackles for loss and one-half sack in 13 starts. Had INT scores against Tulsa, Nebraska and Michigan. Had surgeries on Jan. 31 to repair a labrum tear and hernia and did not work out at the Combine as a result.

Strengths: Good body length with long arms and the biggest hands (10 3/4 inches) of any defensive back at the Combine. Exceptional range and ball skills to leverage either half and play center field. Superb recovery speed to adjust and even bait quarterbacks to throw the ball. Natural interceptor who plays the deep ball like a receiver. Reads quarterbacks' eyes and adjusts his path, with a knack for undercutting routes. Exceptional athlete with the ball in his hands returning interceptions. Outstanding man cover skills and zone instincts. Very explosive popping out of his breaks. Highly competitive. Has been a gunner on the punt team and on the edge for the field-goal block team.

Weaknesses: Thin and leggy and needs to add some mass to his frame to better withstand contact. Only a one-year starter and is still learning the nuances of diagnosing route concepts. Can be overaggressive biting on double moves (see get beat vs. Indiana). Still developing awareness. Can be a choppy in his pedal. Allows some separation at the top of routes in man coverage. Could stand to do a better job of breaking down in the open field and securing tackles in space.

Future: An athletic phenom with a rare combination of range, ball skills and playmaking ability on the back end to emerge as a perennial Pro Bowler. If he can add some bulk to his frame and avoid injury, the sky is the limit. Has the greatest upside at the safety position in this year's draft, though injury situation will likely leave him on the PUP list to begin the season and introduces a lot of risk about how he will recover. Hooker is easily the most talented, rangy ballhawk and top safety prospect in the draft from a talent perspective, though grade reflects durability concerns.

Draft projection: First-round pick.

Scout's take: "Hooker is the best player on the (Ohio State) team. He is still raw, though his ball skills are exceptional. He is lean like a basketball player and his range is unbelievable. He has a frame to be 215 to 220 pounds. His biggest knock is that he is just inexperienced. He is still learning. I can't imagine with proper coaching how good he can be. I've scouted some of the best — Ed Reed and Earl Thomas. (Hooker) can be as good as any of them. He is so good you will make excuses for him on film when he (makes mistakes)."

RCB MARLON HUMPHREY, #26 (Soph-3)
ALABAMA   ▶ GRADE: 5.96
Ht: 6-0 1/4 | Wt: 197 | 40: 4.43 | Arm: 32 1/4 | Hand: 8 3/4

History: Father, Bobby, was an All-American running back for the Crimson Tide and a Broncos 1989 supplemental first-round pick. Marlon is a product of powerhouse Hoover (Ala.) High, where he won a pair of state championships and dominated as a track athlete (won seven state titles). Blue chipper and consensus All-American. Redshirted in 2014. In '15, stepped into the lineup opposite Cyrus Jones — recorded 45 tackles, eight pass breakups and three interceptions with 3 1/2 tackles for loss and two forced fumbles in 15 starts. Made 14 starts in '16, and logged 36-5-2 (TD) with three tackles for loss and one forced fumble. Suffered a right hamstring injury against Auburn, and did not play against Florida. Did not perform shuttles because at the Combine because of back tightness and opted not to jump.

Strengths: Has prototype size and press strength to hem receivers at the line and disrupt releases. Recorded the fastest 20-yard split (2.40 seconds) of any player at the Combine, indicative of exceptional sustained burst desired in a Cover 2 shell where much action for a cornerback comes in a small outside zone. Coachable with good football intelligence. Caught the ball well over his head downfield at the Com-

bine. Has served as a gunner on the punt team.

Weaknesses: Very small hands. Has some tightness in his hips, and the quick passing game gets on top of him quickly. Not fluid moving in reverse and transitioning out of his breaks — frequently uses a bail technique, takes some extra steps transitioning and gets beat down the field. Not natural with his back to the ball (see LSU) and is too easily spun. Average eyes, anticipation and downfield ball skills. Does not consistently come to balance in the open field to secure tackles, and tackle production is low from often being late to arrive.

Future: Big, fast, athletic, high-hipped, long-limbed corner ideally suited for a No. 2 role in an aggressive press man coverage defense such as Seattle, Pittsburgh or Baltimore. Many evaluators believe Humphrey will be overdrafted based on his pedigreed last name and contribution to a national championship team. Concerns remain about his limited instincts, ball skills and toughness and how well they will transfer to the pro game.

Draft projection: Top-50 pick.

Scout's take: "(Humphrey) is a man cover guy. He's not very good pedaling. He understands concepts and can squat on routes, but he panics down the field."

NCB-RS ADOREE' JACKSON, #2 (Jr-3)
USC   ▶ GRADE: 6.09
Ht: 5-10 | Wt: 186 | 40: 4.42 | Arm: 31 3/8 | Hand: 9 1/4

History: Grew up in Illinois, 30 miles southeast of St. Louis, but moved in with his sister in California in order to take advantage of better athletic opportunities. Prepped at Serra High, a private school which also previously produced Trojans and NFL receivers Marquise Lee (Jaguars) and Robert Woods (Bills). Parade and USA Today All-American played all over the field, and starred as a basketball player and sprinter and long jumper (state champion). Made an immediate impact in 2014 — started 10-of-13 games at cornerback, and recorded 49 tackles, 10 pass breakups and zero interceptions with four tackles for loss and one forced fumble. Also contributed as a receiver and kick returner — caught 10 balls for 138 yards (13.8-yard average) and three touchdowns; returned 23 kickoffs for 684 yards (29.7-yard average, including two scores; and returned two punts for 12 yards (6.0-yard average). Against Notre Dame, was the first Trojan to start on both sides of the ball since the 1960s. Was team MVP in '15 when he started all 14 games — 12 at corner, one (UCLA) at safety and one (Utah) at receiver. Accumulated 35-8-1 (TD) with one forced fumble; seven carries for 36 yards (5.1-yard average) and zero

DEFENSIVE BACKS

touchdowns; 30-690-0 (23.0) on kickoffs; and 24-251-2 (10.5) on punts. Suffered an abdominal strain in the season opener against Arkansas State, but did not miss a start. In '16, won the Thorpe Award and was a finalist for the Hornung Award and Lott IMPACT Trophy, as the Pac-12 Defensive Player of the Year and team MVP registered 55-11-5 with two tackles for loss in 13 starts. Added 7-51-0 (7.3) on the ground, 26-767-2 (29.5) on kickoffs and 20-315-2 (15.8) on punts. Injured his right ankle in the Rose Bowl against Penn State. Team captain. Tied NCAA records for most career touchdowns on kick returns (eight) and all runbacks (nine). Two-time All-American for the USC track and field team thanks to back-to-back Pac-12 long jump championships. Turns 22 on Sept. 18. Did not bench or perform shuttles at the Combine because of right ankle surgery.

Strengths: Exceptional athlete with very good ball skills and body control to make acrobatic interceptions. Carries a swagger and plays with supreme confidence. Has rare track speed and big-time playmaking ability as a slot receiver and return man. Recorded a 1.53-second 10-yard split, indicative of exceptional short-area acceleration and burst. Dynamic with the ball in his hands and explosive accelerating out of cuts. Outstanding man cover skills to ride the hip of receivers. Has explosive recovery speed to catch up when he falls out of position. Outstanding ball skills. Very natural interceptor with exceptional hands. Quick learner.

Weaknesses: Very diminutive frame that could struggle to withstand the rigors of the pro game. Tied for having the smallest hands of any player at the Combine. Is undisciplined jumping routes and lets receivers by him (see Washington). Is not an aggressive tackler and turns down some contact — plays small. Scouts have been turned off by his on-field body language and worried he plays with too much of a track mentality as a tackler. Track interests could continue to compete with football in the future.

Future: A diminutive playmaking returner and offensive weapon with the reactive quickness, explosive burst and ball skills to produce covering the slot. Has drawn comparisons from scouts to Titans' 2005 6th overall pick and Bengals CB Adam Jones, having elite burst and play-making talent, yet Jackson does not bring with him the same character concerns.

Draft projection: First-round pick.

Scout's take: "Jackson is small and undisciplined, but you have to respect him for his return ability. He had eight returns for TD's. He was an All-American jumper at USC on the track team and can flat out fly. He runs track at 175 (pounds). He played between 177-180 during the year. I don't know how well he is going to hold up at our level, but I like what he does with the ball in his hands."

FS-PR EDDIE JACKSON, #4 (Sr-4)

ALABAMA ▶ GRADE: 5.24

Ht: 6-0 3/8 | Wt: 201 | 40: 4.55e | Arm: 32 1/4 | Hand: 9 1/4

History: Did not play his sophomore and junior years of high school while getting his academics in order. As a true freshman in 2013, started 4-of-7 games played at cornerback, and tallied 19 tackles, three pass breakups and one interception with one tackle for loss. Sprained his ankle against Georgia State, and sat out against Kentucky. Five other DNPs were coach's decision. Tore his right ACL in April '14. Returned in Week Two — started all 11 games played, and managed 41-6-1 with two tackles for loss, one sack and two forced fumbles. Did not play against Florida or Ole Miss (quad). Transitioned to strong safety in '15 when he secured 46-2-6 (two TD) with three tackles for loss and one forced fumble. In '16, put up 24-2-1 (TD) with 2 1/2 tackles for loss in eight starts before suffering a season-ending broken left leg injury against Texas A&M. Added 11 punt returns for 252 yards (23.0-yard average), including two scores. Team captain. Graduated. Did not participate in Combine or pro day because of left leg injury.

Strengths: Good size and athletic ability. Fine zone awareness. Has loose hips, good balance and movement skill to come off spots. Very natural interceptor who extends outside his frame and catches with ease in stride like a receiver. Good football intelligence. Has flashed some punt return skill, with the vision, run skill and traffic burst to be effective with the ball in his hands. Has a passion for the game.

Weaknesses: Has small hands. Needs to get stronger at the contact point. Too often shoots low and will whiff on run fills and open-field tackles. Benefitted from a very strong supporting cast. Durability must be evaluated given history of injuries.

Future: Good-sized, athletic, ball-hawking free safety who must show he will be the same player post-injury that he was before and improve as a tackler. Has intriguing return ability to factor in multiple phases if he clears medically.

Draft projection: Fourth- to fifth-round pick.

Scout's take: "They put a rod in his leg, and his career might be shortened. He's injury-prone. He's a talented player, but the injury will knock him down."

DEFENSIVE BACKS

SS **RAYSHAWN JENKINS**, #26 (Sr-5)

MIAMI (FLA.)　　　　　　　▶ GRADE: 5.33

Ht: 6-1 | Wt: 214 | 40: 4.49 | Arm: 32 3/4 | Hand: 9 5/8

History: Has a son. Florida native and state champion hurdler. While in high school, suffered a broken right ankle and fractured ribs. As a true freshman in 2012, tallied 27 tackles, three pass breakups and one interception in 10 games (started final two). Missed a pair of October contests (concussion). Started 12-of-13 games in '13, and produced 46-5-3 with one tackle for loss. Missed the '14 season after having surgery to repair a herniated disk. Played all 13 games in '15, starting the final seven, and contributed 52-4-3 with 2 1/2 tackles for loss. Was ejected for targeting in the bowl game against Washington State. Started 12-of-13 games in '16, and totaled 76-7-2 with 4 1/2 tackles for loss and 1 1/2 sacks. Sprained his right ankle against Virginia Tech. Did not run the shuttles at the Combine because of hamstrings tightening.

Strengths: Outstanding size-speed ratio with long arms. Active supporting the run. Has a 37-inch vertical jump, indicative of outstanding lower-body explosion and athletic ability. Flashes ability to play centerfield and track the deep ball. Good zone awareness to recognize route concepts and break on the ball. Experienced three-year starter.

Weaknesses: Has some tightness in his body transitioning and could struggle matching up with NFL tight ends in man coverage. Barely adequate ball skills. Measured 15.4% body fat at the Combine, among the highest for defensive backs and a potential indicator of a lack of stamina. Durability needs to be evaluated carefully given long history of injuries (ankle, ribs, concussion, back, hamstrings).

Future: An athletic, interchangeable safety with enough range on the back end and enough strength in the box to become a serviceable starter, though could be most ideally suited for a No. 3 role. Has core special teams potential. Durability must be a consideration given lengthy injury history.

Draft projection: Third- to fourth-round pick.

Scout's take: "He's stiff and has average ball skills. Coming out of the school (in the fall), I thought he was a fourth-rounder."

SS-CB **LORENZO JEROME**, #22 (Sr-4)

ST. FRANCIS (PA.)　　　　▶ GRADE: 5.22

Ht: 5-10 1/2 | Wt: 204 | 40: 4.68 | Arm: 30 5/8 | Hand: 8 5/8

History: Also played basketball as a prep in Florida, where he went overlooked as an option quarterback. As a true freshman in 2013, was the Northeast Conference Defensive Rookie of the Year when he started all 11 games — eight at free safety, three at cornerback — and recorded 56 tackles, four pass breakups and six interceptions (TD) with one tackle for loss and one forced fumble. Played FS his final three years. Was the leading tackler in '14 when he produced 79-13-3 (TD) with two tackles for loss and one forced fumble in 11 starts. Started all 11 games in '15, and tallied 58-7-3 with 5 1/2 tackles for loss and 2 1/2 sacks. Also led the FCS in kickoff return average by returning 17 kickoffs for 531 yards (31.2-yard average), including two scores. Started 8-of-10 games played in '16, and managed 59-5-6 with 5 1/2 tackles for loss and 2 1/2 sacks, while returning kickoffs 14-405-1 (28.9). Added a 48-yard receiving score and an 89-yard fumble recovery score. Suffered an MCL sprain against Duquesne — did not play against Sacred Heart or Central Connecticut, and was limited in non-starts against Wagner and Villanova. Buck Buchanan Award (FCS Defensive Player of the Year) finalist led the FCS with 18 career interceptions. Had 39 career punt returns for 295 yards (7.6-yard average), including one score, as well as a pair of completions for 86 yards. Two-year captain. Aiming to become the first SFU player drafted since 1945. On track to graduate with a criminal justice degree.

Strengths: Extremely competitive. Very good, football-playing instincts and ball skills put on display in post-season all-star competition when he recorded two interceptions in the East-West Shrine game and followed up with an encore performance at the Senior Bowl with two more and a forced fumble. Experienced, four-year starter. Plays faster than his timed speed. Aggressive tackler. Vocal team leader. Has a love for the game.

Weaknesses: Produced the fewest bench-press reps (12) among all strong safeties at the Combine. Tied for recording the slowest 10-yard split (1.71 seconds) of any defensive back at the Combine, indicative of ordinary initial burst off spots. Also recorded the slowest 20-yard shuttle (4.72) and 3-cone drill time (7.66) of any defensive back, indicative of marginal lateral agility, balance and burst. Pedals a bit tall and upright.

Future: Similar to former Cardinals undrafted free agent and current Ravens SS Tony Jefferson, Jerome is not much of an athletic tester and does not meet the requisite speed requirements for the safety positon. However, he plays faster than his timed speed and made a huge impact during the post-season all-star circuit, proving he could not only hang with but excel as a Johnny-on-the-Spot (right time, right place)

DEFENSIVE BACKS

against better competition. Could warrant consideration as a short-area, zone corner.

Draft projection: Fourth- to fifth-round pick.

FS JADAR JOHNSON, #18 (Sr-4)

CLEMSON ▶ GRADE: 5.21
Ht: 6-0 3/8 | Wt: 206 | 40: 4.64 | Arm: 32 | Hand: 9 1/4

History: South Carolina native. Lost his high school sophomore season after tearing his left labrum in Week One and undergoing season-ending surgery. As a true freshman in 2013, notched12 tackles, one pass breakup and zero interceptions in 11 appearances. Played all 13 games in '14, drawing one start, and tallied 13-3-2 (TD) with two tackles for loss and one sack. Played all 15 games in '15, drawing one start, and collected 15-1-2 with one-half tackle for loss, one blocked punt and a safety. Was behind Jayron Kearse (Vikings) and T.J. Green (Colts) until '16 when he started all 15 games at strong safety, and produced 61-7-5 with two tackles for loss and two forced fumbles. Exited the Florida State contest with a calf strain. Team captain. Graduated with sociology degree.

Strengths: Good size. Fine agility, body control and ball skills. Tracks the ball well in the air and highpoints it. Good hands and solid improving interception production (9). Football smart. Adequate instincts — active and effortful. Solid production. Has special teams experience and served as a gunner. Caught the ball naturally like a receiver in the gauntlet drills at the Combine.

Weaknesses: Has small hands. Tentative, drag-down tackler with a soft approach — retreats when ball carriers run at him (see Alabama) and gets knocked backward. Takes questionable angles working from high to low and needs to improve his functional football-playing strength as a tackler. Only a one-year starter. Lacks eye discipline. Processes too much and is not sudden off spots.

Future: A functional, finesse cover safety lacking the toughness, physicality and striking ability desired in the run game. Flash player who will tease with some timely big plays in coverage, though has yet to prove consistent or well-rounded enough to become an NFL starter and lacks a desirable temperament for special teams.

Draft projection: Fifth- to sixth-round pick.

Scout's take: "(Johnson) is only an average special teams player. He's too soft. I don't think he will hold up in the run game. And when live bullets are flying on kickoffs, he'll be looking for cover. Someone will draft him to play special teams and be a reserve safety though. We'll pass."

FS-LCB JOHN JOHNSON, #9 (Sr-4)

BOSTON COLLEGE ▶ GRADE: 5.42
Ht: 6-0 1/2 | Wt: 208 | 40: 4.61 | Arm: 32 | Hand: 9 7/8

History: Also played basketball as a Maryland prep. Was a backup cornerback/special teams player as a true freshman in 2013, recording four tackles, zero pass breakups and zero interceptions with one tackle for loss. Played eight games in '14, drawing two starts at right cornerback, and tallied 25-2-0 with one sack. Missed five games while recovering from left wrist surgery. Transitioned to safety, and changed his number from No. 43 to No. 9. Started all 12 games in '15 — first nine at strong safety, final three at left cornerback — and posted 63-3-3 with 1 1/2 tackles for loss, two forced fumbles and one blocked kick. Played free safety in '16 when he logged 77-9-3 with 2 1/2 tackles for loss, one sack and one forced fumble. Team captain. Scheduled to graduate in May. Turns 22 on Dec. 19.

Strengths: Very good size and athletic ability. Fine eyes, instincts and anticipation. Good range. Takes good angles and plays the cutback. Plays with urgency and fills fast. Competitive run defender. Solid, wrap tackler. Has a 37 1/2-inch vertical jump, indicative of outstanding lower-body explosion. Good burst out of his break. Solid Senior Bowl week performance. Plays hard and leaves everything on the field. Strong special teams contributor. Versatile and has played corner and safety. Tough, smart and durable.

Weaknesses: Struggles some in transition in man coverage and will be outmatched by quick slot receivers. Press technique could use refinement. Could stand to iron out his pedal and transition. Not a physical, drive-through tackler.

Future: Solid all-around player who excels vs. the run and pass and contributes in all phases on special teams.

Draft projection: Third- to fourth-round pick.

FS-SS JOSH JONES, #11 (Jr-4)

NORTH CAROLINA STATE ▶ GRADE: 5.72
Ht: 6-1 3/8 | Wt: 220 | 40: 4.41 | Arm: 32 | Hand: 9 3/8

History: Safety-running back from Michigan. Redshirted in 2013. Started all 12 games played at strong safety in '14, and recorded 61 tackles, eight pass breakups and two interceptions. Was suspended, with six teammates, against Louisville for his role in a BB gun incident. Started 11-of-13 games at SS in '15, and secured 63-2-1 with 2 1/2 tackles for loss and one-half sack. Transitioned to free (boundary) safety, and changed his jersey number from 2

DEFENSIVE BACKS

to 11. Started 11-of-13 games in '15, and was credited with 63-2-1 with 2 1/2 tackles for loss and one-half sack. In '16, was the Wolfpack's leading tackler — started all 13 games at FS, and notched 109-8-3 with four tackles for loss and one sack. Did not run shuttles at the Combine because of a quad injury.

Strengths: Well-built and looks the part with good musculature. Explosive striker. Very physical in run support. Tied for the most bench-press reps (20) among all strong safeties at the Combine. Outstanding movement skill for a 220-pound safety and hits with physicality. Good closing burst. Tough and aggressive football playing temperament. Sacrifices his body around piles. Has a 37 1/2-inch vertical. Experienced, three-year starter. Came across as smart and articulate in the interview process.

Weaknesses: Has some tightness in his movement and transition. Lacks fluidity in man coverage to stay in the hip pocket of receivers. Can be lured by play-action and be overaggressive reacting to the run and lose positioning. A bit choppy in his backpedal. Misses some tackles lunging and leaving his feet too early and could do a better job of coming to balance in space and playing under control. Needs to play with more discipline in coverage and avoid mental mistakes. Fights the ball at times and is not a natural catcher. Immature early and has some abrasiveness. Was not always receptive to coaching.

Future: A hard-hitting, impact tackler with good straight-line speed and striking ability. Has played both safety positions and can interchange high to low, though is best suited for a physical, in-the-box hammer role. Has immediate starter potential and the physicality desired on special teams.

Draft projection: Second- to third-round pick.

Scout's take: "(Jones) has been flying under the radar all year. Physically he has everything you want. He busts coverages a little more than you'd like and he's a little rough around the edges, but he is a good football player and will be a good pro."

RCB SIDNEY JONES, #26 (Jr-3)

WASHINGTON ▶ GRADE: 5.40

Ht: 6-0 | Wt: 186 | 40: 4.52 | Arm: 31 1/2 | Hand: 9 3/8

History: Prepped in California. As a true freshman in 2014, started 12-of-13 games, and recorded 61 tackles, five pass breakups and two interceptions with 2 1/2 tackles for loss and one forced fumble. Started all 27 games the next two seasons — totaled 45-10-4 (TD) with 3 1/2 tackles for loss, three forced fumbles and

a fumble recovery for a 70-yard touchdown in '15; and 39-6-3 with 2 1/2 tackles for loss and two forced fumbles in '16. Also returned an interception 69 yards for a score in '15. Tore his left Achilles' at his pro day workout on March 11th and is expected to miss at least six to eight months in rehabilitation. Opted not to bench at the Combine.

Strengths: Has good body length and solid press cover skill. Good instincts diagnosing the run quickly. Always around the ball. Six career forced fumbles and heavy production on the ball. Plays with discipline under control, sees the quarterback and jumps routes. Flashes playmaking ability. Competes for the ball in the air. Good man cover skills to mirror receivers. Experienced three-year starter.

Weaknesses: Very skinny. Lacks ideal size and is not a strong tackler. Does not play physical in run support. Has some stiffness in his body with average foot quickness in plant-and-drive. Not clean in his transition. Average ball production and recovery speed. Did not catch the ball cleanly at the Combine. Below-average leaping ability. Turns down some contact. Durability is a serious concern given narrow frame, tight hips and Achilles' injury that will keep him out for most if not all of his rookie season.

Future: A lean, press man corner with second-round athletic traits, Jones is likely to slip a few rounds after rupturing his Achilles' at his pro day workout. Is expected to begin the season on the physically-unable-to-perform list and might need to take a redshirt season. Ceiling is lower than his hype, and willingness to tackle could define his career as opponents are likely to run at him. Uncertainty still lingers about how well he will be able to recover from Achilles' injury.

Draft projection: Third- to fourth-round pick.

Scout's take: "He's a man cover guy who can run. He's lazy with his technique, but he is an athlete. He has been overhyped. He has good length, but he's soft. He is similar to (Buccaneers 2013 second-round pick [43]) Johnthan Banks, who has flopped around the league and doesn't tackle very well."

RCB-PR DAMONTAE KAZEE, #23 (Sr-5)

SAN DIEGO STATE ▶ GRADE: 5.29

Ht: 5-10 1/4 | Wt: 184 | 40: 4.56 | Arm: 30 7/8 | Hand: 8 5/8

History: Pronounced "Kay-zee." Also lettered in basketball and track as a California prep. Redshirted in 2012. Played 12 games in '13, and recorded 41 tackles, two pass breakups and one interception with three tackles for loss,

DEFENSIVE BACKS

one sack, four forced fumbles and a blocked kick. Did not play against New Mexico (concussion). Manned right corner for the Aztecs. Started all 41 games the last three seasons — totaled 58-13-1 with four tackles for loss in '14; and 75-7-8 (TD) with 5 1/2 tackles for loss and two forced fumbles; and 65-8-7 (TD) with three tackles for loss in '16. Also had five punt returns for 70 yards (14.0-yard average), including one score as a junior. Two-time Mountain West Defensive Player of the Year. Owns school interceptions record (17). Team captain. Will be a 24-year-old rookie. Did not run shuttles at the Combine because of hamstrings.

Strengths: Very instinctive. Good ball skills. Produced the game-winning interception against Cal and consistently produces in the clutch. Quick-footed. Aggressive attacking the ball at the top of routes and shows very good anticipation. Exceptional interception production with 15 interceptions the last two years. Has very natural receiving skills. Experienced three-year starter. Competitive tackler willing in run support.

Weaknesses: Undersized, short-armed and small-handed. Overmatched against bigger receivers in man coverage and struggles to keep stride against top speed as seen at the Senior Bowl in one-on-one matchups. Plays a bit recklessly and out of control against the run and will miss tackles not coming to balance.

Future: Tough, scrappy, confident, undersized, quicker-than-fast zone corner who flashes some playmaking ability and could be most ideally suited for a job as a nickel cornerback handling slot receivers. Is a good, feisty football player and would be most ideally suited for a predominantly zone coverage, Tampa-2 type defense where he could utilize his exceptional ball skills to play the ball. Similar to Bears' 2004 fourth-round pick Nathan Vasher.

Draft projection: Fourth- to fifth-round pick.

Scout's take: "He's a zone corner who can't run. He's probably a nickel back. His background will need to be vetted. There's a lot there. He's a good little football player though. I like his ball skills and instincts."

NCB-FS-RS DESMOND KING, #14 (Sr-4)

IOWA ▶ GRADE: 5.56

Ht: 5-9 7/8 | Wt: 201 | 40: 4.60e | Arm: 31 1/8 | Hand: 9 5/8

History: Recruited out of Detroit, where he set the Michigan state record with 29 career interceptions. Also starred as a running back, and lettered four times in track. Jordan Lomax was injured in the first game of the 2013 season, opening the door for King to take over the right cornerback position. As a true freshman in '13, King started 12-of-13 games, and posted 69 tackles, eight pass breakups and zero interceptions with three tackles for loss. Started all 13 games in '14, and produced 64-5-3 with two tackles for loss. Was the Thorpe Award winner in '15 after racking up 72-13-8 with one tackle for loss in 14 games (13 starts). Was benched for the first quarter versus Nebraska as punishment for being late to a team meeting. Also returned 29 kickoffs for 708 yards (24.4-yard average). Started all 13 games in '16, and registered 58-7-3 with 3 1/2 tackles for loss and one forced fumble. Added 27-750 (27.8) on kickoffs. Team captain. Graduated with a degree in mass communications. Opted not to run at the Combine.

Strengths: Outstanding ball skills and hands — natural interceptor with good body control and balance to adjust to the thrown ball. Good eyes and anticipation to sort out routes in zone coverage, see the quarterback and drive on the ball. Reads routes and stays in the hip pocket of receivers in short areas. Strong hands to press receivers with subtle hand use to help keep positioning. Secure tackler quick to fill vs. the run. Extremely competitive. Very durable four-year starter. Has return skills.

Weaknesses: Lacks ideal length. A bit tight and upright in his backpedal. Limited recovery speed — fights to keep stride with average receivers (see North Dakota State and Iowa State) and shows average burst transitioning at the top of routes. Too handsy and could have some man coverage limitations in the pros. Still immature and learning what it means to be a pro.

Future: A tough, confident, zone corner most ideally suited for a nickel role. Lacks ideal length and long speed desired in a starter, yet carries the swagger and possesses the cover instincts, ball skills and eye discipline to make an impact for an aggressive, ball-hawking secondary such as the that of the Cardinals, Giants, Panthers or Chiefs. Could warrant some interest as a safety.

Draft projection: Second- to third-round pick.

Scout's take: "I heard all the hype entering the school and was looking forward to seeing him. I was disappointed. I'm not ready to say he could start for us. …I love his instincts. He's smart and tough. He's just not fast, and ultimately that will catch up to him. …He looks 5-9 when you walk up on him. He's a team's third corner, a nickel. He has had some success as a returner. … It's always easy to say a corner can play safety when they are tough and instinctive. It's different matching up against NFL receivers."

LCB-FS KEVIN KING, #20 (Sr-4)

WASHINGTON ▶ GRADE: 5.42

Ht: 6-3 | Wt: 200 | 40: 4.46 | Arm: 32 | Hand: 9 1/2

History: Oakland, Calif. native also competed in track and field in high school. As a true freshman in 2013, recorded 17 tackles, one pass breakup and zero interceptions in 10 games (two starts at free safety). Missed three games after tearing his left labrum. Started 12-of-13 games played in '14, and produced 65-3-1 with one-half tackle for loss and one forced fumble. Did not play against Stanford (mono). Moved to corner in '15 — started 8-of-11 games played, and managed 39-5-3 with 4 1/2 tackles for loss. Did not play against Arizona (right quad), and missed the bowl game against Southern Miss (concussion). Started all 14 games at CB in '16, and posted 44-13-2 with 3 1/2 tackles for loss.

Strengths: Rare size with a lean, wiry musculature. Solid instincts. Exceptional Combine workout. Recorded a Combine-best 6.56-second 3-cone drill time and the best 20-yard shuttle (3.89) and 60-yard shuttle (11.14) of any defensive back, indicative of exceptional agility, change of direction and short-area burst. Experienced three-year starter. Versatile and has lined up all over the field, as an inside and outside corner and both safety positions. Functional, drag-down tackler. Has gunner and jammer experience.

Weaknesses: Does not play to his size in the run game, and length creates some issues transitioning cleanly in coverage. Needs to do a better job of shooting his hands in press coverage and playing more physical at the line of scrimmage. Stays blocked too long.

Future: Tall, lean, high-cut, press man corner with upside to be groomed for a press coverage defense such as the Ravens or Seahawks if he shows more willingness to improve as a tackler.

Draft projection: Third- to fourth-round pick.

RCB ASHTON LAMPKIN, #6 (Sr-5)

OKLAHOMA STATE ▶ GRADE: 5.15

Ht: 6-0 1/4 | Wt: 189 | 40: 4.53 | Arm: 31 | Hand: 9 3/8

History: Prepped in Texas, where he also ran track. As a true freshman in 2012, recorded 24 tackles, one pass breakup and zero interceptions in 13 games. Played all 13 games in '13, and tallied 18-0-1. In '14, managed 4-3-2 (TD) in four starts before suffering a severe right ankle injury. Was shut down for the season, but was granted a medical hardship waiver. Started 8-of-12 games in '15 — first seven and Sugar Bowl against Ole Miss — and collected 31-5-1 with one tackle for loss. A broken right thumb sidelined him against Texas Tech and cost him starts

in the last four regular season games. Started all 13 games in '16, and totaled 34-3-1 with one forced fumble. Graduated.

Strengths: Good size and press strength, as confirmed with 19 bench-press reps at the Combine, among the highest of all cornerbacks. Competitive in run support. Has served as a gunner in punt coverage and played on all special teams units.

Weaknesses: Marginal production on the ball, with only three career interceptions and skillets for hands. Average long speed. Not quick or explosive out of his breaks and does not anticipate routes. Peeks too much and gets caught flat-footed and loses positioning.

Future: Big, slow-twitch, short-area, developmental zone corner with no distinguishable traits to hang your hat on and must find a way to produce on special teams to stick on a roster. Size and strength give him a chance.

Draft projection: Late draftable pick.

RCB BRENDAN LANGLEY, #21 (Sr-4)

LAMAR (TEX.) ▶ GRADE: 5.22

Ht: 6-0 3/8 | Wt: 201 | 40: 4.44 | Arm: 32 | Hand: 9 1/2

History: Prepped in Georgia, and was named AAAAA Player of the Year. Began his college career at University of Georgia. As a true freshman in 2013 (wore jersey No. 4), played nine games, starting the first four at cornerback, and recorded 12 tackles, two pass breakups and zero interceptions. In '14, notched 4-1-0 with one tackle for loss in five games (one start). Seeking more playing time, transferred to FCS Lamar, where he played receiver initially before settling at cornerback. Played all 11 games in '15, starting three — totaled 21-11-1 (86-yard TD) with one tackle for loss on defense, as well as four catches for 51 yards (12.8-yard average) and one touchdown on offense. Switched from jersey No. 5 to 21. Started all 11 games in '16 at boundary corner, and produced 43-7-6 with two tackles for loss and one forced fumble.

Strengths: Has a long, projectable frame and looks the part. Very good athletic ability, burst and range. Outstanding size-speed combination. Bench-pressed the most reps (22) of 225 pounds of any defensive back at the Combine, indicative of outstanding strength to help press receivers at the line of scrimmage. Tough and durable.

Weaknesses: Exposed in coverage at the Senior Bowl and footwork and technique still have a long way to go. Needs to become more consistent as a tackler and do a better job of securing tackles in the open field. Lacks functional, football-playing strength and needs to learn how to convert his immense physical talents to the field and play with more confidence.

Future: Well-built, long-limbed, developmental press corner with the speed, strength and burst to warrant developing, though has green instincts and was overmatched by the speed of the game in the Senior Bowl against better competition. Will require some time to transition to the NFL, though has undeniable upside and must mature to reach his potential. Has some similarities to Arizona 2016 third-round pick (92) Brandon Williams.

Draft projection: Late draftable pick.

LCB **MARSHON LATTIMORE**, #2 (Soph-3)
OHIO STATE ▶ GRADE: 6.64

Ht: 6-0 | Wt: 193 | 40: 4.37 | Arm: 31 1/4 | Hand: 8 7/8

History: Cleveland Glenville product was a U.S. Army All-American and Ohio's Division II defensive player of the year. Redshirted in 2014 after having surgery to repair a chronic hamstring injury which dated back to his high school track season. Was plagued by hamstring issues again in '15, recording 5-3-0 in seven appearances. Started 12-of-13 games in '16 (entered second play of Michigan game), and produced 41-9-4 (TD) with one tackle for loss. Did not bench at the Combine because of a left shoulder injury and did not perform shuttles after injuring a hip flexor on his second 40-yard dash attempt.

Strengths: Very fluid and quick with outstanding transitional quickness to take away the underneath passing game. Accelerates instantly, as confirmed by 1.50-second 10-yard split. Has a 38 1/2-inch vertical jump, indicative of exceptional lower-body explosion and leaping ability to play the ball in the air. Exceptional hand quickness to re-route receivers at the line. Plays on balance with clean feet and little man movement skills. Outstanding speed to run with receivers down the field. Excellent balance and body control. Natural ball skills — highpoints interceptions and has soft hands. Willing, physical tackler.

Weaknesses: Has very small hands. Durability is a concern given multiple hamstring injuries. Struggled to handle the complexity of covering the slot and worked in a three-man rotation often playing into the boundary. Only a one-year starter.

Future: The most fluid, loose-hipped, smooth-moving, athletic cover man in the draft, Lattimore has just scratched the surface of how good he could become and has not figured it out yet. Possesses the length, balance, burst, agility and transitional quickness to become a Day One plug-and-play starter, though will be best with simple assignments locking down receivers in press man coverage. Similar mold to Bengals' 2006 first-round pick and Texans CB Johnathan Joseph and Lions' 2013 second-round pick (36th) Darius Slay and has perennial Pro Bowl potential if he can stay healthy, as he was treated with kid gloves (diet, yoga, counted reps) following his second hamstring injury.

Draft projection: Top-10 pick.

Scout's take: "(Lattimore) did not excel in the slot when he played there. He struggles when he is around 200. He has the best ball skills and pure upside of any corner to come out of there in recent years, and they have had some good ones."

RCB **JOURDAN LEWIS**, #26 (Sr-4)
MICHIGAN ▶ GRADE: 5.58

Ht: 5-10 1/4 | Wt: 188 | 40: 4.56 | Arm: 31 5/8 | Hand: 9 1/4

History: Detroit Cass Tech product won a pair of state titles, and garnered U.S. Army All-American honors. Played all 13 games in '13, and was credited with 17 tackles, two pass breakups and zero interceptions. Started 7-of-12 games played in '14, and contributed 39-6-0 with 1 1/2 tackles for loss. In '15, set the UM single-season pass breakups record when he started all 13 games, and produced 52-20-2 (TD) with 3 1/2 tackles for loss, one sack and one forced fumble. Also returned 15 kickoffs for 378 yards (25.2-yard average). Sustained a concussion against Oregon State. In '16, was the Big Ten Defensive Back of the Year and a Thorpe Award finalist despite missing the first three games while dealing with back, hamstring and quad injuries. On the season, started all 10 games played, and managed 25-11-2 with 3 1/2 tackles for loss, while returning kickoffs 7-127-0 (18.1). Opted not to run shuttles at the Combine. On March 15, 2017, pled not guilty to a misdemeanor domestic violence charge for an argument involving his live-in girlfriend of three years.

Strengths: Very good cover skills. Outstanding ball production. Very confident and competitive and responds to a challenge. Can make acrobatic adjustments and contort his body in the air to play the ball. Plays bigger than his size and uses his hands well at the line of scrimmage to funnel receivers. Quick to sniff out screens developing and trigger downhill and jump routes. Plays with good balance and maintains good positioning — stays in phase with good hand-eye coordination and can recover when he loses position. Competitive tackler. Has been a gunner in punt coverage and will sacrifice his body on special teams.

Weaknesses: Thin-framed and lacks bulk. Has some struggles matching up against elite

DEFENSIVE BACKS

size and speed, and can be grabby when he loses positioning. Lacks awareness with his back to the ball. Has room to improve press-bail technique. Was repeatedly beaten vs. Ohio State and Florida State and can be challenged by elite speed.

Future: Rangy, athletic, confident cornerback with natural cover skills to transition quickly to the pro game, though skill set could project best to covering the slot. Has the tools to emerge as a solid No. 2 corner, with the confidence and competitiveness to become a very solid pro.

Draft projection: Second- to third-round pick.

Scout's take: "I liked his feet, hips, movement skills and ability to pattern read. He's not flashy and lacks some speed, but he is very solid and steady."

NCB-RS **WILL LIKELY**, #4 (Sr-4)

MARYLAND ▶ GRADE: 5.20

Ht: 5-6 5/8 | Wt: 180 | 40: 4.50e | Arm: 29 | Hand: 9 1/2

History: Belle Glade (Fla.) Glades Central product played all over the field, and was recognized as the state's Gatorade Player of the Year. Also ran track. Was the Terps' special teams player of the year as a true freshman in 2013 — started 11-of-13 games, and produced 70 tackles, six pass breakups and one interception with 4 1/2 tackles for loss. Also returned 28 kickoffs for 729 yards (26.0-yard average) and 16 punt returns for 205 yards (12.8-yard average), including one score. Started all 13 games in '14, and notched 83-9-6 (two TD) with four tackles for loss, one sack and one forced fumble. Also returned kickoffs 16-496-1 (31.0) and punts 20-225-1 (11.2). Started all 11 games played in '15, including a two-way start against Wisconsin (receiver), and tallied 44-11-0 with four tackles for loss and three forced fumbles. Was the Big Ten return specialist of the year after returning kickoffs 35-789-1 (22.5) and punts 23-419-2 (18.2), including 233 punt return yards against Richmond, which broke a 76-year Big Ten record. Sat out against Rutgers (left ankle). In '16, put up 32-3-0 with four tackles for loss, one sack and one forced fumble in six starts before tearing his right ACL. Also returned kickoffs 8-219-0 (27.4) and punts 8-26 (3.2). Graduated with a communication degree. Was a medical exclusion from working out at the Combine because of a right knee injury.

Strengths: Good instincts. Reads and reacts quickly and shows good pattern awareness. Has an efficient pedal. Good closing speed, range and burst. Scrappy run defender who aggressively will fill and has mastered the art of low-wrap, lasso tackling. Is quick, elusive, and has good long speed in the return game. Extremely tough and competitive and is an experienced, four-year starter.

Weaknesses: Poor size. Extremely short (5-6 5/8 inches) and short-armed (29), both measuring the shortest of any defensive back at the Combine. Has small, inconsistent hands and has left too much production on the field with dropped interceptions.

Future: A feisty, diminutive corner with the competitiveness and toughness to earn a role as a starting nickel corner, though will always be challenged by his lack of height, and must prove durable after ending his career with a knee injury that could bleed into his rookie season. Return ability is a plus.

Draft projection: Late draftable pick.

SS **SHALOM LUANI**, #18 (Sr-5)

WASHINGTON STATE ▶ GRADE: 5.14

Ht: 5-11 3/8 | Wt: 202 | 40: 4.54 | Arm: 32 | Hand: 9 3/4

History: Born in American Samoa, where he played soccer growing up. Did not have any offers coming out of high school. Spent a semester at Chabot College (Calif.) — could not afford tuition, but practiced with the team. With his sister backing him financially, got back on the field at City College of San Francisco. Played 11 games in 2013, and posted 49 tackles, one pass breakup and seven interceptions with 3 1/2 tackles for loss, one forced fumble and one blocked kick. Was considered one of the top JUCO safeties in the country in '14 when he registered 69-8-4 with six tackles for loss, one sack, two forced fumbles and one blocked kick. Was a team captain. With the Cougars in '15, started all 13 games at free safety, and notched 90-6-4 (TD) with three tackles for loss and two forced fumbles. Ten days before the '16 season, got in a fight at a pizza place and sustained a concussion. After sitting out the opener against Eastern Washington, started all 12 games — two at FS before transitioning to nickel — and totaled 68-6-4 with 8 1/2 tackles for loss, two sacks and one forced fumble.

Strengths: Very good career interception production (19). Outstanding keying the quarterback and sorting out coverage in front of him. Plays very competitively and fills hard. Has a special teams personality with an all-out approach and proficiency navigating through organized chaos that dates back to his soccer upbringing.

Weaknesses: Has small hands and a thin frame. Undisciplined eyes. Unreliable open-field tackler — plays with too much reckless abandon and does not consistently wrap as a tackler. Takes some questionable angles coming underneath blocks. Has a 31-inch vertical jump, indicative of a lack of lower-body explosion. Bench-pressed 225 pounds only 12 times at the Combine and lacks weight-room strength.

Future: A very aggressive, competitive football player with an undisciplined, freelance approach to the game that leads to many big plays but even more blown coverages and missed assignments. Needs to become more disciplined and learn to play within the scheme of a defense to succeed in the pros. Has the wiring to become a Pro Bowl special teams player.

Draft projection: Late draftable pick.

NCB ART MAULET, #8 (Sr-4)

MEMPHIS ▶ GRADE: 5.06

Ht: 5-9 3/4 | Wt: 189 | 40: 4.66 | Arm: 31 1/4 | Hand: 9 5/8

History: Last name is pronounced "Mal-et." New Orleans native also played basketball and soccer in high school. Spent two seasons at Copiah-Lincoln Community College (Miss.). Played nine games in 2013, and recorded 37 tackles, 14 pass breakups and one interception. Played 11 games in '14, and posted 30-20-5 with one sack and one forced fumble. With the Tigers in '15, contributed 38-7-2 (TD) in 13 games (eight starts). In '16, was the Tigers' team MVP — started all 13 games, and totaled 73-13-2 with 7 1/2 tackles for loss, 4 1/2 sacks and two forced fumbles. Capped his career with 11 tackles and three sacks against Western Kentucky, as he saw time at the "Star" position in place of the injured starter. The Tigers did not employ permanent team captains, but Maulet was a weekly captain 11 times as a senior. Opted not to run shuttles at the Combine.

Strengths: Competitive and physical. Bench-pressed 225 pounds 18 times at the Combine, third-most among cornerbacks, and it shows. Flashes explosive pop in his hands to disrupt the release of bigger receivers and does not back down from a challenge. Fine zone eyes and anticipation, with a knack for jumping routes. Willing tackler.

Weaknesses: Marginal height and foot speed with limited short-area burst and acceleration, as confirmed by 1.65-second 10-yard split at the Combine. Struggles to run with and carry receivers deep and lacks the length and leaping ability to climb the ladder and play the ball in the air. Easily overmatched against size.

Future: A short, instinctive, zone corner with the size most ideally suited to line up in the slot in the pros and compete for a no. 5 or No. 6 role.

Draft projection: Priority free agent.

FS MARCUS MAYE, #20 (Sr-5)

FLORIDA ▶ GRADE: 5.80

Ht: 5-11 3/4 | Wt: 210 | 40: 4.55e | Arm: 32 1/2 | Hand: 9 1/8

History: Florida native. Safety-running back also starred in basketball and ran track in high school. Redshirted in 2012 while recovering from a torn right meniscus. Played all 12 games in '13 — started the first two at strong safety, but was benched; recorded 16 tackles, zero pass breakups and one interception. Sat out the '15 season opener (hamstring) before starting 9-of-11 games played — four at nickel, five at safety — and logged 62-5-1 with three tackles for loss and two forced fumbles. Was suspended for the '15 season opener, but started 12-of-13 games played at free safety alongside Keanu Neal (Falcons), and totaled 82-6-2 with 1 1/2 tackles for loss and five forced fumbles. In '16, tallied 50-6-1 with 1 1/2 tackles for loss and one sack in nine starts at FS before suffering a season-ending broken left arm injury. On pace to graduate. Was a medical exclusion from the Combine because of arm injury.

Strengths: Quick feet, fluid hips and a seamless, smooth pedal. Good eyes and anticipation. Plays alert and sees route concepts unfolding and breaks on the ball. Uses his hands well to disrupt the timing of routes. Zeroes in on the quarterback and anticipates the thrown ball. Very good range to get over the top. Takes good angles and leverages the field. Quick to read keys and react — fills fast vs. the run. Efficient slipping blocks and forcing contain.

Experienced, three-year starter in the Southeastern Conference. Versatile and has lined up all over the secondary, as an interchangeable strong and free safety and over the slot in nickel packages. Has a love of the game and it shows.

Weaknesses: Has small hands that could stand to improve — will make some easy drops and is not a natural catcher. Ball skills are still developing — does not attack the ball in the air like a receiver and could stand to do a better job finishing. Can be challenged by quick-footed receivers. Drag-down tackler lacking thump.

Future: Athletic, interchangeable safety with the movement skill, versatility and football smarts to emerge readily as an NFL starter. Consistently shows up in all phases of the game, and though he needs to finish better, could immediately upgrade many NFL secondaries.

Draft projection: Second- to third-round pick.

DEFENSIVE BACKS

SS-WLB OBI MELIFONWU, #20 (Sr-5)

CONNECTICUT ▶ GRADE: 5.55

Ht: 6-3 7/8 | Wt: 224 | 40: 4.43 | Arm: 32 1/2 | Hand: 9 1/8

History: Last name is pronounced "Melon-FON-wuh." Born in London, and raised in Massachusetts, where the defensive back-running back also competed as a long jumper and high jumper. In August 2012, was arrested by campus police and charged with sixth-degree larceny. Redshirted that year. Manned free safety for the Huskies. Started all 12 games in '13, and produced 70 tackles, five pass break-ups and two interceptions with three tackles for loss and two forced fumbles. Started all 11 games played in '14, and tallied 75-3-0 with 3 1/2 tackles for loss. Sat out the season finale against SMU with a torn right labrum. Started 12-of-13 games in '15, and logged 88-5-2 with two tackles for loss. Was the Huskies' leading tackler in '16 when he piled up 118-3-4 with 2 1/2 tackles for loss. Opted not to run shuttles at the Combine. Measured the heaviest (224) of any defensive back at the Combine.

Strengths: Explosive athlete with a unique 44-inch vertical jump and 11'9" broad jump, both bests among all participants at the Combine and indicative of rare lower-body explosion and athletic ability. Experienced four-year starter. Good weight-room strength. Has the short-area burst and acceleration to track down backs to the perimeter and covers a lot of ground quickly with long strides.

Weaknesses: Average instincts and toughness. Has a bit of a track mentality and does not fill with urgency downhill. Leggy long-strider struggles to get off a track, open his hips and transition quickly. Does not uncoil his hips and strike with explosion or translate the tremendous spring in his legs to the field. Plays too tall and bends at the waist, struggling to adjust with a tight core. Average production on the ball. Scouts describe his personality as quirky and overly analytical processor. Average Senior Bowl showing.

Future: Rare-sized, long-limbed, explosive athlete with a finesse playing temperament not ideally suited for a move inside the box to handle the mini-linebacker role that his body type suggests he is more ideally suited to fulfill. Serious concerns linger about whether he is tough, instinctive and compact enough to function at safety, with his height appearing to be a detriment at times, as he tries to bend and transition against fleet-footed receivers. Looks like the second coming of (49ers' 2010 second-round [49th] pick) Taylor Mays and could be too tall for the safety position. Has

boom-or-bust potential.

Draft projection: Second- to third-round pick.

Scout's take: "(Melifonwu) looks like Tarzan and plays like Jane. He's tall and lanky and not necessarily soft, but he does not look like a safety moving around. Now, if you were handing out sticks to a track team, I would draft him first. Someone needs to show me the tape where he plays 4.4 though. I have not seen any yet, and I've spent a lot of time (tracking) him."

LCB FABIAN MOREAU, #10 (Sr-5)

UCLA ▶ GRADE: 5.52

Ht: 6-0 1/2 | Wt: 206 | 40: 4.37 | Arm: 31 3/8 | Hand: 9

History: Prepped in Florida, where he played running back and receiver. Saw limited action in 11 games as a true freshman, scratching five tackles, zero pass breakups and zero interceptions. Started all 12 games played in '13, and recorded 51-4-0 with one-half tackle for loss. Sat out against USC (right hamstring). Started all 13 games in '14, and produced 53-8-1 with three tackles for loss. In '15, managed 8-1-0 in three starts before suffering a season-ending Lisfranc fracture to his right foot. Started all 12 games in '16, and totaled 31-9-2 with one tackle for loss and one forced fumble. Team captain graduated with a political science degree. Did not bench at the Combine because of a left shoulder injury and a strained pectoral injury at his pro day also kept him from performing planned positional drills. Underwent surgery to repair the torn pectoral muscle he suffered during his pro-day bench press, with an expected recovery time of 4-6 months.

Strengths: Very well built and looks the part with outstanding size and a thick frame. Has a 38-inch vertical jump and 11'4" broad jump, possessing outstanding lower-body explosion. Measured only 4.6% body fat at the Combine, tied for the lowest among defensive backs and indicative of exceptional conditioning and stamina. Good press strength to disrupt receivers at the line. Fine recovery speed.

Weaknesses: Does not play to his size. Too tight in transition and handsy down the field. Takes false steps. Marginal career interception production (3). Lacks physicality and is too inconsistent as a tackler, often taking a passive approach to run support. Average coverage instincts — too content going through the motions. Lacks ball awareness and needs to do a better job seeing, recognizing and anticipating route concepts.

Future: A big, strong, explosive corner filled with upside and looks like a first-round talent

171

DEFENSIVE BACKS

on paper, yet has never been able to put it all together and emerge as an elite cover man, or shake the injury bug. Still very much a work in progress, but has athletic traits to be molded into a starting press corner if he could stay healthy. Still a better athlete than football player at this stage of his development, with undeniable upside, and pectoral surgery could drop his draft status by a round.

Draft projection: Third- to fourth-round pick.

NCB-RS JALEN MYRICK, #5 (Sr-4)

MINNESOTA   ▶ GRADE: 5.24

Ht: 5-9 5/8 | Wt: 200 | 40: 4.31 | Arm: 31 5/8 | Hand: 8 3/4

History: Two-way standout from Georgia, where he also ran track (10.6 100 meters). A special teams player as a true freshman in 2013, was credited with four tackles, zero pass breakups and zero interceptions. In '13, recorded 21-7-1 (TD) with one tackle for loss and one forced fumble in 13 games (one start). Also returned 18 kickoffs for 508 yards (28.2-yard average), including a score. Was the Gophers' nickel corner in '15 when he started 7-of-10 games played, and tallied 27-3-3 (TD) with 3 1/2 tackles for loss and one-half sack. Suffered a collapsed lung against Ohio State, and missed the final three regular season games. Started all 13 games in '16, and produced 41-11-1 with 3 1/2 tackles for loss. Also returned kickoffs 13-287-0 (22.1) and punts 9-44-0 (4.9). On pace to finish his business marketing degree.

Strengths: Rare speed. Good thickness. Recorded the fastest 10-yard split (1.41 seconds) and 40-yard dash (4.28) of any defensive back at the Combine, indicative of exceptional short-area burst and acceleration. Has a 37 1/2-inch vertical jump and good explosive leaping ability. Very good closing speed on backside zone blitzes. Good speed to carry receivers vertically. Has dynamic return ability.

Weaknesses: Lacks ideal height. Plays with too much finesse. Not technique sound. Footwork is choppy. Needs to become more of a student of the game and hone his fundamentals. Not a strong, drive-through tackler and can be slow to trigger in run support. Lacks ideal size and temperament for special teams.

Future: A short, stocky, finesse nickel corner with explosive return capability, Myrick lacks ideal length to match up with NFL receivers on the perimeter and needs to become more tough and feisty to excel in the slot. Best chance to contribute readily in the pros is as a return man, with developmental nickel corner capabilities.

Draft projection: Fourth- to fifth-round pick.

SS MONTAE NICHOLSON, #9 (Jr-3)

MICHIGAN STATE   ▶ GRADE: 5.38

Ht: 6-2 3/8 | Wt: 212 | 40: 4.47 | Arm: 33 3/8 | Hand: 9 1/2

History: Two-way standout was one of the top players in Pennsylvania, where he also played basketball and won three state titles in track (60 meters, 110 hurdles and 400-meter relay). As a true freshman in 2014, played all 13 games, starting three at strong safety, and recorded 31 tackles, zero pass breakups and zero interceptions. In '15, totaled 83-2-3 with 2 1/2 tackles for loss in 14 games (10 starts). Started the first four games at free safety; after being benched in four of the next five games for inconsistent tackling, made other six starts at SS. Started 10-of-11 games played at SS in '16, and was credited with 86-2-1 with two tackles for loss. Was injured against Maryland, did not start against Michigan, and did not play against Illinois. Was a medical exclusion from the bench-press test at the Combine because of a left shoulder injury and did not run the shuttles because of a left ankle injury.

Strengths: Exceptional size. Very good straight-line speed to close downhill in a hurry when he triggers. Is alert in zone coverage and can be seen making pre-snap adjustments. Led team in special teams tackles as a freshman and has dimensions to be effective as a core teams contributor.

Weaknesses: Often plays into the boundary with limited ground to cover. Is tight-hipped and straight-linish and gathers to cut. Does not play to timed speed. Pedals tall and is late out of his transition. Lacks fluidity to match up with tight ends and backs in man coverage. Marginal ball skills. Could stand to do a better job wrapping as a tackler, missing 14 tackles in 2016. Needs to do a better job shedding and disengaging blockers.

Future: A finesse, high-cut, speedy, college free safety who projects best into the box in the pros. Has physical skills to continue developing.

Draft projection: Third- to fourth-round pick.

Scout's take: "I was surprised by the way he ran at the Combine. I was thinking about projecting him to 'Will' linebacker and then he showed up really light at 214. That was surprising."

SS-NCB-WR [F]/RS JABRILL PEPPERS, #5 (Jr-3)

MICHIGAN   ▶ GRADE: 6.16

Ht: 5-10 7/8 | Wt: 213 | 40: 4.46 | Arm: 30 3/4 | Hand: 9 5/8

History: Father, Terry, was imprisoned from the time Jabrill was seven until 2014 for felony firearm and drug charges. Brother, Don, was shot and killed in 2010. Jabrill grew up in East Orange, N.J., where he won four state championships — two at Don Bosco Prep, two at Paramus Catholic. Was named USA Today Defensive Player of the Year, and starred on the track, capturing back-to-back 100- and 200-meter state championships. Posted a 10.52-second 100 meters. Committed to UM and then-head coach Brady Hoke. Had a disappointing true freshman season in 2014 due to early season injuries, managing eight tackles, zero pass breakups and zero interceptions in three games (one start at nickel). Suffered a right ankle injury in the season opener versus Appalachian State then didn't play again after Week Four because of a knee injury. Speaking about the season, Peppers told the Big Ten Network, "I think I kinda let myself get lost in the hype a little bit. Took a lot of things for granted, wasn't playing as hard as I should have been and protecting myself as well as I should have been." Deployed as a hybrid "Sam" linebacker in '15, produced 45-10-0 with 5 1/2 tackles for loss in 12 starts. Sat out the Citrus Bowl against Florida with a right hand injury. In '16, was the Hornung Award winner, Lott IMPACT Trophy winner, Big Ten Defensive Player of the Year, and Big Ten Return Specialist of the Year, as well as a finalist for the Heisman and four other major awards. Started all 12 games at SLB, and totaled 72-0-1 with 16 tackles for loss, four sacks and one forced fumble. Sat out the Orange Bowl against Florida State after pulling his left hamstring in practice. Multipurpose player also had 45 career rushes for 239 yards (5.3-yard average) and five touchdowns; 10 career receptions for 82 yards (8.2-yard average) and zero touchdowns; 18 kickoff returns for 483 yards (26.8-yard average); and 39 punt returns for 510 yards (13.1-yard average), including one score.

Strengths: Ultra-competitive and plays with tremendous energy and intensity. Outstanding size for a strong safety. Very aggressive supporting the run, and consistently made plays behind the line of scrimmage. Superb instincts — is constantly around the football. Plays with physicality at the point of attack. Excellent closing speed and can recover quickly if he missteps. Very dependable tackler with good body control to come to balance in space. Versatile and can be deployed in many alignments and provide a defense with a unique mismatch piece, as one of the only in college football to be aligned at different times as a defensive end, linebacker, safety and cornerback. Aggressive blitzer who times up the snap well. Has creative return skills with elite playmaking ability

when the ball is in his hands. Has alpha-male leadership traits.

Weaknesses: Can be inconsistent tracking the deep ball down the field. Is a bit choppy in his pedal and can get grabby in his transition flipping his hips. Lacks ideal range to play center field and undersized for an every-down linebacker. Did not have a lot of production on the ball as he was moved around to multiple positions, with only one career interception.

Future: A versatile talent and unique athlete with the ball in his hands, Peppers is the most versatile player in this year's draft, with experience that could translate to playing safety, cornerback, running back, dime linebacker, slot receiver and nickel corner in the pros, in addition to handling returns and potentially a wildcat role. Will require a creative football coach that plays to the strengths of his roster to fully maximize his many talents. Is at his best with the ball in his hands making plays and might turn out to be a better offensive skill player than box safety. Will fit best defensively as a Troy Polamalu-esque, hybrid linebacker/safety.

Draft projection: First-round pick.

Scout's take: "I know there are (scouts) that graded him as a running back. I didn't see enough of that to say it. If you are going to draft him early, you need to have a conviction about where to play him and run with it. I think he is a great athlete and will go somewhere in the first (round). I was not fired up with what I saw of him as a safety."

LCB-FS EZRA ROBINSON, #21 (Sr-5)

TENNESSEE STATE ▶ GRADE: 5.09
Ht: 5-11 | Wt: 189 | 40: 4.49 | Arm: 31 1/2 | Hand: 8 3/4

History: Prepped in Florida, where he also played basketball and competed in high jump and triple jump. Began his college career at Michigan State. Tore his left meniscus in the spring of 2012. Redshirted in the fall. In September '13, was arrested for underage drinking and driving. Was a special teams player in the fall, scratching two tackles, zero pass breakups and zero interceptions in 12 appearances. Transferred to FCS Tennessee State in '14, where he recorded 42-1-0 with 5 1/2 tackles for loss and two sacks in 11 games (one start). Did not play against Southeastern Missouri (chest). Played all 10 games in '15, starting four, and collected 30-7-2. Started all 11 games in '16, and produced 42-8-5 (two TD) with one-half tackle for loss. Invited to the Senior Bowl. Did not run shuttles at the Combine because of a right foot injury.

Strengths: Good size and ball skills and carries receivers vertically with ease. Explosive athlete with a 10'10" broad jump. Versatile and has played free safety and corner. Has very good range.

Weaknesses: Has small hands. Lacks the physicality to match up against big receivers. Soft, passive tackler with limited pop on contact. Has a lackadaisical approach to the run game and is selective as a hitter. Only a one-year, full-time starter. Durability has been an issue throughout his career.

Future: Good-sized, off-man corner with athletic traits worthy of developing. Will require a patient, understanding positional coach that will help him focus and learn the finer points of the game. Lack of physicality could limit ability to factor on special teams and limit opportunities.

Draft projection: Late draftable pick.

NCB SOJOURN SHELTON, #8 (Sr-4)

WISCONSIN ▶ GRADE: 5.10

Ht: 5-9 | Wt: 177 | 40: 4.53 | Arm: 31 | Hand: 8 3/8

History: Prepped in Florida (originally verbaled to Florida State before changing his mind). As a true freshman in 2013, started 12-of-13 games, and notched 36 tackles, seven pass breakups and four interceptions with one forced fumble. Started 12-of-14 games in '14, and tallied 33-6-0 with one forced fumble. Started all 27 games the next two seasons — totaled 29-7-1 with one forced fumble in '15; and 31-12-4 with one tackle for loss in '16. Graduated with a degree in life sciences communication.

Strengths: Outstanding quickness and change of direction. Good short-area burst and closing speed. Smooth in his pedal and fluid in his movement. Can shadow and mirror and ride the hip pocket of receivers. Comfortable in man coverage. Experienced, four-year starter in the Big Ten Conference.

Weaknesses: Very small, measuring the lightest (177 pounds) of any defensive back at the Combine. Lacks functional strength in the run game and is a near liability in run support. Lacks length to match up outside. Limited special teams experience.

Future: Diminutive, finesse corner with the agility and cover skills to compete for a job in the slot, though must improve as a tackler to earn a job and could be challenged by the physicality of the NFL game.

Draft projection: Priority free agent.

LCB CHANNING STRIBLING, #8 (Sr-4)

MICHIGAN ▶ GRADE: 5.25

Ht: 6-1 1/4 | Wt: 188 | 40: 4.62 | Arm: 31 1/2 | Hand: 8 1/2

History: Comes from a military family, and moved eight times growing up. Also played basketball as a prep in North Carolina, where he was part of a nationally ranked, state championship football team. As a true freshman in 2013, recorded 16 tackles, zero pass breakups and zero interceptions with one forced fumble in 13 games (one start). Saw limited action in 10 games in '14, and collected 7-0-0 with one-half tackle for loss. Played 11 games in '15, starting four, and tallied 17-3-2 with one-half tackle for loss. Missed two October contests (injured). In '16, led the Big Ten in pass breakups during conference play — started all 13 games at corner, and posted 28-13-4 (TD) with three tackles for loss and one sack. Dislocated his left shoulder against Ohio State.

Strengths: Excellent body length. Effective re-routing receivers at the line. Keeps stride with receivers in press man coverage and has good field awareness and route recognition to anticipate the thrown ball. Good hands. Willing in run support.

Weaknesses: Very small hands. Has some tightness in his hips and ankles. Bench-pressed 225 pounds only 5 times at the Combine, tying for the fewest at the event, and press strength is very limited. Recorded the slowest 20-yard split (2.78 seconds) of any defensive back at the Combine. Very tight-hipped, as confirmed by 4.56 second 20-yard short shuttle time, and allows too much separation. Only a one-year, full-time starter. Does not play strong or physical. Usually uses a bail technique allowing free releases and is often in a trail position. Left a lot of production on the field, especially early in his career.

Future: Very lean, angular, developmental press corner made the most of his senior season and has the size, length and athletic ability to warrant developing. Will need to get stronger to hold up outside against NFL receivers.

Draft projection: Fourth- to fifth-round pick.

Scout's take: "(Stribling) plays a lot in trail technique and his interceptions tend to be underthrown balls that happen to come right to him, not plays that he is making or creating on his own. There's a big difference. Stats can be really good, but if you watch his technique and movement, it leaves more to be desired."

DEFENSIVE BACKS

NCB-PR **CAM SUTTON**, #23 (Sr-4)

TENNESSEE   ▶ GRADE: 5.36

Ht: 5-11 1/4 | Wt: 188 | 40: 4.56 | Arm: 30 | Hand: 8 1/4

History: Cornerback-receiver from Georgia, where he also played basketball and baseball. As a true freshman in 2013, started all 12 games, and recorded 39 tackles, seven pass breakups and two interceptions with four tackles for loss and one sack. With his 36-yard score against Western Kentucky, became the first freshman to return an interception for a touchdown since Eric Berry in '07. Started all 13 games in '14, and produced 37-13-4 with four tackles for loss and one forced fumble. In '15, changed his jersey from No. 23 to 7 as a tribute to injured teammate Rashaan Gaulden. Started all 13 games, and tallied 28-6-1 with three tackles for loss and two forced fumbles. In '16, secured 23-4-1 with two tackles for loss in seven games played. Missed six games after fracturing his right ankle against Ohio. Had 45 career punt returns for 657 yards (14.6-yard average), including three scores. Team captain graduated with a degree in communication studies.

Strengths: Good anticipation reading routes. Has quick feet, fluid hips and good body control, leading to very efficient transitional quickness and recovery speed. Well-versed and comfortable in man and zone coverage. Very focused and driven and carries a quiet confidence. Film junkie. Tough competitor. Experienced, four-year starter.

Weaknesses: Very small with a thin frame. Lacks physicality to re-route receivers at the line. Measured the smallest hands (8 1/4 inches) of any defensive back at the Combine. Weak tackler. Late to support the run and is too selective as a hitter with a pile inspector approach.

Future: Quick, athletic, undersized corner most ideally suited for a role in the slot in the pros, though will need to learn to play more aggressively against the run to hold up. Work habits and passion for the game will carry him to success and allow him to reach his ceiling as an NFL starter in sub-packages.

Draft projection: Third- to fourth-round pick.

Scout's take: "We beat up on him in our meetings because he won't tackle. He still has starter traits, and I think he will be a good pro."

LCB-FS **TEEZ TABOR**, #31 (Jr-3)

FLORIDA   ▶ GRADE: 5.63

Ht: 6-0 1/2 | Wt: 199 | 40: 4.61 | Arm: 32 | Hand: 8 5/8

History: Washington, D.C.'s "Mr. Football." Was cited for marijuana possession in July 2014. As a true freshman in the fall, recorded 31 tackles, eight pass breakups and one interception with four tackles for loss, two sacks and one forced fumble in 12 games (five starts). Was suspended for the '15 season opener against Tennessee after he refused to take a drug test. On the season, started 9-of-13 games, and produced 40-14-4 (two TD) with four tackles for loss and one sack. Was kicked out of practice and suspended for the '16 season opener versus Massachusetts after getting into a fight with teammate C'yontai Lewis. On the season, logged 33-6-4 (TD) with two tackles for loss and one sack in 12 starts.

Strengths: Exceptional size with outstanding length. Good press strength. Very good zone eyes to play the ball in front of him and prey on quarterbacks. Excellent plant-and-drive. Plays the ball well with his back to it. Aggressive blitzer. Plays the ball like a receiver and is disruptive breaking up passes. Good run fits. Strong tackler. Very confident and has displayed playmaking ability.

Weaknesses: A bit leggy and slow to transition, with too much wasted motion in his movement. Bench-pressed only 9 reps of 225 pounds at the Combine and needs to get stronger. Has a very ordinary 31-inch vertical jump, indicative of a lack of lower-body explosion. Marginal long speed shows up downfield. Was repeatedly targeted against Arkansas and Alabama. Will get caught gambling too much jumping routes. Susceptible to the double move. Scouts question his maturity and arrogance, as he can come off too abrasively, and has had a number of issues with discipline throughout his career that will require additional maintenance.

Future: Tough, instinctive, undisciplined, ballhawking press corner that would fit most ideally with teams seeking big, physical press corners such as the Saints, Eagles, Cardinals and Ravens. A poor man's Aqib Talib.

Draft projection: Second-round pick.

Scout's take: "Tabor is athletic and has good ball skills, but he is really soft in run support. He did not interview well with us. I don't think he is going to be drafted nearly as highly as he thinks he is."

LCB **CORDREA TANKERSLEY**, #25 (Sr-5)

CLEMSON   ▶ GRADE: 5.66

Ht: 6-1 1/4 | Wt: 199 | 40: 4.42 | Arm: 32 1/4 | Hand: 9 1/8

History: First name is pronounced "cohr-DRAY." Has a newborn son named Cameron. South Carolina native also ran track in high school. Attended Hargrave Military Academy (Va.) in 2012. Was a reserve/special teams player in '13 — notched 13 tackles (nine on special teams), zero pass breakups and zero interceptions with one-half tackle for loss in 12 games.

DEFENSIVE BACKS

Played all 13 games in '14, and collected 11-0-0, including seven on special teams. Played opposite Mackensie Alexander (Vikings) in '15 — started all 15 games primarily to the boundary, and produced 48-9-5 (TD) with 3 1/2 tackles for loss and one sack. Started all 15 games in '16, and totaled 52-11-4 with six tackles for loss, while being penalized seven times. Graduated with a degree in parks, recreation & tourism management.

Strengths: Exceptional size with outstanding straight-line speed. Good press strength at the line. Carries receivers down the field with ease and keeps stride for stride. Solid production on the ball. Plays with confidence in single coverage and has a feel for routes developing to trace the steps of receivers. Matches up well with size. Quick to jump routes in front of him in zone coverage.

Weaknesses: Has small hands and body-catches most of his interceptions. Grabs and holds too much. Recorded the lowest vertical jump (29 1/2 inches) of any defensive back at the Combine, indicative of marginal lower-body explosion. Average lateral agility. Disinterested run defender stays blocked too long and shows little urgency in filling.

Future: Big, stiff, high-hipped press corner with the size, long speed and ball skills desired in Minnesota, Cincinnati and Pittsburgh, though Tankersley needs to ratchet up the intensity against the run all of the time to reach his potential in the pros.

Draft projection: Second- to third-round pick.

Scout's take: "(Tankersley) is going to have a bunch of penalties in the pros. He's big and fast, but he's not tough and won't tackle anyone — it's a bad combination to me."

FS TEDRIC THOMPSON, #9 (Sr-4)
COLORADO ▶ GRADE: 5.68
Ht: 6-0 | Wt: 204 | 40: 4.56 | Arm: 31 1/2 | Hand: 9 5/8

History: First name is pronounced "tehdrick." Brother, Cedric, is a safety for the Vikings. Tedric prepped in California. As a true freshman in 2013, recorded 32 tackles, three pass breakups and zero interceptions in 12 games (three starts — two at strong safety, one at free safety). In '14, compiled 59-4-3 with three tackles for loss and one forced fumble in eight starts at SS before his season was cut short by a concussion against UCLA. Started all 13 games at SS in '15, and produced 80-9-3 with five tackles for loss. In '16, was CU's most outstanding defensive player after leading the nation in passes defended (25) by racking up 75-18-7 with three tackles for loss, including two INTs and four PBUs in

a win that sent the Buffs to the Pac-12 championship.

Strengths: Good size and athletic ability. Has fluid hips and very good field vision and anticipation to read the quarterback's eyes and adjust. Smooth in his pedal. Can cover the slot in man coverage. Plays fast and has a very good coverages instincts. Has 13 career interceptions and very good hands. Fluid catcher. Experienced, three-year starter.

Weaknesses: Not a strong, physical tackler and tends to shoot low and take some questionable backside angles to lasso ball carriers. Needs to do a better job wrapping up and securing tackles in space. Marginal 10-yard splits (1.64) indicate a lack of initial burst and acceleration. Has a low 32 1/2-inch vertical jump and is not an explosive athlete.

Future: A very rangy, athletic, interchangeable cover safety that plays more in the deep hole than he does in the box and created more ball production as a senior than any other defender in the country. Serviceable in run support and though he lacks elite range, athletic ability and top-end speed, he is very effective working deep to short and making plays.

Draft projection: Second- to third-round pick.

Scout's take: "Everyone talks about how good (Ohio State FS) Malik Hooker is, but I actually like Thompson just as much if not more. He has more experience and better instincts and makes a lot of plays on the ball."

RCB JACK TOCHO, #29 (Sr-4)
NORTH CAROLINA STATE ▶ GRADE: 5.19
Ht: 6-0 1/4 | Wt: 202 | 40: 4.52 | Arm: 31 5/8 | Hand: 9 3/8

History: Last name is pronounced "TOE-choe." Son of Kenyan immigrants. Defensive back-running back also ran track as a North Carolina prep. Played with a broken finger on his right hand as a true freshman in 2013 — played all 12 games, starting the final seven at left cornerback, and recorded 25 tackles, three pass breakups and two interceptions. Left the Syracuse contest with a shoulder injury. Started all 13 games at LCB in '14, and tallied 41-11-1. Was slowed by injuries and shared snaps with Mike Stevens in '15, as he managed 20-3-1 in 11 games (three starts at LCB). Bruised his right knee against Troy, and did not play against Eastern Kentucky. Sat out against Boston College (concussion). Started all 13 games at LCB in '16, and totaled 37-9-2 with two tackles for loss and one sack. Team captain has an accounting degree. Did not run shuttles at the Combine because of tightness.

Strengths: Bench-pressed 225 pounds 21 times at the Combine and has good functional strength. Good tackler. Carries receivers down the field and maintains good inside leverage and positioning. Fine route recognition to trail and mirror receivers. The game is important to him.

Weaknesses: Extremely stiff in his hips with mechanical movement and limited knee extension. Struggles to locate the ball in the air quickly. Lacks flexibility and stumbled and tripped during drills at the Combine. Labors to change direction and is easily challenged by any type of quick-cutting crossing routes.

Future: Well-built, strong, stiff-hipped, straight-line corner with enough strength and movement skill to function outside in a defense employing a lot of press coverage and would be at his best in short zones.

Draft projection: Late draftable pick.

Scout's take: "(Tocho) is tight as a drum. He's very stiff and cannot run. He doesn't play 4.52, and he panics when the ball is in the air."

SS DAMARIUS TRAVIS, #7 (Sr-5)

MINNESOTA ▶ GRADE: 5.24

Ht: 6-0 7/8 | Wt: 206 | 40: 4.64 | Arm: 31 3/4 | Hand: 9

History: Prepped in Florida, where he was once won a state championship with Packers CB Damarious Randall. As a true freshman in 2012, recorded eight tackles, zero pass breakups and zero interceptions with one-half for loss in 13 appearances, seeing primary action on special teams. Played all 13 games in '13, starting three at strong safety, and tallied 28-4-0. Started 7-of-13 games in '14 — five at SS, two at nickel — and contributed 61-5-2 with 3 1/2 tackles for loss and one forced fumble. Sprained his right ankle against Illinois. Had 10 tackles in the '15 season opener against TCU before suffering a season-ending torn left hamstring injury (granted medical hardship waiver). Was the Gophers' outstanding defensive player and leading tackler in '16 when he piled up 83-4-2 with five tackles for loss in 13 starts at SS. Graduated with a sports management degree. Opted not to run shuttles at the Combine.

Strengths: Solid size. Physical, knockback hitter. Will deliver some decleating hits (see Wisconsin). Craves contact and takes pride in delivering punishment. Will submarine lead blockers and stack up a hole. Fine zone awareness. Attacks the flats like a missile when threatened. Good football intelligence. Makes the secondary calls and gets the defense lined up. Solid personal and football character.

Weaknesses: Has small hands. Tight in the hips and has just adequate transitional quickness. Limited foot speed and deep range to play on the back half. Only four career interceptions. Is seldom asked to handle man coverage and

tends to shuffle more than pedal.

Future: Strong, high-cut, physical tackler with the football smarts and toughness to eventually push for a starting job as a strong safety and could readily compete as a core special teams contributor.

Draft projection: Fourth- to fifth-round pick.

RCB-SS MIKE TYSON, #5 (Sr-4)

CINCINNATI ▶ GRADE: 5.21

Ht: 6-11/8 | Wt: 204 | 40: 4.59 | Arm: 31 3/4 | Hand: 9 1/4

History: Has a son (Michael Jai). Norfolk, Va., native attended prep school at Hargrave Military Academy (Va.). Played nine games as a freshman in 2013, and was credited with 18 tackles, one pass breakup and two interceptions with one-half tackle for loss. Played all 13 games in '14, starting three at strong safety, and tallied 41-1-0 with one-half tackle for loss. Sat out the first two games of the '15 season while healing a right ankle injury, but chipped in 32-4-0 with two tackles for loss in 11 games played (four starts in a linebacker/nickel back role). Started 9-of-10 games played in '16, and totaled 46-5-5 with 4 1/2 tackles for loss. Sat out against Temple and BYU (ankle). Did not run shuttles at the Combine because of a right hamstring injury.

Strengths: Excellent size with natural movement skills for a big man. Highpoints the ball and plays it well in the air, with good body control to adjust. Makes athletic interceptions above his head and takes the ball away from receivers. Has safety experience and is still very willing in run support. Strong personal and football character and has matured a lot. Has a love of the game and is very competitive. Is tough and will battle through injuries.

Weaknesses: Not initially quick off spots. Only a one-year starter and never survived a full-season healthy. Registered 16.4% body fat at the Combine, among the highest of defensive backs and indicative of a lack of endurance. Durability has been an issue throughout his career. Can be stressed by elite speed vertically. Lacks ideal size and savvy for the safety position.

Future: A big, athletic nickel corner who plays faster than his timed speed and is at his best with simplified assignments where he could concentrate on locking down a receiver. Has the ability to fend for a job as a No. 5 or 6 corner and earn a job on special teams.

Draft projection: Late draftable pick.

Scout's take: "Tyson gets listed as a free safety, but he plays nickel for them. I projected him to cornerback. He struggles mentally too much to handle playing safety, but you can hide the mistakes at corner and simplify his

DEFENSIVE BACKS

job. I wanted to put him in the seventh (round) so we would talk about him but thought he was a free agent."

RCB **MARQUEZ WHITE**, #27 (Sr-4)

FLORIDA STATE ► GRADE: 5.23
Ht: 5-11 3/4 | Wt: 194 | 40: 4.64 | Arm: 32 1/8 | Hand: 10

History: Has a daughter (Alayla). Prepped in Alabama, where he also averaged 19 points and 10 rebounds on the hardwood. As a true freshman in 2013, recorded 12 tackles, zero pass breakups and one interception with one tackle for loss. Saw limited action in '14, and notched 3-0-0 in 12 appearances. Stepped into the lineup at the field corner in '15 when he logged 25-2-1 with two tackles for loss in 13 starts. Suffered a broken right hand in the spring of '16 (required surgery). In the fall, started all 13 games at FCB, and posted 25-4-2 with two tackles for loss. Team captain. Did not bench press at the Combine because of a right shoulder injury and missed the shuttles because of a headache.

Strengths: Has long arms, loose hips and quick feet. Has a 36-inch vertical jump and good leaping ability to highpoint the ball in the air. Good feet to shadow and mirror. Competes for the ball in jump ball situations.

Weaknesses: Pedals upright and plays too tall. Lacks bulk and playing strength and is a low, cut tackler. Has an underdeveloped frame that looks like it has not seen the weight room. Recorded 18.5% body fat at the Combine, the highest of any defensive back and indicative of a lack of endurance. Average ball production, with only six career pass breakups and four interceptions.

Future: Upright, high-hipped, developmental corner with a very passive playing temperament and will need to spend more time in the weight room and show more willingness defending the run to earn a roster spot.

Draft projection: Late draftable pick.

RCB-NCB-PR **Tre'DAVIOUS WHITE**, #18 (Sr-4)

LSU ► GRADE: 6.14
Ht: 5-11 1/4 | Wt: 192 | 40: 4.49 | Arm: 32 1/8 | Hand: 9 1/8

History: Name pronounced "true-Day-vee-us." Louisiana native starred as a cornerback, quarterback and kick returner. Highly recruited U.S. Army All-American and all-state basketball player. As a true freshman in 2013, played all 13 games, starting the final 11 at right cornerback, and recorded 55 tackles, seven pass breakups and two interceptions with 2 1/2 tackles for loss. Started all 13 games at RCB in '14, and produced 33-6-2 with three tackles for loss and one sack. Also returned 25 punts for 273 yards (10.9-yard average), including one score. Started all 11 games played at RCB in '15, and

had 44-7-0 with 1 1/2 tackles for loss, while returning punts 20-229-1 (11.5). Did not play against Western Kentucky (left MCL sprain). Started all 12 games in '16 — six at RCB, six at nickel — and totaled 35-14-2 with four tackles for loss and one-half sack. Also returned punts 24-186-1 (7.8). Was a finalist for the Thorpe and Senior CLASS Awards, and was recognized as a member of LSU's all-time Strength and Conditioning Team. Team captain wore revered jersey No. 18 the last two seasons, an honor bestowed upon the player who epitomizes what it means to be an LSU player on and off the field. Graduated with a sports administration degree.

Strengths: Very experienced, four-year starter in the Southeastern Conference. Uses his long arms well to re-route receivers. Does not back down from a challenge. Stays in phase in man coverage and has outstanding feet to shadow and mirror his man. Good route recognition, zone instincts and ball skills. Willing in run support. Outstanding personal and football character. So committed to the weight room that he will overtrain and needs to be told to rest. Very competitive and is always looking for ways to improve. Football smart and instinctive. Has the vision and run strength to be effective returning punts, with three career TDs.

Weaknesses: Thin-framed. Not a strong or physical tackler and uses too much finesse. Has a low 32-inch vertical jump and ordinary leaping ability. Recorded a 4.32-second 20-yard shuttle, indicative of limited lateral agility. Is not a ballhawk.

Future: Good-sized, high-cut, long-limbed, experienced press corner with the feet, hips and athletic ability to become a plug-and-play starter. Exits a program known for churning out quality starting NFL cornerbacks as much as any other in the country and comes doubly stamped by way of their esteemed #18 jersey as one of the most revered team leaders. Has the cover talent, strength of character and added punt-return ability to become a strong contributor immediately.

Draft projection: Late first-round pick.

Scout's take: "He is not flashy or twitchy. He is big, fast and dependable and returns punts, but he's not special (as a returner). He's so big that he can get hit and knocked back five yards and keep his feet and convert."

FS-LCB **MARCUS WILLIAMS**, #20 (Jr-3)

UTAH ► GRADE: 5.96
Ht: 6-0 5/8 | Wt: 202 | 40: 4.59 | Arm: 32 1/2 | Hand: 9 1/2

History: Receiver-safety from California, where he also played basketball and competed in track and field. Played free safety for the

Utes. As a true freshman in 2014, started 6-of-13 games, and contributed 59 tackles, zero pass breakups and one interception with one tackle for loss and two forced fumbles. Started all 13 games in '15, and produced 66-5-5 with two tackles for loss. Started all 11 games played in '16, and posted 64-3-5 with one tackle for loss and two forced fumbles. Did not play against UCLA and Washington (knee). Will be a 21-year-old rookie.

Strengths: Very smooth and fluid mover. Outstanding range — plays faster than his timed speed and closes fast to the sideline. Excellent hands and concentration (see Arizona). Smooth in his pedal. Quick to change direction and flip his hips. Good, wrap tackler. Plays the cutback very well. Takes good angles and plays the ball well in the air. Rare leaping ability, as displayed at the Combine with a 43 1/2-inch vertical jump, and uses it to climb over the top of receivers and pluck the ball out of the air (see Arizona State). Very football smart and lines up the secondary and sees the whole field.

Weaknesses: Needs to add some bulk for the safety position. Tied for recording the slowest 10-yard split (1.71 seconds) of any defensive back at the Combine, indicating he can be slow off spots at times. Is not a knockout hitter and will catch contact too much when approaching the strike point too upright and straight-legged, leaking yardage.

Future: A very athletic, instinctive, field-fast free safety with plug-and-play potential as a centerfielder. Finesse style, leaping ability and ball skills might even be more naturally suited for the cornerback position.

Draft projection: Top-50 pick.

Scout's take: "(Williams) is a really good player. He played at 195 but has a frame to be 210 easy. He is athletic like a cornerback. He's an okay tackler but not a big hitter. I really like his movement skills."

NCB HOWARD WILSON, #6 (Soph-3)

HOUSTON ▶ GRADE: 5.38
Ht: 6-0 5/8 | Wt: 184 | 40: 4.57 | Arm: 31 3/8 | Hand: 9 5/8

History: Lightly recruited Texas native. As a true freshman in 2014, recorded 48 tackles, three pass breakups and three interceptions with one tackle for loss in 13 games (three starts at nickel). In '15, was credited with 5-2-1 in three games before suffering a season-ending torn right ACL injury and being granted a medical redshirt. Returned to start all 13 games at cornerback in '16, posting 54-10-5 (TD) with 2 1/2 tackles for loss. Opted not to perform the bench-press test at the Combine.

Strengths: Good length with loose hips and thin ankles and is extremely smooth in and out of transition. Fluid mover. Efficient man cover skills to ride the hip pocket of receivers. Has exceptional lateral quickness and agility, as measured in the 20-yard short shuttle (3.94 seconds) and 3-cone drill (6.68) at the Combine. Outstanding ball skills and hands. Measured only 5.8% body fat at the Combine, among the lowest and indicative of exceptional conditioning and stamina. Skilled cut tackler.

Weaknesses: Extremely thin and lacks bulk and tackling strength. Missed 10 tackles in 2016 shooting low. Only a one-year starter and did not regularly match up against top competition. Needs to get stronger to match up against NFL outside receivers.

Future: A lean, lanky, quicker-than-fast, underdeveloped corner who showed intriguing athletic traits, instincts and ball skills to become a No. 3 or No. 4 corner and special teams contributor.

Instinctive football player ideally suited for a slot role in the pros but must prove he can stay healthy.

Draft projection: Third- to fourth-round pick.

RCB-FS QUINCY WILSON, #6 (Jr-3)

FLORIDA ▶ GRADE: 5.85
Ht: 6-1 1/2 | Wt: 211 | 40: 4.56 | Arm: 32 1/4 | Hand: 9 5/8

History: Father, Chad, played cornerback for the Miami Hurricanes (1992-94), and is a high school defensive coordinator. Florida native also ran track in high school. As a true freshman in 2014 (wore jersey No. 12), tallied 22 tackles, three pass breakups and one interception with one tackle for loss and one forced fumble in 12 games (two starts). Started 9-of-14 games in '15 — seven at CB, two at nickel — and chipped in 29-5-2. Underwent off-season surgery to repair a sports hernia. Started all 13 games in '16, and produced 33-6-3 (TD) with 3 1/2 tackles for loss and one sack.

Strengths: Exceptional size and length to match up with big receivers and smother them at the line. Has strong hands to re-route receivers at the line of scrimmage. Outstanding short-area quickness, as confirmed by 20-yard shuttle (4.02 seconds) at the Combine. Plays with good balance in his feet and has good body control. Strong, aggressive tackler. Good football intelligence. Fine route recognition. Outstanding hands. Caught the ball extremely well in Combine drills. Very confident and competitive. Team player. Brings energy and emotion to the field. Served as the jammer on the punt return team.

Weaknesses: Tends to rise in his pedal and lacks top-end speed to carry elite speed receiv-

DEFENSIVE BACKS

ers down the field. Needs to get stronger in the weight room. Struggles with off-man coverage, allowing separation against quick-cutting receivers.

Future: Exceptional-sized, tough, physical press corner with the length, football smarts and toughness to potentially convert to free safety. Confident and competitive and can contribute readily wherever he lines up.

Draft projection: Second- to third-round pick.

Scout's take: "Wilson is a prototypical Seattle Seahawks corner. He is stiff and can't play off (coverage). The further he carries (receivers) in coverage, the more they separate."

RCB AHKELLO WITHERSPOON, #23 (Sr-4)
COLORADO   ▶ GRADE: 5.27

Ht: 6-2 3/4 | Wt: 198 | 40: 4.49 | Arm: 33 | Hand: 9 7/8

History: Full name is James Ahkello Elec Witherspoon. Goes by second name pronounced "ah-kellow." Played soccer growing up before playing basketball and baseball until his senior year of high school when he tried football for the first time after growing about 7 inches in 16 months as a late bloomer. Played at Sacramento (Calif.) City College in 2013, and was credited with 21 tackles, seven pass breakups and three interceptions with a forced fumble in eight games. With the Buffs in '14, notched 12-2-0 in nine games (one start at right cornerback). Sat out the season opener (back), as well as two more games (coach's decision). Started 8-of-13 games at left corner in '15, and chipped in 36-3-2. In '16, led the nation in pass breakups — started 12-of-13 games at RCB, and tallied 23-22-1 with one forced fumble. Played through a shoulder injury in the Alamo Bowl against Oklahoma State.

Strengths: Unique size-speed ratio with outstanding arm length. Highpointed and caught the ball very well at the Combine. Rare leaping ability (40 1/2 inches) combined with the longest wingspan (79 3/8) of any cornerback in the draft creates a unique cover radius that helped contribute to leading the nation in pass breakups (22) in 2016. Unique recovery length and quickness. Has a lot of upside.

Weaknesses: Very lanky frame that needs to add some mass and strength to survive the rigors of the NFL. Liability in run support and will consistently be run at (see Michigan). Very leggy and is not smooth in his transition — could be too tall for the cornerback position. Could stand to refine his footwork and pedal technique (tends to rise and gather). Only had one interception as a senior and tackle production (22) was poor for a 12-game starter. Benefit-

ted from playing in a very talented secondary. Shoulder injury requires closer scrutiny.

Future: One of the most unique athletes in the draft, Witherspoon possesses the length, speed, leaping ability and ball skills to negate mismatches in the passing game and could neutralize big receivers in nickel situations. However, he must learn to play off blocks and support the run better if he is to earn a starting job in the pros.

Draft projection: Fourth- to fifth-round pick.

Scout's take: "(Witherspoon) is a height-weight-speed prospect who won't hit anyone. He plays very soft. How often have you seen a player with more (pass breakups) than tackles? I don't remember seeing it in 30 years in this business."

SS XAVIER WOODS, #7 (Sr-4)
LOUISIANA TECH   ▶ GRADE: 5.16

Ht: 5-11 1/8 | Wt: 197 | 40: 4.54 | Arm: 30 3/8 | Hand: 9 3/8

History: Louisiana native won a state championship, and chose the Ragin' Cajuns over offers from Stanford and Houston. Was used as a nickel and safety during his true freshman 2013 season (wore jersey No. 39) — recorded 61 tackles, two pass breakups and zero interceptions with three tackles for loss in 12 games (10 starts). Started all 40 games the next three seasons as a field safety — totaled 71-7-6 (two TD) with 3 1/2 tackles for loss, one sack, three forced fumbles and one blocked field goal attempt in '14; 56-3-3 with 7 1/2 tackles for loss and two forced fumbles in '15; and 89-6-5 with 6 1/2 tackles for loss, three sacks and one forced fumble in '16. Team captain. Had three defensive coordinators in four years. Graduated.

Strengths: Efficient in his pedal and is quick to jump routes. Aggressive run defender. Strikes hard and seeks to punish. Plays downhill. Very competitive. Example leader. Experienced four-year starter. Very intelligent and football smart. Film junkie. Superb football character. Good career interception production (14).

Weaknesses: Undersized for the safety position. Lacks man cover skills to match up with backs and tight ends and is used mostly in zone coverage. Takes some questionable angles in run support, and needs to be more consistent with his wild tackling technique. Lacks lower-body strength.

Future: Smart, aggressive, tough college field safety who would be best suited in the box in the pros. Is going to have to make a mark on special teams to earn a role.

Draft projection: Late draftable pick.

DEFENSIVE BACKS

SPECIALISTS

P TOBY BAKER, #37 (Sr-5)

ARKANSAS   ▶ GRADE: 5.09

Ht: 6-3 1/8 | Wt: 210 | 40: 5.00e | Arm: 31 5/8 | Hand: 9 1/4

History: Memphis prep quarterback also played basketball and soccer. Redshirted in 2012. Did not appear in any games in '13. Saw very limited action in two games in '14. In '15, punted 43 times for an average of 41.2 yards, including 23 downed inside the 20-yard line. Awarded a scholarship after the regular season. Punted 57-44.4 in '16 while pinning six inside the 10-yard line. Did not have a punt blocked the last two seasons. Graduated with a finance degree. Averaged a distance of 47.8 yards per punt at the Combine with a 1.48-second toe-to-toe time and 4.49 hang-time.

Future: Very good-sized, two-year starter with the leg strength and mental fortitude to earn a punting job. Needs to hasten his delivery. Kicks with precision and accuracy, though could improve working on the coffin corner. Could be drafted late.

Draft projection: Late draftable pick.

PK HARRISON BUTKER, #87 (Sr-4)

GEORGIA TECH   ▶ GRADE: 5.12

Ht: 6-3 7/8 | Wt: 199 | 40: 4.93 | Arm: 31 3/4 | Hand: 8 3/4

History: Georgia native also played soccer and basketball in high school. Started all 13 games as a true freshman in 2013 and led Georgia Tech in scoring after converting 10-of-14 field goals (71.4 percent) with a long of 49 and 53-of-54 extra point attempts. Also had 73 kickoffs for a 62.9-yard average and 30 touchbacks. Once again led team in scoring in '14 by making FGs 11-18-L53 (61.1) and 65-of-66 PATs. Also kicked off 87-63.3-52. Connected on FGs 7-11-L53 (63.6) and 44-of-44 PATs. Booted 61-64.2-41 on kickoffs. In '16, converted 15-17-52 (88.2) FGs and all 46 PATs. Kicked off 73-64.5-54. Graduated with a degree in industrial engineering. Averaged a Combine-best 73.6 yards on kickoffs with a 4.2-second hang time. Missed only one kick from the right hash 35 yards out of his 15 attempts from 20 through 40 yards.

Future: Rare-sized, experienced, four-year starter with the leg strength to drive the ball through the end zone on kickoffs. Smooth, two-step, right-footed placekicker with good accuracy. Works at his craft and should have a chance to earn a job after an impressive showing at the Combine.

Draft projection: Late draftable pick.

PK JAKE ELLIOTT, #46 (Sr-4)

MEMPHIS   ▶ GRADE: 5.14

Ht: 5-9 1/4 | Wt: 167 | 40: 4.73 | Arm: 29 | Hand: 9

History: Also played soccer and tennis as a West suburban Chicago prep. Started all 12 games as a true freshman in 2013 — made 16-of-18 field goals (88.9 percent), including a career-long 56-yarder. Kicked off 50 times for a 62.0-yard average with 21 touchbacks. In '14, started all 13 games, and converted FGs 21-32-L54 (65.6), while kicking off 87-64.0-51. Started all 13 games in '15 and made FGs 23-28-L53 (82.1), while kicking off 99-64.3-74. In '16, converted 21-26-L50 (80.8), while booting 94-63.7-64 on kickoffs. Never missed an extra point (202), and is third on the Memphis' all-time scoring list behind Stephen Gostkowski and DeAngelo Williams. Did miss a game-winning kick vs. Houston. Averaged 71.6 yards on kickoffs with a hang-time of 4.32 seconds and connected on 13-of-15 kicks from 20-to-40 yards at the Combine, missing one each from 30 and 40 yards out.

Future: Diminutive, four-year starter with excellent leg snap to drive the ball long range on kickoffs, with nearly 75 percent going through the end zone. Efficient, two-step, right-footed placekicker with mental toughness to bounce back from adversity.

Draft projection: Late draftable pick.

PK ZANE GONZALEZ, #5 (Sr-4)

ARIZONA STATE   ▶ GRADE: 5.28

Ht: 6-0 1/2 | Wt: 202 | 40: 4.91 | Arm: 29 1/2 | Hand: 9

History: Grew up playing soccer in Texas, where his football coach was former Rams long snapper Chris Massey. Tied the FBS record for most made field goals as a freshman in 2013 when he converted 25-of-30 field goals (83.3 percent) with a long of 44 and 63-of-65 extra point attempts. Kicked off 106 times for a 62.2-yard average and 39 touchbacks. Was the runner-up for the Lou Groza Award in '14, when he converted FGs 22-27-L49 (81.5) and 50-of-52 PATS. In '15, made FGs 26-34-L48 (76.5) and PATs 52-of-52, and had the highest touchback rate in the FBS with 88-64.56-66. Broke the

FBS record for most-career-made field goals in '16 when he hit 23-25-L59 (92.0) and 39-of-40 PATs, while kicking off 79-64.4-60. Gonzalez is the first kicker ever in FBS history to finish with 20+ made field goals in all four seasons. Averaged 71 yards with a hang-time of 4.02 seconds at the Combine and converted on 13-of-15 field goals, missing one each from 30 and 40 yards out. Should be the first kicker drafted, an immediate starter and on trajectory to become a steady 15-year pro. Averaged 71 yards with a hang-time of 4.02 seconds at the Combine and converted on 13-of-15 field goals, missing one each from 30 and 40 yards out.

Future: Extremely accurate, four-year starter with a weapon of a leg to connect from long range, connecting on 7-of-9 beyond 50 yards as a senior. Has a very swift, rapid swing and the ball pops off his foot. Generates excellent distance on kickoffs. Very disciplined and works at his craft. Could be drafted in the middle rounds and plugged in to stabilize a kicking job for the next 10-plus years. Should be the first kicker drafted, an instant starter and on trajectory to become a steady 10-plus year pro.

Draft projection: Third- or fourth-round pick.

LS COLIN HOLBA, #49 (Sr-5)

LOUISVILLE ▶ GRADE: 4.90
Ht: 6-4 1/4 | Wt: 248 | 40: 5.17 | Arm: 33 5/8 | Hand: 9 5/8

History: Graduated as valedictorian from the largest high school in Kentucky, where he also played baseball (did not play football as a senior). Walked on in 2012, but did not factor until his junior season. Started all 26 games 2015-16. Earned invitations to the Senior Bowl and Combine, where his snaps ranged from 0.76 to .82 seconds and averaged .79.

Future: Smart, exceptional-sized, long snapper with consistent snap times. Can be overly focused on his follow-thru and inconsistent with his location, yet snaps with excellent velocity and is a solid tackler in coverage.

Draft projection: Priority free agent.

P HAYDEN HUNT, #49 (Sr-5)

COLORADO STATE ▶ GRADE: 5.00
Ht: 5-11 3/4 | Wt: 212 | 40: 5.09 | Arm: 29 7/8 | Hand: 9 1/4

History: Long Beach (Calif.) Poly product also played baseball in high school. Redshirted in 2012. In '13, booted 68 punts for a 41.9-yard average, including 14 inside the 20-yard line. Was a Ray Guy Award finalist in '14 after punting 51-43.8 with 14 inside the 20. In '15, punted 52-46.0 with 24 inside the 20. In '16, totaled 56-44.1 with 26 inside the 20. For his career, was credited with 13 touchbacks, 57

fair catches and three blocked. Graduated with a degree in political science and minors in history and business. Averaged only 37.5 yards at the Combine with a 1.46 touch-to-toe time and 4.23 hang-time.

Future: Average-sized, three-step, right-footed punter who will need to hasten his approach to survive in the pros. Experienced, four-year starter with good directional control, though does not drive the ball and leg strength has room to improve.

Draft projection: Priority free agent.

P CAMERON JOHNSTON, #95 (Sr-4)

OHIO STATE ▶ GRADE: 5.07
Ht: 5-11 | Wt: 194 | 40: 4.89 | Arm: 31 | Hand: 9

History: Former Australian Rules Football player. As a true freshman in 2013, punted 49 times for a 44.0-yard average, including 31 pinned inside the 20-yard line. Totaled 48-45.1 in '14, including 26 inside the 20. In '15, booted 58-43.9 with 26 inside the 20. Punted 56-46.7 with 26 inside the 20 in '16. Averaged 46.8 yards per punt at the Combine with a 1.43-second average touch-to-toe times and a Combine-best 5.04-second average hang-time.

Future: Right-footed, experienced, four-year starter that varies between using a running, Australian-style, four-step approach and traditional, three-step, straight-ahead approach. Also is able to shorten his approach to two steps when needed. Outstanding hang-time and varied approach for any situation.

Draft projection: Priority free agent.

LS BRADLEY NORTHNAGEL, #48 (Sr-5)

CALIFORNIA ▶ GRADE: 4.87
Ht: 6-2 3/8 | Wt: 243 | 40: 5.29 | Arm: 32 1/2 | Hand: 10

History: California native also played basketball and baseball in high school. Joined Cal as a walk-on in 2012, and did not take over snapping duties until his junior season. Started all 25 games 2015-16. Graduated with a bachelor's degree in Social Welfare. Averaged between .76 and .83 seconds on long snaps at the Combine with an average of .79 seconds.

Future: Very-good sized, two-year starting long snapper has average speed and strength (11 reps) to factor in punt coverage. Could receive late looks in the draft and earn a job.

Draft projection: Priority free agent.

P AUSTIN REHKOW, #5 (Sr-4)

IDAHO ▶ GRADE: 5.10
Ht: 6-2 7/8 | Wt: 214 | 40: 4.90e | Arm: 31 7/8 | Hand: 9 7/8

History: Punted and kicked as a prep in Washington, where he made a 67-yard field

SPECIALISTS

goal. As a true freshman in 2013, led the NCAA in punt average —recorded 75 punts for a 47.8-yard average, including 24 inside the 20-yard line. Was a Ray Guy Award finalist for the second straight year in '14 when he matched his freshman average with 44-47.8, including 17 inside the 20. Kicked 49-45.7 in '15 with 14 pinned inside the 20, while having two punts blocked. Totaled 56-41.6, including 26 inside the 20 in '16. For his career, had 16 touchbacks, 58 fair catches and three blocked. Did it all for the Vandals — converted 70-of-92 field goal attempts (76.1 percent) with a career-long of 50 yards; made 135-of-140 extra points; booted 254 kickoffs for a 60.5-yard average, including 96 touchbacks and 14 out of bounds; and served as the team's primary holder. Averaged 63 yards on kickoffs at the Combine with hang-time of 4.2 seconds. Also averaged 43.7 yards per punt at the Combine with a Combine-best 1.37 average touch-to-toe times and 4.5-second average hang-time.

Future: Outstanding-sized, experienced, four-year starter who handled field goals, kickoffs and punts, a true jack of all trades, though best chance will come as a punter where he has shown proficiency pinning opponents. A right-footed, three-step punter with a quick get-off and outstanding hang-time.

Draft projection: Late draftable pick.

P RIGOBERTO SANCHEZ, #43 (Sr-5)

HAWAII   ▶ GRADE: 4.95
Ht: 6-0e | Wt: 185e | 40: 5.15e | Arm: NA | Hand: NA

History: Also played soccer as a California prep. Spent two years at Butte Junior College. In 2012, made 11-of-19 field goal attempts (57.9 percent) with a long of 54, as well as 43-of-44 extra points. In '13, punted 50 times for a 38.5-yard average, including 20 inside the 20-yard line, 12 fair catches and three touchbacks. Also kicked FGs 11-16-L50 (68.8) and PATs 76-of-77. Redshirted at Hawaii in '14. Started 12 games in '15 (missed the Louisiana-Monroe game for a family funeral) — totaled 74-45.1 punting, including 28 inside the 20; 8-11-L50 (72.7) FGs; 49-of-50 PATs; and 22-64.2 kickoffs, including 14 touchbacks. In '16, totaled 67-44.6 punting with 20 inside the 20; 12-12-L55 (100.0) FGs; 49-of-50 PATs; and 71-61.0 kickoffs, including 25 touchbacks. Did not attend the Combine.

Future: Two-year Hawaii starter who handled punts, kickoffs and extra points. Two-step, right-footed punter with a 4.4-second hang-time. A jack of all trades most optimally suited to punt or kickoff and could serve as an emergency placekicker.

Draft projection: Priority free agent.

PK CONRAD UKROPINA, #34 (Sr-5)

STANFORD   ▶ GRADE: 4.95
Ht: 5-11 7/8 | Wt: 190 | 40: 4.92 | Arm: 31 3/8 | Hand: 9 1/8

History: Pronounced "you-crow-pee-nuh." California native joined the Cardinal as a walk-on. Redshirted in 2012. Primarily a kickoff specialist in '13, booted 42 kickoffs for a 60.5-yard average, including four touchbacks. Also made 2-of-4 field goals (50.0 percent) with a long 31 yards, as well as 12-of-13 extra point attempts. Was a non-factor in '14. Earned a scholarship during the '15 season when he kicked field goals 18-20-L52 (90.0), PATs 67-of-67 and kickoffs 31-60.7 (seven touchbacks). Also kicked a 45-yard, game-winner against Notre Dame. In '16, totaled 22-27-L52 (81.5) on FGs and 34-of-34 on PATs (did not handle kickoffs). Working on master's degree in communication (media studies). Averaged 65.8 yards on kickoffs at the Combine with a hang-time of 4.17 seconds. Connected on all 15 field goals between 20 and 40 yards.

Future: Average-sized, two-year-starting, right-footed placekicker with very good accuracy up to 50 yards, using a very consistent approach with a loose follow-thru. Smart, tough and has shown he can produce in the clutch.

Draft projection: Priority free agent.

P-KO JUSTIN VOGEL, #16 (Sr-5)

MIAMI (FLA.)   ▶ GRADE: 5.12
Ht: 6-4 1/2 | Wt: 219 | 40: 4.71 | Arm: 32 1/2 | Hand: 9

History: Father, Paul, starred at linebacker at South Carolina. Justin, a Florida native, began his college career at University of Florida, where he did not see the field 2012-13. Transferred to Miami in '14 when he punted 52 times for a 42.8-yard average with 21 inside the 20-yard line. In '15, punted 67-42.5 with 21 inside the 20. In '16, totaled 64-43.8 with 25 inside the 20. Averaged 63 yards on kickoffs at the Combine with a hang-time of 3.95 seconds. Also averaged a Combine-best 49.8 yards with a 1.45-second touch-to-toe time and 4.63-second hang-time.

Future: Excellent-sized, three-year-starting, right-footed, two-step punter with inconsistent directional placement. Also serves as the holder on field goals and handles kickoffs, though lacks ideal length strength to boom it. Has an explosive swing, and the ball explodes off his foot.

Draft projection: Late draftable pick.

SPECIALISTS

PLAYER RANKINGS

GRADE SCALE

9.0 — A once-in-a-generation player (e.g. Bo Jackson, Deion Sanders).

8.00-8.99 — Perennial All-Pro (e.g. Anthony Munoz).

7.00-7.99 — Eventual All-Pro.

6.50-6.99 — Sure-fire first-rounder should make immediate impact.

6.00-6.49 — Likely first-rounder capable of starting readily.

5.60-5.99 — Likely second-rounder with immediate starter potential.

5.40-5.59 — Likely third-rounder minimally with sub-starter potential.

5.21-5.39 — Should make a roster and contribute on special teams

5.11-5.20 — Potential late-rounder with fair chance to earn a roster spot.

4.75-5.10 — Late draftable or priority free agent capable of battling for a roster spot.

4.00-4.75 — Solid free agent capable of being invited to an NFL training camp.

ALERT SYMBOLS

Soph-3 — Player is a third-year sophomore.

Jr-3 — Player is a true, third-year junior.

Jr-4 — Player is a redshirt, fourth-year junior.

QB — Can also play quarterback or the position that is listed, such as RS for return specialist.

Ch. — Character (i.e. history of arrests, team suspensions or off-field problems) can affect draft status.

X — Has a current injury situation that could affect camp status.

XX — Past or present durability concerns could affect draft status.

XXX — Serious injury concern.

About the player rankings: Players are ranked according to their grades, not necessarily in the order they will be drafted. Factors such as a drafting team's needs and the abundance or scarcity of available talent at a given position can cause a player to be drafted higher or lower than his grade would indicate. All grades take into account workouts up to and including the Indianapolis Scouting Combine. Post-Combine workouts were seldom factored except in extreme cases (injury).

QUARTERBACKS

RK NAME	SCHOOL	GRADE	NOTES
1. Deshaun Watson	Clemson	6.18	Jr-3
2. Mitchell Trubisky	North Carolina	6.12	Jr-4
3. Patrick Mahomes	Texas Tech	5.98	Jr-3
4. DeShone Kizer	Notre Dame	5.62	Soph-3
5. Davis Webb	California	5.42	
6. Josh Dobbs	Tennessee	5.38	
7. Nathan Peterman	Pittsburgh	5.36	
8. C.J. Beathard	Iowa	5.29	
9. Brad Kaaya	Miami (Fla.)	5.27	Jr-3
10. Trevor Knight	Texas A&M	5.21	
11. Alek Torgerson	Penn	5.19	
12. Jerod Evans	Virginia Tech	5.18	Jr-4
13. Chad Kelly	Mississippi	5.10	X, Ch.
14. Mitch Leidner	Minnesota	5.09	
15. Cooper Rush	Central Michigan	5.07	
16. Wes Lunt	Illinois	5.06	X
17. Seth Russell	Baylor	5.04	X
18. Brady Gustafson	Montana	4.97	
19. Antonio Pipkin	Tiffin (Ohio)	4.96	
20. Sefo Liufau	Colorado	4.94	
21. Nick Mullens	Southern Mississippi	4.92	
22. Zach Terrell	Western Michigan	4.90	
23. Gunner Kiel	Cincinnati	4.85	
24. Bart Houston	Wisconsin	4.80	
25. Taysom Hill	BYU	4.75	
26. Tommy Armstrong Jr.	Nebraska	4.75	
27. Garrett Fugate	Central Missouri State	4.60	
28. P.J. Walker	Temple	4.50	
29. Philip Nelson	East Carolina	4.50	
30. Greyson Lambert	Georgia	4.50	
31. Sean Maguire	Florida State	4.50	
32. Drew Hare	Northern Illinois	4.40	
33. Skyler Howard	West Virginia	4.35	
34. Steven Cluley	William & Mary (Va.)	4.30	
35. Grant Rohach	Buffalo	4.30	
36. Jack Nelson	Winona State (Minn.)	4.25	
37. Luke Papilion	Sioux Falls (S.D.)	4.25	

38. Drew Bauer	Minnesota-Duluth	4.25	
39. Patrick Towles	Boston College	4.25	
40. Jordan West	Eastern Washington	4.25	
41. Dakota Prukop	Oregon	4.20	

FULLBACKS

RK NAME	SCHOOL	GRADE	NOTES
1. Freddie Stevenson	Florida State	5.16	
2. Sam Rogers	Virginia Tech	5.12	
3. Shane Smith	San Jose State	5.09	
4. Darrin Laufasa	UTEP	5.07	RB
5. Marquez Williams	Miami (Fla.)	5.05	
6. Alex Armah	West Georgia	5.02	DE
7. Algernon Brown	BYU	4.97	
8. Tyler McCloskey	Houston	4.85	
9. Joe Bacci	Central Michigan	4.75	
10. John Robinson-Woodgett	Massachusetts	4.60	
11. Emmanuel Holder	Towson	4.50	
12. Ricky Ortiz	Oregon State	4.50	
13. Dreon Johnson	Towson	4.40	
14. Bobby Wolford	Boston College	4.30	

RUNNING BACKS

RK NAME	SCHOOL	GRADE	NOTES
1. Leonard Fournette	LSU	7.70	Jr-3
2. Christian McCaffrey	Stanford	6.33	Jr-3, WR, RS
3. Dalvin Cook	Florida State	6.06	Jr-3, Ch.
4. Curtis Samuel	Ohio State	5.92	Jr-3, WR, RS
5. Samaje Perine	Oklahoma	5.64	Jr-3
6. Alvin Kamara	Tennessee	5.48	Jr-4, PR
7. Joe Mixon	Oklahoma	5.44	Soph-3, KR, Ch.
8. D'Onte Foreman	Texas	5.42	Jr-3
9. Donnel Pumphrey	San Diego State	5.37	
10. James Conner	Pittsburgh	5.35	Jr-4, X
11. Matt Dayes	North Carolina State	5.33	
12. Corey Clement	Wisconsin	5.32	X
13. Elijah McGuire	Louisiana-Lafayette	5.30	X, RS
15. Kareem Hunt	Toledo	5.29	
14. Wayne Gallman	Clemson	5.28	Jr-4
16. Jeremy McNicholas	Boise State	5.27	Jr-3
17. T.J. Logan	North Carolina	5.25	KR
18. De'Veon Smith	Michigan	5.24	
19. Marlon Mack	South Florida	5.24	Jr-3
20. Brian Hill	Wyoming	5.23	Jr-3
21. Jamaal Williams	BYU	5.22	
22. Dare Ogunbowale	Wisconsin	5.21	
23. Aaron Jones	UTEP	5.21	Jr-3
24. Tarik Cohen	North Carolina A&T St.	5.21	RS
25. Elijah Hood	North Carolina	5.17	Jr-3
26. Joe Williams	Utah	5.15	
27. De'Angelo Henderson	Coastal Carolina	5.13	
28. Boom Williams	Kentucky	5.12	Jr-3, KR
29. Chris Carson	Oklahoma State	5.12	
30. LeShun Daniels	Iowa	5.10	
31. Khalfani Muhammad	California	5.09	RS
32. Jahad Thomas	Temple	5.08	RS
33. Justin Davis	USC	5.07	KR
34. Devine Redding	Indiana	5.06	Jr-3
35. Rushel Shell	West Virginia	4.94	
36. Tion Green	Cincinnati	4.92	
37. Mario Pender	Florida State	4.87	
38. Tarean Folston	Notre Dame	4.80	Jr-4
39. De'Shawn Jones	Campbell (N.C.)	4.80	
40. Taquan Mizzell	Virginia	4.80	
41. Brandon Radcliff	Louisville	4.80	
42. William Stanback	Virginia Union	4.80	
43. Akeem Judd	Mississippi	4.75	
44. Devante Mays	Utah State	4.75	
45. Leon Allen	Western Kentucky	4.75	
46. I'Tavius Mathers	Middle Tennessee St.	4.70	
47. Kalif Phillips	UNC Charlotte	4.70	
48. Shock Linwood	Baylor	4.70	
49. Joseph Yearby	Miami (Fla.)	4.65	Jr-3
50. Joel Bouagnon	Northern Illinois	4.60	
51. Darius Victor	Towson	4.60	
52. Anthony Wales	Western Kentucky	4.60	
53. Terrell Newby	Nebraska	4.50	
54. Jovon Robinson	ex-Auburn	4.50	
55. Jody Webb	Youngstown	4.45	RS
55. Jordan Johnson	Buffalo	4.40	
56. Lenard Tillery	Southern A&M	4.40	
57. Kade Harrington	Lamar (Tex.)	4.40	
58. Jamal Towns	Illinois State	4.35	
59. Aaron Bailey	Northern Iowa	4.30	QB
60. Jarveon Williams	UTSA	4.30	
61. Marcus Cox	Appalachian State	4.30	
62. Jela Duncan	Duke	4.30	
63. Malik Brown	Southern Utah	4.30	
64. Kody Walker	Arkansas	4.30	
65. Barry Sanders	Oklahoma State	4.30	
66. Tyvis Smith	Northern Iowa	4.30	

WIDE RECEIVERS

RK NAME	SCHOOL	GRADE	NOTES
1. John Ross	Washington	6.34	X, Jr-4, RS
2. Mike Williams	Clemson	6.11	Jr-4
3. JuJu Smith-Schuster	USC	5.97	Jr-3
4. Corey Davis	Western Michigan	5.84	X
5. Chris Godwin	Penn State	5.68	Jr-3
6. Zay Jones	East Carolina	5.63	
7. ArDarius Stewart	Alabama	5.59	Jr-4
8. Cooper Kupp	Eastern Washington	5.48	PR
9. KD Cannon	Baylor	5.45	Jr-3
10. Josh Reynolds	Texas A&M	5.44	
11. Malachi Dupre	LSU	5.42	Jr-3
12. Amara Darboh	Michigan	5.41	
13. Dede Westbrook	Oklahoma	5.40	Ch.
14. Taywan Taylor	Western Kentucky	5.39	
15. Bug Howard	North Carolina	5.38	
16. Jehu Chesson	Michigan	5.37	KR
17. Josh Malone	Tennessee	5.36	Jr-3
18. Mack Hollins	North Carolina	5.34	X
19. Kenny Golladay	Northern Illinois	5.33	
20. Carlos Henderson	Louisiana Tech	5.32	Jr-4, KR
21. Isaiah Ford	Virginia Tech	5.31	Jr-3
22. Isaiah McKenzie	Georgia	5.31	Jr-3, RS
23. Robert Davis	Georgia State	5.30	
24. Shelton Gibson	West Virginia	5.29	Jr-4, KR
25. Chad Hansen	California	5.29	Jr-4
27. Ryan Switzer	North Carolina	5.28	PR
26. Amba Etta-Tawo	Syracuse	5.27	
28. Zach Pascal	Old Dominion (Va.)	5.26	KR
29. Quincy Adeboyejo	Mississippi	5.25	
30. Jamari Staples	Louisville	5.24	
31. Fred Ross	Mississippi State	5.23	X, PR
32. Stacy Coley	Miami (Fla.)	5.22	RS
33. Keevan Lucas	Tulsa	5.22	Jr-4
34. Travin Dural	LSU	5.21	
35. Artavis Scott	Clemson	5.20	Jr-3, KR
36. Trent Taylor	Louisiana Tech	5.19	PR
37. Krishawn Hogan	Marian (Ind.)	5.18	
38. Jalen Robinette	Air Force	5.13	
39. Travis Rudolph	Florida State	5.13	Jr-3
40. Bobo Wilson	Florida State	5.12	PR

RK	NAME	SCHOOL	GRADE	NOTES
41.	Austin Carr	Northwestern	5.09	
42.	Noah Brown	Ohio State	5.08	H-B
43.	Rodney Adams	South Florida	5.08	KR
44.	Keon Hatcher	Arkansas	5.07	
45.	Noel Thomas	Connecticut	5.07	
46.	Darreus Rogers	USC	5.05	
47.	Speedy Noil	Texas A&M	5.05	Jr-3, RS, Ch.
48.	Victor Bolden	Oregon State	5.04	RS
49.	James Quick	Louisville	5.03	Ch., RS
50.	Kendrick Bourne	Eastern Washington	5.03	
51.	Kermit Whitfield	Florida State	5.02	KR
52.	Gabe Marks	Washington State	5.01	X
53.	Ishmael Zamora	Baylor	5.01	Soph-3, Ch., Age
54.	Greg Ward	Houston	5.01	QB
55.	Damore'Ea Stringfellow	Mississippi	5.00	Jr-4, Ch.
55.	Dontre Wilson	Ohio State	4.99	X, RS
56.	Drew Morgan	Arkansas	4.99	
57.	Jerome Lane	Akron	4.97	Jr-4, H-B
58.	Domonique Young	Purdue	4.96	X
59.	Michael Rector	Stanford	4.90	
60.	Michael Clark	Marshall	4.90	Jr-4
61.	R.J. Shelton	Michigan State	4.85	RS
62.	Jordan Westerkamp	Nebraska	4.85	X
63.	River Cracraft	Washington State	4.85	X
64.	Thomas Sperbeck	Boise State	4.85	
65.	DeAngelo Yancey	Purdue	4.85	
66.	Chad Williams	Grambling State	4.85	
67.	Daikiel Shorts	West Virginia	4.85	
68.	Deon-Tay McManus	Marshall	4.80	Jr-4
69.	Jhajuan Seales	Oklahoma State	4.80	
70.	David Moore	East Central (Okla.)	4.80	
71.	Tim Patrick	Utah	4.80	
72.	Tim White	Arizona State	4.80	
73.	Kevonn Mabon	Ball State	4.77	
74.	Derrick Griffin	Texas Southern	4.75	Jr-4, TE
75.	Corey Robinson	Notre Dame	4.75	X
76.	Janarion Grant	Rutgers	4.75	RS
77.	Brian Brown	Richmond (Va.)	4.70	
78.	Karel Hamilton	Samford (Ala.)	4.70	
79.	Dominique Reed	Arkansas	4.70	
80.	Alonzo Moore	Nebraska	4.70	X
81.	JoJo Natson	Akron	4.65	
82.	Rokeem Williams	Miami (Ohio)	4.65	
83.	Kenneth Walker	UCLA	4.65	RS
84.	Dan Arnold	Wisconsin-Platteville	4.65	
85.	Trey Griffey	Arizona	4.60	
86.	Deante Burton	Kansas State	4.60	
87.	Brandon Reilly	Nebraska	4.60	
88.	Rob Wheelwright	Wisconsin	4.60	
89.	Tanner Gentry	Wyoming	4.60	
90.	Nate Cole	Cincinnati	4.55	
91.	Joey Augustin	Charleston (W.V.)	4.55	
92.	Justin Hardee	Illinois	4.50	
93.	Robert Tonyan	Indiana State	4.50	
94.	Corey Smith	Ohio State	4.50	
95.	Dwayne Stanford	Oregon	4.50	X
96.	Teriyon Gipson	New Mexico	4.50	
97.	Jamir Tillman	Navy	4.50	
98.	Cory Butler-Byrd	Utah	4.45	
99.	Lance Lenoir	Western Illinois	4.45	

TIGHT ENDS

RK	NAME	SCHOOL	GRADE	NOTES
1.	O.J. Howard	Alabama	6.21	
2.	David Njoku	Miami (Fla.)	6.16	Soph-3
3.	Evan Engram	Mississippi	6.04	WR
4.	Gerald Everett	South Alabama	5.58	H-B
5.	Jordan Leggett	Clemson	5.56	
6.	Bucky Hodges	Virginia Tech	5.47	Jr-4
7.	Jake Butt	Michigan	5.40	X
8.	Jeremy Sprinkle	Arkansas	5.38	
9.	Adam Shaheen	Ashland	5.36	Jr-4
10.	Jonnu Smith	Florida International	5.33	H-B
11.	George Kittle	Iowa	5.28	X, H-B
12.	Cole Hikutini	Louisville	5.23	H-B
13.	Michael Roberts	Toledo	5.22	
14.	Cethan Carter	Nebraska	5.21	H-B
15.	Eric Saubert	Drake	5.19	H-B
16.	Darrell Daniels	Washington	5.17	WR
17.	Billy Brown	Shepherd (W.V.)	5.16	WR
18.	Scott Orndoff	Pittsburgh	5.12	
19.	Ricky Seals-Jones	Texas A&M	5.09	Jr-4, WR
20.	Hayden Plinke	UTEP	5.04	X, Ch.
21.	Pharaoh Brown	Oregon	5.02	Ch.
22.	Josiah Price	Michigan State	4.95	
23.	Evan Baylis	Oregon	4.90	
24.	Jacob Hollister	Wyoming	4.90	
25.	Blake Jarwin	Oklahoma State	4.85	
26.	James Summers	East Carolina	4.85	H-B, RB
27.	Sean Culkin	Missouri	4.80	
28.	Anthony Auclair	Laval (Can.)	4.80	
29.	Keith Towbridge	Louisville	4.75	
30.	Tyrone Swoopes	Texas	4.75	QB
31.	Mason Schreck	Buffalo	4.75	
32.	Nate Iese	UCLA	4.75	
33.	DJ Dowdy	Cincinnati	4.70	
34.	Taylor McNamara	USC	4.70	
35.	Anthony Firkser	Harvard	4.70	H-B
36.	Colin Jeter	LSU	4.65	
37.	Phazahn Odom	Fordham	4.60	X
38.	Sam Cotton	Nebraska	4.60	
39.	Anthony Kukwa	Lake Erie (Ohio)	4.55	LS
40.	Natron Brooks	Mississippi Valley State	4.55	
41.	DeSean Smith	LSU	4.50	
42.	Mike Estes	Gardner-Webb (N.C.)	4.50	
43.	Andrew Price	UNLV	4.50	
44.	Connor Cella	Rice	4.50	
45.	Josiah Thropay	Azusa Pacific	4.45	
46.	Erich Schneider	Duke	4.40	
47.	Caldon Bloom	Central Florida	4.40	
48.	Keith Rucker	Georgia State	4.40	H-B
49.	Johnny Mundt	Oregon	4.35	
50.	Jordan Powell	New Hampshire	4.35	
51.	Terry Pettis	Middle Tennessee St.	4.35	WR
52.	Ryan Owens	Wagner (N.Y.)	4.35	H-B
53.	Caleb Smith	Oregon State	4.30	

CENTERS

RK	NAME	SCHOOL	GRADE	NOTES
1.	Pat Elflein	Ohio State	5.76	OG
2.	Ethan Pocic	LSU	5.67	OT, OG
3.	Tyler Orlosky	West Virginia	5.36	
4.	Jon Toth	Kentucky	5.29	
5.	Kyle Fuller	Baylor	5.23	OG
6.	Chase Roullier	Wyoming	5.22	
7.	J.J. Dielman	Utah	5.21	X, OG, OT
8.	Erik Austell	Charleston Southern	5.16	OT, OG
9.	Daniel Brunskill	San Diego State	5.09	OT
10.	Dan Voltz	Wisconsin	4.85	X
11.	Anthony McMeans	New Mexico State	4.80	
12.	Cameron Tom	Southern Mississippi	4.80	
13.	Freddie Burden	Georgia Tech	4.75	X

RK	NAME	SCHOOL	GRADE	NOTES
14.	Cam Keizur	Portland State	4.70	OG
15.	Gavin Andrews	Oregon State	4.65	OT
16.	Casey Dunn	Jacksonville State (Ala.)	4.65	
17.	Brandon Kublanow	Georgia	4.60	OG
18.	Deyshawn Bond	Cincinnati	4.50	
19.	Bret Treadway	Lamar (Tex.)	4.50	X, OG
20.	Parker Collins	Appalachian State	4.50	OG
21.	Lucas Crowley	North Carolina	4.50	
22.	Andrew Lewis	Virginia Military Institute	4.45	OT, TE
23.	Jay Guillermo	Clemson	4.45	
24.	Jamaal Clayborn	Mississippi State	4.40	
25.	Austin Stephens	Utah State	4.35	

OFFENSIVE GUARDS

RK	NAME	SCHOOL	GRADE	NOTES
1.	Forrest Lamp	Western Kentucky	5.81	OT, C
2.	Dan Feeney	Indiana	5.68	X, OT, C
3.	Dorian Johnson	Pittsburgh	5.65	OT
4.	Isaac Asiata	Utah	5.52	
5.	Taylor Moton	Western Michigan	5.48	OT
6.	Nico Siragusa	San Diego State	5.42	OG
7.	Danny Isidora	Miami (Fla.)	5.37	
8.	Jordan Morgan	Kutztown (Pa.)	5.35	OT
9.	Jessamen Dunker	Tennessee State	5.32	OT, Ch.
10.	Cameron Lee	Illinois State	5.26	OT
11.	Jermaine Eluemunor	Texas A&M	5.24	OT
12.	Damien Mama	USC	5.28	Jr-3
13.	Collin Buchanan	Miami (Ohio)	5.17	OT
14.	Ben Braden	Michigan	5.14	
15.	Sean Harlow	Oregon State	5.12	X, OT, C
16.	Nate Theaker	Wayne State (Mich.)	5.11	X, OT
17.	Corey Levin	Tenn.-Chattanooga	5.10	
18.	Ethan Cooper	Indiana (Pa.)	5.01	OT
19.	Kyle Kalis	Michigan	4.99	X
20.	Skyler Phillips	Idaho State	4.90	
21.	Levon Myers	Northern Illinois	4.90	OT
22.	Jake Eldrenkamp	Washington	4.85	
23.	Adam Pankey	West Virginia	4.75	OT
24.	Kareem Are	Florida State	4.75	
25.	Kent Perkins	Texas	4.75	OT
26.	Johnny Caspers	Stanford	4.70	
27.	Richard Levy	Connecticut	4.70	
28.	Zackary Johnson	North Dakota State	4.65	
29.	Joshua Boutte	LSU	4.60	
30.	Anton Wahrby	Wofford (S.C.)	4.60	OT
31.	Jordan Roos	Purdue	4.55	
32.	Evan Goodman	Arizona State	4.55	OT
33.	Travis Averill	Boise State	4.55	
34.	Sam Ekwonike	Coastal Carolina	4.50	
35.	Geoff Gray	Manitoba (Can.)	4.50	
36.	Greg Pyke	Georgia	4.50	OT
37.	Miguel Machado	Michigan State	4.45	OT
38.	Cameron Hunt	Oregon	4.45	
39.	Jake Simonich	Utah State	4.40	
40.	Leo Koloamatangi	Hawaii	4.40	C
41.	Tyler Catalina	Georgia	4.40	
42.	Ryan Melton	Texas State	4.30	OT
43.	Maurquice Shakir	Middle Tennessee St.	4.30	OT
44.	Kyle Avaloy	Illinois State	4.30	
45.	Alex Kozan	Auburn	4.30	
46.	Chris Borrayo	California	4.25	
47.	Chris Bordelon	Nicholls State (La.)	4.25	OT
48.	Caleb Peterson	North Carolina	4.25	
49.	Elijah Wilkinson	Massachusetts	4.25	OT
50.	Connor Bozick	Delaware	4.25	OT
51.	Jacob Henry	Nevada	4.25	X, OT

OFFENSIVE TACKLES

RK	NAME	SCHOOL	GRADE	NOTES
1.	Cam Robinson	Alabama	6.35	Jr-3
2.	Ryan Ramczyk	Wisconsin	6.26	Jr-4, OG
3.	Garett Bolles	Utah	5.74	Jr-3
4.	Dion Dawkins	Temple	5.62	OG
5.	Zach Banner	USC	5.47	
6.	David Sharpe	Florida	5.46	Jr-3
7.	Julien Davenport	Bucknell	5.34	
8.	Antonio Garcia	Troy	5.31	
9.	Adam Bisnowaty	Pittsburgh	5.27	OG
10.	Chad Wheeler	USC	5.26	X, Ch.
11.	Conor McDermott	UCLA	5.25	
12.	Aviante Collins	TCU	5.25	
13.	Avery Gennesy	Texas A&M	5.24	
14.	Justin Senior	Mississippi State	5.23	
15.	Roderick Johnson	Florida State	5.20	Jr-3
16.	Cole Croston	Iowa	5.17	
17.	Jerry Ugokwe	William & Mary (Va.)	5.17	
18.	Sam Tevi	Utah	5.12	
19.	Javarius Leamon	South Carolina State	5.10	
20.	Will Holden	Vanderbilt	5.01	
21.	Dan Skipper	Arkansas	4.97	
22.	Landon Lechler	North Dakota State	4.95	
23.	Dieugot Joseph	Florida International	4.95	
24.	Jylan Ware	Alabama State	4.90	
25.	Dimitric Camiel	Indiana	4.90	X
26.	Jonathan McLaughlin	Virginia Tech	4.85	
27.	Storm Norton	Toledo	4.85	
28.	Erik Magnuson	Michigan	4.85	
29.	Tyshon Henderson	Clark-Atlanta	4.80	
30.	Robert Leff	Auburn	4.80	
31.	Jonah Pirsig	Minnesota	4.75	
32.	Peter Bateman	Minnesota-Duluth	4.65	
33.	Michael Dunn	Maryland	4.60	
34.	Chauncey Briggs	SMU	4.55	
35.	Taylor Gadbois	Southeastern Louisiana	4.55	
36.	Eric Smith	Virginia	4.50	
37.	Jon Heck	North Carolina	4.50	
38.	Brad Seaton	Villanova	4.45	
39.	Victor Salako	Oklahoma State	4.45	
40.	Andreas Knappe	Connecticut	4.40	
41.	Eric Olson	Northwestern	4.40	
42.	Mason Zandi	South Carolina	4.40	
43.	Brandon Greene	Alabama	4.35	TE
44.	Andrew Lauderdale	New Hampshire	4.30	
45.	Cole Gardner	Eastern Michigan	4.30	
46.	Andrew Jelks	Vanderbilt	4.30	
47.	Austin Schmidt	Illinois	4.25	

DEFENSIVE ENDS

RK	NAME	SCHOOL	GRADE	NOTES
1.	Myles Garrett	Texas A&M	7.90	Jr-3, OLB
2.	Solomon Thomas	Stanford	6.37	Jr-3, DT
3.	Charles Harris	Missouri	6.18	Jr-4, OLB
4.	Takkarist McKinley	UCLA	5.92	OLB
5.	Taco Charlton	Michigan	5.90	DT
6.	Jordan Willis	Kansas State	5.88	
7.	Tim Williams	Alabama	5.72	Ch., PRS
8.	Malik McDowell	Michigan State	5.70	Jr-3, DT
9.	Daeshon Hall	Texas A&M	5.66	OLB
10.	Dawuane Smoot	Illinois	5.56	OLB
11.	Carl Lawson	Auburn	5.52	Jr-4, OLB, X
12.	DeMarcus Walker	Florida State	5.48	OLB
13.	Tarell Basham	Ohio	5.45	
14.	Tanoh Kpassagnon	Villanova	5.44	
15.	Derek Rivers	Youngstown	5.38	OLB
16.	Isaac Rochell	Notre Dame	5.36	DT
17.	Deatrich Wise Jr.	Arkansas	5.32	X

18. Trey Hendrickson	Florida Atlantic	5.32	OLB
19. Fadol Brown	Mississippi	5.24	
20. Avery Moss	Youngstown	5.24	Ch., OLB
21. Keionta Davis	Tenn.-Chattanooga	5.23	
22. Garrett Sickels	Penn State	5.21	Jr-4, OLB
23. Bryan Cox	Florida	5.18	OLB
24. Ejuan Price	Pittsburgh	5.15	PRS
25. Noble Nwachukwu	West Virginia	5.14	OLB
26. Ifeadi Odenigbo	Northwestern	5.13	PRS
27. Ken Ekanem	Virginia Tech	5.09	OLB
28. Dylan Donahue	West Georgia	5.05	OLB, PRS
29. Tashawn Bower	LSU	5.02	OLB
30. Al-Quadin Muhammad	ex-Miami (Fla.)	5.01	Jr-4, OLB, Ch.
31. Jonathan Calvin	Mississippi State	4.95	
32. Hunter Dimick	Utah	4.90	
33. Karter Schult	Northern Iowa	4.90	
34. Se'Von Pittman	Akron	4.85	
35. Jhaustin Thomas	Iowa State	4.85	
36. Pat O'Connor	Eastern Michigan	4.85	
37. Alejandro Barrett	San Diego State	4.80	
38. Jeremiah Valoaga	UNLV	4.75	
39. Cameron Malveaux	Houston	4.75	
40. Darius English	South Carolina	4.65	
41. JT Jones	Miami (Ohio)	4.60	X
42. Terence Waugh	Kent State	4.60	
43. Isaiah Irving	San Jose State	4.60	
44. Sydney Omameh	Grand Valley St. (Mich.)	4.50	
45. Cassidy Weitl	Northwest Missouri St.	4.50	
46. A.J. Jefferson	Mississippi State	4.45	
47. Patrick Gamble	Georgia Tech	4.40	X, DT
48. Marquavius Lewis	South Carolina	4.40	
49. Courtney Miggins	Kentucky	4.40	
50. Gimel President	Illinois	4.35	
51. Hendrick Ekpe	Minnesota	4.25	
52. Terrence Daniel	Oregon	4.25	

DEFENSIVE TACKLES

RK NAME	SCHOOL	GRADE	NOTES
1. Jonathan Allen	Alabama	7.40	DE
2. Chris Wormley	Michigan	5.78	DE
3. Caleb Brantley	Florida	5.65	Jr-4
4. Dalvin Tomlinson	Alabama	5.58	X
5. Jaleel Johnson	Iowa	5.50	NT
6. Carlos Watkins	Clemson	5.47	
7. Montravius Adams	Auburn	5.46	
8. Davon Godchaux	LSU	5.38	Jr-3, DE, NT
9. D.J. Jones	Mississippi	5.32	NT
10. Larry Ogunjobi	UNC Charlotte	5.31	X, NT
11. Elijah Qualls	Washington	5.29	Jr-4
12. Ryan Glasgow	Michigan	5.28	X
13. Treyvon Hester	Toledo	5.25	NT
14. Nazair Jones	North Carolina	5.24	Jr-4
15. Jarron Jones	Notre Dame	5.24	
16. Tanzel Smart	Tulane	5.22	
17. Eddie Vanderdoes	UCLA	5.21	Jr-4
18. Stevie Tu'ikolovatu	USC	5.21	NT
19. Charles Walker	Oklahoma	5.12	Jr-4, DE, X
20. Jeremiah Ledbetter	Arkansas	5.10	
21. Vincent Taylor	Oklahoma State	5.09	Jr-4
22. DeAngelo Brown	Louisville	5.01	NT
23. Chucky Clements	Illinois	4.97	
24. Collin Bevins	NW Missouri State	4.95	DE
25. Jeremy Faulk	Garden City CC	4.95	Jr-4
26. Josh Tupou	Colorado	4.90	NT, Ch.
27. Joey Ivie	Florida	4.90	X
28. Lewis Neal	LSU	4.90	DE
29. Josh Banks	Wake Forest	4.90	
30. Ralph Green	Indiana	4.90	NT
31. Harold Brantley	NW Missouri State	4.85	

32. Travis Tuiloma	BYU	4.85	
33. Tyrique Jarrett	Pittsburgh	4.85	NT
34. Christian Brown	West Virginia	4.80	DE
35. Grover Stewart	Albany (Ga.) State	4.80	
36. Devaroe Lawrence	Auburn	4.80	
37. Samson Kafovalu	Colorado	4.75	DE
38. Omarius Bryant	Western Kentucky	4.75	
39. Rashaad Coward	Old Dominion (Va.)	4.75	
40. Adam Butler	Vanderbilt	4.75	X
41. Woody Baron	Virginia Tech	4.75	
42. Dylan Bradley	Southern Mississippi	4.75	
43. Roderick Henderson	Alabama State	4.70	NT
44. Ondre Pipkins	Texas Tech	4.65	NT
45. Josh Augusta	Missouri	4.65	
46. Rob Barber	Washington State	4.65	NT
47. Isaiah Golden	McNeese State	4.60	Jr-4
48. Eli Ankou	UCLA	4.60	
49. Jon Taylor	Southeastern Louisiana	4.60	NT, Ch.
50. Jordan Carrell	Colorado	4.60	DE
51. Patrick Ricard	Maine	4.50	X
52. Matt Godin	Michigan	4.50	
53. Cornelius Henderson	Jackson State (Miss.)	4.50	
54. Nick James	Mississippi State	4.45	NT
55. Jason Carr	West Georgia	4.40	DE
56. Imarjaye Albury	Florida International	4.40	
57. B.J. Singleton	Houston	4.40	NT
58. Casey Sayles	Ohio	4.35	
59. Winston Craig	Richmond (Va.)	4.35	
60. Monty Nelson	North Carolina State	4.35	
61. Izaah Lunsford	Bowling Green	4.35	NT
62. Jordan Wade	Oklahoma	4.35	NT
63. Rickey Hatley	Missouri	4.30	
64. Maurice Swain	Auburn	4.30	
65. Robert Bain	Illinois	4.30	NT
66. Desmond Owino	Jacksonville State (Ala.)	4.30	
67. Truman Gutapfel	Boston College	4.25	
68. Waylon Roberson	Arkansas State	4.25	NT
69. Viliami Latu	Arizona State	4.25	
70. Scott Ekpe	Minnesota	4.25	
71. Nigel Williams	Virginia Tech	4.25	

INSIDE LINEBACKERS

RK NAME	SCHOOL	GRADE	NOTES
1. Reuben Foster	Alabama	6.32	X, OLB
2. Raekwon McMillan	Ohio State	5.68	Jr-3
3. Kendell Beckwith	LSU	5.52	X
4. Anthony Walker	Northwestern	5.39	Jr-4
5. Ben Gedeon	Michigan	5.27	
6. Harvey Langi	BYU	5.25	DE, FB
7. Connor Harris	Lindenwood (Mo.)	5.23	
8. Hardy Nickerson	Illinois	5.20	
9. Tanner Vallejo	Boise State	5.16	X, SS
10. Brooks Ellis	Arkansas	5.12	
11. Kevin Davis	Colorado State	5.11	
12. Riley Bullough	Michigan State	5.04	
13. Ben Boulware	Clemson	5.01	
14. Keith Kelsey	Louisville	4.97	
15. Jordan Evans	Oklahoma	4.96	
16. Steven Taylor	Houston	4.95	OLB
17. Ukeme Eligwe	Georgia Southern	4.90	X
18. Dylan Cole	Missouri State	4.90	
19. Eric Wilson	Cincinnati	4.85	
20. Shaan Washington	Texas A&M	4.85	
21. Michael Scherer	Missouri	4.80	
22. Calvin Munson	San Diego State	4.80	OLB
23. Richie Brown	Mississippi State	4.75	OLB
24. Jermaine Grace	ex-Miami (Fla.)	4.75	Jr-4
25. Nyeem Wartman	Penn State	4.70	X

24. Austin Calitro	Villanova	4.65	OLB
25. Kenneth Olugbode	Colorado	4.65	
26. Josh Banderas	Nebraska	4.60	
27. Andrew King	Army	4.60	
28. Jerrol Garcia-Williams	Hawaii	4.50	
29. Anthony Williams	Utah State	4.50	
30. Jordan Herdman	Simon Fraser (Can.)	4.50	
31. Josh Letuligasenoa	Cal Poly State	4.45	OLB
32. Brandon Bell	Penn State	4.40	OLB
33. Tau Lotulelei	UNLV	4.40	OLB
34. Tre'Von Johnson	Weber State	4.40	
35. Jack Lynn	Minnesota	4.35	OLB
36. Lucas Wacha	Wyoming	4.30	
37. Chase Allen	Southern Illinois	4.25	
38. Caleb Saulo	Oregon State	4.25	OLB
39. Matt Galambos	Pittsburgh	4.25	
40. Devante Averette	Oklahoma State	4.25	

OUTSIDE LINEBACKERS

RK NAME	SCHOOL	GRADE	NOTES
1. Derek Barnett	Tennessee	6.17	Jr-3, DE
2. Haason Reddick	Temple	6.15	DE, ILB
3. Jarrad Davis	Florida	6.13	X, ILB
4. Zach Cunningham	Vanderbilt	5.90	Jr-4, ILB
5. Ryan Anderson	Alabama	5.88	DE
6. T.J. Watt	Wisconsin	5.62	Jr-4, DE
7. Duke Riley	LSU	5.48	
8. Tyus Bowser	Houston	5.46	PRS
9. Vince Biegel	Wisconsin	5.44	
10. Carroll Phillips	Illinois	5.38	DE, PRS
11. Alex Anzalone	Florida	5.37	X, Jr-4
12. Jalen Reeves-Maybin	Tennessee	5.28	X, ILB
13. Devonte' Fields	Louisville	5.27	X, Ch., DE
14. Josh Carraway	TCU	5.26	X, DE
15. Blair Brown	Ohio	5.25	ILB
16. Matt Milano	Boston College	5.24	SS
17. Elijah Lee	Kansas State	5.22	Jr-3
18. Pita Taumoepenu	Utah	5.18	DE
19. Marquel Lee	Wake Forest	5.17	
20. Jayon Brown	UCLA	5.14	ILB
21. JoJo Mathis	Washington	5.12	X, DE
22. James Onwualu	Notre Dame	5.08	
23. Denzel Johnson	TCU	5.07	SS
24. Jamal Marcus	Akron	5.05	DE
25. Kennan Gilchrist	Appalachian State	5.03	
24. Keion Adams	Western Michigan	5.00	DE
25. Jimmie Gilbert	Colorado	4.90	
26. Donavin Newsom	Missouri	4.85	
27. Folarin Orimolade	Dartmouth	4.85	
28. Marcus Oliver	Indiana	4.85	Jr-4
29. Dayon Pratt	East Carolina	4.80	
30. Corey Vereen	Tennessee	4.80	DE
31. Charmeachealle Moore	Kansas State	4.75	X, ILB
32. Samson Ebukam	Eastern Washington	4.75	DE
33. Deon Hollins	UCLA	4.75	
34. Praise Martin-Oguike	Temple	4.75	DE
35. Tim Kimbrough	Georgia	4.75	Jr-4
36. Nick Usher	UTEP	4.60	DE
37. Javancy Jones	Jackson State (Miss.)	4.50	
38. Avery Williams	Temple	4.50	
39. Jordan Burton	Oklahoma State	4.45	
40. Christian Tago	San Jose State	4.40	X
41. Psalm Wooching	Washington	4.35	
42. Christian Kuntz	Duquesne	4.35	
43. Deondre Barnett	Southern Illinois	4.35	DE
44. Ryan Watson	Air Force	4.25	DE
45. Scott Felix	USC	4.25	

CORNERBACKS

RK NAME	SCHOOL	GRADE	NOTES
1. Marshon Lattimore	Ohio State	6.64	Soph-3
2. Gareon Conley	Ohio State	6.26	Jr-3
3. Tre'Davious White	LSU	6.14	PR
4. Adoree' Jackson	USC	6.09	Jr-3, RS, WR, X
5. Marlon Humphrey	Alabama	5.96	Soph-3
6. Quincy Wilson	Florida	5.85	Jr-3, FS
7. Chidobe Awuzie	Colorado	5.82	FS
8. Budda Baker	Washington	5.68	Jr-3, FS
9. Cordrea Tankersley	Clemson	5.66	
10. Teez Tabor	Florida	5.63	Jr-3
11. Jourdan Lewis	Michigan	5.58	RS
12. Desmond King	Iowa	5.56	FS, RS
13. Fabian Moreau	UCLA	5.52	X
14. Shaquill Griffin	Central Florida	5.50	FS
15. Kevin King	Washington	5.42	FS
16. Sidney Jones	Washington	5.40	Jr-3, X
17. Howard Wilson	Houston	5.38	Soph-3, X
18. Rasul Douglas	West Virginia	5.37	
19. Cam Sutton	Tennessee	5.36	PR
20. Corn Elder	Miami (Fla.)	5.31	RS
21. Damontae Kazee	San Diego State	5.29	PR
22. Ahkello Witherspoon	Colorado	5.27	
23. Channing Stribling	Michigan	5.25	
24. Jalen Myrick	Minnesota	5.24	RS
25. Marquez White	Florida State	5.23	
26. Treston DeCoud	Oregon State	5.22	X
27. Brendan Langley	Lamar (Tex.)	5.22	
28. Brian Allen	Utah	5.21	WR
29. Mike Tyson	Cincinnati	5.21	SS
30. Jack Tocho	North Carolina State	5.19	
31. Ashton Lampkin	Oklahoma State	5.15	
32. Will Likely	Maryland	5.13	RS, WR
33. Sojourn Shelton	Wisconsin	5.10	
34. Ezra Robinson	Tennessee State	5.09	X
35. Nate Hairston	Temple	5.08	
36. Art Maulet	Memphis	5.06	
37. Jeremy Clark	Michigan	5.06	X
38. Cole Luke	Notre Dame	5.04	
39. Aarion Penton	Missouri	5.00	RS, Ch.
40. Gregory Mabin	Iowa	4.95	
41. Jeremy Cutrer	Middle Tennessee St.	4.95	
42. Joshua Holsey	Auburn	4.90	
43. David Rivers	Youngstown	4.90	
44. Breon Borders	Duke	4.90	
45. Des Lawrence	North Carolina	4.90	Ch.
46. Tony Bridges	Mississippi	4.90	
47. D.J. Jones	Mississippi	4.85	WR
48. Titus Howard	Slippery Rock	4.80	Jr-3
49. Brad Watson	Wake Forest	4.80	
50. Josh Thornton	Southern Utah	4.75	
51. DJ Dean	Arkansas	4.65	
52. Michael Davis	BYU	4.65	
53. Devon Edwards	Duke	4.65	
54. Reggie Porter	Utah	4.60	
55. Tyquwan Glass	Fresno State	4.60	
56. Dwayne Thomas	LSU	4.60	
57. Taylor Reynolds	James Madison (Va.)	4.55	X
58. Jared Collins	Arkansas	4.55	
59. Dashaun Amos	East Carolina	4.50	
60. JR Nelson	Montana	4.50	
61. Jamal Agnew	San Diego	4.50	
62. Torry Mctyer	UNLV	4.50	
63. Ryan Lewis	Pittsburgh	4.50	
64. Daquan Holmes	American International	4.45	FS
65. Jomal Wiltz	Iowa State	4.30	FS

66. Torren McGaster	Vanderbilt	4.30	
67. Ja'Darion Harmon	Kentucky	4.25	
68. Ryan Reid	Baylor	4.25	
69. Xavier Coleman	Portland State	4.25	
70. D.J. Killings	Central Florida	4.25	
71. Marnez Ogletree	Kansas	4.25	X
72. Dontrell Nelson	Memphis	4.25	

STRONG SAFETIES

RK NAME	SCHOOL	GRADE	NOTES
1. Jamal Adams	LSU	6.27	Jr-3
2. Jabrill Peppers	Michigan	6.16	Jr-3, WR, RS, CB
3. Justin Evans	Texas A&M	5.88	CB, KR
4. Josh Jones	North Carolina State	5.72	Jr-4, FS
5. Obi Melifonwu	Connecticut	5.55	FS, WLB
6. Montae Nicholson	Michigan State	5.38	Jr-3, FS
7. Rayshawn Jenkins	Miami (Fla.)	5.33	FS, X
8. Rudy Ford	Auburn	5.28	CB, KR
9. Josh Harvey-Clemons	Louisville	5.26	
10. Delano Hill	Michigan	5.25	
11. Damarius Travis	Minnesota	5.24	
12. Nate Gerry	Nebraska	5.23	
13. Lorenzo Jerome	St Francis (Pa.)	5.22	CB, RS
14. Xavier Woods	Louisiana Tech	5.16	
15. Shalom Luani	Washington State	5.14	
16. Jamal Carter	Miami (Fla.)	5.08	
17. Damariay Drew	California	5.00	
18. Ahmad Thomas	Oklahoma	4.95	FS, OLB
19. Jordan Sterns	Oklahoma State	4.95	
20. Orion Stewart	Baylor	4.90	
21. Brandon Wilson	Houston	4.90	CB, RS
22. Weston Steelhammer	Air Force	4.90	
23. Malik Smith	San Diego State	4.85	
24. Rickey Jefferson	LSU	4.85	
25. Michael Egwuagu	UTSA	4.85	
26. Tony Annese	Central Michigan	4.80	FS
27. Devin Chappell	Oregon State	4.80	
28. Malik Golden	Penn State	4.80	
29. Darrion Millines	SMU	4.75	
30. Randall Goforth	UCLA	4.75	
31. Dominique May	Wyoming	4.70	ILB
32. Jordan Moore	UTSA	4.70	
33. DeJuan Rogers	Toledo	4.65	
34. Dravious Wright	North Carolina State	4.65	X
35. B.T. Sanders	Nicholls State (La.)	4.60	
36. Quincy Mauger	Georgia	4.60	
37. Leon McQuay	USC	4.55	
38. Fish Smithson	Kansas	4.50	
39. D'Nerius Antoine	Southern Mississippi	4.50	
40. Dymonte Thomas	Michigan	4.50	FS
41. Adrian Colbert	Miami (Fla.)	4.50	
42. Maurice Smith	Georgia	4.50	
43. Austin Tennessee	Stevenson (Md.)	4.40	FS, CB
44. Dante Barnett	Kansas State	4.35	
45. Marcus McWilson	Kentucky	4.35	
46. Guy Stallworth	Grambling State	4.35	
47. Nathan Holley	Kent State	4.30	FS
48. Leroy Alexander	Youngstown	4.30	
49. Tahaan Goodman	UCLA	4.25	

FREE SAFETIES

RK NAME	SCHOOL	GRADE	NOTES
1. Malik Hooker	Ohio State	6.24	Soph-3, X
2. Marcus Williams	Utah	5.96	Jr-3, CB
3. Marcus Maye	Florida	5.80	CB
4. Tedric Thompson	Colorado	5.68	SS
5. John Johnson	Boston College	5.42	
6. Eddie Jackson	Alabama	5.24	X, PR
7. Chuck Clark	Virginia Tech	5.22	
8. Jadar Johnson	Clemson	5.21	
9. David Jones	Richmond (Va.)	5.05	
10. Kai Nacua	BYU	5.00	
11. Demetrious Cox	Michigan State	4.95	
12. Alex Gray	Appalachian State	4.95	
13. Zach Edwards	Cincinnati	4.90	
14. Charlie Miller	Dartmouth	4.90	
15. Richie Sampson	Coastal Carolina	4.75	
16. Aaron Peak	Butler Comm. College	4.40	Jr-3, CB
17. Bobby Baker	Georgia State	4.40	SS
18. Khari Vanderbilt	California	4.30	
19. Kelvin Rainey	Virginia	4.25	X
20. Tre'Vaughn Sullivan	Shepherd (W.V.)	4.20	
21. Willie Bailey	Virginia Union	4.20	
22. Tevon Mutcherson	Central Florida	4.20	
50. Nate Andrews	Florida State	4.20	
51. Laiu Moeakiola	Arizona State	4.20	OLB
52. Tellas Jones	Arizona	4.20	
53. Nicholas Morrow	Greenville (Ill.)	4.20	OLB
54. Trey Robinson	Furman (S.C.)	4.20	

PLACEKICKERS

RK NAME	SCHOOL	GRADE	NOTES
1. Zane Gonzalez	Arizona State	5.28	
2. Jake Elliott	Memphis	5.14	
3. Harrison Butker	Georgia Tech	5.12	
4. Conrad Ukropina	Stanford	4.95	
5. Kenny Allen	Michigan	4.90	
6. Andy Phillips	Utah	4.75	
7. Jonathan Gonzales	Portland State	4.65	
8. Jay Mattox	UTEP	4.60	KO
9. Nick Weiler	North Carolina	4.60	
10. Cameron Van Winkle	Washington	4.50	
11. Lance Geesey	St Francis (Pa.)	4.20	X

PUNTERS

RK NAME	SCHOOL	GRADE	NOTES
1. Justin Vogel	Miami (Fla.)	5.12	
2. Austin Rehkow	Idaho	5.10	PK
3. Toby Baker	Arkansas	5.09	
4. Cameron Johnston	Ohio State	5.07	
5. Hayden Hunt	Colorado State	5.00	
6. Rigoberto Sanchez	Hawaii	4.95	
7. Matthew Haack	Arizona State	4.95	
8. Dayton Balvanz	Louisiana-Monroe	4.91	
9. Nick Conte	Virginia	4.90	
10. Worth Gregory	East Carolina	4.85	
11. Eric Keena	North Texas	4.80	
12. Miles Bergner	South Dakota	4.80	
13. Alex Boy	Nevada	4.75	
14. Chris Fraser	Cornell	4.75	
15. Dalton Schomp	Florida Atlantic	4.50	
16. Tate Lewis	Southern Utah	4.30	
17. Lumi Kaba	Texas State	4.25	KO
18. Dalton Parks	Tulsa	4.25	
19. Colby Wadman	Cal-Davis	4.25	
20. Alex Knight	Southeast Missouri St.	4.20	

LONG SNAPPERS

RK NAME	SCHOOL	GRADE	NOTES
1. Colin Holba	Louisville	4.90	
2. Bradley Northnagel	California	4.87	
3. Nolan Dowling	Western Kentucky	4.80	
4. Cole Mazza	Alabama	4.75	
5. Mark Amann	San Jose State	4.40	
6. Billy Shipman	Cal Poly State	4.40	OG

BEST PLAYER AVAILABLE BY GRADE

RK.	POS, NAME, SCHOOL	GRADE	NOTES
1.	DE Myles Garrett, Texas A&M	7.90	Jr-3, OLB
2.	RB Leonard Fournette, LSU	7.70	Jr-3
3.	DT Jonathan Allen, Alabama	7.40	DE
4.	CB Marshon Lattimore, Ohio State	6.64	Soph-3
5.	DE Solomon Thomas, Stanford	6.37	Jr-3, DT
6.	OT Cam Robinson, Alabama	6.35	Jr-3
7.	WR John Ross, Washington	6.34	X, Jr-4, RS
8.	RB Christian McCaffrey, Stanford	6.33	Jr-3, WR, RS
9.	ILB Reuben Foster, Alabama	6.32	X, OLB
10.	SS Jamal Adams, LSU	6.27	Jr-3
11.	CB Gareon Conley, Ohio State	6.26	Jr-3
12.	OT Ryan Ramczyk, Wisconsin	6.26	Jr-4, OG
13.	FS Malik Hooker, Ohio State	6.24	Soph-3, X
14.	TE O.J. Howard, Alabama	6.21	
15.	QB Deshaun Watson, Clemson	6.18	Jr-3
16.	DE Charles Harris, Missouri	6.18	Jr-4, OLB
17.	OLB Derek Barnett, Tennessee	6.17	Jr-3, DE
18.	SS Jabrill Peppers, Michigan	6.16	Jr-3, WR, RS, CB
19.	TE David Njoku, Miami (Fla.)	6.16	Soph-3
20.	OLB Haason Reddick, Temple	6.15	DE, ILB
21.	CB Tre'Davious White, LSU	6.14	PR
22.	OLB Jarrad Davis, Florida	6.14	X, ILB
23.	QB Mitchell Trubisky, North Carolina	6.12	Jr-4
24.	WR Mike Williams, Clemson	6.11	Jr-4
25.	CB Adoree' Jackson, USC	6.09	Jr-3, RS, WR, X
26.	RB Dalvin Cook, Florida State	6.06	Jr-3, Ch.
27.	TE Evan Engram, Mississippi	6.04	WR
28.	QB Patrick Mahomes, Texas Tech	5.98	Jr-3
29.	WR JuJu Smith-Schuster, USC	5.97	Jr-3
30.	CB Marlon Humphrey, Alabama	5.96	Soph-3
31.	FS Marcus Williams, Utah	5.96	Jr-3, CB
32.	RB Curtis Samuel, Ohio State	5.92	Jr-3, WR, RS
33.	DE Takkarist McKinley, UCLA	5.92	OLB
34.	DE Taco Charlton, Michigan	5.90	DT
35.	OLB Zach Cunningham, Vanderbilt	5.90	Jr-4, ILB
36.	DE Jordan Willis, Kansas State	5.88	
37.	OLB Ryan Anderson, Alabama	5.88	DE
38.	SS Justin Evans, Texas A&M	5.88	CB, KR
39.	CB Quincy Wilson, Florida	5.88	Jr-3, FS
40.	WR Corey Davis, Western Michigan	5.84	X
41.	CB Chidobe Awuzie, Colorado	5.82	FS
42.	OG Forrest Lamp, Western Kentucky	5.81	OT, C
43.	FS Marcus Maye, Florida	5.80	CB
44.	DT Chris Wormley, Michigan	5.78	DE
45.	C Pat Elflein, Ohio State	5.76	OG
46.	OT Garett Bolles, Utah	5.74	Jr-3
47.	DE Tim Williams, Alabama	5.72	Ch., PRS
48.	SS Josh Jones, North Carolina State	5.72	Jr-4, FS
49.	DE Malik McDowell, Michigan State	5.70	Jr-3, DT
50.	WR Chris Godwin, Penn State	5.68	Jr-3
51.	OG Dan Feeney, Indiana	5.68	X, OT, C
52.	ILB Raekwon McMillan, Ohio State	5.68	Jr-3
53.	CB Budda Baker, Washington	5.68	Jr-3, FS
54.	FS Tedric Thompson, Colorado	5.68	SS
55.	C Ethan Pocic, LSU	5.67	OT, OG
56.	DE Daeshon Hall, Texas A&M	5.66	OLB
57.	CB Cordrea Tankersley, Clemson	5.66	
58.	OG Dorian Johnson, Pittsburgh	5.65	OT
59.	DT Caleb Brantley, Florida	5.65	Jr-4
60.	RB Samaje Perine, Oklahoma	5.64	Jr-3
61.	WR Zay Jones, East Carolina	5.63	
62.	CB Teez Tabor, Florida	5.63	Jr-3
63.	QB DeShone Kizer, Notre Dame	5.62	Soph-3
64.	OT Dion Dawkins, Temple	5.62	OG
65.	OLB T.J. Watt, Wisconsin	5.62	Jr-4, DE
66.	WR ArDarius Stewart, Alabama	5.59	Jr-4
67.	TE Gerald Everett, South Alabama	5.58	H-B
68.	CB Jourdan Lewis, Michigan	5.58	RS
69.	DT Dalvin Tomlinson, Alabama	5.58	X
70.	TE Jordan Leggett, Clemson	5.56	
71.	DE Dawuane Smoot, Illinois	5.56	OLB
72.	CB Desmond King, Iowa	5.56	FS, RS
73.	SS Obi Melifonwu, Connecticut	5.55	FS, WLB
74.	OG Isaac Asiata, Utah	5.52	
75.	DE Carl Lawson, Auburn	5.52	Jr-4, OLB, X
76.	ILB Kendell Beckwith, LSU	5.52	X
77.	CB Fabian Moreau, UCLA	5.52	X
78.	DT Jaleel Johnson, Iowa	5.50	NT
79.	CB Shaquill Griffin, Central Florida	5.50	FS
80.	RB Alvin Kamara, Tennessee	5.48	Jr-4, PR
81.	WR Cooper Kupp, Eastern Washington	5.48	PR
82.	OG Taylor Moton, Western Michigan	5.48	OT
83.	DE DeMarcus Walker, Florida State	5.48	OLB
84.	OLB Duke Riley, LSU	5.48	
85.	TE Bucky Hodges, Virginia Tech	5.47	Jr-4
86.	OT Zach Banner, USC	5.47	
87.	DT Carlos Watkins, Clemson	5.47	
88.	OT David Sharpe, Florida	5.46	Jr-3
89.	DT Montravius Adams, Auburn	5.46	
90.	OLB Tyus Bowser, Houston	5.46	PRS
91.	WR KD Cannon, Baylor	5.45	Jr-3
92.	DE Tarell Basham, Ohio	5.45	
93.	RB Joe Mixon, Oklahoma	5.44	Soph-3, KR, Ch.
94.	WR Josh Reynolds, Texas A&M	5.44	
95.	DE Tanoh Kpassagnon, Villanova	5.44	
96.	OLB Vince Biegel, Wisconsin	5.44	
97.	QB Davis Webb, California	5.42	
98.	RB D'Onte Foreman, Texas	5.42	Jr-3
99.	WR Malachi Dupre, LSU	5.42	Jr-3
100.	OG Nico Siragusa, San Diego State	5.42	OG
101.	CB Kevin King, Washington	5.42	FS
102.	FS John Johnson, Boston College	5.42	
103.	WR Amara Darboh, Michigan	5.41	
104.	CB Sidney Jones, Washington	5.40	Jr-3, X
105.	WR Dede Westbrook, Oklahoma	5.40	Ch.
106.	TE Jake Butt, Michigan	5.40	X
107.	WR Taywan Taylor, Western Kentucky	5.39	
108.	ILB Anthony Walker, Northwestern	5.39	Jr-4
109.	QB Josh Dobbs, Tennessee	5.38	
110.	WR Bug Howard, North Carolina	5.38	
111.	TE Jeremy Sprinkle, Arkansas	5.38	
112.	DE Derek Rivers, Youngstown	5.38	OLB
113.	DT Davon Godchaux, LSU	5.38	Jr-3, DE, NT
114.	OLB Carroll Phillips, Illinois	5.38	DE, PRS
115.	CB Howard Wilson, Houston	5.38	Soph-3, X
116.	SS Montae Nicholson, Michigan State	5.38	Jr-3, FS
117.	RB Donnel Pumphrey, San Diego State	5.37	
118.	WR Jehu Chesson, Michigan	5.37	KR
119.	OG Danny Isidora, Miami (Fla.)	5.37	
120.	OLB Alex Anzalone, Florida	5.37	X, Jr-4
121.	CB Rasul Douglas, West Virginia	5.37	
122.	QB Nathan Peterman, Pittsburgh	5.36	
123.	WR Josh Malone, Tennessee	5.36	Jr-3
124.	TE Adam Shaheen, Ashland	5.36	Jr-4
125.	C Tyler Orlosky, West Virginia	5.36	
126.	DE Isaac Rochell, Notre Dame	5.36	DT
127.	CB Cam Sutton, Tennessee	5.36	PR
128.	RB James Conner, Pittsburgh	5.35	Jr-4, X
129.	OG Jordan Morgan, Kutztown (Pa.)	5.35	OT
130.	WR Mack Hollins, North Carolina	5.34	X
131.	OT Julien Davenport, Bucknell	5.34	
132.	RB Matt Dayes, North Carolina State	5.33	
133.	WR Kenny Golladay, Northern Illinois	5.33	
134.	TE Jonnu Smith, Florida International	5.33	H-B
135.	SS Rayshawn Jenkins, Miami (Fla.)	5.33	FS, X
136.	RB Corey Clement, Wisconsin	5.32	X
137.	WR Carlos Henderson, Louisiana Tech	5.32	Jr-4, KR
138.	OG Jessamen Dunker, Tennessee State	5.32	OT, Ch.
139.	DE Deatrich Wise Jr., Arkansas	5.32	X
140.	DE Trey Hendrickson, Florida Atlantic	5.32	OLB
141.	DT D.J. Jones, Mississippi	5.32	NT
142.	WR Isaiah Ford, Virginia Tech	5.31	Jr-3
143.	OT Antonio Garcia, Troy	5.31	
144.	WR Isaiah McKenzie, Georgia	5.31	Jr-3, RS
145.	DT Larry Ogunjobi, UNC Charlotte	5.31	X, NT
146.	CB Corn Elder, Miami (Fla.)	5.31	RS
147.	RB Elijah McGuire, Louisiana-Lafayette	5.30	X, RS
148.	WR Robert Davis, Georgia State	5.30	
149.	DT Elijah Qualls, Washington	5.29	Jr-4
150.	CB Damontae Kazee, San Diego State	5.29	PR

PLAYER INDEX